Related Books of Interest

Enterprise Master Data Management
An SOA Approach to Managing Core Information

By Allen Dreibelbis, Eberhard Hechler, Ivan Milman, Martin Oberhofer, Paul Van Run, and Dan Wolfson
ISBN: 0-13-236625-8

The Only Complete Technical Primer for MDM Planners, Architects, and Implementers

Enterprise Master Data Management provides an authoritative, vendor-independent MDM technical reference for practitioners: architects, technical analysts, consultants, solution designers, and senior IT decision makers. Written by the IBM® data management innovators who are pioneering MDM, this book systematically introduces MDM's key concepts and technical themes, explains its business case, and illuminates how it interrelates with and enables SOA.

Drawing on their experience with cutting-edge projects, the authors introduce MDM patterns, blueprints, solutions, and best practices published nowhere else—everything you need to establish a consistent, manageable set of master data, and use it for competitive advantage.

Understanding DB2
Learning Visually with Examples, Second Edition

By Raul F. Chong, Xiaomei Wang, Michael Dang, and Dwaine R. Snow
ISBN: 0-13-158018-3

IBM® DB2® 9 and DB2 9.5 provide breakthrough capabilities for providing Information on Demand, implementing Web services and Service Oriented Architecture, and streamlining information management. *Understanding DB2: Learning Visually with Examples, Second Edition*, is the easiest way to master the latest versions of DB2 and apply their full power to your business challenges.

Written by four IBM DB2 experts, this book introduces key concepts with dozens of examples drawn from the authors' experience working with DB2 in enterprise environments. Thoroughly updated for DB2 9.5, it covers new innovations ranging from manageability to performance and XML support to API integration. Each concept is presented with easy-to-understand screenshots, diagrams, charts, and tables. This book is for everyone who works with DB2: database administrators, system administrators, developers, and consultants. With hundreds of well-designed reviewquestions and answers, it will also help professionals prepare for the IBM DB2 Certification Exams 730, 731, or 736.

Listen to the author's podcast at: ibmpressbooks.com/podcasts

Related Books of Interest

DB2 pureXML Cookbook
Master the Power of the IBM Hybrid Data Server

By Matthias Nicola and Pav Kumar-Chatterjee
ISBN: 0-13-815047-8

Hands-On Solutions and Best Practices for Developing and Managing XML Database Applications with DB2

Two leading experts from IBM offer the practical solutions and proven code samples that database professionals need to build better XML solutions faster. Organized by task, this book is packed with more than 700 easy-to-adapt "recipe-style" examples covering the entire application lifecycle–from planning and design through coding, optimization, and troubleshooting. This extraordinary library of recipes includes more than 250 XQuery and SQL/XML queries. With the authors' hands-on guidance, you'll learn how to combine pureXML "ingredients" to efficiently perform virtually any XML data management task, from the simplest to the most advanced.

Viral Data in SOA
An Enterprise Pandemic

By Neal A. Fishman
ISBN: 0-13-700180-0

"This book is a must read for any organization using data-integration or data-interchange technologies, or simply any organization that must trust data. Neal takes the reader through an entertaining and vital journey of SOA information management issues, risks, discovery, and solutions. He provides a fresh perspective that no corporation should overlook; in fact, corporations might head blindly into SOA implementations without this awareness."

–Kevin Downey, Senior Partner, Xteoma Inc., Canada

Leading IBM information forensics expert Neal Fishman helps you identify the unique challenges of data quality in your SOA environment–and implement solutions that deliver the best results for the long term at the lowest cost.

Listen to the author's podcast at:
ibmpressbooks.com/podcasts

Related Books of Interest

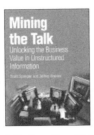

Mining the Talk
Unlocking the Business Value in Unstructured Information

By Scott Spangler and Jeffrey Kreulen
ISBN: 0-13-233953-6

Leverage Unstructured Data to Become More Competitive, Responsive, and Innovative

In *Mining the Talk*, two leading-edge IBM researchers introduce a revolutionary new approach to unlocking the business value hidden in virtually any form of unstructured data—from word processing documents to websites, emails to instant messages.

The authors review the business drivers that have made unstructured data so important—and explain why conventional methods for working with it are inadequate. Then, writing for business professionals—not just data mining specialists—they walk step-by-step through exploring your unstructured data, understanding it, and analyzing it effectively.

Understanding DB2 9 Security

Bond, See, Wong, Chan
ISBN: 0-13-134590-7

DB2 9 for Linux, UNIX, and Windows

DBA Guide, Reference, and Exam Prep, 6th Edition
Baklarz, Zikopoulos
ISBN: 0-13-185514-X

Lotus Notes Developer's Toolbox

Elliott
ISBN: 0-13-221448-2

IBM Lotus Connections 2.5

Planning and Implementing Social Software for Your Enterprise
Hardison, Byrd, Wood, Speed, Martin, Livingston, Moore, Kristiansen
ISBN: 0-13-700053-7

Mainframe Basics for Security Professionals

Getting Started with RACF
Pomerantz, Vander Weele, Nelson, Hahn
ISBN: 0-13-173856-9

The Art of Enterprise Information Architecture

The Art of Enterprise Information Architecture

A Systems-Based Approach for Unlocking Business Insight

Mario Godinez, Eberhard Hechler, Klaus Koenig, Steve Lockwood, Martin Oberhofer, Michael Schroeck

IBM Press
Pearson plc
Upper Saddle River, NJ • Boston • Indianapolis • San Francisco
New York • Toronto • Montreal • London • Munich • Paris • Madrid
Cape Town • Sydney • Tokyo • Singapore • Mexico City

Ibmpressbooks.com

IBM Press Program Managers: Steven M. Stansel, Ellice Uffer
Cover design: IBM Corporation
Associate Publisher: Greg Wiegand
Marketing Manager: Kourtnaye Sturgeon
Acquisitions Editor: Katherine Bull
Publicist: Heather Fox
Development Editors: Kendell Lumsden and Ginny Bess Munroe
Managing Editor: Kristy Hart
Designer: Alan Clements
Project Editor: Anne Goebel
Copy Editor: Ginny Bess Munroe
Indexer: Lisa Stumpf
Compositor: Jake McFarland
Proofreader: Debbie Williams
Manufacturing Buyer: Dan Uhrig

Published by Pearson plc
Publishing as IBM Press

IBM Press offers excellent discounts on this book when ordered in quantity for bulk purchases or special sales, which may include electronic versions and/or custom covers and content particular to your business, training goals, marketing focus, and branding interests. For more information, please contact:

U. S. Corporate and Government Sales
1-800-382-3419
corpsales@pearsontechgroup.com.

For sales outside the U. S., please contact:

International Sales
international@pearson.com.

Library of Congress Cataloging-in-Publication Data is on file.

Text printed in the United States on recycled paper at R.R. Donnelley in Crawfordsville, Indiana. First printing March 2010.

To my family, for the support and encouragement

they gave me during this effort.

M.G.

To my wife Irina and my sons, Lars and Alex—

who so greatly supported me in this endeavor.

E.H.

To my wife Astrid and my children Nicola and Florian,

for all their support and tolerance.

K.K.

To my wife Vanessa and my three children Emma, Chris, and Kate,

for helping me throughout the long hours.

S.L.

To my beloved wife Kirsten—you are my inspiration.

M.O.

To my family and colleagues, thank you for your patience, support,

and encouragement throughout my career.

M.S.

Contents

Appendixes can be found online at www.ibmpressbooks.com/artofeia

Foreword

Ron Tolido

In the past two years, I have become more involved in what my company, Capgemini, has fondly started to describe as the "business technology agora," a place where IT and business people meet, discuss, make decisions, and prepare for action. Like in the old Greek cities, this agora proves to be a catalyst for dialogue, a gathering place for different stakeholders to reach out to the others and improve understanding.

By using the principles of the Business Technology Agora, we carefully identify the most important business drivers of an organization, map these to technology solutions in different categories, and discuss impact, timing, and implementation issues. Categorizing solutions in different areas helps to simplify the technology landscape, but it also provides us with a wealth of insight into what areas of IT truly matter to the business of our clients.

If there is one dominant category that we have identified in these two years of business technology sessions across the world, it is no doubt "Thriving on Data." The abundant, ubiquitous availability of real-time information proves to be the single most important requirement to satisfying the needs of the business.

Organizations envision thriving on data in many different ways. One way might be to simply get more of a grip on corporate performance by creating a more integrated view of client-related information and having management dashboards that truly show the actual state of the business. Another way, being used more often, is to carefully analyze data from inside and outside of the enterprise to predict and understand what might happen next. Above all, the exchange of meaningful data is the glue that binds all the actors (man, machine, anything else) in the highly interconnected, network of everything that nowadays defines our business environment; data literally gets externalized and becomes the main tool for organizations to reach out to the outside world.

Given the extreme importance of data today, it is surprising that many organizations do not seem to be able to govern their data properly, let alone use data in a strategic way to achieve their objectives. Data is often scattered across the enterprise. There are no measures to guarantee consistency, and ownership is unclear. The situation becomes even more difficult when different business entities are involved or when data needs to be shared between organizations. This is a truly complex problem and businesses need a much more architectural approach for leveraging their data.

In my other role as a board member of The Open Group, I have come to value the role of architecture as a tool not only to bring structure and simplification to complex situations, but also to bridge the views of the different stakeholders involved. If we are to achieve boundary-less information flow inside and between organizations, which is the ultimate goal of The Open Group, we need standards. Standards aren't only about the terms of definitions and semantics but about the methodologies we apply and the models that we build on. After all, ever since the rise and fall of the Tower of Babel, we know that successful collaboration depends on the ability to share the same ways of working, to share the same objectives, to build on a common foundation, and to be culturally aligned. Essentially, it is about speaking the same language in the broadest sense of the word.

The authors of this book aim for nothing less than creating an architectural perspective on enterprise information, and they have embarked on a mission of epical proportions. By bringing together insights and best practices from all over the industry, they provide us with the models, methodologies, diagnostics, and tools to get a grip on enterprise information. They show us how enterprise information fits into the broader context of enterprise architecture frameworks, such as The Open Group Architecture Framework (TOGAF). They introduce a multi-layered information architecture reference model that has the allure of a standard, common foundation for the entire profession. They also show us how Enterprise Information Architecture (EIA) alludes to emerging, contemporary topics such as SOA, business intelligence, cloud-based delivery, and master data management.

However, most of all, they supply us with a shared, architectural language to create oversight and control in the Babylonic confusion that we call the enterprise information landscape. When the business and IT side of the enterprise share the same insights around the strategic value of information and when they mutually agree on the unprecedented importance of information stewardship, they start to see the point of this book—how to unleash the power of enterprise information and how to truly thrive on data.

Ron Tolido
VP and Chief Technology Officer, Capgemini Application Lifecycle Services
Board Member, The Open Group

Foreword

Dr. Kristof Kloeckner

Senior business and technical executives are becoming increasingly concerned about whether they have all the critical information at their disposal to help them make important decisions that might impact the future of their companies. They need to anticipate and adequately respond to business opportunities and proactively manage risk, while also improving operational efficiency. At the same time, the world's political leaders are being challenged with the opportunity to improve the way the world works. As populations grow and relocate at a faster pace, we are stressing our aging infrastructures. Smarter transportation, crime prevention, healthcare, and energy grids promise relief to urban areas around the world.

What these business, political, and technical leaders have come to realize is that a key enabler across all these pressure points is *information*. During the past 20 plus years, the IT industry has focused primarily on automating business tasks. Although essential to the business, this has created a complex information landscape because individual automation projects have led to disconnected silos of information. As a result, many executives do not trust their information. Redundancy reigns—both logically and physically. This highly heterogeneous, costly, and non-integrated information landscape needs to be addressed. Value is driven by unlocking information and making it flow to any person or process that needs it—complete, accurate, timely, actionable, insightful information, provided in the context of the task at hand. Advanced insight, new intelligence, predictive analytics, and new delivery models, such as Cloud Computing, must be fully leveraged to support decisions within these new paradigms.

These information-centric capabilities help enable a fundamental shift to a smarter, fact-based *Intelligent Enterprise* and eventually enable building a *Smarter Planet*—city by city, enterprise by enterprise. To facilitate these changes, an innovative, comprehensive, yet practical, *EIA* is required. It is one that technically underpins a more analytical information strategy and paves the way for more intelligent decisions to build a smarter planet within the enterprise and globally.

The Art of Enterprise Information Architecture delivers a practical, comprehensive cross-industry reference guide that addresses each of the key elements associated with developing and implementing effective enterprise architectures. Industry-specific examples are included; for instance, the intelligent utility network is discussed and how EIA enables the new ways in which energy and utility companies operate in the future. It also elaborates on key themes associated with unlocking business insight, such as Dynamic Warehousing and new trends in business analytics and optimization. Crucial capabilities, such as Enterprise Information Integration (EII) and end-to-end Enterprise Metadata Management, are presented as key elements of the EIA. The role of information in Cloud Computing as a new delivery model and information delivery in a Web 2.0 World rounds off key aspects of the EIA. This book serves as a great source to the information-led transformation necessary to becoming an intelligent enterprise and to building a smarter planet. It delivers an architectural foundation that effectively addresses important business and societal challenges.

Moreover, the authors have applied their deep practical experience to delivering an essential guide for every practitioner from EIA to leaders of information-led projects. You will be able to apply many of the best practices and methods provided in this book for many of your information-based initiatives.

Enjoy reading this book.

Dr. Kristof Kloeckner
CTO, Enterprise Initiatives
VP, Cloud Computing Platforms
IBM Corporation

Preface

What Is This Book About?

EIA has become the lifeline for business sustainability and competitive advantage today. Firms of all sizes search for practical ways to create business value by getting their arms around information and correlating insights so business and technical leaders can confidently predict outcomes and take action. For all business and technical executives around the world, the information era poses unique challenges: How can they unlock information and let it flow rapidly and easily to people and processes that need it? How can they cost-effectively store, archive, and retrieve a –virtual explosion of new information? How do they protect and secure that information, meet compliance requirements, and make it accessible for business insight where and when it is needed? How can they mitigate risks inherent in business decision making and avoid fraudulent activities in their own operations?

Senior leaders have come to realize that intelligence, information, and technology will radically and quickly change how business is done in the future. Globally integrated enterprises require that business become more intelligent and more interconnected day by day. With these changes come amazing opportunities for every business: It is now possible to gain intelligence of information created by millions of smart devices that have been and even more will be deployed and connected to the Internet. The fundamental nature of the Internet has changed into an Internet of interconnected devices communicating with one another. Individuals are also creating millions of new digital footprints with transactions, online communities, registrations, and movements. To cope with this explosion of data, creating new data centers with exponentially larger storage and faster processing is necessary but by itself is not sufficient. Businesses now require new intelligence to manage the flow of information and surface richer insights to make faster, better decisions.

Consequently, what business leaders realize is that a new approach to EIA is needed. They realize that an architectural foundation is necessary to effectively address these business challenges to provide best practices for how to unlock business insight and for how to apply architectural patterns to business scenarios supported by reference models, methodologies, diagnostics, and tools. With *The Art of Enterprise Information Architecture: A Systems-Based Approach for Unlocking Business Insight*, we've outlined the right methods and tools to architect information management solutions. We've also outlined the right environment to enable the transformation of information into a strategic asset that can be rapidly leveraged for sustained competitive advantage.

This book explains the key concepts of information processing and management, the methodology for creating the next generation EIA, how to architect an information management solution, and how to apply architectural patterns for various business scenarios. It is a comprehensive architectural guide that includes architectural principles, architectural patterns, and building blocks and their applications for information-centric solutions. The following is what you can expect from reading the chapters of this book:

- **Chapter 1, "The Imperative for a New Approach to Information Architecture"**—In this chapter, we introduce business scenarios that illustrate how intelligence, information, and technology are radically changing how business will be conducted in the future. In all these scenarios, we outline how new sources and uses of enterprise data are brought together in new ways to shake the foundation of how companies will compete in the "New Economy."

- **Chapter 2, "Introducing Enterprise Information Architecture"**—This chapter introduces the major key terms and concepts that are used throughout this book. The most important foundational concept is Reference Architecture, which we apply to the key terms, such as Information Architecture and EIA, to finally derive our working model of an EIA Reference Architecture.

- **Chapter 3, "Data Domains, Information Governance, and Information Security"**—This chapter introduces the scope associated with the definition of data in the EIA and the relevant data domains which are Metadata, Master Data, Operational Data, Unstructured Data, and Analytical Data. We describe their role and context, and most important, we briefly describe how these domains can be managed successfully within the enterprise though a coherent Information Governance framework. This chapter also takes a brief look at the current issues surrounding Information Security and Information Privacy.

- **Chapter 4, "Enterprise Information Architecture: A Conceptual and Logical View"**—This chapter first introduces the necessary capabilities for the EIA Reference Architecture. From that, we derive the conceptual view using methods such as an Architecture Overview Diagram that groups the various required capabilities. We introduce architecture decisions that we then use to drill-down in a first step from the conceptual view to the logical view.

- **Chapter 5, "Enterprise Information Architecture: Component Model"**—This chapter introduces the component model of the EIA Reference Architecture covering the relevant services with its descriptions and interfaces. We describe the functional components in terms of their roles and responsibilities, their relationships and interactions to other components, and the required collaboration to allow the implementation of specified deployment and customer use case scenarios.

- **Chapter 6, "Enterprise Information Architecture: Operational Model"**—This chapter describes the operational characteristics of the EIA Reference Architecture. We introduce the operational-modeling approach and provide a view on how physical nodes can be derived from logical components of the component model and related deployment scenarios. We also describe with the use of operational patterns how Information Services can be constructed to achieve functional and nonfunctional requirements.

- **Chapter 7, "New Delivery Models: Cloud Computing"**—This chapter covers the emerging delivery model of Cloud Computing in the context of Enterprise Information Services. We define and clarify terms with regard to Cloud Computing models with its different shapes and layers across the IT stack. Furthermore, we provide a holistic view of how the deployment model of Enterprise Information Services will change with Cloud Computing and examine the impact of the new delivery models on operational service qualities.

- **Chapter 8, "Enterprise Information Integration"**—In this chapter, we outline the fundamental nature of an Enterprise Information Integration (EII) framework and how it can support business relevant themes such as Master Data Management (MDM), Dynamic Warehousing (DYW), or Metadata Management. We describe a large number of capabilities and technologies to choose from which include replication, federation, data profiling, or cleansing tools, and next generation technologies such as data streaming.

- **Chapter 9, "Intelligent Utility Networks"**—This chapter covers business scenarios that are typical for the utility industry demanding for improved customer services and insight, improved enterprise information, and integration. We introduce specific Information Services for the Intelligent Utility Network (IUN), such as automated metering, process optimization through interconnected systems, and informed decision making based on advanced analytics.

- **Chapter 10, "Enterprise Metadata Management"**—This chapter details new aspects in the generation and consumption of Metadata. We describe the increasing role of enterprise-wide Metadata Management within information-centric use case scenarios. Primarily, we concentrate on the emerging aspects of Metadata and Metadata Management, such as Metadata to manage the business, aligned Business and Technical Metadata, Business Metadata to describe the business, or Technical Metadata to describe the IT domain.

- **Chapter 11, "Master Data Management"**—In this chapter, we describe relevant sub-components and provide component deep dives of MDM solutions. We explore relevant capabilities and how architects can apply them to specific business scenarios. With the use of Component Interaction Diagrams, we discuss the applicability of MDM Services of exemplary use cases, for instance the Track and Trace aspects of a Returnable Container Management solution in the automotive industry.

- **Chapter 12, "Information Delivery in a Web 2.0 World"**—This chapter covers the use of Mashups as part of the next phase of informational applications. We describe how Mashups fit into a Web 2.0 world and then outline the Mashup architecture, its place within the Component Model, and some scenarios that use Mashups. This should allow the architect to understand and to design typical Mashup applications and how to deploy them in operational environments.

- **Chapter 13, "Dynamic Warehousing"**—This chapter explores the role of the EIA components in the new Dynamic Warehousing approach. We address the challenges imposed by demands for real-time data access and the requirements to deliver more dynamic business insights by integrating, transforming, harvesting, and analyzing insights from Structured and Unstructured Data. We focus on satisfying the shrinking levels of tolerance the business has for latency when delivering business intelligence.

- **Chapter 14, "New Trends in Business Analytics and Optimization"**—The business scenarios discussed in this chapter provide examples of the newer trends in the use of advanced and traditional Business Intelligence (BI) strategies. We explore powerful infrastructures that enable enterprises to model, capture, aggregate, prioritize, and analyze extreme volumes of data in faster and deeper ways, paving the road to transform information into a strategic asset.

Who Should Read This Book

The Art of Enterprise Information Architecture: A Systems-Based Approach for Unlocking Business Insight has content that should appeal to a diverse business and technical audience, ranging from executive level to experienced information management architects, and especially those new to the topic of EIA. Whether newcomers to the topic of EIA or readers with strong technical background, such as Enterprise Architects, System Architects, and predominately Information Architects, should enjoy reading the technical guidance for how to apply architectural models and patterns to specific business scenarios and use cases.

What You Will Learn

This book is intended to provide comprehensive guidance and understanding of the importance and nature of the different data domains within EIA, the need for an architectural framework and reference architecture, and the architectural modeling approach and underlying patterns. Readers learn the answers to questions such as:

- How to keep up with ever-shortening cycle times of information delivery to the lines of business by applying architectural patterns?
- How to design Information Services with a methodological approach, beginning from conceptual and functional building blocks down to operational requirements satisfying specific service levels?
- How to apply advanced technologies and tools to systematically mine new Structured and Unstructured Data?
- How to outline new intelligence leveraging more and more real-time operating capabilities?
- How to create instant reaction and proactive applications in smarter businesses by applying architectural building blocks for specific business scenarios?
- How to design next generation EII connecting data and leveraging the flow of information?

How to Read This Book

There are several ways to read this book. The most obvious way is to read it cover to cover to get a complete end-to-end picture of the next generation of EIA. However, the authors organized the content in such a way that there are basic reading paths and appropriate deep dives with related business scenarios and application of architectural patterns.

To understand the key design concepts of the EIA Reference Architecture and the architectural patterns that can be applied ranging from conceptual views to logical views and down to physical views, we suggest reading Chapter 1 through Chapter 6. This should provide the reader with a clear understanding of EIA and how to design and implement the relevant components in the enterprise. Additionally, Chapter 7 provides a view of how Enterprise Information Services will change with Cloud Computing. To understand detailed solution patterns, we suggest reading Chapters 5 and 6 to understand the Component Model and the Operational Model of the EIA. Chapters 8 through 14 can be investigated in any order the reader desires to learn about industry solutions such as Intelligent Utility Networks, or focus on more details of Enterprise Information Services such as Enterprise Information Integration, Enterprise Metadata Management, Master Data Management, Mashups, Dynamic Warehousing, and Business Analytics and Optimization.

The scope of this book is a discussion of EIA from a business, technical, and architectural perspective. Our discussion of EIA is not tied to specific vendors' software and thus is not a feature-oriented discussion. However, based on the solid architecture guidance provided, an IT architect can make appropriate software selections for a specific, concrete solution design. To give an IT architect a quick start when performing the software mapping as part of the Operational Model design, we provided a complementary Web resource on www. ibmpressbooks.com/artofeia. This online resource lists software offerings from IBM and some other vendors by functional area. We decided to put this section online because we also provide links to the corresponding product homepages for easier access. There are numerous standards relevant for EIA and information management in general. These standards range from the *lingua franca* SQL for databases or more recent ones such as RSS for information delivery in Web 2.0. Whenever a standard or a technical acronym is mentioned where the reader might be interested, we provide an online appendix for Standards and Specifications (Appendix B) and Regulations (Appendix C). See the Web page http://www.ibmpressbooks.com/artofeia where we list all technical standards and acronyms used throughout the book. Because references to standard or regulation documents and other resources are in most of the cases online resources, the reader should have easier access by just following the online links provided.

Acknowledgments

From conceptual design of the book through reviewing the complete manuscript, numerous external professionals and well-known industry experts provided valuable feedback to the book. The author team would like to express a special thanks to Ron Tolido, member of the Board of Directors of The Open Group and CTO of Capgemini Europe, for his valuable feedback provided during the manuscript review and the foreword he provided for the book. Mark Sobotka from Bank of America also reviewed the manuscript and provided valuable and encouraging feedback for which the author team is grateful. Aaron Zornes, chief research officer at The MDM Institute, earns a thank you for his feedback during the conceptual design of the book and for his insightful comments in reviewing various chapters. Maria Villar, managing partner at Business Data Leadership, reviewed various chapters of the manuscript and was a big help for the author team with all her comments and insights. For their review of chapters, the authors would like to express their thanks to Jon Collins, managing director and CEO from Freeform Dynamics and Alex Kwiatkowski, lead analyst at DataMonitor. The author team would also like to thank Claudia Imhoff, president of Intelligent Solutions, for her feedback during the conceptual design of the book.

The author team also would like to say thank you to a number of IBM colleagues for their support. First, we would like to express our gratitude to Kristof Kloeckner, CTO of Enterprise Initiatives and vice president for Cloud Computing Platforms, for his foreword. Harish Grama, vice president of InfoSphere Development, earns special thanks as our executive sponsor.

The author team would like to also give a special thank you to Allen Dreibelbis, the lead architect and owner of the MDM Reference Architecture Asset in the IBM Software Group. The MDM topic discussed in this book is heavily influenced by his work. We would also like to thank the following IBM colleagues from the IBM technical expert community for their contributions:

Holt Adams, Michael Behrendt, Gerd Breiter, Kavita Chavda, Chris Couper, Christopher Grote, Michael Hofmeister, Peter Husar, Patrick Jelinek, Ronald Leung, Karim Madhany, Louis Mau, Barbara McKee, Ivan Milman, Paulo Pereira, Margaret Pommert, Rick Robinson, Sandra Tucker, Paul van Run, Mike Wells, and Dan Wolfson.

The IBM Information Management publishing department provided valuable support. Susan Visser guided the author team through the publication process. Martin would like to thank Susan in particular for the second time providing outstanding insight and guidance for managing a book project. In addition, we would like to say thanks to Steven Stansel and Elissa Wang for helping the author team through the legal processes related to a book project.

Pearson publishing provided a strong team for this book. In particular, the author team would like to thank Katherine Bull, Kendell Lumsden, Anne Goebel, and Ginny Bess Munroe for their support.

About the Authors

Mario Godinez is an executive IT architect and IBM senior certified IT architect (SCITA) at IBM's Worldwide Information On Demand Architecture team. He cofounded IBM Software Group's Information Management Technical Enablement team and has spent 15+ years helping IBM banking, financial, and industrial customers architect and implement complex enterprise solutions.

Mario Godinez

After working as a data architect for various U.S. and Canadian IT companies involved in successful solution designs and implementations for large corporations in Singapore, Canada, and the U.S., Mario joined the IBM Toronto Software Development Lab in Canada in 1993 as an advanced software engineer working in the DB2® development organization in the areas of software development, performance optimization and benchmarking, and solution architecture involving enterprise-packaged applications in the ERP, SCM, and Business Intelligence areas and leading efforts that delivered industry record breaking benchmark results and several patents.

Mario's main expertise includes the areas of IOD architectures and solutions for banking and financial services industries, information integration and master data management, and information system and technical solution architectures. He has authored several technical papers and was awarded the "Leader in Technology" designation by the NSBE-BEYA in 2006. Mario holds a bachelor's degree in Computer Sciences from the University of Toronto and a Software Engineering degree from the University of Havana.

Eberhard Hechler is the chief architect of the IBM Information On Demand (IOD) Technical Center of Excellence, and as a senior certified IT architect (SCITA) and executive IT architect, he is one of the technical leaders in the Information Management organization of the IBM Germany Research and Development Lab.

He joined the IBM Boeblingen Lab, Germany in 1983 as a junior programmer. After a two-and-a-half year international assignment to the IBM Kingston Lab in New York, he has worked in software development, performance optimization and benchmarking, solution architecture and design, software product planning, technical consultancy, and IT architecture. In 1992, Eberhard began to work with DB2 for MVS, focusing on testing and performance measurements of new DB2 versions. Since 1999, his focus is on Information Management and DB2 on distributed platforms.

Eberhard Hechler

His main expertise includes IOD architectures and industry solutions, information integration and master data management, information system and technical solution architecture, information management in risk and compliance solutions, and physical data modeling and data placement.

He coauthored the book *Enterprise Master Data Management: An SOA Approach to Managing Core Information*. Eberhard holds a bachelor's degree in Electrical Engineering—Telecommunication (Diplom–Ingenieur [FH]) from Kassel University of Applied Sciences, and a master's degree in Pure Mathematics (Diplom—Mathematiker) from Hamburg University. He is a member of the IBM Academy of Technology.

Klaus Koenig is an IBM Distinguished Engineer and the CTO and chief architect for Integrated Technology Services within IBM Global Technology Services, Germany. Klaus is member of the global IBM Academy of Technology and member of the global CTO team while collaborating with senior partners and fellows across the IBM divisions.

He is responsible for technical leadership and solution design in complex client environments. Klaus provides senior management support on technical solution design and infrastructure management in various client engagements. For many years, he has conducted strategy consulting and solution workshops for prominent clients on implementing comprehensive IT transformation and information management programs.

Klaus Koenig

Klaus has more than 20 years of experience in IT systems integration and information infrastructure. His main expertise includes the areas of architecture modeling and infrastructure solution design, the enablement of business/IT alignment, information management in risk and compliance solutions, IT service management, and related business optimization solutions.

Klaus holds a master's degree in Electrical Engineering (Diplom—Ingenieur, Univ.) from Technical University of Munich, Germany.

Steve Lockwood is an executive information architect who has been involved in IT for more than 20 years; he has successfully completed roles as an information architect, consultant, application development analyst, and project manager.

After joining IBM in 1997, he worked in Strategic Outsourcing and Global Business Services® before coming to rest in SWG Services six years ago.

Working in the IBM Software Group, he acts as the lead information architect for that group in the UK and has been involved in many of the aspects in the development of information-related projects, covering Data Warehousing and Business Intelligence, Information Integration, Master Data solutions, and

Steve Lockwood

SAP-based solutions. These have encompassed the entire lifecycle of such projects from business discovery to implementation, support, and maintenance. His core technical skills are in DB technologies, and he has used DB2, Teradata, Sybase, SQL Server®, Ingres, Oracle, and BI Tools such as Cognos®, Microstrategy, and Business Objects.

Steve has experience working across a broad number of sectors; he has successfully completed projects in retail, insurance, banking, and government, and he now runs a team of architects who drive IBM's Information Agenda message into the marketplace.

Steve holds a degree in Physics and Electronic engineering and an MBA from Loughborough University in the UK.

Martin Oberhofer joined IBM in the IBM Silicon Valley Labs in the United States at the beginning of 2002 as a software engineer. In an architect role for Enterprise Information Integration (EII) and MDM, he works with large enterprises around the globe shaping the Enterprise Information Architecture (EIA) foundation solving information-intense business problems.

His areas of expertise are MDM, EII, database technologies, Java development, and IT system integration. Martin is particularly interested in MDM and EII with SAP applications. He provides Enterprise Information Architecture and Solution workshops to customers and major system integrators. In a lab advocate role, he provides expert advice for Information Management to large IBM clients.

Martin Oberhofer

Martin coauthored the book *Enterprise Master Data Management: An SOA Approach to Managing Core Information*. Martin holds a master's degree in mathematics from the University of Constance/Germany.

Michael Schroeck is a Partner and the Global Analytics Solutions Team/Center of Competency Leader for IBM, Business Analytics and Optimization, Global Business Services. Mike is considered an industry thought leader and visionary.

He has authored several articles on Business Intelligence, performance management, and analytics, has been a featured speaker at many industry conferences and major seminars, and is frequently quoted in leading business and technical publications.

Mr. Schroeck was twice named as one of the world's top "25 Most Influential Consultants" by *Consulting* magazine and was named a Distinguished Engineer by IBM for his outstanding and sustained technical achievement and leadership.

Michael Schroeck

## CHAPTER 1

The Imperative for a New Approach to Information Architecture

The scenarios in Table 1.1 illustrate how intelligence, information, and technology will radically change how business is done in the future. In each of these scenarios, new sources and uses of enterprise data are brought together and analyzed in new ways to shake the foundation of how companies will operate in this "smarter" world.

Unfortunately, most businesses struggle with even the most basic applications of information. Many companies have difficulty getting timely, meaningful, and accurate views of their past results and activities, much less creating platforms for innovative and predictive transformation and differentiation.

Executives are increasingly frustrated with their inability to quickly access the information needed to make better decisions and to optimize their business. More than one third of business leaders say they have significant challenges extracting relevant information, using it to quantify risk, as well as predict possible outcomes. Today's volatile economy exacerbates this frustration. Good economies can mask bad decisions (even missed opportunities), but a volatile economy puts a premium on effective decision making at all levels of the enterprise. Information, insight, and intelligence must be fully leveraged to support these decisions.

This concept is shown in Figure 1.1 where you can see the results of a recent IBM survey.[1] While executives rely on dubious and incomplete information for decisions, they simultaneously struggle with the complexity and costs of the larger and oftentimes redundant information environments that have evolved over time. The inefficiencies and high costs associated with maintaining numerous, redundant information environments significantly hinder an organization's capability to meet strategic goals, anticipate and respond to changes in the global economy, and use information for sustained competitive advantage. The redundant environments might also

---

[1] For more details on the IBM Institute for Business Value (IBV) Study see [1].

Table 1.1   New Business Scenarios

#	Scenario	Description
1	Imagine getting good stock picks from... Facebook.	Imagine a financial advisor who can understand investor decisions not only from precise monitoring of each and every stock transaction, but from mining every broker e-communication, and every company's annual report in the same instant.
2	Imagine a... talking oil rig.	Imagine an oil rig that constantly "speaks" to its production supervisors by being connected to their control room, and that control room is connected to their supply chain planning systems, which is connected to the oil markets. The oil markets are connected to the pump. Each change in the actual petroleum supply can inform the entire value chain.
3	Imagine if car insurance policies used... cars.	Imagine a car insurer measuring policy risk not only by tracking claim data, but by putting that together with the collective Global Positioning System (GPS) record of where accidents take place, police records, places of repair, and even the internal vehicle diagnostics of an automobile's internal computer.
4	Imagine if every employee had... a thousand mentors.	Imagine students and young employees using social networks to find experts and insight as they grow into their chosen career, enabling them to have a thousand virtual mentors.
5	Imagine an ocean shipping lane that was... always sunny.	Imagine orchestrating a global logistics and international trade operation that was impervious to changes in the weather because of an uncanny capability to predict how global weather patterns affect shipping routes.
6	Imagine if repairmen learned how to fix things... while they fixed things.	Imagine a new breed of super repairmen who service thousands of different complex power grid devices. The intelligent grid senses its own breakdowns and inefficiencies through sensors in the network and intelligent metering. The repairmen are deployed automatically based on their location and availability. Upon arriving to do the repair, they are fed every metric they need, the troubleshooting history of the equipment they are repairing, and likely solutions. Schematics are "beamed" to screens within their goggles, overlaying repair instructions over the physical machine. Their own actions, interpretations, and the associated data patterns are stored in the collective repair history of the entire grid.
7	Imagine energy consumers... able to predict their energy consumption.	Imagine a portal based consumer interface that allows energy consumption to be predicted on a customer-specific basis over a defined period of time. Furthermore, allowing individual energy consumers to choose from a set of available services and pricing options that best match their energy consumption patterns, which leverages predictive analytics to provide advanced consumer insight.

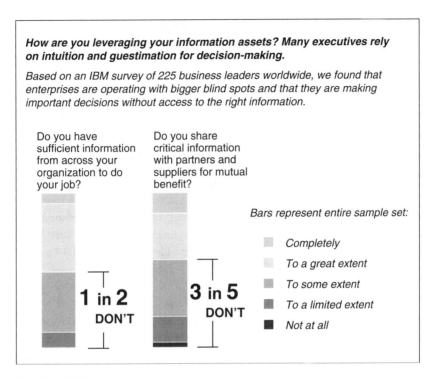

How are you leveraging your information assets? Many executives rely on intuition and guestimation for decision-making.

Based on an IBM survey of 225 business leaders worldwide, we found that enterprises are operating with bigger blind spots and that they are making important decisions without access to the right information.

Do you have sufficient information from across your organization to do your job?

Do you share critical information with partners and suppliers for mutual benefit?

Bars represent entire sample set:

1 in 2 DON'T

3 in 5 DON'T

Completely

To a great extent

To some extent

To a limited extent

Not at all

Figure 1.1   The IBV Study

provide inconsistent information and results which increases executives' apprehension about the quality and reliability of the underlying data.

A new way forward is required. That new way must revolve around an Enterprise Information Architecture and it must apply advanced analytics to enable a company to begin operating as an "Intelligent Enterprise."

1.1 External Forces: A New World of Volume, Variety, and Velocity

Our modern information environment is unlike any preceding it. The volume of information is growing exponentially, its velocity is increasing at unprecedented rates, and its formats are widely varied. This combination of quantity, speed, and diversity provides tremendous opportunities, but makes using information an increasingly daunting task.

1.1.1 An Increasing Volume of Information

Even in the "primitive" times of the information age, where most data was generated through transactional systems, data stores were massive and broad enough to create processing and analytical challenges. Today, the volume is exploding well beyond the realm of these transaction applications. Transistors are now produced at a rate of one billion transistors for every individual on Earth every year.[2] In capturing information from both people and objects, these transistor-based "instruments" are able to provide unprecedented levels of insight—for those organizations that can successfully analyze the data. For example, individuals can now be identified by GPS position and genotype. In the world of intelligent objects, it's not only containers and pallets that are tagged for traceability, but also banalities such as medicine bottles, poultry, melons and wine bottles that are adding deeper levels of detail to the information ecosystem. How is it possible for organizations to make sense of this virtually unlimited data?

1.1.2 An Increasing Variety of Information

Data is no longer constrained to neat rows and columns. It comes from within and from outside of the enterprise. It comes structured from a universe of systems and applications located in stores, branches, terminals, workers' cubes, infrastructure, data providers, kiosks, automated processes and sensor-equipped objects in the field, plants, mines, facilities, or other assets. It comes from unstructured sources, too, including: Radio Frequency Identification (RFID) tags, GPS logs, blogs, social media, images, e-mails, videos, podcasts, and tweets.

1.1.3 An Increasing Velocity of Information

The speed at which new data and new varieties of data are generated is also increasing.[3] In the past, data was delivered in batches, and decision makers were forced to deal with historical and often out-dated post-mortems that provided snapshots of the past but did little to inform them of today or tomorrow. Today, data flows in real time. This has resulted in a world of real time decision making. Therefore, business leaders must be able to access and interpret relevant information instantaneously and they must act upon it quickly to compete in today's changing and more dynamic world.

Other external business drivers contribute to the increasing complexity of information. Globalization, business model innovation, competition, changing and emerging markets, and increasing customer demands add to the pressures on business decision makers. Business leaders are also now looking beyond commercial challenges to see how their enterprises contribute to and interact with societies, including how they impact the environment, use energy, interact with governments and populations, and how they conduct their business with fairness and ethics.

In the context of this changing external environment, information becomes an important differentiator between those who can't or won't cope with this information challenge and those ready to ride the wave into the future.

---

[2] For more details on the growth rate, see [2] and [3].

[3] The speed of increasing volumes during data generation reached in some scenarios is at a point where the volume of data can't even be persisted anymore. This demands the capability to analyze data while the data is in motion. Stream analytics are a solution to this problem and are introduced in several solution scenarios in Chapters 8 and 14.

1.2 Internal Information Environment Challenges

Chief Information Officers (CIOs) and business leaders are starting to take a careful look inward to see how their own Enterprise Information environment is evolving, and the results are not encouraging. Some of the existing information challenges are:

- Accurate, timely information is not available to support decision-making.
- A central Enterprise Information vision or infrastructure is not in place or commonly accepted. The information environment was built from the bottom up without central planning.
- Data repositories number in the hundreds, and there is no way to count or track systems.
- A governance of systems across function, business lines, or geography is lacking.
- Severe data quality issues exist.
- System integration is difficult, costly, or impossible.
- Significant data and technology redundancy exists.
- There is an inability to tie transactional, analytical, planning, and unstructured information into common applications.
- Business leadership and IT leadership are at constant loggerheads with each other.
- Analytic information is severely delayed, missing, or unavailable.
- System investments are justified only at the functional level.
- The IT project portfolio is prioritized in a constant triage mode, and it is slow to respond to new business imperatives.
- The Total Cost of Ownership (TCO) is very high.

1.3 The Need for a New Enterprise Information Architecture

In this decade, businesses have leveraged technologies such as Enterprise Resource Planning (ERP) and Customer Relationship Management (CRM) to help enable their business process transformation efforts, propelling them to greater efficiencies and productivity. Today, it is the advances in information management and business intelligence that drive the level of transformation that empowers businesses and their people.

What "smart" company leaders realize is that a new approach to Enterprise Information Architecture is needed. The current chaotic, unplanned environments do not provide enough business value and are not sustainable over the longer term. The proclivity for system build outs over the years has created too much complexity and is now at a point where enterprise oversight and governance must be applied.

By embracing an enterprise approach, information-enabled companies optimize three interdependent business dimensions:

- **Intelligent profitable growth**—Provides more opportunities for attracting new customers, improving relationships, identifying new markets, and developing new products and services
- **Cost take-out and efficiency**—Optimize the allocation and deployment of resources and capital to improve productivity, create more efficiency, and manage costs in a way that aligns to business strategies and objectives
- **Proactive risk management**—Reduces vulnerability and creates greater certainty in outcomes as a result of an enhanced ability to predict and identify risk events, coupled with an improved ability to prepare and respond to them.

For the information-enabled enterprise, the new reality is this: Personal experience and insight are no longer sufficient. New analytic capabilities are needed to make better decisions, and over time, these analytics will inform and hone our instinctual "gut" responses. The information explosion has permanently changed the way we experience the world: Everyone—and everything— creates real time data with each interaction. This "New Intelligence" is now increasingly embedded into our Smarter Planet.™

CASE IN POINT: SMARTER POWER AND WATER MANAGEMENT

IBM works with local government agencies, farmers, and ranchers in the Paraguay-Paraná River basin, where São Paulo is located, to understand the factors that can help safeguard the quality and availability of the water system.

Malta is building a smart grid that links the power and water systems; it will also detect leakages, allow for variable pricing, and provide more control to consumers. Ultimately, it will enable this island country to replace fossil fuels with sustainable energy sources.

1.3.1 Leading the Transition to a Smarter Planet

Today, Enterprise Information and Analytics is helping to *change the way the world works*—by making the planet not just smaller and "flatter," but *smarter*. At IBM, we have coined the term *Smarter Planet* to describe this information-driven world. A central tenet of Smarter Planet is "New Intelligence,"[4] a concept that is focused on using information and analytics to drive new levels of insight in our businesses and societies. We envision an Intelligent Enterprise of the future that is far more of the following:

- **Instrumented**—Information that was previously created by people will increasingly be machine-generated, flowing out of sensors, RFID tags, meters, actuators, GPS, and

---

[4] See [4] for more information on "New Intelligence."

more. Inventory will count itself. Containers will detect their contents. Pallets will report exceptions if they end up in the wrong place. People, assets, materials, and the environment will be constantly measured and monitored.

- **Interconnected**—The entire value chain will be connected inside the enterprise and outside it. Customers, partners, suppliers, governments, societies, and their corresponding IT systems will be linked. Extensive connectivity will enable world-wide networks of supply chains, customers, and other entities to plan and make interactive decisions.

- **Intelligent**—Advanced analytics and modeling will help decision makers evaluate alternatives against an incredibly complex and dynamic set of risks and constraints. Smarter systems will make many decisions automatically, increasing responsiveness and limiting the need for human intervention.

1.4 The Business Vision for the Information-Enabled Enterprise

As we've discussed, the future information environment will have unprecedented volumes and velocity, creating a virtual and constant influx of data, where enterprises that leverage this information will gain a significant competitive advantage over those that do not.

What does the information-enabled enterprise look like? What new capabilities set it apart and above the information powers of today? Looking forward, we can envision new characteristics for an information-enabled enterprise that empower it to combine vast amounts of structured and unstructured information in new ways, integrate it, analyze it, and deliver it to decision-makers in powerful new formats and timeframes, and give the organization a line of sight to see the future and anticipate change.

We can think of this as an evolution from traditional reporting to advanced predictive analytics. Many organizations still struggle with becoming effective reporters, meaning that even their weekly, monthly, or quarterly views of the past are not reliable or complete enough to help them fix what is broken. Some firms are beginning to advance to a level of being able to "sense and respond" where they can measure and identify performance, risks, and opportunities quickly enough to take corrective action based on a workable level of immediacy that is responsive to business stimuli. Then there are a few of the most sophisticated who are on a path to advance to the next step in analytic maturity that involves having the capability to "anticipate and shape." In this mode, they leverage information in order to predict the road ahead, see future obstacles and opportunities, and shape their strategies and decisions to optimize the results to their ultimate advantage. This concept is shown in Figure 1.2 where you can see the evolution of the information-enabled enterprise.

In an information-enabled enterprise, these capabilities are achieved through better intelligence that is obtained through the sophisticated use of data, empowered by a new analytical vision of Enterprise Information Architecture. Table 1.2 describes characteristics of each phase of this evolution.

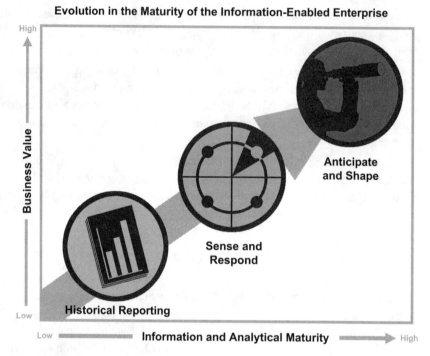

Figure 1.2   Information-enabled Enterprise Maturity

Table 1.2   Phases of Evolution

Focus Area	Historical Reporting	Sense and Respond	Anticipate and Shape
Information sources	Information is collected from internal transactional systems.	Event-based information is collected and integrated from transactional, planning, CRM, and external data providers.	Actionable data is analyzed and collected from many sources, including external sources, new instrumented data, and unstructured and societal data.
Processing	Some large databases are processed in batches and create snapshots of the past.	Large quantities of data process and deliver information quickly.	Large quantities of Structured and Unstructured Data are processed in real time.

Table 1.2 Phases of Evolution

Focus Area	Historical Reporting	Sense and Respond	Anticipate and Shape
Source of insight	Personal experience and informed guess-work are used to make decisions.	Many of the most important decision points are supported by data-driven facts.	Analytical tools are pervasive and user-friendly. Information is delivered anytime, anywhere, over the channels and devices of the user's choice.
Ability to see backward and forward	Historical data is used for "post-mortem" reporting and tracking.	Insights garnered through events enable decision makers to smartly consider future actions.	Sophisticated simulations and modeling are performed to more accurately predict outcomes.
Events	Events are identified and analyzed "after the fact."	Events are tracked in real time, and sophisticated rules enable the automation and rapid speed of response.	Events are anticipated and actions are taken before the event occurs.
Performance and risk	Although some performance measuring is in place, there is minimal measurement of risk factors.	Action is taken after a risk event occurs.	Actions are taken that mitigate risk and improve performance.
Knowing the facts	Information is coded and interpreted differently by Line of Business (LOB) and departments.	Many departments have integrated views of information.	The organization has "one version of the truth," which is defined and understood in the same way across the enterprise.
Summaries and details	Information has limited levels of detail and summary.	Information has many levels of detail and summary.	The needs of the individual and the environment are understood at different levels and delivered in personalized views.
Unstructured Data	Content and unstructured information is used only transactionally. For example, it is used for its primary purpose and then discarded or archived.	Vast stores of content are managed and analyzed, including e-mail, voice, Short Message Service (SMS), images, and video on a stand-alone basis.	Unstructured information is integrated with structured data and used for decision making and as knowledge at the point of interaction/use.

Table 1.2   Phases of Evolution

Focus Area	Historical Reporting	Sense and Respond	Anticipate and Shape
Wisdom and knowledge	Expertise and wisdom are products of experience and networking.	Information is gathered, stored, and accessed through knowledge systems.	New collective wisdom is generated via information and collaboration.
Lifetime of insight	Information is used for monthly, quarterly, and annual reporting.	Relevant information is used across the enterprise, having implications both up and down the value chain (for example, the flow from suppliers to customers).	Information is turned into institutional knowledge and accessed and used in new ways across the extended enterprise.
Integration	Linking of information across boundaries is difficult.	Key systems are integrated to capture important events.	People, systems, and external entities constantly connect and "speak" to each other seamlessly.
Timeliness and access	Users are not provided the information they need to make timely decisions.	Information is delivered in ways that are useful to the context of the situation.	Analytical results are timely, personalized, and actionable.
People	Significant time is spent "chasing and reconciling" data.	Time is spent responding to events as they occur.	People focus on planning, innovation, performance improvement, and risk mitigation.
Innovation	Innovation is seen as a discrete function of research and development or product managers.	Knowledge workers provide innovative responses to events.	Innovation is derived from all segments of the enterprise and from external sources.
Resource management	The enterprise continues to deploy more people to information management.	The enterprise actively seeks to optimize performance by making information more readily available.	Skills and culture are focused on improved analytical decision making at all levels of the organization.

Table 1.2   Phases of Evolution

Focus Area	Historical Reporting	Sense and Respond	Anticipate and Shape
Decision approval	Most decision making is top down and based on financial results.	Formal decision-making processes are in place to expedite approvals and executive sign-off.	Decision-making authority is delegated to more people and requires less managerial and administrative oversight. Employees are encouraged to solve issues immediately and locally.
Incentives	Incentives are aligned to key financial measures.	Incentives are performance- and decision-based.	Incentives are aligned to balanced performance measures with an emphasis on innovation.

These characteristics begin to "color in" the information-enabled enterprise. This said, the specific characteristics and capabilities for each enterprise are defined and built based on the needs and priorities of each organization. Determining this mix and establishing a vision for becoming an Information-Enabled Enterprise are the first and most important steps an organization can take on their enterprise information journey.

CASE IN POINT: SMARTER TRAFFIC IN STOCKHOLM

Traffic is a global epidemic. For example, U.S. traffic creates 45 percent of the world's air pollution from traffic and in the UK, time wasted in traffic costs £20B per year. Stockholm was faced with similar challenges and decided to take action to reduce city traffic and its impact on the environment, especially during peak periods.

Critical to addressing this challenge was providing the city of Stockholm with the ability to access, aggregate, and analyze the traffic flow data and patterns required to develop an innovative solution. State of the art information integration capabilities for structured and unstructured (for example, video streams from traffic cameras) data are, thus, a key technical foundation of the solution.

As a result of performing this analysis, a new strategy was created that included "congestion charges" to influence the levels of traffic at peak times by using cost incentives to drivers. To accurately apply these charges, the city knew that the system had to be accurate on day one. Eight entrances were equipped with cameras that photograph cars from the front and back. These images are sent to a central data system to read the license plates via an optical character recognition (OCR) system to ensure the right cars are charged. Information is collected, aggregated and analyzed with the resultant simulations and algorithms used to determine fee structures based on road usage and traffic patterns.

Continued on the next page

Stockholm was able to implement the system within two months, and the results have been quite impressive.[5] Over 99 percent of cars are identified correctly. The traffic has gone down 22 percent and air pollution has improved by 14 percent since deployment of the system. Besides innovating a new traffic business model, these improvements were made possible with an information-centric approach and by providing advanced and predictive analytical models to better understand and improve traffic patterns, especially during peak periods.

Other cities and countries are interested in the system. The "Smarter Traffic" system does more than paint a picture for the future; it demonstrates how information can be leveraged in new ways to help "drive" a Smarter Planet.

1.5 Building an Enterprise Information Strategy and the Information Agenda™

Enterprises need to achieve information agility, leveraging trusted information as a strategic asset for sustained competitive advantage. However, becoming an Information-Enabled Enterprise through the implementation of an enterprise information environment that is efficient, optimized, and extensible does not happen by accident. This is why companies need to have an Information Agenda[6]—a comprehensive, enterprise-wide approach for information strategy and planning. An *Information Agenda* as shown in Figure 1.3 is an approach for transforming information into a trusted source that can be leveraged across applications and processes to support better decisions for sustained competitive advantage. It allows organizations to achieve the information agility that permits sustained competitive advantage by accelerating the pace at which companies can begin managing information across the enterprise.

Like building a bridge, the architects and engineers must start by showing what the bridge will do and look like, and then carefully plot each component and system so that individual project teams can implement new or enhanced systems that are consistent with the long-term vision. Unlike a bridge, an enterprise continually changes. Therefore, the roadmap must be adaptable to accommodate changing business priorities.

Unlike past planning approaches that have typically been suited for single applications or business functions, the Information Agenda must take a pervasive view of the information required to enable the entire value chain. It must incorporate new technologies, an ever-growing portfolio of business needs, and the impact of new channels (for example, social networks or blogs). The Information Agenda must also take into account the significant investments and value associated with existing systems. The challenge becomes how to combine the existing information environment with new and evolving technology and processes to create a flexible foundation for

---

[5] See [5] for more information on this scenario and its results.

[6] See [6] for more information on IBM's Information Agenda approach.

the future. New information management practices such as Master Data Management (MDM), Information Services within a Service-Oriented Architecture (SOA) environment, and Cloud Computing provide capabilities to further facilitate both the breadth and depth of capabilities required for a true Enterprise Information Architecture.

The Information Agenda must include the strategic vision and roadmap for organizations to:

- Identify and prioritize Enterprise Information projects consistent with the business strategy and based on delivering real business value.
- Identify what data and content is most important to the organization.
- Identify how and when this information should be made available to support business decisions.
- Determine what organizational capabilities and government practices are required to provision and access this data.
- Determine what management processes are required to implement and sustain the plan.
- Align the use of information with the organization's business processes.
- Create and deploy an Enterprise Information Architecture that meets current and future needs.

The Information Agenda becomes the central forum for business and IT leaders to begin taking a serious look at their information environment. It enables leadership to begin formulating a shared vision, developing a comprehensive Enterprise Information Strategy, and ultimately designing the detailed blueprints and roadmaps needed to deliver significant business value by truly optimizing the use and power of Enterprise Information.

Figure 1.3 displays the four key dimensions of the Information Agenda.

The following sections provide an overview of the four key phases associated with developing an Enterprise Information Agenda. Each of these represents a phase of work and decision making, and a set of specific work products that comprise an effective Information Agenda.

1.5.1 Enterprise Information Strategy

The key to building a successful Enterprise Information Strategy is to closely align it to your business strategy. In so doing, the development process is often as important as the strategy it produces. This process enables business leaders to consider, evaluate, reconcile, prioritize, and agree on the information vision and related roadmap. It should compel business executives to actively gain consensus, sponsor the strategy, and lead their respective organizations accordingly. This includes "leading by example" and, in some cases, delaying projects benefiting executives' own functions and departments to accelerate others that are in the best interests of the corporation. To this end, great care should be taken in defining the strategy development approach and ensuring that the right decision makers participate in its development and execution.

From a technology perspective, the information strategy establishes the principles which will guide the organization's efforts to derive an Enterprise Information Architecture and exploit

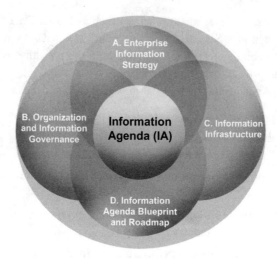

Figure 1.3   Information Agenda

the trusted information and advanced analytical insight that the architecture enables. As such, the enterprise information strategy provides an end-to-end vision for all aspects of the information.

As part of this process, there are three key steps that must be performed to establish the vision and strategy:

1. Define an Enterprise Information vision based on business value.
2. Determine future-state business capabilities.
3. Justify the value to the organization.

1.5.1.1 Define an Enterprise Information vision based on business value

From the outset, IT and business leadership must develop a comprehensive, shared vision for their Enterprise Information environment. This vision describes a long-term, achievable future-state environment, documenting benefits and capabilities in business terms and showing how information is captured and used across the enterprise. This vision must be driven from, and aligned with, the business strategy. In this sense, the information vision never evolves independently, but is always tied to the business strategy via its objectives and performance metrics. It includes operational, analytical, planning and contextual information, and it is designed to benefit almost everyone in the enterprise, from executive leadership to line workers, and from automated systems to end-customers and suppliers. The alignment and mapping of business and technical metadata, which is a key aspect of the Enterprise Information Architecture, enables this interlock between the information vision and the business strategy.

1.5.1.2 Determine your future-state business capabilities

This phase frames the key comparison between the current state ("where are we now?") with the desired future state ("where do we want to be?") from a business value perspective. The result is a gap analysis that identifies what needs to be changed and to what extent, or in other words, what effort is required to close the gap between where we are and where we want to be.

It is useful to develop an understanding of both current and future state by thinking in terms of maturity. Maturity is a measure of establishment, competence, or sophistication in a given capability. At this point in the strategy development process, both the maturity model and gap analysis are likely limited to a very high-level point of reference: This point of reference provides meaningful information on how much change is required within the enterprise information environment and provides guidance to ensure that the blueprint and roadmap are realistic and achievable. Its creation might require subjective opinions and the process might spark energetic debate between different business units and IT leaders. This said, it is not detailed enough to frame initiatives or transformation work. This happens within the blueprint and roadmap process.

1.5.1.3 Justify the value to the organization

Justifying the value to the organization provides a documented, value-based economic justification for enabling the process, organization, and technology capabilities set forth in the Information Agenda Roadmap. Although it is listed here as an end-product, the process of building the value case (also known more plainly as a "business case") is an ongoing, iterative process throughout the entire strategy development cycle, and an ongoing measurement and maintenance activity throughout design and implementation.

The value case frames the benefits to the organization, typically expressed both in business-terms and quantifiable metrics, whenever possible. The value case is instrumental in the decision-making process and is also used to maintain commitment and energy for the transformation throughout the entire lifecycle. It is not uncommon for leaders to lose focus as they become involved in other important areas, yet the value case stands as an important reminder of their commitment and the reasons to continue with difficult project work.

Key components of the strategy are value drivers, or, in other words, the specific measurable benefits and attributes that create value, such as identifying new revenue opportunities, reducing costs, or improving productivity. These value drivers can number in the hundreds or even thousands for an enterprise, but generally are logically grouped by: customers, products, employees, financial management, supply chain, or other operational and functional areas.

By having a timely line-of-sight into these value drivers, executives can better identify those opportunities that represent the greatest value and return on investment for the corporation.

1.5.2 Organizational Readiness and Information Governance

After the vision and strategy are completed, the next step is to evaluate the readiness of the organization to embrace and implement these plans. While Enterprise Information is often thought of in terms of systems and technology, it is the people, processes, organization, and culture that ultimately contribute heavily to success.

Information Governance is a critical component in aligning the people, processes, and technology to ensure the accuracy, consistency, timeliness and transparency of data so that it can truly become an enterprise asset. Information Governance can help unlock the financial advantages that are derived by improved data quality, management processes, and accountability. Business performance and the agility of the Enterprise Information Architecture are also dependent on effective enterprise information definition and governance. This is done via common definitions and processes that drive effective strategy development, execution, tracking, and management. To this end, Information Governance is an important enabler for the Enterprise Information Architecture.

At the outset, it is essential to assess the organization's current information governance framework and processes to determine whether they are robust enough to sustain a competitive, long-term Information Agenda. To manage information as a strategic asset, managing the quality of data and content is critical and can be accomplished only with the right governance and processes in place, supported by appropriate tools and technology.

1.5.3 Information Infrastructure

Assessing and planning the Information Infrastructure is an integral part of developing the Information Agenda. And while there is a strong affinity of all phases of the Information Agenda to the Enterprise Information Architecture, it is an integral part of the Information Infrastructure phase. The ability to govern the Information Infrastructure and to analyze the efforts needed to get from the "as-is" state to the "to-be" state supporting new business needs requires a comprehensive map of all information systems in the enterprise. This map for the Information Infrastructure is the Enterprise Information Architecture and is thus an integral part of the Information Agenda blueprint. This architecture must include a company's current tools and technologies while at the same time incorporating the newer technologies that provide the requisite enterprise scalability and sustainability necessary to address both short term and longer term business priorities.

There are two important steps. First, you must understand the current information infrastructure environment and capture this in an Enterprise Information Architecture showing the current state. Second, you need to define the future information infrastructure and capture this in an Enterprise Information Architecture showing the future state. You can then identify important gaps determining what is needed to get from current to future state.

1.5.3.1 Understand your current Information Infrastructure Environment

This activity involves understanding the company's existing Information Infrastructure with a goal of leveraging, to the greatest extent possible, the investments that have already been made. The current state architecture can then be compared to the future state architecture to identify those technology areas where there might be redundant tools and technologies or, on the other hand, those areas where additional technology might be required now or in the future.

1.5.3.2 Define your future Information Infrastructure

As much as the business vision is essential in describing the desired future state, defining the future Enterprise Information Architecture describes a longer-term and achievable "to-be" state for the Enterprise Information technology environment. Many different information stakeholders should participate in this process, including: Enterprise Architecture, Information Management, Business Intelligence, and Content Management, to name a few. The remainder of this book will describe the Enterprise Information Architecture process in much more detail.

1.5.4 Information Agenda Blueprint and Roadmap

The final step in the development of an Information Agenda is the most important. The three previous steps have each primarily focused on a single important dimension. In developing the Information Agenda Blueprint and Roadmap, these three elements come together and are expressed in the Blueprint via the end-state vision. This is complemented with a short-term tactical plan and a higher level, longer-term strategic plan included in the Roadmap. This Blueprint and Roadmap help ensure that the Information Agenda creates value for the organization, remains aligned with business dynamics and requirements, and prioritizes the necessary projects in the right sequence based on the delivered value.

In essence, the Blueprint describes the "what" the organization is going to do and "where" they are going, as it relates to the information management vision. And the Roadmap defines "how" to achieve this vision. Two key work streams guide this process to successful completion:

1. Develop the Information Agenda Blueprint.
2. Develop the Information Agenda Roadmap and Project Plans.

1.5.4.1 Develop the Information Agenda Blueprint

In this step of the Information Agenda development process, an operational view of the proposed Enterprise Information capabilities is developed, rendered, and described relative to how it exists in its proposed end state. It is a fusion of business capabilities, organizational design, and technologies required to enable the transformation. The Blueprint answers the question "What are we going to build?" This Blueprint, if fully developed, is the to-be state of the Enterprise Information Architecture.

Much like the blueprint for a house containing structural elements, such as plumbing, electrical, mechanical, and so on, the Information Agenda Blueprint provides the design for the new Enterprise Information environment.

Different from the vision, the Blueprint is described in operational terms. To continue the house analogy, the vision for the house might describe its size, number of rooms, whether it's modern, has a warm design, or is ergonomic, and so on. The Blueprint is stated in terms of bricks, mortar, pipes, wires, and so on. In the Information Agenda context, the vision might be voiced in statements such as "Users are able to access real time performance data," whereas the Blueprint might describe "an online performance data dashboard supported by a business intelligence database and rules engine."

Although we describe the Blueprint as an end-state, a good Blueprint is designed for future extensibility, meaning that it will provide a flexible foundation for the future, as the business strategy, requirements, and technologies change over time.

1.5.4.2 Develop the Information Agenda Roadmap and project plans

This work stream involves creating the roadmap of prioritized Enterprise Information initiatives and projects designed to build out the processes, architecture, and capabilities designed in the Blueprint. The Blueprint answers the question "What are we trying to build?" The Roadmap answers the question "How are we going to build it?"

The ultimate product of the Roadmap is a prioritized portfolio of initiatives, projects, and waves that build out the features of the Blueprint. Each project (or group of projects) typically focuses on delivering specific functionality and includes an underlying work plan. These project plans typically include goals, resources, schedules, deliverables, milestones, activities, responsibilities, and budgets. Because of the relative complexity and magnitude of work required at an enterprise-level, a good roadmap needs to integrate these plans in a way that delivers short-term value "quick hits" while also specifying the longer term approach, consistent with the business priorities and the Information Blueprint. To this end, the following techniques are often used to develop the Information Blueprint Roadmap:

- **Varying levels of summary and detail in the roadmap**—These are used to describe progress and plans with different audiences. It is typical to develop a macro view of the entire roadmap, usually expressed on a single page with large, telegraphic chevrons that show the entire picture at an executive level. Supporting this will be detailed work plans developed for the first project(s).

- **Sequential prioritization of groups of projects**—These are usually defined as "waves," which are collections of projects that happen in a sequence (for example, Wave 1, Wave 2, Wave 3, and so on) based on their importance to the organization, their likelihood to deliver immediate benefits or payback, commonality of the projects, and the dependency of their completion for future waves. Smartly organized and sequenced waves maximize the benefits of the projects to the organization. Oftentimes, companies are able to "fund" future waves with the benefits generated from the early waves.

- **A portfolio approach**—This is used to manage multiple, parallel projects to ensure the best use of valuable resources, to reduce and improve coordination among the various teams, to reconcile efforts with existing or in-flight projects, and to manage the resource impact (be it people or investment dollars) on the organization.

- **Center of Excellence (COE) or Center of Competency (COC)**—This is an organizational item—the previous bullets were project-related items. The COEs and COCs are deployed to accomplish this portfolio approach at many organizations. These centers are an effective way of building and enhancing key information management skills and then leveraging those skills across multiple projects.

The Roadmap represents the final and most important product produced from the Information Agenda process because it brings together the results from each of the other three Phases. However, many well-intentioned managers have the urge to skip the other phases of the Information

Agenda development process and attempt to draft their own individual project plans from the start, or perhaps right after the vision is set. From an enterprise perspective, this is a "recipe for disaster" as it commonly enables these teams to develop their own designs and select their own technologies for specific capabilities and functions without a view of the overall environment. In fact, this is how many Enterprise Information environments became the "jungle" that they are today when projects are spawned from the "bottom up" and not guided by a central vision, strategy, and plan.

The process described previously, while generalized, describes a proven and high-quality approach to an Information Agenda development. Each enterprise should tailor, weigh, and prioritize activities to suit its individual needs and situation. Different organizations will want to customize or add certain steps based on their individual circumstances and priorities. In general, these four activities represent the major decision points and deliverables needed to create a comprehensive, pragmatic, and flexible Information Agenda.

1.6 Best Practices in Driving Enterprise Information Planning Success

The Information Agenda development process is often challenging, with each situation requiring its own balance of structured approach, sensitivity to company culture, and the meshing of strong personalities and opinions from diverse teams. Based on IBM's experience working with multiple organizations, the following sections discuss best practices and considerations for how to develop and deploy a successful Information Agenda.

1.6.1 Aligning the Information Agenda with Business Objectives

The top priority in developing an Information Agenda is ensuring that core business objectives drive the agenda. At a high level, these business objectives might be strategic in nature, such as revenue generation, competitive differentiation, cost avoidance, efficiency, or performance. At a line item or feature level they might be described in terms of "being able to mine voice data" or "access to sales data in real time."

It is also important to be realistic and practical in defining the Information Agenda. Most leaders are wary of "boil the ocean" type strategies that appear too expansive and exhaustive to be practically implemented. Along these lines, being realistic with expected returns can be important when setting expectations. When a projected benefit looks too good to be true, it might be viewed with skepticism and disbelief. Lastly, pragmatism in the Blueprint and design approach might require choosing tactics that fit the organization's strengths, even if it does not represent leading-edge thinking within the industry.

1.6.2 Getting Started Smartly

There are typically multiple entry points, competing priorities, and methods for getting started. Sometimes a case for an Enterprise Strategy finds its start in a specific area, such as data quality or risk management, that when examined, is revealed to be endemic of a larger organizational data issue. Other times, the process starts from a strategic enterprise level, where the strategy is based on goals such as global integration, enterprise agility, and competitive differentiation. Regardless, the smart Information Agenda should ultimately take a strategic purview and be supported by advocates for improving the overall business, not just changing the technology, while at the same time identifying opportunities for deriving short-term benefits. It is essential to garner support and advocacy by cross-departmental or cross-functional leadership that includes and spans beyond IT. Although the CIO is a likely candidate to lead the Information Agenda initiative, he or she should have the full support of other top leaders in understanding, championing, and funding the Information Agenda process.

1.6.3 Maintaining Momentum

Constant, quality communications with the right stakeholders is an important way to ensure the project stays on track. Communication should be bidirectional, with the team accepting and responding to stakeholder input and reporting results and decisions.

Since the Information Agenda process will involve many different types of stakeholders, it is important to communicate in the various 'languages' they speak and understand. For example, a CEO might think in terms of competitive differentiation and shareholder value. The CFO will look for hard numbers and speak in financial terms. A CRM or marketing leader might think in terms of customer experience. The IT leaders think in terms of data and systems. Because of this, it is important to describe strategy in ways that engage these different audiences.

1.6.4 Implementing the Information Agenda

The Information Agenda is only as good as an organization's capability to implement it. For the Information Agenda Roadmap to be successful, it must compel the organization forward toward the vision. At the same time, after the implementation begins, the organization cannot lose sight of the strategy. The vision, the Blueprint, and the value case must live on through the implementation as the "guiding lights" and "touchstones." The ultimate strategic output is the Roadmap, as it is the short-term and long-term plan toward achieving the vision.

Lastly, a formal metrics and measurement program needs to be instituted and maintained. At the project level, milestones, schedules, and budgets should be tracked to ensure that the projects are executed on time and on budget. At a strategic business level, the value drivers should be monitored and quantified as the new Information Agenda operations come online.

1.7 Relationship to Other Key Industry and IBM Concepts

The concepts discussed in this book are related to, include, and span many other titles, practices and themes within the realm of using Enterprise Information Architecture. The wide use of different lexicon needn't be a point of confusion or conflict; Enterprise Information practices are broad and varied, requiring many different terms, each with their own nuances and places. Many concepts overlap to a degree, and few claim to be exhaustive in their scope or vision.

This said, within all of these concepts there persists a central thread of *developing excellence in business performance and execution through the use of superior intelligence derived from enterprise information.*

During the past few years, the IBM Corporation and the industry have introduced several new terms that relate to the subject of Enterprise Information, some of which are used in this chapter and throughout this book. Therefore, to avoid confusion and to tie a few of these concepts together, we have taken the liberty to define a few of these key terms on the following pages.

The Relationship to Information On Demand (IOD): Information On Demand[7] describes the comprehensive, enterprise-wide end-state environment, along with the competencies associated with an Information-Enabled Enterprise. These organizations have a masterful ability to capture, analyze, and use the right, critical, powerful information at the point of decision. Inherent within IOD is an extensible Enterprise Information Architecture that provides the technical foundation for gaining and sustaining a competitive advantage through the better use of information. First coined by IBM in 2006, the term IOD has been adopted by many in the industry.

The Relationship to Information Agenda Approach: Whereas IOD represents the end-state vision (the Blueprint), the Information Agenda (and its approach) explains *how* and with *whom* an organization can achieve it. The Information Agenda is a strategy and approach (the Roadmap) for the organization to move forward toward pursuing its IOD objectives.

The Relationship to the Intelligent Enterprise and the Information Enabled Enterprise: Both of these terms connote an organization that is progressing toward achieving their IOD objectives and has mastered the Enterprise Information strategies, programs, and capabilities to be exemplars in analytic and information optimization practices. They refer to "best in class" analytical companies, and their key uses are as models for organizations to emulate as they devise their own specific visions for the future.

The Relationship to Smarter Planet and New Intelligence: Smarter Planet and its sub-domain of New Intelligence are IBM-coined visions of how companies, governments, and societies utilize information, innovation, and analytics to improve quality of life and drive significant value in today's changing world. Different from other concepts listed here, Smarter Planet's purview goes beyond any one enterprise or functional area to describe relationships between global systems, people, and their environments. The Intelligent Utility Network outlined in Chapter 9 is one concrete example of Smarter Planet.

The Relationship to Business Analytics and Optimization (BAO): BAO is the next-generation practice and management discipline for the consulting services industry. It is how practitioners in this space identify the work they do or would characterize the skills that they have. It also describes the practices and disciplines organizations undertake, to deliver on the promise of IOD and Information Agenda. BAO includes all Information Management and Analytics disciplines, including: Business Intelligence (BI), Corporate Performance Management (CPM), Data

---

[7] See Chapter 2 for more discussion on Information On Demand.

Mining and Predictive Analytics, Master Data Management (MDM), and Enterprise Content Management (ECM). It is a sub-domain of the Enterprise Information Architecture. Some of the new trends in this space are discussed in Chapters 13 and 14 in the context of solution scenarios such as Predictive Analytics in Healthcare or Dynamic Pricing in Financial Services Industry. These scenarios are of course just a subset of relevant ones across all industries where BAO is applicable.

1.8 The Roles of Business Strategy and Technology

This chapter sets a business and "how-to" context for what is primarily a technical manuscript to both introduce and reinforce the message that an organization's Enterprise Information Architecture and associated strategy and objectives must be centered around the business value that enterprise information can deliver.

The business value conversation is critically important to even technical audiences. As has been noted throughout this chapter, organizations are not be able to effectively compete without having access to better and more timely information. At the strategic level, IT professionals must partner with business managers in devising, approving, funding, and enabling new capabilities.

At the tactical level, good business knowledge helps the technology professional better understand his or her own priorities and frame of reference as he or she creates technical solutions, by continuing to question *"What value is this creating for the organization or our customers? How will this solution best drive innovation, increase revenue, or improve efficiency?"* These types of inquiries can keep the Enterprise Information Architecture discussion firmly planted within the reality of the larger business context.

This book is the technology companion to an upcoming business discussion on analytics titled *"The Information-Enabled Enterprise: Using Business Analytics to Make Smart Decisions"* by Michael Schroeck. Those readers seeking a deeper business understanding of Enterprise Information Management should consider this book, as it will provide a more detailed discussion into the true value of enterprise information and business analytics.

1.9 References

[1] IBM Whitepaper: *Business Analytics and Optimization for the Intelligent Enterprise.* ftp://ftp.software.ibm.com/common/ssi/pm/xb/n/gbe03211usen/GBE03211USEN.PDF or http://www-935.ibm.com/services/us/gbs/bao/ideas.html (accessed December 15, 2009).

[2] *Semiconductor Industry Association Annual Report, 2001.* http://www.sia-online.org/galleries/annual_report/SIA_AR_2001.pdf (accessed December 15, 2009).

[3] IBM. *Smarter Healthcare.* http://www.ibm.com/ibm/ideasfromibm/us/smartplanet/topics/healthcare/20090223/index.shtml (accessed December 15, 2009).

[4] IBM. *New Intelligence – New thinking about data analysis.* http://www.ibm.com/ibm/ideasfromibm/us/smartplanet/topics/intelligence/20090112/index1.shtml (accessed December 15, 2009).

[5] IBM. *Driving change in Stockholm.* http://www.ibm.com/podcasts/howitworks/040207/index.shtml (accessed December 15, 2009).

[6] IBM. IBM Continues to Help City of Stockholm Significantly Reduce Inner City Road Traffic. http://www-03.ibm.com/press/us/en/pressrelease/24414.wss (accessed December 15, 2009).

[7] IBM. Unlock the business value of information for competitive advantage with IBM Information On Demand. http://www.ibm.com/software/data/information-on-demand/ (accessed December 15, 2009).

## CHAPTER 2

Introducing Enterprise Information Architecture

Chapter 1 elaborates on the information-intense business challenges of the next years to come, and it describes the business value context of tomorrow's intelligent enterprise. This chapter defines the terms Information Architecture and Enterprise Information Architecture (EIA). It positions EIA in the context of Enterprise Architecture. We define the term Reference Architecture. Understanding the concept of a Reference Architecture and its typical description with its various work products, views, and aspects is vital to be able to follow this book.

We discuss how the concept of a Reference Architecture is applied to the Information domain in order to arrive at the most important term and concept that is used throughout the entire book—the Enterprise Information Architecture Reference Architecture (EIA Reference Architecture). You certainly need to study the entire book to appreciate the new emerging aspects of the EIA Reference Architecture and its various facets. However, reading through this chapter will enable you to understand the key concepts that we discuss throughout this book.

This chapter also describes the context of the EIA in terms of its relationship to well known technical frameworks and themes, such as IBM's Information On Demand (IOD) initiative, The Open Group Architecture Framework (TOGAF™), and the concept of Information as a Service (IaaS) in a Service-Oriented Architecture (SOA) environment. You will also explore important methods and models (such as the Information Maturity Model) being used by many organizations to better position the EIA as an enabler of business value.

2.1 Terminology and Definitions

Delivering working solutions in the Information Technology space is always preceded by a process in which the to-be environment is *architected*, a process that helps us to better understand how the solution-building process should be done. Hence, architecture is a key requirement to achieve a high quality solution while reducing costs. The architecture should help to minimize both data and process redundancy. The architecture serves to deliver a better understanding and guidance about how a complex solution should be built. It is used to scope and plan incremental delivery of solutions in the context of a roadmap. During the last decade, there has been an increased emphasis on information architects to better align themselves with the business domain and many practitioners in the field routinely include business strategy as a core component of the Enterprise Information Architecture discipline.

Let's clarify now what we mean by the term *architecture*, well knowing that the meaning of this term might be obvious to most readers. The term *architecture* is widely used in all different domains, going far beyond the Information Technology (IT) domain. There are architectures for houses, gardens, landscapes, cities, automobiles, airplanes: the list is endless. The term architecture might be interpreted and even defined differently within each domain. For our specific purpose, we start with the following definition of *architecture* as it is used in ANSI/IEEE Std 1471-2000,[1] where architecture is defined as:

> "The fundamental organization of a system, embodied in its components, their relationships to each other and the environment, and the principles governing its design and evolution."

Although this ANSI/IEEE definition concentrates on design and evolution, we believe there are other aspects and characteristics that need to be considered by architectures such as guidelines and principles for implementation, operations, administration and maintenance (not just design and evolution). Another essential attribute is the *description* of the architecture—that is, how it is structured and described in a formal way, often by providing generic and detailed diagrams. Furthermore, a description should provide a definition and an explanation about the components and other building blocks of the architecture, its properties and collaboration among each other. The architecture description should enable subsequent steps and tasks in building the overall system. Example steps include the ability to define the Operational Architecture description derived from the Logical Architecture and the ability to perform a technology and product mapping for the implementation. The point is that the architecture is needed to guide you through all aspects (both technical and business) of planning, implementing, testing, deploying and maintaining business and IT systems. IBM's developerWorks® articles[2] are another source on this topic of software architecture.

Building architectures should be supported by an *architecture framework*. An architecture framework is based on an abstraction from multiple implementations and leverages a set of tools (such as pattern modeling and management tools,[3] or tools for logical and physical data

---

[1] See [1] for more information.

[2] See [2] for more information.

[3] See [3] for more information on IBM's Rational Software Architect (RSA) tool which is one example in this space.

modeling) that use a domain-specific taxonomy, methods, guidelines and best practices that already incorporate important aspects, such as standards and regulations. Architecture frameworks should ease and accelerate the development of a broad range of different architectures. They should also accelerate the integration of architecture patterns in other architecture deliverables. TOGAF[4] is a great example of a comprehensive industry standard architecture framework and a methodology that enables the design, evaluation and implementation of the right architecture for an enterprise.

2.1.1 Enterprise Architecture

As we have seen in the previous section, the term architecture is used in a rather broad way and there are different types of architectures such as Business Architecture, Application Architecture, Information Architecture, Infrastructure Architecture, Integration Architecture, Operational Architecture, Security Architecture, and Network Architecture. Although rather long, this list is far from complete. All of these architectures address specific situations or problems to be solved within an enterprise and are thus related in some way to the overall Enterprise Architecture.

We won't explain all these different architectures; this would simply consume too much space. But we would still like to spend some time to introduce on a high-level the Enterprise Architecture and its major layers. This provides a map on which we can locate and position EIA.

Enterprise Architecture provides a framework for the business to add new applications, infrastructure, and systems for managing the lifecycle and the value of current and future environments. Enterprise Architecture provides the alignment across business strategy, IT strategy, and IT implementation. It tightly integrates the business and IT strategies to create an ongoing way to use IT to sustain and grow the business.

Abundant material—both printed and online—is available and covers the Enterprise Architecture area. Online Enterprise Architecture community resources are also available, such as the Enterprise-Wide IT Architecture (EWITA)[5] which includes interesting points of view and history and evolution of Enterprise Architecture. Because of the completeness it offers, we use IBM's Enterprise Architecture definition[6] in this book:

> "An Enterprise Architecture is a tool that links the business mission and strategy of an organization to its IT strategy. It is documented using multiple architectural models that meet the current and future needs of diverse user populations, and it must adapt to changing business requirements and technology."

---

[4] See [4] for more information on The Open Group Architecture Framework (TOGAF™) Version 9.1 "Enterprise Edition."

[5] See [5] for more information.

[6] See [6] for more information.

Enterprise Architecture links the enterprise's business strategy to its IT investments by ensuring a tight integration between the Business, Application, Information, and Infrastructure architecture layers, as shown in Figure 2.1. Each of these areas describes integrated sets of *architecture building blocks (ABBs)* that are used by the enterprise as a whole. These building blocks should be selected so that the enterprise can achieve its overall business objectives. They also need to be made available so that projects can use them in the design, development and deployment of IT-based business systems.

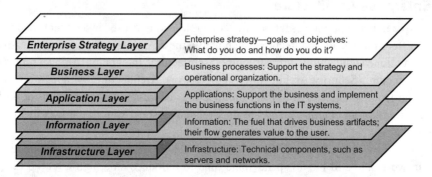

Figure 2.1   The Enterprise Architecture layers

As you can see in Figure 2.1, it's a common approach to describe the complexity of the Enterprise Architecture with a representation based on a collection of architectural layers: each layer supports the needs of the one above it, with the top one directly supporting the capabilities needed by the business strategy. Let's have a closer look at the five layers depicted in Figure 2.1:

- **Enterprise Strategy Layer**—For most institutions, strategic planning and the efficient execution of related IT projects are hampered by lack of enterprise-wide views of the current business and IT landscape and it is difficult to establish a flexible, adaptable, and business-driven IT strategy. Therefore, this layer predominately describes an enterprise strategy concerning product portfolio and appropriate customer segments, appropriate delivery and distribution channels in the given market environment, competitors and core competencies, and capabilities of the company.

- **Business Layer**—Developing an Enterprise Architecture involves providing the process and integrated tools to capture the as-is state of the organization—the business and IT ecosystem—and the desired, to-be state. Enterprise Architecture facilitates the creation of enterprise blueprints that show how business processes are now and how they can be implemented, exploiting the full range of capability of underlying IT architectural building blocks.

- **Application Layer**—The proliferation of applications, systems and the platforms and their interdependencies makes the process of adding and enhancing IT capabilities a risky proposition for the business unless there is an Enterprise Architecture strategy. The Applications Layer supports the business and describes the required business functions in the underlying IT application systems.

- **Information Layer**—Information is the fuel that drives business artifacts; their flow generates value to the user. To transform raw data into meaningful information that provides additional insight and value to the business is one of the key objectives of the Enterprise Architecture. As you can easily imagine, the information layer correlates to our theme of the Art of Enterprise Information Architecture.

- **Infrastructure Layer**—The Infrastructure Layer consists of the network, server and storage infrastructure supporting higher-level functions such as applications, databases or e-mail servers. Due to cost pressure, business stakeholders demand more flexibility and agility also from this layer leading to higher degrees of virtualization and systems consuming less energy, reducing electricity costs.

To summarize, Enterprise Architecture gives the business and IT stakeholders the big-picture perspective across business processes, information systems and technologies. Applying Enterprise Architecture improves the predictability and consistency of project outcomes across the portfolio. Consistently repeatable and thus predictable project success is of utmost importance to achieve an orderly change required for driving effective and lasting transformations such as SOA initiatives while managing associated, inherent risks.

2.1.2 Conceptual Approach to EAI Reference Architecture

This book elaborates on information-centric business challenges, and how they can be creatively addressed by an Enterprise Information Architecture and furthermore by an EIA Reference Architecture. These two architectures describe the Information layer discussed in the previous section from an architecture point of view. To progress with the development of these architectures we first need to develop a concept that can serve as a framework in describing the key design points. In addition, we need a description for what we mean when using the terms Information Architecture, Enterprise Information Architecture and EIA Reference Architecture. Thus, the two-fold purpose of this section is:

- To introduce the conceptual *Reference Architecture* approach
- To introduce a first working description of the term EIA Reference Architecture

Figure 2.2 is a high-level depiction of this conceptual approach. It shows the roadmap to define the relevant information architecture terms. An Information Architecture might exist for each business unit or department in an enterprise. Applying an enterprise-wide business context to the Information Architecture with the objective to get an overall, consistent view leads to the EIA. Finally, when you apply the concept of a Reference Architecture to the EIA it reveals the EIA Reference Architecture. As you can see, there are multiple steps required to define the term EIA Reference Architecture and we sharpen, refine, and detail it as we progress. Chapters 9 to 14 dive into various, chosen aspects of it showing it from various angles.

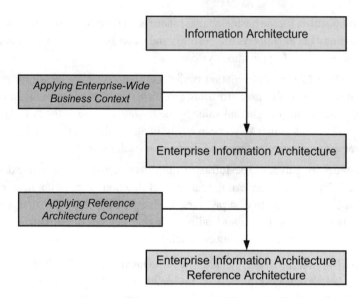

Figure 2.2   A conceptual approach to EIA Reference Architecture

2.1.2.1 Information Architecture

The Information Architecture helps develop the information-centric, technically compatible systems by providing a consistent approach to information technology across a Line Of Business (LOB) or a larger organization. The Information Architecture provides the foundational information-relevant concepts and frameworks for dealing in a consistent and integrated manner with the technology to guarantee the responsiveness and trusted information insight that the business requires from its Information Layer. The Information Architecture identifies the information-centric components of an organization's IT environment and defines its relationship to the organization's objectives.

The Information Architecture also describes the principles and guidelines that enable consistent implementation of information technology solutions, how data and information are both governed and shared across the enterprise, and what needs to be done to gain business-relevant trusted information insight.

Following are some examples of the core principles that guide an Information Architecture:

- **Access and exchange of information**—Information services should provide unconstrained access to the right users at the right time.
- **Service re-use**—Facilitate discovery, selection and re-use of services and whenever possible encourage the use of uniform interfaces.
- **Information Governance**—Adequate information technology should support the efficient execution of an Information Governance strategy.

- **Standards**—A set of coherent standards for data and technology should be defined to promote simplification across the Information Infrastructure.

A well designed and implemented Information Architecture will promote the consistent use of information by all relevant services and business applications, facilitate the access and exchange of information with services, facilitate the discovery and reuse of services, and thus deliver a stable, responsive, and consistent information-centric system behavior.

2.1.2.2 Enterprise Information Architecture

The Enterprise Information Architecture is the framework that defines the information-centric principles, architecture models, standards, and processes that form the basis for making information technology decisions across the enterprise. The Enterprise Information Architecture translates the business requirements into informational strategies and defines what data components are needed by whom and when in the information supply chain. Furthermore, it addresses the need of the business to generate and maintain trusted information that is derived by relevant data components. So why do we distinguish between an Information Architecture and an Enterprise Information Architecture? The *enterprise* in the definition adds the *enterprise-wide business context* to the definition of Information Architecture described in the previous section.

The challenges faced by most organizations, from government to public enterprises, depend upon consistent decision making across multiple business units, departments, and individual projects. The EIA is a core component of the required framework for effective decision making by defining the guiding principles that dictate the organization's strategy to address business needs and the information-centric technology infrastructure that supports them. The EIA defines the technical capabilities and processes the organization needs to manage data and information over its lifetime, optimize content-based operational and compliance processes, establish, govern and deliver trusted information, and optimize business performance.

By aligning business needs with the technology and the information flows in the supply chain, EIA delivers flexibility, agility and responsiveness to the business process and the organization as a whole. The primary goal of the EIA is to reduce complexity and thereby contribute to the elimination of all the factors that act as the inhibitors to change and address new business paradigms.

Primary characteristics that can be used to distinguish a well-defined EIA implementation include the following:

- **Gaining transparency**—The information remains independent from application specifications, application implementations, and user interfaces. It provides a transparency layer between the information and application domains.

- **Considering enterprise business requirements**—The architecture takes into account the overall information needs of the entire enterprise and specific LOBs or individual organizations.

- **Avoiding inconsistencies**—It helps identify inconsistencies, conflicts, overlaps, and gaps in the data and information, and offers a concept, framework, and methods to resolve this, and it is useful to select adequate solutions.

- **Managing Service Level Agreements (SLA)**—It provides mechanisms for the definition and management of information-centric SLAs which can be monitored and enforced.

- **Enabling decision making**—The architecture enables more consistent and efficient IT decision making that is linked to business needs. It does this because it is both flexible and extensible.

- **Addressing reusability aspects**—Enforcing an EIA means that information assets are shared and reused, avoiding data duplication and thus reducing development, service, and support costs.

- **Addressing data scope**—The Information Reference Model (see Chapter 3) used by the enterprise describes the scope of the used data and information supported by the EIA.

- **Defining a technology strategy**—It establishes the framework upon which the technology strategies adopted by the enterprise depend. In addition, it defines the set of principles that guide how an organization's information systems and technology infrastructure are engineered.

2.1.2.3 Reference Architecture

Reference Architecture is an important concept in this book. So what is it? What are the key imperatives and design points? Well, let's start with a generic definition.

The Reference Architecture provides a proven template for architecture for a particular domain or area of application that contains the supporting artifacts to enable their use. The Reference Architecture incorporates best practices resulting from work on a particular field and it also provides a common vocabulary to enable a common understanding while facilitating discussions around implementations.

A Reference Architecture encapsulates at an abstract level the results and best practices derived from multiple deployments of solutions to a given business problem. They enable the logical sequence of tasks required to build a complete system. Reference Architectures provide a common format that facilitates the design and deployment of solutions repeatedly in a consistent manner. Thus, they are a valuable tool for IT Architects to help identify and assess gaps and reduce risks in the solution development cycle.

Based on the requirements in a given area of an application, there are certain components shared between systems in the same area. The Reference Architecture identifies these components and indicates how they interconnect. It is the blueprint that identifies the common components that all conforming systems and environments share.[7] The following are some key Reference Architecture characteristics:

---

[7] For example, in [7] the Reference Architecture concept is applied to the SOA architecture style.

- **Major foundational components or building blocks**—They help to describe an end-to-end architecture solution.

- **Common language**—It simplifies communication when talking about systems of a given type.

- **Framework**—The Reference Architecture is a framework for scope identification, roadmap definition, risk assessment, and gap assessment.

- **Foundation**—It is a proven foundation for all solution designs in a domain (e.g., e-business solutions).

The Reference Architecture leverages ideas from successful past implementations and lessons learned from troubled or failed projects and concentrates on simplification, reuse, and usability, avoiding the complex details of the specific technology. It has the potential to evolve over time, meaning that after it has been constructed, it requires maintenance with harvesting of best practices from projects as they are completed, including changes or additions to the Reference Architecture to handle situations that were not addressed.

Within the wider solution architecture and deployment scope, there are significant advantages to using Reference Architectures. This list is not comprehensive, and you can probably think of examples from your own experience, but following are a few examples:

- **Best practices**—A solution architecture based on an up-to-date Reference Architecture that consistently incorporates available best practices for a specific business domain or an area of application.

- **Consistency and repeatability**—Solution architectures that leverage current RAs are more consistent and often repeatable. Using technology similarly across different solutions delivers significant cost reductions in support activities.

- **Efficiency**—As architects and software developers gain familiarity with the architecture and the technologies used, they become much more efficient at delivering solution outlines.

- **Flexibility and extendibility**—These are enhanced for systems designed and built in compliance with well-conceived RAs.

Reference Architectures in the IT space often define the architecture blueprints for addressing specific technology areas such as Data Security (Data Security Reference Architecture). They can be created to describe areas such as Business Performance Management (Business Performance Management Reference Architecture) or to guide the how-to for a solution of a particular industry problem, such as delivering an IT Reference Architecture for Rapid Product and Service Assembly for Communication Service Providers (CSPs).

The IBM Insurance Application Architecture[8] and the Master Data Management (MDM) Reference Architecture are further examples of well-documented Reference Architectures for different domains that encapsulate best practices in the form of business process, business objects, business rules, architecture patterns, data models, and other artifacts that have been successfully used by many practitioners in the field.

We could actually view a Reference Architecture or part of one to be derived from architecture patterns over time. Architecture patterns for a specific domain, for instance Business Intelligence (BI), MDM, and so forth, have the potential to be developed into a more comprehensive and pervasive Reference Architecture. In any case, the creation of a Reference Architecture is aimed to achieving efficiency and consistency in the assembly process of the Enterprise Architecture by incorporating proven best practices in the specific area.

The description of a Reference Architecture is decomposed into several distinct levels as shown in Figure 2.3.

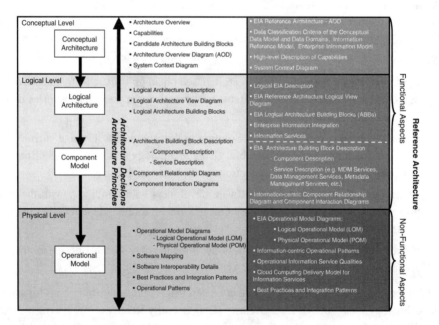

Figure 2.3   Reference Architecture Levels

---

[8] [8] contains more information on this architecture.

- **Conceptual Level**—This level is closest to business definitions, business processes, and enterprise standards. It is stable over time but can be augmented as new business needs arise. The Reference Architecture at the Conceptual Level is called Conceptual Architecture. It describes which architecture building blocks are required and what concepts and capabilities they will display. This is depicted in an Architecture Overview Diagram (AOD). It is owned by (enterprise) architects and architecture governance groups.

- **Logical Level**—This level of the Reference Architecture translates conceptual design into logical design. It takes into consideration existing data elements, functions, processes, and their relationships. The level of detail used to describe the architecture at this level is still understood by most business users in addition to IT professionals. This level is composed of two parts, which are owned by enterprise architects and business analysts. They are:

  - **Logical Architecture**—The Logical Architecture shows the relationships of the different data domains and functionalities required to manage each type of information. The Logical Architecture is depicted with a Logical Architecture Diagram and the description of relevant architecture layers and ABBs.

  - **Component Model**—Technical capabilities and the architecture building blocks that execute them are used to delineate the Component Model. It is shown through a Component Relationship Diagram (static view) and Component Interaction Diagrams showing how the components interact with each other. On this level components are fully described regarding their functional scope.

- **Physical Level**—This level of the Reference Architecture translates the logical design into physical structures and often products. This level includes the technical description and operational services within each architecture building block including the implementation of non-functional requirements. At this level, the Component Model is further formulated to derive to the Operational Model that details integration and operational patterns. It is usually dynamic and evolves with technology advancements. It is owned by IT Architects, designers and system administrators.

2.1.2.4 Enterprise Information Architecture Reference Architecture

Now we can describe the EIA in the context of the Reference Architecture. In addition to the more traditional information capabilities such as data integration or content management, this book explores the new and emerging capabilities required to deliver the vision of a Next-Generation Enterprise Information Architecture. Following are just a few of these new themes that must be considered when developing the EIA Reference Architecture:

- **Cloud Computing[9]**—To facilitate the role of data and content in the Cloud, this, for instance, will require improved capabilities and even new concepts regarding multi-tenancy, the ease-of-use of programming models, and more flexible scalability properties.

- **Metadata Management**—It facilitates business-initiated exploitation of Business and Technical Metadata to gain a pervasive end-to-end insight into coherences in the information infrastructure (for example, data lineage) and also links the business and technical domains.

- **Mashup**—Capabilities to deliver data and information for Web 2.0 and other similar situational applications to essentially deliver new functions and insights.

- **Dynamic Warehousing**—This addresses the new aspects of Data Warehousing, such as optimizing business processes through real-time information insight and analytics as well as integrating Unstructured Data into the analytical domain.

- **New Trends in Business Analytics and Optimization (BAO)**—The Intelligent Enterprises exploits smarter more advanced analytics to optimize business performance.

Our EIA Reference Architecture is described in a set of work products. These Reference Architecture work products address the themes from the business environment and a high-level AOD, to non-functional aspects and the Operational Model. Table 2.1 contains a brief description of these EIA Reference Architecture work products (we introduced some of them earlier).

We next look at the Reference Architecture levels to determine and customize the key Reference Architecture components for the specifics of the Enterprise Information Architecture. To apply the Reference Architecture concept to the Enterprise Information Architecture, let's briefly discuss the four key components of the Reference Architecture levels. This customization of the Reference Architecture concept to incorporate the key EIA aspects is depicted in the dark grey shaded column on the right in Figure 2.3.

Following are the four key components of the EIA Reference Architecture:

- **Conceptual Architecture**—This includes a more detailed level of the Architecture Overview Diagram for the EIA, the description of the data classification criteria, and data domains, and it includes a high-level description of the capabilities, key architecture principles for EIA, and architecture decisions. It also includes IT governance and Information Governance topics.

- **Logical Architecture**—This contains the logical EIA description, the EIA Reference Architecture Logical View diagram (including the data domains in the context of this diagram), key aspects of the enterprise information integration, and a high-level description of the information services.

---

[9] Gartner claims that Cloud Computing is as influential as e-Business (see [9]). Chapter 7 discusses the information-centric aspects of Cloud Computing.

Table 2.1   EIA Reference Architecture Work Products

#	EIA Reference Architecture Work Products	High-Level Description
1	Business Context Diagram	Contains the Business Context Diagram that documents the identity of the enterprise and its interactions with other entities in its environment
2	System Context Diagram	Highlights important characteristics and constraints of the system events and data and information the system receives and generates
3	User Profiles	Contain detailed descriptions of the relevant characteristics of each user category and their responsibilities in interfacing with the system
4	Use Case Model	Describes a model of functional characteristics of use cases of the system, to include use cases such as user registration, archiving BI reports, updating data content, and so on
5	Architecture Overview Diagram	Represents governing ideas and candidate building blocks as part of the conceptual architecture
6	Architectural Decisions	Documents important architectural decisions made
7	Architecture Principles	Architecture principles are a set of fundamental imperatives (or laws) the architecture needs to comply with. An example would be a principle to decouple master data from applications or another to comply with open standards.
8	Service Qualities (Non-functional Requirements)	Identify considerations affecting Quality of Service (QoS) and constraints for the system; examples are security, continuous performance, availability, and scalability.
9	Logical Architecture Diagram	Elaborates on the relationships of the different information types and the functionalities that will use this information. This contains the Logical Architecture Diagram.
10	Component Relationship Diagram & Component Interaction Diagrams	Describes the entire hierarchy of components, their responsibilities, static relationships, and their interactions with other components
11	Operational Model Relationship Diagram, Operational Patterns	Focuses on deployment of components to the infrastructure and describes the operation of the IT system, taking into account the non-functional requirements

- **Component Model**—This is a detailed description of the EIA building blocks and their functionality including a detailed description of the EIA components, a service description (for instance MDM Services, Data Management Services, Metadata Management Services and so on), an information-centric Component Relationship Diagram, and Component Interaction Diagrams (including some exemplary scenario descriptions).

- **Operational Model**—This includes the Logical Operational Model (LOM) and Physical Operational Model (POM); information-centric Operational Patterns; Service Qualities applicable for information services; the Cloud Computing delivery model for information services; best practices and integration patterns.

This concludes the discussion of the Reference Architecture conceptual approach and how the key term EIA is mapped to the Reference Architecture concept.

2.2 Methods and Models

After introducing the relevant terms, we now introduce an architecture methodology and a maturity model. Both are highly relevant to the EIA Reference Architecture.

2.2.1 Architecture Methodology

A number of Enterprise Architecture methodologies have been developed since the origins of the Enterprise Architecture field in 1987. In his publication from 1987, J. A. Zachman[10] laid a vision of Enterprise Architectures that has guided this field for the past several decades. Zachman described what was, in his perception, the major challenge in the IT field at that time to manage the complexity of increasingly distributed systems. The cost involved and the success of the business, which depended increasingly on its information systems, required a disciplined approach to the management of those systems. Currently, the architecture methodology field has several leading methods developed by governments and other large institutions. Among the most recognized methodologies in the EIA field are the following four:[11]

- The Open Group Architectural Framework (TOGAF)
- The Zachman Framework for Enterprise Architectures
- The Federal Enterprise Architecture
- The Gartner Methodology (formerly Meta Framework)

Each of these architecture methodologies has areas of strengths and dedicates a significant part of its content to the creation of an Information Architecture and an EIA as a core component of an Enterprise Architecture. For many organizations, a complete EIA solution

---

[10] See [10] for more information.

[11] See [11] for more information as well as for a comparison based on a comprehensive assessment of these four architecture methodologies. Details on these four methodologies can be found in [4], [12], [13], [14] and [15].

requires choosing useful areas from each methodology and modifying them according to the specific needs of the organization.

One of the earliest attempts at creating an EIA methodology was carried out by the U.S. Department of Defense based on Zachman's principles. This effort took place in 1994 and was known as the Technical Architecture Framework for Information Management (TAFIM).[12] In 1995, TAFIM was used as the core for the original development of TOGAF Version 1. In terms of the relevance of Zachman's principles and the TOGAF framework to the overall architecture development cycle, they are universally applicable to the TOGAF Architecture Development Method (ADM) and the broader governance disciplines.

Many information-specific frameworks and methodologies have been created since Zachman's original publication and they are all used as guidance during the process of creating an EIA. Equally abundant is the number of documented strategies that are used as a guidance to successfully manage the process of creating, changing, and using the EIA. Adopting one or more of these methods to guide the strategy around information in an organization is crucial.

The development of an EIA should be managed as a formal program by an Enterprise Information Architecture Department with strong participation of business users and clear accountability measures for its success. The EIA must provide the flexibility to accommodate the changes that result from the changing business environment in the organization; consequently, the enterprise information architect plays a key role as an agent of change.

The effective implementation of the EIA requires a clear set of processes that can be used by the business and IT areas alike to continuously assess and enforce compliance with the Enterprise Architecture. Bypassing these requirements should rarely occur and when it does it should be done only after careful and detailed business case analysis. When the organization does not put in place a consistent governance program there is a significant risk that changes and new systems will not meet the organization's business needs or will be incompatible, and there will be a noticeable increase in the costs associated with systems development, maintenance and integration.

Although the details may vary from one EAI method to another, the basic elements of every successful EIA can be described as follows:

1. Complete the initial analysis and start-up activities using the Information Maturity Model we describe in the next section.

2. Define the as-is and the to-be state of the EIA, including the gap assessment. For this purpose, the as-is state can be captured using the System Context Diagram deliverable we describe in Chapter 3.

3. Develop a plan to address the gaps, including the execution of the plan.

---

[12] See [16] for more information.

2.2.2 Information Maturity Model

This section describes an approach to assess the maturity of a given EIA Reference Architecture by looking at the following core measurements of agility:

- Maturity of information use
- Business value delivered to the organization

The Information Maturity Model can be used as an assessment technique upfront in the overall EIA development cycle. To assess how mature an EIA is, you measure the maturity of the enterprise capabilities against the following criteria. This assessment provides prescriptive actions for the enterprise to better support its information requirements. To achieve the desired agility and responsiveness, the enterprise requires succeeding in the following areas:

- Reducing the time needed to access information
- Reducing information complexity
- Lowering costs through an optimized infrastructure
- Gaining insight through analysis and discovery
- Leveraging information for business transformation
- Gaining control over master data
- Managing risk and compliance via a single version of truth

By evaluating a baseline of the current enterprise information management infrastructure against best practices and establishing current and target maturity levels and using a rapid analysis of all the significant dimensions including integration, security, standards, governance, availability, and quality, you can assess gaps in the maturity level and establish a high-level business case for aligning the EIA to reach the target information maturity level.

The objective of this assessment is to understand how information is managed currently (in the as-is state), compare it to the industry best practices, and determine what needs to be done to enable the agility in the EIA in terms of driving toward a higher maturity level of the information use.

The assessment process begins by compiling background information on the organization's EIA, including the inventory of all data repositories and systems including DWs and data marts, the data and information handling processes, and their purposes. This is then mapped to a hierarchy level view of the Business Architecture and projects and initiatives that relate to the data and related processes. Furthermore, data quality needs to be analyzed and compared against target levels. Also, without an assessment of the maturity of Information Governance in the organization, the assessment regarding Information Maturity is incomplete.

To measure the maturity, use the following areas that define the architecture:

- **Information Strategy**—Is there one and is it articulated consistently? Is it linked to business goals?

- **Information Users**—Is organizational leadership on board? Are enterprise architect roles defined? Does the organization have the required level of skills?

- **Information Processes**—Are formal processes defined in the various information areas? Is a security and privacy policy in place?

- **Information Governance**—Is there an Information Governance program in place?

- **Data**—Are architecture and standards in place? Is the organization exploiting Master Data Management? What are the processes around information integration and data quality? Is there a metadata strategy?

- **Information Technology**—Are quality and security controls in place?

Figure 2.4 provides the overall maturity model as part of the EIA Reference Architecture. This model includes high-level characteristics for each level of maturity. Each of the six areas above can be assessed against these characteristics. Each of these six areas might have its own detailed definition for each step in the levels of maturity.

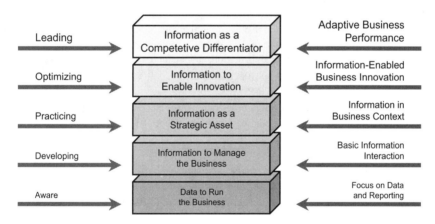

Figure 2.4   Information Maturity Model

The maturity model reflects a structured approach to achieve a specific set of maturity goals. The investment over the past few years was focused on using data and content to automate the business that ensures transactions flowed seamlessly across different applications without manual intervention.

This approach did not address the proliferation of information silos. Organizations have begun to move their focus to managing the core pieces of enterprise information that span across the many systems that exist to treat information as a strategic asset. This refocus enables them to use information in new ways and outside of the context of any individual system. As organizations progress up this maturity curve, they see an enormous increase in the business value derived from their information.

The information maturity models described are loosely based on the Capability Maturity Model Integration (CMMI) maturity models for software development organizations as well as IBM's Information On Demand Maturity Model.[13] Table 2.2 summarizes our discussion on the Information Maturity Model, where we begin with the lowest level of maturity.

Table 2.2   Information Maturity Model

#	Level	Maturity Summary
1	Aware	Data to run the business: An organization that has few of the required capabilities, enabled generally through manual processes with little automation or *heroic* efforts by individuals is the *immature* organization regarding a certain ability of information use. Processes to manage data are undocumented, uncontrolled, reactive, and chaotic.
2	Developing	Information to manage the business: An organization that has a rudimentary, loosely-woven set of capabilities – the basic operational organization regarding a certain ability of information use. Processes, information, and technology are underdeveloped and lack integration across touch points, though they might be deployed within isolated touch points or functional areas. Some data processes are documented and repeatable with consistent results, but there is no continuous improvement plan in place to maintain processes.
3	Practicing	Information as a strategic asset: An organization that has implemented basic capabilities that are consistent with industry norms: the industry-competitive organization in a given capability. Capabilities have been deployed with business results in key touch points, but not all. Data processes are documented with repeatable consistent results with a continuous improvement plan. There is some consistency of data processes across a single LOB.
4	Optimizing	Information to enable innovation: An organization that has not only developed the required capabilities but also actively integrates them into its daily operations – the leading practice regarding a certain ability of information use. This organization has a high degree of cross-functional integration. Data processes are documented with repeatable, consistent results, and there is continuous improvement of data processes across a single LOB. In some instances, there is a consistent data process across multiple LOBs.

[13] See [17] for CMMI and [18] for the IOD maturity model details.

Table 2.2 Information Maturity Model

#	Level	Maturity Summary
5	Leading	Information as a competitive differentiator:
		An organization that has differentiated itself based upon its capabilities and simultaneously redefined those capabilities – the *bleeding edge* regarding a certain ability of information use. Systems are fully integrated.
		Data processes are documented with repeatable consistent results, they continuously improve, and there is consistency of data processes across multiple LOBs.

2.3 Enterprise Information Architecture Reference Architecture in Context

In this section, we put the EIA Reference Architecture into a wider context because within an enterprise other architectures and methods might be in use. Knowing its relationship to them[14] is thus important, but we only position it for the following four which we considered the most relevant:

- Information On Demand (IOD) initiative
- Information Agenda (IA) approach
- Open Group Architecture Framework (TOGAF)
- Service-Oriented Architecture (SOA) architectural style

2.3.1 Information On Demand

IBM's IOD approach is introduced in Chapter 1 from a business perspective. But what does IOD have to do with our concept of the EIA Reference Architecture? For an enterprise to flourish and adapt to quickly changing conditions, the EIA Reference Architecture needs to enhance its capabilities and maturity to better support business-oriented solutions. The IOD approach offers for this purpose a framework, suitable processes as well as capabilities and tools to reach this goal. The core architectural capabilities delivered by IOD to enable critical abilities in the EIA are:

- **Information as a Service (IaaS)**—In SOA architecture, information services enable business processes to gain access to information they need in a timely fashion and in conformance with open industry standards.
- **Data virtualization**—It enables access to heterogeneous data sources through techniques such as federation.

---

[14] For example, more details on IOD, the Information Agenda, and TOGAF™ can be found in [19], [20], and [21] respectively.

- **Unconstrained access**—All users in the enterprise need unconstrained access to the data and information relevant to perform their job whether the work within an office on company ground or remotely (for example from home).

- **Single version of the truth**—This is central management of the master enterprise copy for core business entities such as customers, suppliers, partners, products, materials, bill of materials, charts of account, locations, employees, and so on.

- **Advanced analytics, Business Intelligence, and performance management**—These provide a better understanding of and optimization of business performance.

- **Advanced search**—Robust search to uncover inherent meaning, user intent, and application context to deliver meaningful information that are easily actionable within a required business process.

- **End-to-end metadata management**—This enables the generation and exploitation of business and technical metadata for acceleration, consistency, ease of deployment, and improved insight.

- **Information integration capabilities**—This includes understanding, cleansing, transformation, information delivery, replication, and other information integration capabilities.

To summarize, the EIA Reference Architecture substantiates the IOD imperatives by delivering an information-centric Reference Architecture. Leveraging the EIA Reference Architecture facilitates the deployment of open and agile technology to leverage existing information assets for speed and flexibility.

2.3.2 Information Agenda Approach

As we have already elaborated on the Information Agenda approach in Chapter 1, this chapter focuses on its affinity to the EIA Reference Architecture. The following sections point out how they are linked to the EIA Reference Architecture.

2.3.2.1 Information Strategy

Information strategy establishes the principles that will guide the organization's efforts to derive an EIA and exploit the trusted information that the architecture enables. The information strategy provides an end-to-end vision for all components of the Information Agenda and is driven by an organization's business strategy and operating framework. The organization's ongoing framework and guiding set of principles ensures that current and future investments in people, processes and technologies align and support an agile and flexible EIA. IT will need the assistance and even guidance of LOB users including executive sponsorship from the very beginning to make sure the EIA aligns with the information strategy defined by the Information Agenda. Once the organization business imperatives are identified and reviewed, goals are defined to help set the priorities upon which to derive an appropriate EIA Reference Architecture. The information strategy is a critical component of an Information Agenda and it is also within the initial phase of the EIA Reference Architecture methodology.

2.3.2.2 Information Definition and Information Governance

Information definition and Information Governance are the most difficult challenges companies face. They require the enterprise to be able to find answers to questions such as:

- What information do you have, where is it stored, and what value does it have?
- How does your business use it and for what purpose?
- How good (or bad) is the information quality?
- What information do you keep and what do you archive?

To begin to adequately answer these questions, there needs to be alignment and consistent understanding across IT and business functions and users enabled by an enterprise data dictionary where business and technical terms are related to each other. The EIA Reference Architecture enables such an enterprise data dictionary with appropriate end-to-end metadata management capabilities. Some of the objectives of information definition and Information Governance that need to be reflected by the EIA Reference Architecture include:

- Defining governance processes, infrastructure, and technology
- Establishing common data and information domain definitions
- Monitoring and ongoing improvement of data quality
- Establishing necessary executive sponsorship, organizational policies, and cross-organizational oversight

Business performance and the agility of the EIA Reference Architecture can also be improved as a result of information definition and Information Governance. This is done via common definitions and processes that drive effective strategy development, execution, tracking and management. Information Governance is a key theme for our EIA Reference Architecture.

2.3.2.3 Information Infrastructure

To enable the organization to manage information as a strategic asset over time, it must commit to establishing an EIA Reference Architecture. Within the context of an Information Agenda, an EIA Reference Architecture identifies the technology required to integrate current investments with future technologies, helping to optimize return on investment.

During this stage, a set of tasks that can be mapped to the EIA methodology can be identified. The work required with defining the *as-is* EIA, assessing how ready and aligned the architecture is to the business imperatives already identified, what would be the *to-be* EIA and figuring out the gaps. The EIA Reference Architecture needs to include at least the element's Enterprise Information Integration (EII), Metadata Management, MDM, Data Management, Enterprise Content Management (ECM), Dynamic Warehousing (DYW), BI, and performance management.

You will see throughout the various chapters that all of these elements are vital to our EIA Reference Architecture. Thus, the Information Infrastructure dimension of the Information Agenda is well linked to the scope of our EIA Reference Architecture.

2.3.2.4 Information Roadmap

The Information Agenda includes the deployment roadmap for both the near and long term. For the roadmap to be most effective, the process needs to show where the organization and the EIA stands now in terms of the maturity of its information use, and where it wants to go in the future. This information roadmap influences the evolution of the EIA Reference Architecture because it contains the what and when of changing business requirements to which it must adapt by a step-by-step approach according to an implementation master plan.

2.3.3 The Open Group Architecture Framework

The Open Group Architecture Framework (TOGAF) is an architecture framework that enables practitioners to design, evaluate, and build the right architecture for a particular business. TOGAF doesn't specify the architecture style; it is a generic framework. Therefore, the EIA Reference Architecture or the SOA architecture style can serve as an architecture framework within TOGAF.

We consider now specifically the TOGAF Architecture Development Method (ADM).[15] We intend to demonstrate that our concept of the EIA Reference Architecture is well aligned with the key principles of the TOGAF framework and especially the ADM method. TOGAF and the EIA Reference Architecture are iterative methods that identify and produce—if not the same—artifacts and deliverables, such as AODs, enterprise information models (as-is and to-be), architecture component models, and also development and governance processes that are very similar to working top-down from the business needs.

Like the approaches discussed by TOGAF for developing an EIA, we also encourage dedicating special attention to defining the scope and a roadmap for the EIA Reference Architecture effort. Complex enterprise-wide architecture efforts are difficult to manage. In addition, an enterprise-wide scope appears to be more difficult in terms of getting firm sponsorship from the organization's executives. Segmenting the effort and establishing a pragmatic step-by-step roadmap enables the incremental development of the architecture while maintaining the structured approach of the architecture framework.

Figure 2.5 is a depiction of the TOGAF ADM method, where we highlight a few exemplary relationship points to the EIA Reference Architecture. This comparison and interconnection between the TOGAF ADM and the EIA Reference Architecture is far from complete. However, with the exemplary discussion of some relationships it is clear in which direction an in-depth elaboration would go. We concentrate on the following three TOGAF ADM areas:

---

[15] See [21] for more information on the ADM from TOGAF.

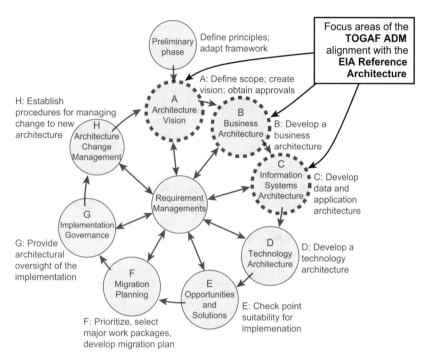

Figure 2.5   Interconnection of the TOGAF ADM Method with the EIA Reference Architecture

Reprinted with small modification and permission from The Open Group™

- Architecture vision
- Business Architecture
- Information Systems Architecture

In addition to these three areas, TOGAF and the EIA Reference Architecture are aligned in other areas, too. For instance, The Information Agenda approach strengthens and underpins TOGAF and our EIA Reference Architecture with a methodological approach in identifying business-relevant, information-centric themes.

2.3.3.1 Architecture Vision

The objectives of this phase are to:

- Ensure proper recognition and endorsement from business sponsors.
- Validate the business principles, business goals, and strategic business drivers.
- Define the scope of the current architecture effort.
- Define the relevant stakeholders and their concerns and objectives.

- Define the key business requirements and the constraints.
- Articulate an Architecture Vision that addresses requirements and constraints.
- Secure formal approval to proceed.
- Understand the impact on and of other enterprise architecture development cycles.
- Develop a business case for SOA for this architecture cycle.

The EIA Reference Architecture can be used to map the existing landscape and the proposed target landscape. At the logical level of the EIA Reference Architecture, a set of architectural principles can be first established. They are used as guidelines and imperatives in building an EIA Reference Architecture. It can also be used as a discussion document to inform and achieve alignment with end users and governance bodies (related to the business, data and information, business or IT-related processes, corporate themes, SOA-related topics, and so on).

Furthermore, security requirements for new initiatives, impact analysis, and Risks, Assumptions, Issues, and Dependencies (RAID) and themes derived from the high-level logical mapping can be addressed.

2.3.3.2 Business Architecture

The objectives of the Business Architecture phase are to:

- Describe the Baseline Business Architecture.
- Develop the Target Business Architecture.
- Analyze the gaps between the Baseline and Target Business Architectures.
- Select the relevant architecture viewpoints.
- Select the relevant tools and techniques for viewpoints.

The Business Architecture addresses business objectives. In the context of the EIA Reference Architecture, the Business Architecture can be used to further refine the requirements of the business to understand which business services must be supported. This stage can also be used to define many of the business terms and semantics that drive business service identification. This identifies relevant data from the existing data repositories to build a view of particular entities that are consumed by business services. This definition of terms and semantics is crucial in deriving consistent services that can be used across the enterprise for many business processes. Without a clear representation of these terms, the services lack the crucial reuse capabilities.

2.3.3.3 Information Systems Architecture

In this phase, target architectures are developed covering either or both the Data and Application Systems domains. The scope depends significantly on the concrete project requirements. The logical architecture of the EIA Reference Architecture can be used to describe the high-level functional components that are needed for the overall solution. It covers existing or new data repositories as well as the services required to turn that data into a reusable information service that can be consumed when required. This step takes the high-level logical architecture and decomposes it into a set of components with a clear functional scope. It can be used as a *first* cut component list to identify dependencies across the landscape. This Information Systems Architecture is also very nicely aligned with the Component Model of the EIA Reference Architecture and even the non-functional requirements that are typically addressed in the Operational Model covering topics such as security, performance, continuous availability, scalability, and so on.

The EIA Reference Architecture describes operational aspects which are part of the Technology Architecture in Figure 2.5 as well as complementary aspects to the TOGAF framework by addressing the new requirements in areas such as Dynamic Warehousing or Cloud Computing.

2.3.4 Service-Oriented Architecture and Information as a Service

When organizations adopt the services paradigm and the approach is implemented correctly, the enterprise becomes more flexible, adaptable, and agile. SOA is an architectural style designed with the goal of achieving loose coupling among interacting services based on open standards and protocols. A service is a unit of work done by a service provider to achieve desired end results for a service consumer. Both provider and consumer are roles played by organizational units and software agents on behalf of their owners. Fine-grained services can be composed into coarse-grained services. Business processes are executed by choreographing a series of services.

An EIA capable of satisfying the SOA information requirements must be able to deliver information consistently across the organization and this requires information to be componentized using services of various degrees of granularity. This way of packaging information into easily reusable services that are based on universally adopted standards removes the complexity of the languages, platforms, locations, and formats of source systems is a main enabler of an efficient SOA architecture. It permits business processes to use enterprise data without having to bind themselves to the sources of the data.

By embracing the vision of Information as a Service (IaaS), all the technical disparities are insulated by layers of abstraction that introduce a globally accepted standard for representing information and this offers an enormous potential for organizations because many of the traditional challenges faced by ever-changing IT environments can be directly addressed through the application of these standardized layers.

2.3.4.1 Information Services in an SOA Environment

To understand the relationship of Information Services[16] to other services shown in the SOA solution stack, it is important to understand the relationship of services to service components.

Services provide the formal contracts between the service consumer layer and the service provider layer. From the top down, the service layer provides the mapping from the business

---

[16] See [22] and [23] for more information on the concept of Information as a Service.

process to the service implementation. Service components provide the implementation layer for services. From the bottom up, the service layer exposes interfaces from the service component layer. There is a many-to-many relationship between service interfaces and service components. There are many implementation alternatives available for realizing service components. A service component can be developed entirely as new code, but it is common to use the service component layer as a wrapper or connector to existing components in operational systems.

Figure 2.6 illustrates this approach and some of the typical combinations of the services and service components with the underlying application and information services. Figure 2.6 identifies the potential opportunities for delivering information services that can be delivered within an SOA environment. The service metadata would be available via the Service Registry and Repository (SRR) to ensure developers can search, find, understand, and reuse such services based on their metadata. Let's have a closer look into the various opportunities that are depicted in Figure 2.6.

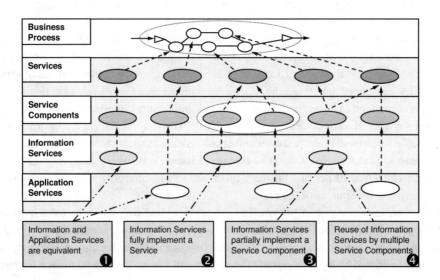

Figure 2.6   Information Services in the SOA Stack

2.3.4.2 Relationship to Application Services

Information services can be used directly like any other application SOA services (see #1 in Figure 2.6). In other words a pure Information Service can be required to deploy a fully enabled service to the outside world. An example is a banking scenario in which several customer accounts and core customer information are brought together into one consistent service that can be exposed to any business service that needs this single version of the customer truth. The service layer identifies, finds, and retrieves the service and enables any suitable security mechanism such as authentication and authorization. The service component layer has the actual specific points of integration that access the data sources and manages (potentially) federated queries across heterogeneous data sources.

2.3.4.3 Relationship to Service Components

An information service can provide the full implementation of a service component that is then wrapped with other service components to implement the service (see #2 in Figure 2.6). For this case the information service provides the implementation of only a part of the service.

An example of such a scenario is an information service that returns a query to forecast availability days of a particular product for a new promotion. This information might be used to drive an additional service, which alerts relevant individuals in the organization to review the stock levels. This result might have an impact to review and change the algorithm associated with how availability of the product is determined in the future.

An information service can provide a partial implementation of the service component (see #3 in Figure 2.6). An example is a business process that requests submission of an order, where the implementation can be the combination of a simple application actually updating the order, with another information service that identifies the most appropriate warehouse from which to service the order.

2.3.4.4 Reusability Aspects

An information service can be re-used in more than one service component and consequently in more than one service (see #4 in Figure 2.6). Thus an information service must be re-usable, such that the level of granularity of the service is not too coarse (only useful to a very small number of services or even a single one) and not too fine (it becomes nothing less than a simple Create, Read, Update, Delete [CRUD] style operation against some form of data source that adds little or no value). These high-level logical abstractions can be seen as a simple set of generic services tied to various existing platforms and applications to support the development of an information-centric solution.

2.3.4.5 Opportunity Patterns

In this section, we explore typical patterns to determine when it makes sense to expose information through services for consumption. There are five best practices to follow regarding when to expose information through services.

The first and obvious pattern is service enabling of legacy data. With a wealth of corporate data stored on the mainframe and a significant part of it being locked in information silos and in hard-coded applications, it is important and useful to unlock this information and make it available across the enterprise via platform-independent services. Although this assessment is true for other platforms as well, this opportunity pattern is specifically concentrating on the mainframe platform.

The second opportunity is to create cleansing and federation services (for more details see Chapter 8) that combine data from a variety of heterogeneous data sources in an efficient manner, and with consistency, accuracy, and trustworthiness.

The third entry point is to create Content Services in order to surface a unified view across a variety of unstructured content such as e-mails, images, documents, and so on. This information can be leveraged throughout the corporation, including the traditional database applications that typically work only on structured data.

The fourth and very common opportunity that we observe for information services in an SOA context is MDM that essentially provides a single authoritative source of information and a management interface for enterprise entities like customers, products, and other core information.

The fifth opportunity is to manage XML data centrally. The most common implementation of services in SOA is Web services, and these typically rely on XML messages in a SOAP envelope (the SOAP Envelope element is the root element of a SOAP message). The ability to store these messages in a central repository and then analyze, summarize, transform, and finally resurface the relevant portions as services becomes a key opportunity for Information as a Service.

2.3.4.6 Opportunity Anti-Patterns

Don't forget the anti-patterns around developing information services where it is not useful to expose information as a service. If your proposed information service exhibits one or more of the following characteristics, there is a good chance that it shouldn't be implemented as a service:

- **Lack of reusability**—The information service must have high potential for reuse. If the capability is likely to be used by a single application only, there is little point in implementing it as a service.

- **Performance requirements**—If performance is absolutely critical, adding a service layer can have a negative impact. After you start exposing data through services, there is a natural temptation to force all users of that data to use the service interface. For OLTP applications, this information services-based implementation might be too cumbersome.

- **Degree of flexibility**—As a service provider, you will not know the potential users of your service. Consequently, you need to be conscious about how much flexibility is implemented in the service interface. For example, accepting free format queries is difficult to control after deployment, so it is better to deploy only services that have a controlled and well understood range of behaviors.

To summarize, the relationship of our EIA Reference Architecture to SOA is mainly through the concept of *Information as a Service*.

2.4 Conclusion

This chapter detailed the key terms and concepts that are used throughout this book. The most important foundational concept is the Reference Architecture which we have applied to the term EIA and as a result were able to define the EIA Reference Architecture. We also discussed the EIA Reference Architecture in the context of existing frameworks and initiatives such as SOA or IOD. With this foundational understanding and a good overview on the structure of the book, we hope to have inspired an interest in diving into the subsequent chapters where you will gain a more detailed understanding of the EIA Reference Architecture.

2.5 References

[1] IEEE Standards Association. IEEE Standard 1471-2000. *IEEE Recommended Practice for Architectural Description of Software–Intensive Systems–Description.* 2004. http://standards.ieee.org/reading/ieee/std_public/description/se/1471-2000_desc.html (accessed December 15, 2009).

[2] Eeles, P. *What is a Software Architecture?* IBM developerWorks. 2006. http://www.ibm.com/developerworks/rational/library/feb06/eeles/ (accessed December 15, 2009).

[3] Chessell, M. et al. *Patterns: Model-Driven Development Using IBM Rational Software Architect.* IBM Redbooks, 2005. SG24–7105–00.

[4] The Open Group (TOG): *The Open Group Architecture Framework (TOGAF™).* 2009. http://www.opengroup.org/togaf/ (accessed December 15, 2009).

[5] Enterprise-Wide IT Architects (EWITA) homepage: *Enterprise Architecture (EA).* http://www.ewita.com/ (accessed December 15, 2009).

[6] IBM: *Leveraging Patterns and Reference Architectures in Enterprise Architecture Definition.* 2004. http://w3.itso.ibm.com/abstracts/redp3811.html (accessed December 15, 2009).

[7] Allam, A., Arsanjani, A., Channabasavaiah, K, Ellis, M., Zhang, L. J. *Design an SOA Solution using a Reference Architecture.* IBM developerWorks, 2008. http://www.ibm.com/developerworks/library/ar-archtemp/ (accessed December 15, 2009).

[8] IBM homepage: *Insurance Application Architecture.* http://www-03.ibm.com/industries/insurance/us/detail/resource/N800197Y63090H34.html (accessed December 15, 2009).

[9] Gartner: *Gartner Says Cloud Computing Will Be As Influential As E-business.* Gartner Press Release, 2008. http://www.gartner.com/it/page.jsp?id=707508 (accessed December 15, 2009).

[10] Zachman, J.A. *A Framework for Information Systems Architecture.* IBM Systems Journal, Volume 26, Number 3, 1987.

[11] Microsoft Developer Network (MSDN). *Building Distributed Applications—A Comparison of the Top Four Enterprise-Architecture Methodologies.* Roger Sessions, ObjectWatch, Inc. 2007. http://msdn.microsoft.com/en-us/library/bb466232.aspx (accessed December 15, 2009).

[12] Fishman, N., O'Rourke, C., Selkow, W. *Enterprise Architecture using the Zachman Framework.* Course Technology. 2003.

[13] The White House: *Federal Enterprise Architecture (FEA)—FEA Consolidated Reference Model Document Version 2.3.* 2007. http://www.whitehouse.gov/omb/assets/fea_docs/FEA_CRM_v23_Final_Oct_2007_Revised.pdf (accessed December 15, 2009).

[14] Bittler, R. S., Kreizman, G. *Gartner Enterprise Architecture Process: Evolution.* 2005. Gartner Report ID: G00130849.

[15] Gall, N., Handler, R. A., James, G. A., Lapkin, A. *Gartner Enterprise Architecture Framework: Evolution 2005.* 2005. Gartner Report ID: G00130855.

[16] Department of Defense: *Technical Architecture Framework for Information Management. Vol. 3.* 1996. http://www.dtic.mil/srch/doc?collection=t2&id=ADA321174 (accessed December 15, 2009).

[17] Software Engineering Institute of Carnegie Mellon: *Capability Maturity Model Integration (CMMI) Models and Reports.* 2009. http://www.sei.cmu.edu/cmmi/models/index.html (accessed December 15, 2009).

[18] IBM homepage: *Information on demand maturity model—Assessment tool.* 2009. http://www-01.ibm.com/software/uk/itsolutions/leveraginginformation/assessment/ (accessed December 15, 2009).

[19] IBM homepage: *Information On Demand—Unlocking the Business Value of Information for competitive Advantage.* 2009. http://www-01.ibm.com/software/data/information-on-demand/overview.html (accessed December 15, 2009).

[20] IBM homepage: *IBM Information Agenda for your Industry.* 2009. http://www-01.ibm.com/software/data/information-agenda/industry.html (accessed December 15, 2009).

[21] The Open Group (TOG): *Introduction to the ADM.* http://www.opengroup.org/architecture/togaf8-doc/arch/chap03.html (accessed December 15, 2009).

[22] IBM homepage: *Service Oriented Architecture (SOA) Entry Points—What is information as a service?* 2009. http://www-01.ibm.com/software/solutions/soa/entrypoints/information.html (accessed December 15, 2009).

[23] Gilpin, M., Yuhanna, N. *Information-As-A-Service: What's Behind This Hot New Trend?* Forrester Report, 2007. http://www.forrester.com/Research/Document/Excerpt/0,7211,41913,00.html (accessed December 15, 2009).

## CHAPTER 3

Data Domains, Information Governance, and Information Security

Building on the architecture terminology introduction in Chapter 2, this chapter sets out to elaborate on:

- The data domains that define the information scope of the EIA Reference Architecture
- The IT Governance and Information Governance aspects that provides the framework for defining and governing the EIA
- The Information Security and Information Privacy that defines the requirements to appropriately secure information and to comply with Information Privacy legislation
- The System Context Diagram as a methodological approach to iteratively roll out or upgrade the EIA in a given context

3.1 Terminology and Definitions

In this chapter, we introduce data domains that classify information assets used for specific purposes where the purpose identifies usage patterns with a dedicated set of capabilities. As outlined in the previous chapter, any Reference Architecture can be described in terms of views, such as the functional view or the security view. Because this book is about EIA, we are obliged to elaborate on the *data* view. The data-centric view describes the data domains that are derived from classification criteria, the relationship between data domains, and the flow of data through the components of the EIA Reference Architecture. The underlying model describing the criteria and capabilities of data domains is also known as the Conceptual Data Model. The relationship between defined information entities based on their data domain classification is known as the Information Reference Model. Both the Conceptual Data Model and the Information Reference Model constitute the Enterprise Information Model (EIM), a key ingredient of our EIA Reference

Architecture on the Conceptual Level. As the EIM is fundamental to adopting a way in which to describe the data assets and structure of a business's operations, we will discuss in detail the classification criteria of the Conceptual Data Model and the Information Reference Model alongside the data domains.

Furthermore, we discuss IT Governance and Information Governance.[1] Without good governance, decisions will continue to be ad-hoc, poorly managed and coordinated, and cost businesses real money. IT Governance is defined as a discipline of managing IT to deliver value for a business and managing the risks associated with IT. Decision making is driven from good governance which requires accountability (assigning responsibility and ownership) and some form of measurement and performance management to ensure compliance and effectiveness. IT Governance is also key to deriving architectural decisions. Typically, issues arise in decision making through the complexity of ways in which a solution can be implemented and then identifying the most appropriate solution. In these cases, architectural principles or policies must be used to drive architectural decisions that must be adhered to during at least the life of a development cycle of any program of work. For information-centric decision making, Information Governance is a discipline that governs information assets throughout their lifecycles. Information Governance is exercised through Information Stewards following governance processes enabled by technology. We will discuss why governing the EIA throughout the evolution over its lifecycle is easier and more successful with strong Information Governance in place.

We also look at Information Security aspects of managing and controlling security around the information assets. Information Security is defined as management discipline to address security in business and IT where the risk of allowing information to be corrupted, destroyed, or used unscrupulously has never been higher. For example, developing a single source of truth can increase risk unless proper Information Security is applied. As a consequence, developing a Master Data Management (MDM) solution means accumulated, high value, and sensitive data now residing in one place becomes a prime time target for attackers, increasing risk unless proper security measures have been applied.

Finally, we introduce the System Context Diagram as a methodological approach to introduce or upgrade the EIA. An EIA is almost never implemented or changed on the green field. A given IT environment must be considered, and changes or improvements in the EIA are typically not deployed in a big-bang approach. More often, this is a phased approach. Thus, there is an as-is state that affects the to-be state. Using a System Context Diagram, the current state can be captured, which is a key input for defining the next step. The System Context Diagram is a high-level view of the new system with the dependent systems and actors (users) and external data sources that it uses or feeds around. It maps the flow of data and functions of the system across the system boundaries for the new solution. Thus, building a System Context Diagram helps to focus on the

---

[1] We use the term "Information Governance" on purpose to distinguish it from the older—but better known—term "Data Governance." We explain what we consider new in Information Governance later in this chapter.

areas of interest and define what's in and what's out of scope of the EIA that will be needed to support the solution.

3.2 Data Domains

On a daily basis, employees use data. In some cases, this data exists only in the minds of the employees, and in some cases, it is shared via verbal communication. In other cases, data is captured by writing it on paper, such as with meeting minutes someone captures with a pen. Yet another type of data is *digitalized*. Digitalized data is data that can be processed by computing systems such as desktops, laptops, personal digital assistants (PDA), smart phones, sensors, servers, and mainframes. Different applications process and use this data for various purposes. Well-known examples include applications used by many enterprises today such as:

- **Enterprise Resource Planning (ERP) applications**—An ERP application is often used to process orders and a related business process is the Order-To-Cash (OTC) process. The data processed by this type of application often includes customer, product, order, shipment, fulfillment, and billing related data. This type of data processing is typically performed in a transactional context. This means that several processing steps must be completed successfully or not at all. Otherwise data integrity is lost.

- **A Data Warehouse (DW)**—The DW is based on a normalized data model in a relational database. It supports a diverse set of analytic requirements. Data marts are optimized for specific analytical purpose often using data mining[2] and other techniques. The DW and the data marts generally use a star or snowflake schema deployed on a departmental or enterprise-wide level.

- **E-mail applications**—The data processed by this type of application is typically a mixture of Structured Data (e-mail header with recipient and sender address, subject, and so on), Unstructured Data given by the free-form text (the *body* of the e-mail), and possible documents attached to the e-mail.

As you can see from the examples, certain types of data might be used enterprise-wide and others might be used only locally within a department or a Line of Business (LOB). The data might be structured (for example, an order) or unstructured (for example, a scanned contract document). The data might also differ from a retention perspective indicating how long the data must be stored. We see the following five data domains:

- **Metadata Domain**—Defined as "data about the data." Metadata (see details in Chapter 10) is the information that describes the characteristics of each piece of corporate data asset and other entities.

---

[2] For more details on these concepts and Data Warehouses see [1].

- **Master Data Domain**—Refers to instances of data describing the core business entities, such as customer or product data.

- **Operational Data Domain**—Also referred to as transactional data capturing data, which is derived from business transactions.

- **Unstructured Data Domain**—Also known as content, typically managed by an enterprise content management application.

- **Analytical Data Domain**—Usually derived through transformation from operational systems to address specific requirements of decision support applications.

These data domains will be further detailed after understanding the classification criteria of these domains.

3.2.1 Classification Criteria of the Conceptual Data Model

The following explores the criteria that help identify the introduced data domains.

3.2.1.1 Format

In the scope of this book, we discuss two formats for data:

- **Structured Data**—For a business object (for example, an order or a customer), Structured Data uses the same relational data model given by a fixed set of attributes defining the representation consistently for all instances. Structured data is typically persisted and maintained in tables in a relational database system.

- **Unstructured Data**—As the name implies, this data is characterized by a lack of structure due to the lack of a data model. A collection of Word, Excel or OpenOffice[3] documents representing meeting minutes and project plans for several departments on a file share, or a mixture of free text, presentations, and PDFs in a wiki[4] are typical examples for this format. We do not distinguish Unstructured Data from Semi-Structured Data in this book. Semi-structured data is characterized as data that doesn't comply with the rigid structures of tables and relational database systems. It has tags or markers to separate elements or hierarchies within the document. Documents represented in XML and e-mail are the most well-known examples for semi-structured data.

3.2.1.2 Purpose

A digital piece of data serves a specific purpose in the context of an application. On a high level, we see the following purposes of data:

---

[3] This is an open source office software suite; for details see [2].

[4] A wiki is a set of Web pages where a group of people with access collaborate for creating and maintaining the content available through the wiki. The most well-known wiki is Wikipedia (http://wikipedia.org/).

- **Operational purpose**—Business transactions in the daily operations of a business, such as order entry, order fulfillment, or billing operate on this type of data. It is found in many applications such as Customer Relationship Management (CRM), ERP, Enterprise Content Management (ECM), and call-center applications, and it can be Structured or Unstructured Data.

- **Analytical purpose**—In an analytical context, the data is processed to compute results to gain insight into the past (for example, revenue by product in the last quarter), insight into the present (for example, uncover hidden relationships between people), or insight into the future (for example, predict how certain changes in the route-to-market affect product success).

- **Metadata purpose**—Metadata is used to describe data. It provides the context to data and enables understanding.

- **Master data purpose**—This data represents the essential business entities such as customers, products, suppliers, accounts, and locations to name a few. This core enterprise data is used in many different business processes and many dependent data entities such as opportunities, orders, and bills. Thus, they are considered master objects serving the purpose of being the information foundation for many operational processes.

Note that an instance of data can serve one purpose and then in another context serve another purpose—even at the same time. For example, if Master Data is reused in an order-entry system to create an order and then stored in a DW, it becomes part of the operational purpose in that particular system and part of the analytical purpose in the DW system.

3.2.1.3 Scope of Integration

This criterion defines the scope of integration required for the data:

- **Local scope**—This scope means the data is used only within a team, department, or a LOB. An example is competitive market analysis (which is needed only by the executive board), a design document for a software component (which is needed only in the IT department), or a support ticket (which is processed only by the support organization).

- **Enterprise-wide scope**—This scope indicates that the data is used enterprise-wide. Customer and product master data are examples of data with enterprise-wide scope. Data with enterprise-wide scope of integration might be used across enterprises (such as a portion of product information in a supply chain scenario).

- **Cross-enterprise scope**—This scope indicates that the data is used across enterprises but is not necessarily used across all LOBs internally. It might have less enterprise-wide scope internally, but it is shared with other enterprises. An example of cross-enterprise data is supply-chain data.

3.2.1.4 Accuracy

The accuracy of data is a measure that indicates the level of compliance that a stored piece of data has with its actual value. Inaccurate data is often considered bad data because it affects the business success negatively. For example, bad data is responsible for mail that doesn't reach the recipient due to the wrong address, loss of customer trust, loss of customers, and incorrect revenue reports. As a consequence, data accuracy significantly influences the level of trusted data.

Improving data accuracy is one aspect of data quality improvements. Various measures and techniques are available to improve data accuracy; for example data standardization, data matching, data deduplication, and data validation (these techniques are further discussed in Chapter 14). In addition, Information Governance helps to define processes to govern information and assign Information Stewards for data objects responsible to ensure proper information quality.

3.2.1.5 Completeness

The completeness of data is determined by the degree to which it contains all relevant attributes, entities, and values to represent the object it describes in the real world. Business context affects the decision about whether data is considered complete. For example, having the customer name and the address available to put on the envelope for a bill is considered complete customer information from a billing perspective. However, this might be considered incomplete customer information for the sales representative who needs to know the relationships in the household of that customer to identify a proper cross- and up-sell strategy.

3.2.1.6 Consistency

If you look for the same data entity in various applications, the specific value is considered consistent if and only if you receive the same values for all attributes of this data entity from the various applications. For example, the information relating to a customer can be used in a CRM application, an ERP application, and an e-commerce application across the enterprise. If data is replicated across those applications, data consistency questions immediately arise. Thus, it is beneficial to consider at least two concepts of data consistency: absolute consistency and converging consistency.

Absolute consistency exists when, across all replicas, the information is identical at any given point in time. In the example of the customer information in a heterogeneous application environment, you receive the same information for this customer from all these applications. Two-phase commit protocols[5] that are supported by most distributed databases and messaging systems are typically used to implement absolute consistency in distributed environments by grouping transactions into units of work that either all succeed or are all rolled back to their previous statuses.

---

[5] See [5] for more details.

With *converging consistency* in a distributed set of systems, the idea is to replicate changes from one system where a change has been applied to the other systems to keep them synchronized. There are two major approaches to do this: Either *replicate* the changes (probably near real time) or accumulate and consolidate the changes in a batch process. Both of these techniques are discussed further in Chapter 8.

3.2.1.7 Timeliness

Timeliness of data has two aspects. The first one is the *propagation of changes*. If a customer reports a change such as an address due to a move, this change might be reflected in a call center application. However, it usually takes some time to be reflected in other applications. The delay of the change made and the time it is propagated into other systems have an impact on data quality. The risk for arising issues increases the longer the change is not available in a timely manner. From this perspective, insufficient timeliness has a negative impact on consistency. For example, a DW application that receives updates from operational applications on a monthly schedule via a batch process might not be aware of that change due to the delay in propagation.

The second aspect is the *freshness of data*. Data stored in an IT system gets out of sync with the real-world entities it represents due to the changes of the real-life entities over time; not all these changes make it back to the captured data.

3.2.1.8 Relevance

This measure indicates the degree to which the data satisfies the need of the data consumer. It measures how applicable and connected the data is to a given topic. Relevance is also context dependent. For example, it might be crucial to know the exact date when a product is bought with a guarantee. This date is completely irrelevant when describing the product from a master data perspective.

Data becomes more relevant if the unnecessary information for the task is removed. Finally, the relevance measure is affected by time. What is relevant in the context of business requirements today might be irrelevant tomorrow.

3.2.1.9 Trust

To generate and maintain trusted data, the user must at least know that the data complies with the appropriate levels regarding its accuracy, completeness, consistency, timeliness, and relevance.

Furthermore, you must know and understand the data—this is often enabled through proper Metadata. In addition, knowing that the data is governed with proper processes, managed by Information Stewards, and proper access controls are in place increases our trust in the data. Understanding data lineage (see details in Chapter 10), that is, where the data comes from, also increases our trust.

3.2.2 The Five Data Domains

We can now identify the five data domains further detailed below and used in this book and identify their key characterizations. Figure 3.1 shows the five pillars of enterprise information.

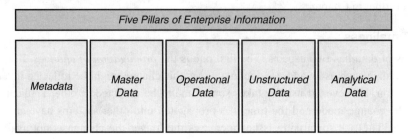

Figure 3.1   The five pillars of Enterprise Information

3.2.2.1 Metadata domain

Defined as data about the data, *Metadata* is the information that describes the characteristics of corporate data assets and other entities. Metadata is the data domain that converts raw data into usable information about the business.

Metadata can be viewed as the collection of data and information used to measure, develop, and operate a business environment. It also includes critical business information or links to that information (business intelligence reports, statistics, and other strategic information) that resides outside the traditional pure view of data about the data. Metadata is often divided into Technical and Business Metadata.[6] In Chapter 10, we describe these elements of Metadata in more detail.

Often, Technical and Business Metadata is not captured or is only partially captured. Even if it is captured, the Metadata management does not assure completeness, accuracy, or consistency. Then, efficient communication between business and IT people is limited due to a missing enterprise dictionary linking Business Metadata to Technical Metadata. This is often a critical mismatch that impedes the business and technical communities from working together in a well integrated manner.

Providing data lineage or impact analysis information also requires accurate Metadata. For these criteria, Metadata has stringent demands. Concerning the timeliness classification criteria, the requirements for Metadata vary greatly depending on the scenario. For example, the physical data model of a database might need to be available only when the next upgrade of the application is designed. Thus, a weekly propagation of the physical data model to an appropriate Metadata repository might be good enough. However, in a Mashup environment where external feeds

---

[6] See [6] for a complete discussion on Business Metadata.

are often subject to unplanned changes, gathering Metadata frequently from these sources is important.

3.2.2.2 Master Data domain

The Master Data domain refers to instances of data describing the core business entities. The Master Data domain itself consists of different domains of Master Data—the domain determines which Master Data business object is managed. Typical Master Data domains include customer, product, account, location, and contract. Software solutions for this component tailored toward Customer Data Integration (CDI) for the customer domain and Product Information Management (PIM) for the product domain dominated during the last few years. Since 2008, we see an ever-increasing shift towards multi-domain implementations where software solutions support more than one Master Data domain and manage the relationships between Master Data domains such as customer-product relationships.

Regarding the criteria accuracy, completeness, consistency, timeliness, relevance, and trust, the Master Data domain has high requirements because Master Data has the enterprise-wide scope of integration, implying that many applications reuse it from a centrally managed MDM system. Master Data appears in the Operational Data domain (for example, part of an order), the Unstructured Data domain (for example, part of a contract), and in the Analytical Data domain.

3.2.2.3 Operational Data domain

The Operational Data domain covers Operational Data. It applies to Structured Data created or used by business transactions and thus is also known as transactional data describing what happened in a business. We use the term Operational Data and transactional data interchangeably. It is fine-grained information with the operational purpose of representing the details of the daily business of an enterprise. In many industries, business transactions such as sales orders, invoices, and billing information are considered Operational Data as part of the Operational Data domain.

Operational Data often incorporates Master Data. An example is customer and product information used to create an order. However, when characterizing Operational Data, the requirements for accuracy, completeness, consistency, timeliness, relevance, and trust are often not as high as for Master Data or Analytical Data. This is motivated by the fact that Operational Data is often used only within a department or LOB. Master Data, for example, is propagated across the enterprise. Thus poor data quality would affect more consumers.

This does not mean we should not strive to drive the accuracy of Operational Data to be as high as possible. It is always better to start with valid, complete data than to have to fix it at a later stage through some complex cleansing or transform routines. (See Chapter 8 for more details on them.)

3.2.2.4 Unstructured Data domain

Unstructured Data is also known as *content*. The purpose of this data is operational. We call the domain Unstructured Data domain for reasons of completeness because it is broader than what is typically managed by an ECM. Consider an employee of an insurance company that might be using large amounts of Unstructured Data through OpenOffice documents or screenshots that is not managed by an ECM application. The existence of this Unstructured Data is often unknown to other employees or has limited availability. The insurance company might also have a centralized scanning application for all insurance contracts signed by customers where the scanned contracts are managed by an enterprise-wide ECM application across the lifecycle of the contracts. The difference between the two is that the Unstructured Data in the first example is not managed and governed on the same level as the contracts in the second example.

The accuracy, completeness, consistency, timeliness, relevance, and trust of the Unstructured Data domain vary greatly. For example, a bullet list of half-complete sentences in a Word document representing meeting minutes might be considered accurate and complete on the day the meeting occurred. However, six months later when the details have faded partially from memory, this might not be the case. Another example is a completely scanned insurance contract, which is still considered accurate after six months if no contract changes occur.

In many cases, the scope of integration is local. However, there might be some cases where Unstructured Data is integrated with an enterprise-wide scope, or even cross-enterprise if documents need to be shared across parties. For example, e-mails might be such a classification of Unstructured Data.

Note that the Operational Data and the Unstructured Data domain share the characteristics of data used in the operational purpose. We introduce two different data domains because we realize the difference in the required capabilities. (See Chapter 4 for further exploration on capabilities.)

3.2.2.5 Analytical Data domain

Analytical Data is usually derived by putting Operational Data into an analytical context. In some cases, the Analytical Data is produced by executing reports directly on the operational system. However, the more common case is data movement of Operational Data into dedicated analytical systems such as DWs or Identity Analytics systems. In the case of a DW, particularly if it has an enterprise scope, data movement from multiple operational systems into the DW is necessary. For this purpose, an Enterprise Information Integration (EII) capability can be harnessed.

For Analytical Data in a DW environment, the requirements for accuracy, consistency, and relevance are typically high because decisions based on strategic and tactical Business Intelligence (BI) reports have far-reaching impact. Therefore, Operational Data is typically standardized, cleansed, harmonized, and deduplicated to achieve accuracy and consistency while moved into a DW. The relevance aspect for Analytical Data implies that only relevant Operational and Master Data should move into DW, which is required to satisfy the reporting needs.

Accuracy, consistency, and relevance requirements are also typically high in Identity Analytics applications. If hidden relationships between customers are discovered, high quality customer Master Data as input for Identity Analytics improves results.

From a data completeness point of view, not all attributes are relevant for reporting purposes. Thus, certain attributes of business objects such as bills or customers might not be needed in the analytical environment and remain in their operational or MDM systems. Timeliness for Analytical Data depends on the analytical purpose. If a DW, for example, is used only for strategic or tactical BI reporting, it might suffice to have the last completed month of Operational Data loaded into the DW and the last couple of days of Operational Data not loaded yet. However, if accurate reporting on a daily basis is required, the timeliness for getting the Operational Data being moved into the DW is significantly higher. The scope of integration for the Analytical Data domain varies: There are BI solutions on department or LOB level with a local scope of integration; however, some enterprises also run DW with an enterprise-wide scope of integration.

3.2.3 Information Reference Model

The Information Reference Model is a framework for describing the relationship between the five data domains. Figure 3.2 introduces an abstraction of this relationship.

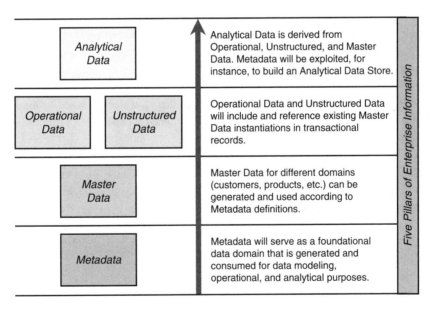

Figure 3.2   Information Reference Model

As shown in Figure 3.2, Metadata is the foundational data domain, which serves as a specification and enabler to generate instantiations of higher-level data domains. However, Metadata is generated and consumed for data modeling, operational, and analytical purposes. Master Data domains required by the business can then be generated and used according to the Metadata definitions. For instance, for the *customer* data domain, the specification and attribute definition of what makes up a customer record, is captured in Metadata and exploited as a guideline for those Master Data instantiations. When we move up the hierarchy of data domains, you can see that the Operational and Unstructured Data reside in the same layer with their common purpose to manage transaction records. Both Operational and Unstructured Data include and reference existing Master Data instantiations in transactional records. The last and final data domain—Analytical Data—is derived from Operational, Unstructured, and Master Data records. In addition, even Metadata is used in the modeling and definition of the DW systems that host Analytical Data.

In summary, the Information Reference Model provides for a better understanding of the relative use of each data domain within their business.

3.3 IT Governance and Information Governance

As introduced in Section 3.1, IT Governance is the key to deriving architectural decisions. Rather than trying to define what *good* architectural decisions are (nearly impossible because it is problem and context specific), this section describes a typical governance framework to help drive architectural principles, policies, and decisions that can be agreed and policed by all relevant parties. We briefly cover the wider issue of IT Governance first and the drivers that go to make up good governance. Then we consider the role of Information Governance specifically within this model.

For IT Governance, many standards do exist—a common one is the COBIT standard (**C**ontrol **Ob**jectives for **I**nformation and related **T**echnology), which is owned by the IT Governance Institute.[7] From the COBIT perspective, IT Governance is considered a framework to govern IT assets over their lifecycle.

Good IT Governance ensures that the IT group supports and extends the company strategies and business objectives. The decision making process—how information systems are planned and organized, acquired and implemented, delivered and supported, as well as monitored and evaluated—should therefore be just another strategic agenda item that the board addresses. IT Governance is tightly coupled with IT principles, IT architecture, IT infrastructure strategies, functional business requirements, and prioritization of IT investments, which form the core decisions that need to be made within any governance framework.

In this context, IT principles are high-level statements about how IT will be used to create business value and a generic information-centric set. IT architecture is about the set of technical choices that guide the enterprise in satisfying business needs. IT infrastructure strategies describe the approach to building shared and standard IT services across the enterprise. Functional business requirement needs refer to applications that need to be acquired or built. Finally, the prioritization of IT investments covers the whole process of IT investments, including where they should be focused and the procedures for progressing initiatives, their justification, approval, and accountability.

---

[7] The IT Governance Institute (ITGI) was established in 1998 in recognition of the increasing criticality of IT to enterprise success. See more details in [7].

Within the context of decision making, Information Governance[8] specifically details the area associated with managing issues such as incomplete data, poor or untimely access to data, lack of or poor Metadata, and managing and resolving duplicate (or similar) data. As introduced in Section 3.1, Information Governance is defined as the orchestration of people, processes, and technology to enable an organization to leverage information as an enterprise asset.

The development of effective Information Governance drives value into companies in many ways, including:

- Compliance and regulatory adherence satisfies auditors and regulators by developing data management environments leveraging technology and process to ensure adherence to specific requirements.

- Enhanced BI capabilities using high-quality information drives new opportunities for organic growth (for example, by identifying opportunities for increased effectiveness in cross-selling and retaining existing customers)

- Enhanced alignment of IT initiatives with business strategies drives more value and enables the business through data availability and enrichment, which enables insightful strategic planning and execution.

- Improved platforms measure, monitor, and improve business performance by tying operational metrics to business performance measures and facilitating reporting and management of critical processes.

- Reduced environmental complexity improves business flexibility and accelerates strategic initiatives by providing comprehensive and predictable information environments that support effective business decision making.

To enable such goals, key objectives of an Information Governance program[9] need to first establish a culture that recognizes the value of information as an enterprise asset. This requires real discipline and possibly the creation of new roles within the business that didn't exist previously (for example, Information Stewards for information assets). Additionally, the formal structure running a new set of processes and rules must be enabled. For example, the development of the policies and decisions mentioned previously; the approach to measuring, monitoring, and managing any rules around information assets; ensuring new operational activities (maintaining Metadata, reporting on data lineage or ongoing data quality management with regular profiling) are in line with the overall corporate business performance metrics; and finally ensuring that the new regime adheres to compliance and regulatory pressures.

---

[8] We use the term Information Governance instead of Data Governance to indicate that we cover all the data domains, not just the operational data domain. Consequently, we will use the term Information Steward instead of Data Steward.

[9] The Data Governance Institute is a provider of in-depth, vendor-neutral information about tools, techniques, models, and best practices for the governance/stewardship of data and information. See more details in [8], [9], and [10].

Figure 3.3 illustrates how these various groups and processes must come together to enable the new regime. Business and IT must coordinate, especially across Information Stewards and Information Management teams to enable best practices around managing, maintaining, measuring, and deploying information across the enterprise.

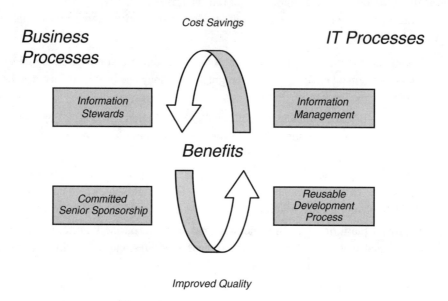

Figure 3.3   Information Governance

Information Stewards are required to manage and maintain information as a corporate asset for use throughout the enterprise. To do this effectively, the Information Steward must be empowered by the organization to make decisions regarding information, resolve conflicts in the use of information, and establish enterprise standards around the creation and use of that information. They are responsible for setting policies, procedures, and definitions of information.

The Information Management team is responsible for actually storing and maintaining the validity of the information, for being able to express the definitions of that information clearly when asked to do so, and for maintaining the quality and lifecycle of that information. They are responsible for the physical form of the information.

The senior sponsorship team is accountable overall for the enterprise-wide information assets and directs the way in which the business continues to use information, add new information, and use information to add value to the business.

The development process of applications using data and information assets is required to become reusable. This will improve the quality of developments and provides better focus on key information and its usage pattern.

Governing the Enterprise Architecture—including the EIA—throughout the evolution over its lifecycle is easier and more successful with strong IT and Information Governance processes in place. Information Security and Information Privacy is another aspect of managing and controlling the information assets which are exposed to a growing number of security threats today.

3.4 Information Security and Information Privacy

This section takes a brief look at the current issues surrounding Information Security and Information Privacy. First, we consider why we need to ensure Information Security and Information Privacy is covered for our business information, and then we look at the potential areas in which information could be seen to be under risk in a typical enterprise information scenario. Today, we see a number of trends around the security aspects of business systems:

- Across the globe there has been a growing number of attacks on major enterprises with (internal inspired) threats still high.

- Business infrastructures, such as utility networks for water or electricity, are increasingly equipped with sensors to capture information. The information is used, for example, to predict peak consumptions—one aspect of the intelligent utility network solution outlined in Chapter 9.

- The Cloud Computing delivery model (see details in Chapter 7) requires new means to federate identities across internal and external systems to protect data from unauthorized access.

- Regulatory compliance pressures around the world across all industries demand strict enforcement of data access and Information Privacy.

- Access by partners to internal systems is ever increasing as the new trends to distributed solutions and cooperation across business boundaries take place.

- As systems design leads to more consolidated data sets (around core enterprise-wide DW and MDM capabilities), the opportunity to hack one's critical resource can actually increase.

3.4.1 Information Security

There are many areas in which we must address Information Security in our business. Figure 3.4 illustrates these areas to define business services required around security, to define the IT related security services, and to help set policies around how to manage these differing areas, specifically:

- **Business Security Services**—Defined as security aspects of the business that must be specified, owned, and managed for successful and secure operations of an enterprise. These are driven by regulatory concerns, partnerships, competitive influences, and more.

- **IT Security Services**—Form the core technical components that must be designed and deployed around our data domains to deliver the security functions as defined in the Business Security Services layer. This means that the IT Security Services layer is responsible for addressing how the business security services are physically deployed.

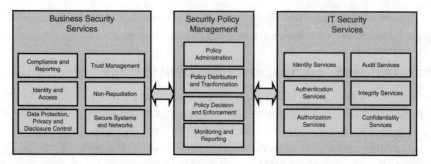

Figure 3.4   The three pillars of Information Security

• **Security Policy Management**—Defined as a set of policies and principles that ensure that the Business Security Services are managed in a consistent manner with IT. Therefore, the Security Policy Management links the business-related and IT-related security services together.

This book is not intended to elaborate in detail[10] all these areas, but we will briefly describe each one for reasons of completeness.

3.4.1.1 Business Security Services

Business Security Services are typically decomposed in six services types as shown in the left pillar in Figure 3.4:

• **Compliance and Reporting Services**—Measure the performance of the business and IT systems against the metrics established by the business. This uses audited and other information regarding overall system activity to compare actual system behaviors against expected system behavior. (See Chapter 6 for more details on these services.)

• **Identity and Access Services**—Manage the creation and deletion of user identities across the enterprise. Often, they also ensure self-management of that identity after it is created.

• **Data Protection, Privacy, and Disclosure Control Services**—Deal with the protection of data across all five domains. The control points of these services are areas such as publishing a privacy policy, managing user consent to these policies, capturing user preferences around how to be contacted, and reporting on who has accessed what information.

• **Trust Management Services**—Manage the identification of trusted relationships between various differing entities within a business; for example, relationships among user IDs, security domains, or different applications. A set of well managed business rules is defined that permits the related entities to transfer information and do business together.

---

[10] For more details, we recommend reading [11] regarding a comprehensive SOA Security Architecture and [12] for a detailed discussion on cryptography algorithms which can be used to implemented IT security services.

- **Non-Repudiation Services**—Ensure that any two parties involved in a transfer of data between each other cannot falsely deny that the communication has taken place. Note that it does not protect the data itself but does ensure that the two parties involved have received and sent the data and cannot refute this claim.

- **Secure Systems and Networks Services**—Cover areas such as intrusion detection, operating system security, malware detection, and patch management processes.

3.4.1.2 IT Security Services

IT Security Services are typically decomposed in six services types as shown in the right pillar in Figure 3.4:

- **Identity Services**—Usually, Identity Services must be able to manage the core function associated with storing and managing information around organizational entities, such as user, a role or user groups. This information is stored in some form of repository such as an LDAP directory. There might be multiple repositories within the enterprise, and these might need synchronizing through provisioning policies to ensure that identity information is consistent across the enterprise.

- **Authentication Services**—Authenticating the users within the enterprise is done through Authentication Services. These services could support multiple different approaches such as user name and password, hardware token based, or even biometric solutions to authenticate an individual based on fingerprinting or retinal pattern recognition.

- **Authorization Services**—After any authentication service, generally, an authorization service follows. This service determines if the user is authorized to perform the requested operation on the target resource. To allow authenticated users to perform tasks for which they have been authorized, there must be policies in place that describe the authorization decision for the appropriate authenticated service.

- **Audit Services**—For example, to meet certain compliance requirements or to perform incident analysis, audit trails must be available to show who accessed what and when. Audit Services maintain logs of critical activities. Typical examples of logged activity can be login failures, unauthorized attempts to access systems, modification of security and identity policies, and so on.

- **Integrity Services**—This service group attempts to monitor traffic intra- and inter-enterprise wide to identify if data has been maliciously altered in some manner. Typically cryptographic techniques such as message integrity codes, authentication codes, and digital signatures are used.

- **Confidentiality Services**—They are applied to prevent disclosure of sensitive information traveling through untrusted communication networks, widely used over the Web. Even if a user is authenticated and authorized, the data requested must still be protected as it moves across systems boundaries.

3.4.1.3 Security Policy Management

Now that we have taken a look at the Business Security and IT Security Services, we take a quick look at the Security Policy Management pillar to understand how we link the two differing areas in a controlled and understood manner. This layer must manage the security policies through the lifecycles of all applications. Security Policy Management is typically decomposed in four disciplines as shown in the middle pillar in Figure 3.4:

- **Policy Administration Services**—They maintain changes to security policies over the lifetime of the application. The policies need to be described in terms that make sense to the underlying architecture. For example, if used in an SOA context, then the policy Metadata should contain information about the services used and other information like the strength of encryption.

- **Policy Distribution and Transformation Services**—They distribute policies defining access to the applications or services themselves to the places where they are enforced. The policies themselves can be deployed using known standards such as WS-Policy or WS-Security Policy, so that the service or requestor can enable the security using its own local techniques.

- **Policy Decision and Enforcement Services**—They are logically connected to Policy Enforcement Points (PEP), which admin users use to update security requirements. The PEPs in turn rely on Policy Deployment Points (PDP) or nodes to physically administer the policies across the enterprise. Challenges of multiple PDPs and PEPs are that different entities might administer them and coordination can become difficult. A central decision function that oversees these functions can sometimes assist greatly.[11]

- **Monitoring and Reporting Services**—This function ensures the business can take the business policies and map them down to the IT services and report successfully on the degree of compliance by the IT Services deployed. It is necessary to keep track of current policies, historic policies, and compliance assessments against corporate policies. Traceability from the corporate polices down to the mechanism utilized to achieve those policies is critical to this function. Changes should be tightly controlled, access to them traced through reporting and monitoring, and audit trails supplied at any point in the process.

3.4.2 Information Privacy: The Increasing Need for Data Masking

Data masking is rapidly gaining prominence when dealing with data such as test databases and the requirement to enable structurally integral data sets without exposing live data to the developers or designers in breach of regulations such as Sarbanes-Oxley (SOX), Health Insurance Portability and Accountability Act (HIPAA), Gramm-Leach-Bliley Act (GLBA). Forrester Research[12]

---

[11] See [14] for information about a typical software product that does this.

[12] See [15] for the Forrester Report which covers the need of data masking becoming part of the security practice.

recently published a paper describing why data masking should be an integrated part of the security practice within an enterprise.

IBM defines *data masking* as "The process of identifying sensitive data and overlaying values that masks the sensitive data, but does not compromise the functional integrity of an application."[13] In today's enterprises, we often see large manual efforts being required to accomplish these goals. Even worse, all too often companies do not actually meet their regulatory requirements around such issues. Clearly the task associated with data masking needs to be repeatable because large companies have hundreds of business applications that are tightly integrated, and they need development and test environments to enable their business. By enabling data masking in the business, it seeks to manage the following issues in today's businesses:

- Meet regulatory compliance needs
- Enhance data security
- Protect against internal or external attacks as the data has little or no external value
- Enable the use of production data within exposing private, sensitive or confidential data to any non trusted party

Clearly this is worth striving for; many companies are coming under sustained attack for their information,[14] and in a number of high profile cases, the costs associated with this are substantial.

Figure 3.5 shows how different techniques can be applied to data masking when moving data from one data source to another.

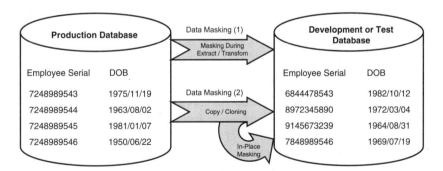

Figure 3.5 Data Masking

The first technique, shown in the figure as Data Masking (1), uses an enhancement to the well known Extract-Transform-Load (ETL) mechanism often used with DW environments, but in this case the process applied is Extract-Mask-Transform-Load (EMTL). This is the process of

---

[13] See [16] for a definition. Furthermore, a brand new technology for data masking named Masking Gateway for Enterprise (MAGEN) has been announced (see [17]).

[14] See [18] for an example of a data breach and its costly settlement.

extracting data from production into flat files while masking the data and finally loading the data into multiple different environments.

The second technique, shown in the figure as Data Masking (2), is in-place data masking where data is first copied from production into multiple environments and then masked in place in those environments. Today, most of the implementation is around using the EMTL technique, which is seen in legacy environments. This technique is often used in conjunction with a number of the components within the EII layer described in Chapter 5, and in more detail in Chapter 8. For example, discovery and profiling techniques might be first employed against production databases to gain more insight into what must be masked. The various algorithms generally considered for data masking fall into the following categories:

- Date aging uses some form of calculation to increment or decrement date values in the database.
- Substitution simply uses some form of realistic value randomly generated or based on character replacement.
- Numeric alternation increases or decreases numeric values by a percentage.
- Shuffling and reorder applies for similar data types where data is moved within a row.
- Custom-defined user-developed algorithms.

Commercially available software packages[15] have functionality to meet the needs mentioned previously and enables right sizing of the data to control growth as well. The software packages' goals are to deidentify production data for privacy protection. For example, with this data masking functionality, businesses are enabled to deploy off-shore testing while still maintaining compliance needs around Information Privacy.

3.5 System Context Diagram

Building any large-scale information-based solution can only be successfully planned and managed if the tasks are broken down into some form of incremental stages (whether using waterfall-based *traditional* or *agile* methods). To do this, some form of scope and understanding of what is proposed to be built is necessary.

As already introduced in section 3.1, the System Context Diagram can be used as a methodological tool to capture the as-is state of an EIA, which forms the foundation to identity the gaps for the to-be state and thus identify the scope of change required. The System Context Diagram describes:

- An event from an external system or user raising an event to which the new system must respond
- An event that the system generates that affects external systems or users

---

[15] An example would be the Optim product suite. See [19] for details and [20] for a description of an implementation example.

- Data flows (batch or real time) inbound that must be managed
- Data flows (batch or real time) outbound that must be managed

The System Context Diagram can also be used to identify any external dependencies (new sources of data and services external to the business) that might be needed and understand how this might impact existing or to-be business processes. Finally, it can be used to gain some understanding of dependencies associated with the new system around non-functional requirements.

Each flow of information into or out of the system is labeled so that the purpose of the interface is known to any reader. Each source of information and actor is also labeled for the same reasons. If possible, at this stage, each flow should be further described to give technical teams a better understanding of the purpose of the interfaces. For example, any specific issues that might be already known can be highlighted here. The following information should be provided:

- Who the users of the system are and what functions they enact
- Description of any external sources of data and services and their owner
- Information on how data flows in and out of the system; for example, daily or weekly batch or real time data access
- Security controls required

Figure 3.6 shows a typical System Context Diagram from a previous project, in this case an MDM solution that includes operational BI reporting and external systems to help extend product definitions from suppliers. Users and systems are clearly depicted and internal, and external elements of the solution are shown.

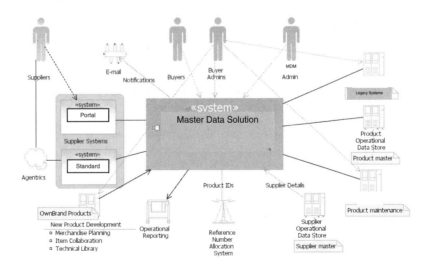

Figure 3.6 System Context Diagram example from a previous MDM project

3.6 Conclusion

In this chapter, we introduced the scope associated with the definition of data in our EIA and the five key data domains (Metadata, Master Data, Operational Data, Unstructured Data, and Analytical Data). From this, we described their role and context, and most importantly, we described how these domains can be managed successfully in the enterprise though a coherent Information Governance framework. Using governed architecture decisions, principles of Information Security and Information Privacy, and the System Context Diagram jointly is a methodological approach to assist in the detailing of the conceptual architecture all the way down to the Operational Model step by step and phase by phase.

In the next chapter, we explain the capabilities needed to manage the differing data domains and extend the thinking into the other areas that are needed to develop a complete, robust EIA on a conceptual and logical level.

3.7 References

[1]   Inmon, W.H. *Building the Data Warehouse*. John Wiley and Sons. 2005.

[2]   OpenOffice.Org Homepage: The Free and Open Productivity Suite. http://www.openoffice.org/.

[3]   Eckerson, W.W. *Data Quality and the Bottom Line, Achieving Business Success Through Commitment to High-Quality Data,* 2002. The Data Warehousing Institute. http://download.101com.com/pub/tdwi/Files/DQReport.pdf (accessed December 15, 2009).

[4]   Dreibelbis, A., Hechler, E., Milman, I., Oberhofer, M., van Run, P., D. *Wolfson Enterprise Master Data Management—An SOA Approach to Managing Core Information*. IBM Press, Pearson plc, 2008.

[5]   Gray, J., Reuter, A. *Transaction Processing: Concepts and Techniques*. Morgan Kaufmann, 1993.

[6]   Inmon, W., O'Neil, B., Fryman, L. *Business Metadata*. Morgan Kaufmann, 2007.

[7]   IT Governance Institute Homepage: Leading the IT Governance Community. http://www.itgi.org/.

[8]   Data Governance Institute Homepage: Data Governance & Stewardship Community of Practice. http://www.datagovernance.com/ (accessed December 15, 2009).

[9]   The Data Governance Blog: http://datagovernanceblog.com/ (accessed December 15, 2009).

[10] IBM Webpage: IBM Data Governance. http://www.ibm.com/ibm/servicemanagement/data-governance.html (accessed December 15, 2009).

[11] Ashley, P., Borret, M., Buecker, A, Lu, M., Mupiddi, S., Readshaw, N. *Understanding SOA Security Design and Implementation*. IBM Redbook, 2008. SG24731001.

[12] Schneier, B. *Applied Cryptography: Protocols, Algorithms, and Source Code in* C. John Wiley & Sons, 1996.

[13] Boubez, T., Hirsch, F., Hondo, M., Orchard, D., Vedamuthu, A., Yalcinap, U., Yendluri, P., (Editors). *Web Services Policy 1.5—Primer*. 2007. http://www.w3.org/TR/ws-policy-primer/ (accessed December 15, 2009).

[14] IBM Webpage: IBM Tivoli Security Policy Manager. ftp://ftp.software.ibm.com/common/ssi/pm/sp/n/tid14029usen/TID14029USEN.PDF (accessed December 15, 2009).

[15] Yuhanna, N. *Why Data Masking Should Be Part of Your Enterprise Data Security Practice*. Forrester Research. 2009. http://www.alacrastore.com/research/forrester-Why_Data_Masking_Should_Be_Part_Of_Your_Enterprise_Data_Security_Practice-54927 (accessed December 15, 2009).

[16] IBM Press Release: IBM Introduces Data Masking Solution. http://www-03.ibm.com/press/us/en/pressrelease/22209.wss (accessed December 15, 2009).

[17] IBM Press Release: Made in IBM Labs: IBM Researchers Develop Shield to Mask Sensitive On-Screen Information. http://www-03.ibm.com/press/us/en/pressrelease/27960.wss (accessed December 15, 2009).

[18] The Free Library Webpage: TJ Maxx Settles Data Breach Charges. http://www.thefreelibrary.com/TJ+Maxx+Settles+Data+Breach+Charges-a01611909452 (accessed December 15, 2009).

[19] Garstang, P. IBM Optim. http://henfield.se/dataserverday2009/IBM_Optim_big_pic_2009_Data_Servers_Day.pdf (accessed December 15, 2009).

[20] Callahan, D. De-identify Flat Files Using Optim Data Privacy Solution and InfoSphere Federation Server. IBM developerWorks. http://www.ibm.com/developerworks/data/library/techarticle/dm-0907optimprivacy/ (accessed December 15, 2009).

Enterprise Information Architecture: A Conceptual and Logical View

In this chapter, we introduce the EIA Reference Architecture on the Conceptual as well as on the first Logical Layer. Both represent well-defined layers describing the EAI Reference Architecture as outlined in Chapter 2 beginning from the top. The conceptual and logical layers are the first elements for a solution design with the latter fleshing out the former.

For the Conceptual Layer, we first outline the necessary capabilities for the EIA Reference Architecture in the context of the architecture terms and the Enterprise Information Model previously introduced. An Architecture Overview Diagram (AOD) shows the various required capabilities in a consistent, conceptual overview for the EIA Reference Architecture.

By introducing architecture principles, we guide the further design of the EIA Reference Architecture. We apply them to drill-down in a first step from the Conceptual to the Logical Layer. We show the Logical View as a first graphical representation of the logical architecture and explain key Architecture Building Blocks (ABB). The architecture principles introduced in this chapter guide the design in subsequent chapters as well.

4.1 Conceptual Architecture Overview

An EIA provides an information-centric view on the overall Enterprise Architecture. Thus, any instantiation of the EIA Reference Architecture enables an enterprise to create, maintain, use, and govern all information assets throughout their lifecycle from a bottom-up perspective. From a top-down perspective, business users and technical users articulate their information needs in the context of business processes shaping the business and application architecture based on the role they perform. We develop the EIA Reference Architecture from a top-down perspective.

We look at information from an end user perspective working with or operating on it to achieve certain goals. Key functional and technical capabilities provide and enable the set of operations on information required by the user community of an enterprise. Thus, we approach the Conceptual View of the EIA Reference Architecture presented in an AOD by introducing from a business perspective the required functional and technical capabilities.

In Chapter 3, we introduced the five data domains as part of the Enterprise Information Model. Not surprisingly, the EIA must cover all five data domains with appropriate capabilities as required by each individual domain.

Furthermore, there are several capabilities required that span across either some or all data domains (for example, EII). Higher-level capabilities such as Business Performance Management (BPM) are based on foundational information capabilities for the five data domains. New delivery models such as the Cloud Computing delivery model demand additional capabilities as well. Thus, for building an EIA Reference Architecture that satisfies the more advanced business requirements of today and the upcoming ones in the future, we see the need for the following additional capabilities:

- Predictive Analytics and Real Time Analytics
- Business Performance Management
- Enterprise Information Integration (EII)
- Mashup
- Information Governance
- Information Security and Information Privacy
- Cloud Computing

We explain these capabilities from a high-level perspective[1] in the following sub-sections and show them conceptually in the AOD jointly afterwards. A company is not required to implement all capabilities introduced in this section as part of an instantiation of the EIA Reference Architecture. IT Architects design the specific IT solutions based on the careful analysis of the specific requirements throughout the design process.[2]

We start with the Metadata management capability and continue aligned with the order of the data domains as shown in the Information Reference Model in Chapter 3.

---

[1] For some of these capabilities, there are dedicated books. (See [1] for an example focusing on just *one* data replication technique.) Thus, it is impossible to reach the same degree of detail for all capabilities here. Furthermore, there are areas which we cannot cover—for example, we will not discuss storage layout optimization supporting Green IT in data centers in the same degree of detail as outlined in [2].

[2] This process includes gap analysis between the current state of the IT and the target state where existing software components might be re-used for the new solution, whereas for a gap a new technology has to be deployed.

4.1.1 Metadata Management Capability

The Metadata management capability addresses the following business requirements:

- This capability helps to establish an enterprise business glossary where business terms are correlated with their technical counterparts; it also enables and facilitates efficient communication between business and IT people.

- Metadata management supports Information Governance which is key to treat information as a strategic asset.

- Metadata is a prerequisite to establish trusted information for business and technical information consumers. A user supposedly trusting information must understand the context of the information and thus must know for example the source of the data or associated data quality characteristics.

- Cost-effective problem resolution in the information supply chain requires data lineage which is based on Metadata.

- Business requirements change over time entailing change in the IT environment. Thus, impact analysis of changes in the IT infrastructure enables the understanding of a change. For example, impact analysis based on Metadata for a data transformation job change which is part of a complex series of transformation jobs would show if and how many subsequent jobs are affected.

Data lineage and impact analysis are detailed in Chapter 10 in the context of a detailed use case scenario.

4.1.2 Master Data Management Capability

The MDM capability[3] (also discussed in more detail in Chapter 11) provides the following functions to the business:

- It creates the authoritative source of Master Data within an enterprise laying the foundation to establish guidelines for the lifecycle management of Master Data.

- Actionable Master Data delivering sustained business value using event mechanism on Master Data changes. (For example, three months before an insurance contract with a customer expires, the customer care representative is notified to proactively contact the customer due to an event rule.)

- Simplification and optimization of key business processes such as new product introduction and cross- and up-sell by providing state of the art business services for Master Data standardizing the way Master Data is used across the enterprise.

---

[3] See more details in [3].

- It reduces cost and complexity with a central place to enforce all data quality, business rules, and access rights on Master Data.

- A centralized MDM solution is a cornerstone for effective Information Governance on Master Data allowing centralized enforcement of governance policies.

- Reporting results are improved in the analytical environment by leveraging consistent Master Data in the dimension tables in a DW.

MDM has a strong dependency on the EII capability during the Master Data Integration (MDI) phase. Using EII functions during the MDI phase, the Master Data is extracted from the current systems, cleansed, and harmonized before it is loaded into the MDM System (and possibly also in a DW system to improve data quality in the dimension tables).

4.1.3 Data Management Capability

The data management capability serves the following business needs:

- Efficient Create, Read, Update, and Delete (CRUD) functions for transactional systems processing structured Operational Data

- Appropriate enforcement of access rights to data to allow only authenticated and authorized users to work with the data

- Low costs for administration by efficient administration interfaces and autonomics

- Business resiliency of the operational applications by providing proper continuous availability functions, including high availability and disaster recovery

In essence, the data management capability provides all functions needed by transactional systems such as order entry or billing applications to manage structured Operational Data across its lifecycle.

4.1.4 Enterprise Content Management Capability

The ECM capability addresses the following business requirements:

- Compliance with legal requirements (for example, e-mail archiving)

- Efficient management of Unstructured Data (for example insurance contracts)

- Delivery of content for web application (for example, images for e-commerce solutions)

- Appropriate enforcement of access rights to Unstructured Data to allow only authenticated and authorized users to work with the data

- Business resiliency of the operational applications by providing proper continuous availability functions, including high availability and disaster recovery

- Comprehensive content-centric workflow capabilities to enable for example workflow-driven management of insurance contracts

This capability enables end-to-end management of Unstructured Data needed in many industries such as the insurance industry. It also enables compliance solutions for e-mail archiving.

4.1.5 Analytical Applications Capability

The analytical applications capability addresses two areas which are DW and Identity Analytics capability, as well as Predictive and Real Time Analytics capability.

4.1.5.1 Data Warehousing and Identity Analytics Capability

The capability area of DW and Identity Analytics applications (mostly focusing by looking into the past) delivers the following functions for a business:

- Identity Analytics can be applied to mitigate fraud or to improve homeland security by discovering non-obvious and hidden relationships.

- DWs are the foundation for reporting for business analysts and report on historical data—the past.

- Integration of analytics to cover Structured and Unstructured Data in a DW is one of the required steps towards a Dynamic Warehousing (DYW, see Chapter 13). For example, analyzing blog posts regarding a product to find out what features customers like or which parts they reported broke most often alongside selling statistics provides new insight. This insight is unavailable with reporting on Structured Data only.

- Discovery mining in a DW allows a business to discover patterns. An example would be association rule mining to find out which products are typically bought together.

Building a DW with enterprise scope where Operational Data from heterogeneous sources must be extracted, cleansed, and harmonized before it is loaded into the DW system has a strong dependency on the EII capability.

4.1.5.2 Predictive Analytics and Real Time Analytics Capability

Building Intelligent Utility Networks (IUN, see Chapter 13), improving medical treatment for prematurely born babies (see Chapter 14), or anticipating trends in customer buying decisions are use cases where companies in various industries are not satisfied with analytic functions reporting on the past. Here, two areas emerge as requirements for satisfying business needs by looking into the present or the future.

- Predictive Analytics are capabilities allowing the prediction of certain values and events in the future. For example, based on the electricity consumption patterns of the past, an energy provider would like to predict spikes in consumption in the future to optimize energy creation and to reduce loss in the infrastructure.

- Real Time Analytics are capabilities to address the need to analyze large-scale volumes of data in real time. Real Time Analytics capabilities consist of the ability of real time trickle feeds (see Chapters 8 and 13 for details on trickle feeds) into the DW, the ability of complex reporting queries executing in real time within the DW, and the ability of real time delivery of analytical insight to front-line applications. Stream analytics are another Real Time Analytics capability, which is introduced in section 4.1.7 and detailed in Chapters 8 and 14.

4.1.6 Business Performance Management Capability

BPM is a capability enabling business users to:

- Define the Key Performance Indicators (KPI) for the business.
- Monitor and measure against the defined KPIs on an ongoing basis.
- Visualize the measurements in a smart way enabling rapid decision making.
- Complement the visualization with trust indices about the quality of the underlying data putting the results in context regarding their trustworthiness.
- Intelligently act if the measurement of the KPIs indicates a need to act.
- Trigger events and notifications to business users if there are abnormalities in the data.

This capability often depends on strong analytical application capabilities.

4.1.7 Enterprise Information Integration Capability

From a business perspective, comprehensive EII (Chapter 8 provides more details on this topic) provides abilities to understand, cleanse, transform, and deliver data throughout its lifecycle. Examples include:

- Data harmonization from various Operational Data sources into an enterprise-wide DW.
- For cost and flexibility reasons, hiding complexity in the various, heterogeneous data sources of new applications should not be implemented in such a way that they are tied to specific versions of these data sources. Thus federated access must be available.
- Re-use of certain data cleansing functions such as standardization services in an SOA to achieve data consistency and improve data quality on data entry must be supported. This requires deploy capabilities of data quality functions as services.

Extract-Transform-Load (ETL) typically identifies EII capabilities to extract data from source systems, to transform it from the source to the target data model, and finally to load it into the target system. ETL thus is most often a batch mode operation. Typical characteristics are that data volumes involved are generally large, the process and load cycles long, and complex aggregations and transformations are required.

During the last two to three years, in many enterprises, ETL changed from custom-built environments with little or no documentation to a more integrated approach by using suitable ETL platforms. Improved productivity was the result of object and transformation re-use, strict methodology, and better Metadata support—all functions provided by the new ETL platforms.

A discipline known as Enterprise Application Integration (EAI)[4] is typically considered for solving application integration problems in homogeneous as well as heterogeneous application environments. Historically, applications were integrated with point-to-point interfaces between the applications—this approach of tightly coupled applications failed to scale with growing number of applications in an enterprise because the maintenance costs were simply too high. Every time an application was changed the point-to-point connections themselves as well as the applications on the other end of the connection had to be changed too. Avoiding these costs and increasing flexibility for evolving applications were drivers of the wide-spread deployment of an SOA. As a result, the applications became more loosely coupled creating more agility and flexibility for business process orchestration. Now, in many cases, applications are application-integrated with an Enterprise Service Bus (ESB)[5] based on message-oriented middleware. With that, an interface change of one application can be hidden from other applications because the ESB (through mediation using a new interface map) can hide this change. Compared to point-to-point connections, this is a significant advantage. Over the years, the discipline of EAI created many architecture patterns, such as Publish/Subscribe. IT Architects now have an abundance of materials[6] available for this domain.

The use of ESB components opened new possibilities from an EIA perspective. High latency is the major disadvantage of traditional ETL moving data from one application to the next. Streams techniques and certain EAI techniques based on ESB infrastructure can be used to solve the problem of high latency for data movement. For example, if a customer places an order through a website of the e-commerce platform and expects product delivery in 24 hours or less, a weekly batch integration to make fulfillment and billing applications aware of the new order is inappropriate. Today, EAI solves this by providing asynchronous and synchronous near real time and real time capabilities useful for data synchronization across systems. EAI can effectively move data among systems in real time, but does not define an aggregated view of the data objects or business entities nor does it deal with complex aggregation problems. It resolves transformations of data generally only managed at the message level. Thus, application integration techniques are often found connecting Online Transactional Processing (OLTP) systems with each other.

To date, the term EII has been typically used to summarize data placement capabilities based on data replication techniques and capabilities to provide access to data across various data sources. Providing a unified view of data from disparate systems comes with a unique set of requirements and constraints. First, the data should be accessible in a real-time fashion, which means that we should be accessing current data on the source systems as opposed to accessing stale data from a previously captured snapshot. Second, the semantics, or meaning, of data needs

---

[4] A minor warning for the reader: EAI (Enterprise Application Integration) and EIA (Enterprise Information Architecture) are very close—thus, read carefully.

[5] See additional collateral in [4].

[6] See additional collateral in [5], [6], [7], and [8].

to be resolved across systems. Different systems might represent the data with different labels and formats that are relevant to their respective uses, but that requires some sort of correlation by the end user to be useful to them. Duplicate entries should be removed, validity checked, labels matched, and values reformatted. The challenges with this information integration technique involve governing the use of a collection of systems in real time and creating a semantic layer that should map all data entities in a coherent view of the enterprise data.

With this overview of the traditional use of the terms ETL, EAI and EII, we propose now the following *new definition* of *EII*:

> EII consists of a set of new capabilities including Discover, Profile, Cleanse, Transform, Replicate, Federate, Stream, and Deploy capabilities. These techniques for information integration are applied across all five data domains: Metadata, Master Data, Operational Data, Unstructured data, and Analytical Data. EII in this new definition includes the former notion of ETL and EII. It also covers the intersection of EII with EAI.

We briefly introduce the new set of EII capabilities which are described in more detail in Chapter 8:

- **Discover capabilities**—They detect logical and physical data models as well as other Technical and Business Metadata. They enable understanding of the data structures and business meaning.

- **Profile capabilities**—They consist of techniques such as column analysis, cross-table analysis, and semantic profiling. They are applied to derive the rules necessary for data cleansing and consolidation of data because they unearth data quality issues in the data, such as duplicate values in a column supposedly containing only unique values, missing values for fields, or non-standardized address information.

- **Cleanse capabilities**—They improve data quality. Name[7] and address standardization, data validation (for example address validation against postal address dictionaries), matching to identify duplicate records enabling reconciliation through survivorship rules, and other data cleansing logic are often used.

- **Transform capabilities**—They are applied to harmonize data. A typical example is the data movement from several operational data sources into an enterprise DW. In this scenario, transformation requires two steps: First, the structural transformation of a source data model to a target data model. Second, a semantic transformation mapping code values in the source system to appropriate code values in the target system.

---

[7] Complementing standardization, you might want to apply Global Name Recognition (GNR) techniques first to more accurately identify cultural variations of names or the gender.

- **Replicate capabilities**—They deliver data to consumers. Typical data replication technologies are database focused using either trigger-based or transactional log-based Change Data Capture (CDC) mechanisms to identify the deltas requiring replication.

- **Federate capabilities**—They provide transparent and thus virtualized access to heterogeneous data sources. From an information-centric view, federation is the topmost layer of virtualization techniques. Federation improves flexibility by not tying an application to a specific database or content management system vendor. Another benefit is to avoid costs with consolidating data into a single system by leaving it in place. The benefits of federation can be used for Structured Data (also known as data federation) and Unstructured Data (also known as content federation).

- **Stream capabilities**—They are a completely new set of capabilities that EIA must cover. The need for enterprises to have them is basically the realization that Structured and Unstructured Data volumes reached levels where the sheer amount of data cannot be persisted anymore. Consider, for example, the total amount of messages exchanged over a stock trading system with automated brokering agents run by large financial institutions. In such an environment, streaming capabilities consist of low-latency data streaming infrastructure and a framework to deploy Real Time Analytics onto the data stream generating valuable business insight and identifying the small fraction of the data that requires an action or is worthwhile to be persisted for further processing.

- **Deploy capabilities**—They provide the ability to deploy EII capabilities as consumable information services. For example, a federated query can be exposed as an information service. In this case, the federated query might be invoked as a real time information service using specific protocols specified at deploy time.

4.1.8 Mashup Capability

Mashup capabilities (see Chapter 12 for more details on Mashups) enable a business to quickly build web-based, situational applications at low cost for typically small user groups (for example, all members of a department). The Mashup capability must allow non-technical users to create new value and insight from the combined information by mashing together information from various sources.

4.1.9 Information Governance Capability

As outlined in Chapter 3, the Information Governance capability is a crucial part for the design, deployment, and control processes of any instantiation of the EIA throughout its lifecycle. The Information Governance capability enables a business to manage and govern its information as strategic assets. More specifically it:

- Aligns people, processes, and technology for the implementation of an enterprise-wide strategy to implement policies governing the creation and use of information.

- Assigns Information Stewards to govern information assets throughout their lifecycle. The Information Stewards govern each information asset in the scope of defined policies, which might be automated regarding enforcement or might require a human being executing a task.

- Assigns a balance sheet describing the value of the information and the impact of loss or improper management from a data quality perspective.

4.1.10 Information Security and Information Privacy Capability

The Information Security and Information Privacy capability are relevant for any enterprise for two major reasons:

- Information Security functions protect information assets from unauthorized access, which prevents the probability of loss of mission critical information.

- Information Privacy functions enable a company to comply for example with legal regulations protecting the privacy of Personally Identifiable Information (PII).

Thus, this capability spans across all other capabilities previously introduced in this section. For example, the Information Governance capability would define the security policies for information, whereas the Data Management capability would either need to deliver the required security features itself or through integration with external systems delivering them. In the Component Model presented in Chapter 5, this capability is decomposed in a number of different components to address all the requirements with coherently grouped functions by component. Foreshadowing them you can anticipate the following components:

- A component providing comprehensive authentication and authorization services.

- A component (known as a De-Militarized Zone [DMZ]) protecting backend systems from external and internal sub-networks using a Reverse Proxy Pattern.

- Base security services such as encryption and data masking services delivered as a security sub-component through the IT Service & Compliance Management Service Component.

4.1.11 Cloud Computing Capability

Due to the business value pledge, the Cloud Computing capability is necessary for many enterprises today and represents a new delivery model for IT. However, the Cloud Computing delivery model is more than just a new way of billing for IT resources. A new set of IT capabilities has been developed and significant changes to existing IT components have been applied. Not surprisingly, the Cloud Computing delivery model also affects the Information Management domain and therefore the EIA within an enterprise. Thus, we briefly introduce functional and technical capabilities relevant for the Cloud Computing delivery model. (See more details on the implication of Cloud Computing in Chapter 7, section 7.4.)

- **Multi-Tenancy capabilities**—They define the sharing of resources as part of the multi-tenancy concept. From a multi-tenancy perspective, there are distinct layers to apply the concept of multi-tenancy such as the application layer, the information layer (for example, shared databases where each tenant has its own schema for maintenance operations), and the infrastructure layer (for example, multiple Operating System [OS] instances on the same hardware).

- **Self-Service capabilities**—They define services to allow the tenant to subscribe to IT services delivered through Cloud Computing with a self-service User Interface (UI). For example, you can subscribe through a web-based self-service UI to collaboration services on LotusLive[8] or use virtualized IT resources in the Amazon Elastic Compute Cloud[9] on a pay-per-use model. While subscribing, you select the parameters for the Service-Level Agreements (SLA) as needed.

- **Full Automation capabilities**—They define services to allow cost reduction on the IT service provider side. Thus, after a tenant subscribes to a service offered, the deployment and management throughout the lifecycle of the service must be fully automated from the point the service is provisioned to the point the service is decommissioned.

- **Virtualization capabilities**—They provide for the virtualization of resources to enable multi-tenancy. From an information perspective, key capabilities are storage hardware virtualization as well as a completely virtualized IO layer. For example, a virtualized IO layer[10] has characteristics such as sharing of storage for multiple consumers with seamless expansion and reduction, high availability and reliability (for example, to allow capacity expansion or maintenance without downtime), policy-driven automation and management, and high performance.

- **Elastic Capacity capabilities**—They provide services to still comply to SLAs even when peak workloads occur. This means the computing capacity needs to be "elastic" in the application, information, and infrastructure layer growing and shrinking as demanded. The assignment, removal, and distribution of resources among tenants has to be autonomic and dynamic to deliver cost efficient workload balancing with optimized use of the available resources.

- **Metering capabilities**—They provide instrumentation and supporting services to know how many resources a certain tenant has consumed. For example, the costs for the services provider offering a database cloud service are affected by the amount of data managed for a tenant who subscribed to this service. More data requires more storage.

---

[8] See more on LotusLive in [9].

[9] See more on Amazon Elastic Compute Cloud in [10].

[10] See an example of file system virtualization in [11].

Higher storage consumption by the service consumer causes an increase of cost for the service provider. For such a cloud service, the ability to meter storage consumption for a database would be a key metering function.

- **Pricing capabilities**—They compute the costs for the tenant of the subscribed services based on resource consumption measured with metering capabilities. It also allows the definition and adjustment of prices over time to reflect an increase or a decrease of costs used by the cloud service provider. Pricing services are invoked by the billing services for bill creation.

- **Billing capabilities**—They are used for accounting purposes. They create and send out the bill to the tenant. Monitoring might affect the billing and pricing services. For example, if the SLA promised to the cloud service consumer haven't been met and the monitoring component measured this fact, the amount of money charged to the service consumer might be reduced as part of the contract.

- **Monitoring capabilities**—They provide management services of a cloud requiring end-to-end monitoring. Monitoring capabilities are an important element of measuring adherence to performance and other requirements of resources and applications. In cloud environments, the task of monitoring becomes more critical due to the highly virtualized environment.

4.2 EIA Reference Architecture—Architecture Overview Diagram

In Section 4.1, we explored which capabilities are needed from a conceptual perspective. This section now takes that framework and the introduced capabilities and jointly shows them conceptually through an AOD in Figure 4.1. In the AOD, you can see various candidates for ABBs[11] representing the discussed capabilities. Note that Information Governance is not shown explicitly, because only parts of Information Governance are technology based.

A framework characteristic of the EIA Reference Architecture represented by the AOD is its industry-agnostic nature. Therefore, for any deployment for a company in a specific industry adaptation to industry-specific requirements must be done. For example, if the EIA Reference Architecture is used by a government to define the EIA for a homeland security solution, integration with external supply chain participants might not be needed, whereas third-party data providers such as terrorist blacklists must be integrated.

A company today typically consists of multiple LOBs or departments. IT systems support the automation of business processes and can be custom-developed, legacy or packaged applications such as ERP, CRM, or Supply Chain Management (SCM). Some of these business processes require integration beyond enterprise scope; examples are end-to-end supply chain integration or information enrichment using third-party information providers such as Dun &

---

[11] Chapter 36 and 37 of version 9 of TOGAF introduce a concise definition of an Architecture Building Block (ABB). TOGAF characterizes a good ABB through a well-defined specification with clear boundaries. For the scope of our discussion, we use a less formal interpretation of ABBs centered on the idea of related functionality or concepts.

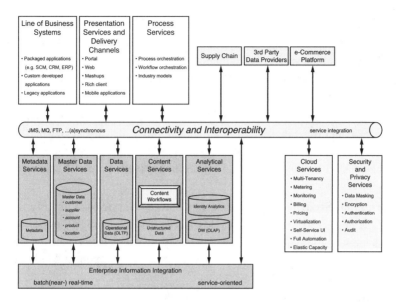

Figure 4.1 Architecture Overview Diagram for the EIA Reference Architecture

Bradstreet, ACXIOM, or LexisNexis.[12] Business users use Presentation Services to access their business functions driven by Process Services. Thus, we get the following candidate ABBs as shown in the AOD in Figure 4.1:

- **Metadata Services**—They provide a common set of functionality and core services for enabling open communication and exchange of information between systems based on consistently managed metadata.

- **MDM Services**—They maintain the core data items in a repository that make up a company's information assets. They manage the lifecycle of Master Data. MDM Services provide for specific quality services and authoring services to author, approve, manage, and potentially extend the definition of that Master Data for a particular LOB.

- **Data Services**—They are implemented using databases to deliver comprehensive functions for structured data to operational applications such as CRM, ERP, or e-commerce.

- **Content Services**—They are frequently delivered by ECM systems. Content Services manage Unstructured Data such as text documents, images, presentations, graphics, e-mail, and provide the necessary functions to search, catalog, and manage that data.

- **Analytical Services**—They enable organizations to leverage information to better understand and optimize business performance. These services support entry points of reporting to deep analytics and visualization, planning, aligned strategic metrics, role-based visibility, search-based access, and dynamic drill-through.

---

[12] See more information in [12], [13], and [14].

- **EII Services**—They provide a uniform way of representing, accessing, maintaining, managing, analyzing, and integrating data and content across heterogeneous information sources. These services take the form of cleansing, transformation and replication services, and services for federated queries to Structured and Unstructured Data spread across different data sources.

- **Cloud Services**—According to the introduction of Cloud Computing capabilities they provide certain functions across other capabilities which we aggregated in this candidate ABB. As we elaborate and detail the EIA Reference Architecture, we break-up this candidate ABB and insert technical capabilities into other areas as appropriate to enable this delivery model.

- **Information Security and Information Privacy Services**—Similarly to Cloud Services they are aggregated in a separate candidate ABB although they consist of a group of heterogeneous functions. We will decompose these heterogeneous functions currently in one ABB into different components in the Component Model while further detailing the EIA Reference Architecture.

- **LOB Systems**—They represent the heterogeneous mix of LOB systems.

- **Presentation Services and Delivery Channels**—They support a broad range of technologies such as Mashups, portals, or rich clients. They are used for dashboarding UIs for BPM, call center applications, or e-commerce platforms.

- **Process Services**—They provide process and workflow orchestration. For many industries, industry models provide comprehensive industry-specific business process templates.

- **Connectivity and Interoperability Services**—They provide for application and service integration within the enterprise and to external participants supporting multitude of different transport and communication protocols. The integration of external participants like e-commerce platforms in the financial industry or the integration of the supply chain is also enabled through this candidate ABB.

Now equipped with an understanding on the conceptual level of the EIA Reference Architecture, we proceed to look at the first layer of the logical architecture whereas architecture principles act as guidance to the solution design process.

4.3 Architecture Principles for the EIA

Architecture principles are a set of logically consistent and easily understood guidelines that direct the design and engineering of IT solutions and services in the enterprise. These principles provide an outline of the tasks, resources, and potential costs to the business for their implementation, and they also provide valuable input that can be used to justify why certain decisions have to be made.

Architecture principles should enable the EIA Reference Architecture as a tool that can help you map between the organization's business goals, business architecture, IT landscape, and the solution delivery, and help the Enterprise Information Architecture to be the conduit to understand the implications of planned new business requirements.

An EIA should be based around many of the principles in Table 4.1. Without such·guiding principles it is likely that any solution will become fragmented or it becomes increasingly difficult to exploit design elements across the enterprise. The architecture principles for EIA shown in Table 4.1 are by their nature generic and would need refining, shaping, and probably adding to in order to usefully serve on any specific instantiation of the EIA Reference Architecture. The column labeled "New" indicates if the architecture principle is a new one due to recent changes in existing or the appearance of new business requirements. The "Domain" column indicates the data domain where the architecture principle is applicable the most. Note that this does not imply that the principle is completely irrelevant in another domain; however, we tried to distinguish strong relevance from minor relevance or irrelevancy in the Domain column. The note of "All" in the Domain column indicates that the architecture principle applies to all data domains. Following the table, each architecture principle is explained in more detail.

Table 4.1   Architecture Principles for the EIA

#	Architecture Principle for the EIA	New	Domain
1	Deploy enterprise-wide Metadata strategies and techniques	Y	Metadata
2	Exploit analytics to the finest levels of granularity		Analytical Data
3	Exploit Real Time and Predictive Analytics for business optimization	Y	Analytical Data
4	Enable KPI-based BPM	Y	Analytical Data, Metadata
5	De-couple data from applications enabling the creation of trusted information which can be shared across business processes in a timely manner	Y	All
6	Strive to deploy an enterprise-wide search capability		All
7	Compliance with all Information Security requirements		All
8	Compliance with all relevant regulations and Information Privacy legislation		All

Table 4.1   Architecture Principles for the EIA

#	Architecture Principle for the EIA	New	Domain
9	Deliver de-coupled, trusted information through Information as a Service (IaaS) so that information services in an SOA are reusable and shareable services for the business like other business services	Y	All
10	Deploy new levels of information lifecycle management creating actionable information	Y	All
11	Apply Cloud Computing delivery model to Information Services	Y	Operational, Unstructured, and Analytical Data
12	Improve cost efficiency of the IT infrastructure, possibly now also using Green IT techniques	Y	All
13	Deliver information with appropriate data quality		All
14	End-to-end inter- and cross-enterprise information integration	Y	All
15	Develop an EII strategy with optimization of data transport, federation and placement		All
16	Virtualize information whenever possible	Y	All
17	Deliver operational reliability and serviceability to meet business SLA to ensure access to Structured and Unstructured Data at all times	Y	All
18	EIA should reduce complexity and redundancy and enable re-use		All
19	EIA should be based on open standards		All
20	Enterprise information assets must have a business owner and be part of end-to-end Information Governance		All
21	Align IT solution with business		All
22	Maximize agility and flexibility of IT assets		All

1. Deploy enterprise-wide Metadata strategies and technologies. Metadata management provides unambiguous definition of data and its history (how it is transformed and manipulated throughout the organization) to enable unified information integration. A comprehensive Metadata management solution improves data quality by providing a full understanding of the data. It is essential to have consistent Metadata enabled to easily build a set of repeatable and reusable IT processes because it centrally and completely documents data and applications. It enables business users and technical developers alike to have a common understanding of the data assets already available to the business and a precise meaning for that data and its usage.

2. Exploit analytics to the finest levels of granularity. The value of data is requiring that ever deeper analytics are exploited to understand smaller events that may influence specific groupings or segments of information such as customers, suppliers or products. This requires not only data access, but that the tooling can crawl through vast quantities of information to extract significant (potentially small but high value) events in a manner that is easily consumed by end users and business processes alike. Techniques such as data mining with visually rich interfaces to understand statistically significant events is one opportunity and being able to slice and dice through OLAP (On-line Analytical Processing) tooling to fine grained data is another. Reporting tools can also be combined with data mining tools to enable mining of data by less qualified end users who see the solution as nothing more than another report that returns a result set (for example scoring a set of customers). Remember that once data has been summarized, that lower level of detail is lost, and if it should prove useful at a later date, may not be retrievable.

3. Exploit Real Time and Predictive Analytics for business optimization. This principle requires new analytical capabilities to be able to derive insight into information in real time when the event occurs. Complex event processing capabilities for reducing loss in water and electricity networks providing real time insight into consumer demand are one example for this real time analytical architecture principle. Predictive Analytics using various algorithms enable an organization to foresee events or values of attributes in the future with a certain probability.

4. Enable KPI-based BPM. In a globally competitive marketplace, the business strategy must be measurable—otherwise it cannot be controlled. This architecture principle thus requires a holistic approach in the EIA to allow the definition, monitoring and reporting on critical business KPIs so that the executive management team can manage an enterprise based on business performance on an ongoing basis. Note that the KPIs themselves could be considered Business Metadata and thus require Metadata management lifecycle capabilities.

5. De-couple data from applications enabling the creation of trusted information which can be shared across business processes in a timely manner. There is a need for a consolidated, accurate, consistent and timely view of the core business entities using a common model for each entity. Without such a view it will be very difficult to define a set of services that can adhere to some common meta-model to drive transformations for data that is held in messages, Master Data solutions, DWs, or Operational Data stores. This view needs to take into account the business definition of data, as well as the physical and logical definitions for that data in any model developed. Difficulties arise if there is no common model whenever there is a need to create and extend enterprise wide business processes, to create consistent reporting, and to re-use services.

In some data domains, such as Master Data, the information is extracted from a variety of sources, harmonized and loaded into a centralized system, managing it and making it available to consumers through services decoupling the data from the consuming applications. Timely and trusted information includes data governing rules that define availability, standardization, quality and integrity. Information requires also associated Metadata describing its source, quality and other relevant attributes so that it can be trusted. This principle is particularly applicable for the Master Data domain because Master Data has the characteristic of high re-use across a large number of business processes. However, there might be applications with too many embedded business rules so that the de-coupling of the data would be cost-prohibitive or even impossible. In such a case it might be appropriate to consider the application itself as information source and consume it through a Cloud Service for example.

6. Strive to deploy an enterprise-wide search capability. One consistent search engine across content repositories, databases, applications, collaborative environments and portals to shorten the time to identify useful information, is becoming a constant requirement for business users. By being able to access all such sources through one simple interface, the job of quickly identifying and making use of the best data for a particular process or job is much simplified. It should not matter whether information is on an intranet page, within a content management system, buried deep inside an ERP application or CRM solution, residing within a legacy database or even in an e-mail system, the search engine deployed should be able to find it. Another dimension of enterprise-wide search is the ability to extend the intranet search to resources such as the Internet in a unified manner.

7. Compliance with all Information Security requirements. This principle includes accounting for several layers of security, identification of a broader risk analysis strategy and the definition of specific rules around Information Security. Basic capabilities are proper authentication and authorization mechanisms which are required by this principle.

8. Compliance with all relevant regulations and Information Privacy legislation. All information assets should be protected regarding information legislation requirements. Also, all information assets must be managed in compliance with all legal regulations such as Sarbanes-Oxley.[13]

9. Deliver de-coupled, trusted information through Information as a Service (IaaS) so that information services in a SOA are reusable and shareable services for the business like other business services. Basically this architecture principle complements the fifth architecture principle. Once information has been decoupled from an application and is trustworthy, it makes sense to deliver it through Information as a Service. Thus, this principle is one of the core components of a well-formed SOA strategy and is part of the definition of the IOD approach to deliver information in context at the right time to the right application or business

---

[13] Sarbanes-Oxley Act (SOX, valid for all US publicly traded companies) was approved in 2002 in the United States as a response to numerous financial scandals such as Enron. The key objectives of SOX are to improve transparency into publicly reported financial information and stricter internal controls.

process. Implementing highly modular, loosely coupled systems and services is the most efficient way of taking advantage of reusable services and minimizing the cost associated with the duplication of processing tasks. This principle also facilitates leveraging services that are provided by other parties. This means that information is packaged as a service to business processes, so that consistent, manageable information is made available to every process in a standardized way that enables re-use and business flexibility. Deploying information services makes them also discoverable in the same way business services are discoverable through a Service Registry and Repository (SRR). (More details on the relationship between an EIA and SOA can be found in Chapter 2.)

10. Deploy new levels of information lifecycle management creating actionable information. This architecture principle requires managing all information assets across their entire lifecycle efficiently. In addition, this principle mandates to create actionable information by emitting notifications and events if information changes and the new values satisfy certain pre-defined conditions and rules. Actionable information can be categorized such as business events (for example, a bank might place a rule that two months before a fixed term deposit expires, a customer care representative must be notified via e-mail to contact the customer), infrastructure events (for example, assignment of a value to each information asset in order to manage storage costs efficiently), and regulatory events (for example, the compliance with legal requirements to retain or delete an information asset in a timely manner such as e-mails related to a certain law suit at court).

11. Apply Cloud Computing delivery model to Information Services. Once information is available through Information Services as indicated with the ninth architecture principle, the Cloud Computing delivery model can be applied to them. With this architecture principle, design consideration must be made for the Operational, Unstructured and Analytical Data domain if these services can be deployed into Cloud Computing environments reducing cost and further improving flexibility. Pushing an SRR into a Cloud Computing environment externally hosted exposes the whole internal SOA infrastructure because now service discovery and service routing is available if and only if the external cloud service provider is available.

12. Improve cost efficiency of the IT infrastructure, possibly now also using Green IT techniques. The EIA is typically not deployed on the green field. A guiding principle for each phase of an iterative rollout of EIA is the improvement of cost efficiency. We consider cost efficiency in this case in three dimensions:

- A Green IT perspective. Energy costs are, for many data centers, the major part of the operational costs. Thus, selecting appropriate hardware platforms as part of this architecture principle that are enabled for Green IT consumes less energy and, hence, reduces costs for the IT infrastructure.[14] Achieving this goal requires, first, analyzing and measuring energy efficiency in the data center with static and dynamic thermal measurements. Once the current situation is assessed, techniques in energy efficient

---

[14] See more information in [2].

system design such as modular systems and the use of new energy efficient systems can be applied. This can be complemented by using virtualization techniques to consolidate or to reduce complexity leading to decreased energy consumption.[15] Further optimization can be achieved using advanced energy management.

- Cost efficiency can be improved by applying advanced IT service management principles. In this category belongs the integration of workload management and traditional facility management in order to manage energy consumption by deploying different measures such as sensor networks in the data center. Another step in the area of advanced IT service management is to reduce complexity in administration thus reducing management overhead.

- Particularly relevant for information aspects is to apply DW and federation principles to align IT and business oriented service management disciplines. Furthermore, if the definition of cost efficiency is interpreted in a broader fashion, this principle demands exploitation of information management capabilities to reduce loss in energy and water networks making these utility networks smarter and therefore friendlier from an environmental perspective. As a side effect, it decreases costs operating these networks by avoiding energy waste, for example. Another scenario for this broader understanding of the cost efficiency principle is the creation of smart traffic systems based on information management capabilities reducing carbon dioxide emissions through reduction of traffic jams. This reduces cost from a perspective of not having the need to reschedule meetings if attendees are stuck in traffic causing decision or project delay, for example.

13. Deliver information with appropriate data quality. Data quality is the cornerstone of decision making—without high quality data results can always be challenged across differing business areas. This leads to impaired decision making, poor coordination across the business and ongoing costs to clean data in a piece meal or siloed fashion. Note that data should be classified in terms of its value and hence its requirement for absolute accuracy, for example, enterprise Master Data is often regarded as highly valuable data because it is used to enable a company to present itself most favorably in all customer interactions. As such it must be highly accurate and is normally considered more valuable than data that is only used within one LOB.

14. End-to-end inter- and cross-enterprise information integration. This principle requires the deployment of comprehensive end-to-end Enterprise Information Integration (EII) capabilities to seamlessly support enterprise information integration initiatives such as Master

---

[15] IBM is running a Big Green IT project using new energy efficient systems as well as virtualization techniques. The key objective of this project is to consolidate approximately 3900 servers on approximately 30 System z mainframes running Linux, reducing energy consumption by 80% and the associated costs significantly as well. Details on this project can be found in [15], [16], [17], [18], and [19].

Data Management, enterprise-wide BI solutions or information integration for cross-enterprise solutions such as an RFID-based Track and Trace solution for e-Pedigree[16] compliance.

15. Develop an EII strategy with optimization of data transport, federation, and placement. This architecture principle expands the previous one regarding an optimization aspect. As well as managing all the data stored in various repositories around the enterprise there is also a pressing need to manage data that is moving around the enterprise at any one time. These data may take the form of flat files being managed in batch, message queues, XML files or replicated data. The alternative to moving data is leaving data in place using federation to access it. This approach tries to ensure that multiple copies of the same data are not proliferated around an organization, being maintained multiple times and potentially having its value reduced if there are multiple update points to it which might result in multiple versions of the truth. Federation might not always be an option for performance reasons, in which case a data movement strategy to ensure data is kept in sync between copies is preferable. By developing a comprehensive strategy to address the need for unified information integration solutions using data movement and federation techniques as appropriate enables the business to be certain that data is consumed in the most effective manner at the right point in a business. This principle is closely tied to the Metadata principle: Without consistent Metadata and governance of that Metadata it becomes very difficult to maintain a company wide approach to movement and placement of data. This can result in fragmented data feeds, the same data being managed in the infrastructure many times in an inconsistent manner, resulting in excessive re-development, costly change, and poor data quality.

16. Virtualize information whenever possible. Storage virtualization and file system virtualization are the basic layers to implement this architecture principle. In Chapter 6 detailing the Operational Model, you can find operational patterns helping to implement this principle.

17. Deliver operational reliability and serviceability to meet business SLA to ensure access to Structured and Unstructured Data at all times. Much of a company's digitized information is unstructured including rich media streaming, website content, facsimiles, and computer output. Unlimited access to such information alongside relational based information is critical to enable a complete view of the entire information available to solve a business need. Today's business solutions require that all company information is available to its employees where necessary. It is becoming increasingly common to see Structured and Unstructured Data residing alongside each other within a set of services that a particular business process needs.

18. EIA should reduce complexity and redundancy and enable re-use. Implementing highly modular, loosely coupled systems and services is the most efficient way of taking advantage of re-usable services and minimizing the cost associated with the duplication of processing tasks. Additionally, this principle also facilitates leveraging services that are provided by other parties.

---

[16] An e-Pedigree is an electronic pedigree showing the complete path of a product from the manufacturer to the point where it is received by the customer.

19. EIA should be based on open standards. This will enable the use of multiple technologies for the interoperability of the systems in the enterprise and external partners. Open standards facilitate interoperability and data exchange among different products or services and are intended for widespread adaptation.

20. Enterprise information assets must have a business owner and be part of end-to-end Information Governance. An Information Steward is responsible for defining the rules for information usage. This eliminates confusion regarding who can maintain, manage and change that information. Information must be viewed as a business asset so it should be managed accordingly to ensure that its value to the organization is maximized.

21. Align IT solution with business. Organizations articulate a set of priorities that serve as a guide where to focus the enterprise efforts.

22. Maximize agility and flexibility of IT assets. This principle requires the IT Architect to consider agility and flexibility aspects of the EIA. For example, the federation techniques mentioned earlier might be used to more loosely couple applications and information sources.

4.4 Logical View of the EIA Reference Architecture

We are now ready to go from the Conceptual View of the EIA Reference Architecture to the first Logical View as shown in Figure 4.2. This diagram and the AOD described previously can be used to start the discussion about how one actually deploys these information components out into an enterprise.

In Figure 4.2, we depict each of the major areas of the EIA Reference Architecture, including the general system and infrastructure components needed to operate and manage any IT landscape. In addition, a set of common requirements that straddle all the layers of the

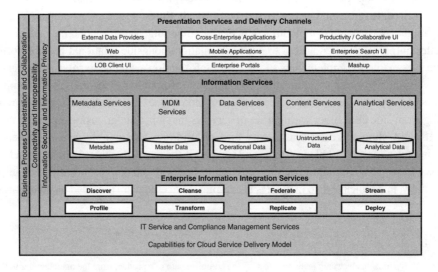

Figure 4.2   Logical View of the EIA Reference Architecture

information architecture—Business Process Orchestration and Collaboration capabilities (not previously discussed), comprehensive Connectivity and Interoperability capabilities, and security-related requirements—all needed to manage and run any solution developed.

Each area is described in more detail in sections 4.4.1 to 4.4.7; this sets the scene for the following chapters on the Component and Operational Models.

The Component Model specifically describes how these functional aspects can be assembled to add value in any solution stack, and the Operational Model details how these functional components can be deployed onto physical assets to deliver the requirements (functional and non-functional) of the design. We now introduce each layer with a brief description.

4.4.1 IT Services & Compliance Management Services Layer

This layer covers the basic requirements upon which any solution must reside—it covers, for example, the set of tools and hardware required to configure, monitor, and manage the solution. Without this layer, no solution can be deployed because no infrastructure exists. Furthermore, there would be no way to manage the solution because there would not be features to monitor performance at the hardware, application, and business level. Also, change implementation and the ability to report back on any issues identified for problem resolution depend on this layer.

Recall that in the AOD we introduced a candidate ABB for Cloud Services and noted that we refine this positioning while detailing the EIA Reference Architecture. In the Logical View, we have the ability to take the first step into this refinement. Cloud Computing capabilities such as Elastic Capacity, a virtualized storage and IO layer, metering, billing, pricing, and monitoring are delivered through this layer. Other aspects of the Cloud Computing delivery model, such as multi-tenancy on the information layer, are discussed in the Component Model in Chapter 5.

4.4.2 Enterprise Information Integration Services

This Logical View shows how IT Architects can begin to manage the various data domains by first ensuring the data is managed, understood, and transformed in the EII layer. This layer is critical to the success of any enterprise-wide venture. It might start around a specific theme, for example, to solve a DW problem, to integrate several differing content repositories, or to manage data movement around the enterprise through an ESB. However, over time, this layer should be used to ensure all information integration workloads are managed through this layer to ensure consistency and re-use of assets.

As introduced in the capability section, EII covers the areas of discovery, profiling, cleansing, transformation, replication, federation, streaming, and deployment of information integration services in the IT environment.

4.4.3 Information Services

Information Services provide a uniform way of representing, accessing, maintaining, managing, and analyzing Structured Data and content across heterogeneous information sources. They are broken down into the following subcategories of logical services based on the data domain reference model previously introduced.

4.4.3.1 Metadata Services

Metadata Services are intended to unify the management of Metadata related to the information solutions supported. Logical and physical data models, data quality metrics, an enterprise business glossary, or Metadata supporting end-to-end data lineage and impact analysis are classified and managed with services in this domain. In the context of an SOA, message models associated with data flows and their service definition, along with service and process definitions, can be held and maintained through these services.

Various user roles perform through various tool operations on Metadata-related artifacts such as data models, data analysis assessment results, or data integration flow specifications. The tooling within this layer links Metadata to enable various different users to gain a 360-degree view of how data is being used and managed throughout the enterprise. For example, in a business glossary for a data model, technical terms can be linked to business terms. In a subsequent step, deriving a set of exposed services that define and enable consistent use of a *business object* such as customer is simplified. Metadata Services ultimately serve an enterprise by enabling trusted information by having the context available as Metadata and improving the consistency of data use wherever possible.

4.4.3.2 MDM Services

MDM Services manage the entities that are most critical to the success of an organization, such as customer, product, contract, or location. Even though the success of an organization relies on them, the Master Data itself is often inconsistent, inaccurate, incomplete, and distributed across application silos. With the deployment of MDM Services, the single version of truth for Master Data in a defined (logically) centralized repository and synchronizes the Master Data across the existing legacy environment. In this way, Master Data can be used by any business service. The service consumer can be confident that (security permitting) a valid set of data for that entity has been managed in a consistent way.

4.4.3.3 Data Services

Data Services provide access to Operational Data stored in any type of data storage. Data Services manage relational data—and if the underlying database supports it—XML data with XQuery support instead of just putting XML (similar to other Unstructured Data) into columns with a data type such as Binary Large Object (BLOB). Through Data Services, queries can be exposed.

Data Services can be divided into two categories: core data operations services including CRUD operations, and the associated housekeeping functions such as logging.

4.4.3.4 Content Services

Content Services manage Unstructured Data such as documents, media, or files. The scope of this layer includes basic CRUD operations and more advanced access mechanisms (content federation and search). The goal of the Content Services is to expose (single source or federated) content as a service and enable these services to be used within content centric workflows.

4.4.3.5 Analytical Services

Analytical Services are typically providing insight after Operational Data has been harmonized, cleansed, enriched, and aggregated in specialized systems such as DWs. For example, a data mining service can be embedded within a reporting service to deliver information to end users without them needing any skills in the use of the mining service employed. They enable the business to adapt to changing market dynamics and everyday operational disruptions. They support a holistic approach to business management enabling basic and deep analytics, aligned information objectives, role-based visibility, contextual insight, and in-time actions.

4.4.4 Presentation Services and Delivery Channels

The Presentation Services and Delivery Channel layer provides various channels for users to access the information and capabilities from the services delivered in the lower levels of the logical stack. This layer will be decomposed into server- and client-side components in the Component Model.

EIA demand ubiquitous access within the users' familiar environment and across multiple delivery channels. Information must be available through servers, laptops, PDAs, or smart phones anywhere and anytime the user needs it. Therefore, it is supported by an enterprise platform, which delivers a consistent view of information to users at the right time, in the right format, and the right language. Users in this case are defined as humans, applications, and business processes.

4.4.5 Information Security and Information Privacy

Information Security and Information Privacy built into any solution are required for security and data assurance policies. They ensure an enterprise is compliant with all internal and (required) external policies. This in itself helps to maintain and even increase enterprise competitiveness.

Thus, these services are needed to create and maintain business-relevant, risk-appropriate solutions to cost-effectively meet and forestall security threats, evolve the enterprise to a posture of continual security and compliance readiness, and optimize response to regulatory, audit, and competitive pressures.

4.4.6 Connectivity and Interoperability

The Connectivity and Interoperability layer provides interoperability between the services within and beyond the enterprise. A typical instantiation of this layer is an ESB providing support for a variety of transport and communication protocols, interface mapping capabilities, and more interoperability functions.

4.4.7 Business Process Orchestration and Collaboration

The Business Process Orchestration and Collaboration layer provides two key capabilities. First, this layer provides end-to-end business process orchestration capabilities based on workflows containing, for example, automated tasks as well as human tasks. These features enable workflows to be driven across differing groups of users and systems to automate and streamline existing processes or to build or even outsource processes beyond the enterprise.

Second, this layer provides the capabilities so that all users in the enterprise can collaborate in an appropriate fashion. Typical examples of collaboration services include instant messaging and e-mail services.

4.5 Conclusion

In this chapter, we introduced the Conceptual Level and the first layer of the Logical Level of the EIA Reference Architecture. In Chapter 5, we provide the Component Model and Component Interaction Diagrams showing the viability of the Component Model describing the EIA Reference Architecture on the second layer of the Logical Level, followed by the Operational Model in Chapter 6.

4.6 References

[1] Alur, N., Briddell, R., Kelsey, D., Takaya, N. *WebSphere Information Integrator Q Replication: Fast Track Implementation Scenarios*. IBM Redbooks, 2007. SG24-6487-00.

[2] Lamb, J. *The Greening of IT: How Companies Can Make a Difference for the Environment*. IBM Press, Pearson plc., 2009.

[3] Dreibelbis, A., Hechler, E., Milman, I., Oberhofer, M., van Run, P., Wolfson, D. *Enterprise Master Data Management—An SOA Approach to Managing Core Information*. IBM Press, Pearson plc., 2008.

[4] Chappell, D. *Enterprise Service Bus*. O'Reilly, 2004.

[5] Fowler, M. *Patterns of Enterprise Application Integration*. Addison-Wesley, 2003.

[6] Hohpe, G., Woolf, B. *Enterprise Integration Patterns*. Addison-Wesley, 2004.

[7] Bieberstein, N., et al. *Service-Oriented Architecture (SOA) Compass,* Pearson Publishing, 2006. ISBN: 0-13-186002-5.

[8] Theissen, M. *Hub-And-Spoke. Getting the Data Warehouse Wheel Rolling*. 2008. http://www.datallegro.com/pdf/white_papers/wp_hub_and_spoke.pdf (accessed December 15, 2009).

[9] IBM LotusLive Cloud Computing offering homepage: *LotusLive*. https://www.lotuslive.com/ (accessed December 15, 2009).

[10] Amazon Elastic Compute Cloud offering homepage: *Amazon Elastic Compute Cloud*. http://aws.amazon.com/ec2/ (accessed December 15, 2009).

[11] IBM General Parallel File System offering homepage: *General Parallel File System*. http://www-03.ibm.com/systems/clusters/software/gpfs/index.html (accessed December 15, 2009).

[12] Dun and Bradstreet homepage: http://www.dnb.com/us/ (accessed December 15, 2009).

[13] AXCIOM homepage: http://www.acxiom.com/Pages/Home.aspx (accessed December 15, 2009).

[14] LexisNexis homepage: http://www.lexisnexis.com/ (accessed December 15, 2009).

[15] IBM Press, *IBM's Project Big Green Spurs Global Shift to Linux on Mainframe*. 2007. http://www-03.ibm.com/press/us/en/pressrelease/21945.wss (accessed December 15, 2009).

[16] IBM Project Big Green. http://www-03.ibm.com/press/us/en/presskit/21440.wss (accessed December 15, 2009).

[17] IBM Green Data Center Resource Library: http://www-03.ibm.com/systems/greendc/resources/literature/index.html (accessed December 15, 2009).

[18] IBM Global Technology Services. *The green data center: cutting energy costs for a powerful competitive advantage*. 2008. http://www-935.ibm.com/services/us/cio/outsourcing/gdc-wp-gtw03020-usen-00-041508.pdf (accessed December 15, 2009).

[19] Ebbers, M., Galea, A., Khiem, M. Schaefer, M., 2008. The Green Data Center: Steps for the Journey. IBM Redpaper: REDP-4413-00, http://www.redbooks.ibm.com/abstracts/redp4413.html (accessed December 15, 2009).

## CHAPTER 5

Enterprise Information Architecture: Component Model

In this chapter, we introduce the Component Model of the Enterprise Information Architecture (EIA) Reference Architecture. Our goal is to show a complete Component Model; thus, we discuss it in a wider context. However, the areas of focus are the information-centric components:

- Mashup Hub
- Metadata Services
- Master Data Management (MDM) Services
- Data Services
- Content Services
- Analytical Services
- Enterprise Information Integration (EII) Services
- IT Service & Compliance Management Services

The scope regarding the previous data domains is to define a complete Component Model that covers metadata, master data, analytical data, operational data, and Unstructured Data.

5.1 The Component Model

In the preceding chapters, the terms *IT architecture* and *Architecture Building Block (ABB)* were introduced. To delve deeper into the architecture description of the EIA, another term is needed: *component*. A *component* represents a logically grouped set of specific capabilities to deliver particular software functionality.

The Component Model is the heart of the EIA. It describes the functional components in terms of their roles and responsibilities, their relationships and interactions to other components, and the required collaboration that enables the implementation of specified deployment and customer use case scenarios. Each component is a relatively independent part of the architecture, where its characteristics are described by its functions, responsibilities, usage aspects, and interfaces. Their usages depend on the required solution capabilities and deployment scenarios. In addition to a detailed description of each component, the main focus of the Component Model is the Component Relationship Diagram and the Component Interaction Diagrams.

- **Component Relationship Diagram**—This diagram is a depiction of the components, interfaces, and relationships that are a part of the Component Model. The interfaces and relationships can be described at different levels. On a basic level, they simply describe directional flows of data between two components. On a more ambitious level, they describe the information content and the usage of protocols to exchange the information content between components. We call this the *static* relationship between the components.

- **Component Descriptions**—In addition to a high-level description, the Component Descriptions also include a detailed description of the main functionalities and the responsibilities of each component. Depending on the nature and functional scope of the component, it also includes the service description and implementation aspects. These implementation aspects might be characterized by various design and service patterns. The component interactions, interfacing capabilities, and functional and non-functional requirements complete the Component Descriptions.

- **Component Interaction Diagrams**—These diagrams depict how components dynamically collaborate to support various required business scenarios. These diagrams capture the most significant *dynamic* relationships between components. The Component Interaction Diagrams focus on the interactions between components and illustrate the derived flow of functionality in the context of a specific deployment scenario. Depending on the deployment scenario and required business scope, an appropriate subset of the functionality of each component might be required. Any customer use case scenario can be easily mapped to the Component Model using the corresponding Component Interaction Diagram (an example is in section 5.4, and you can find more examples in Chapters 7 to 14).

The Component Model can be developed using an iterative approach, driving from higher levels to lower levels with more detailed specifications at each iteration. The higher-level Component Model is definitely an inherent part of the logical model, and consequently, it is product and technology agnostic. The Component Model leads into the Operational Model, which then allows product mapping, a choice of middleware, the implementation of other systems and application technologies, and the selection of the appropriate programming model and communication protocols. (A product mapping for the EIA can be found online in Appendix A.) It is also possible to perform a component-based product mapping after the development of the Component Model, without highlighting the operational aspects right away.

The Component Model is characterized by the following features:

- A comprehensive description of the high-level structure and capabilities of the entire system and its key components and subcomponents.

- A detailed and precise description of the roles and responsibilities, relationships and interfaces, and collaborative capabilities of each component.

- A description of how the application, functional parts, and services of the system components are related to each other. This is especially important for the services concept of the Component Model, which illustrates the possibility of requesting component functionality as a service.

- A specification of how existing, acquired, and developed components are related to each other.

- A definition of the components in the context of the Operational Model to understand the execution and operational management aspects.

5.2 Component Relationship Diagram

Figure 5.1 (on the next page) shows the Component Relationship Diagram for the EIA using various techniques from the domains of Enterprise Application Integration (EAI) and Enterprise Information Integration (EII). In the Component Relationship Diagram, we've included every component we think is necessary for a complete EIA to show its viability and feasibility. However, there are components such as network management that are necessary for a concrete solution deployment but have been omitted because they are not the core area of focus in this chapter.

For the Component Relationship Diagram presentation, we applied the following color codes:

- The dark gray boxes represent the information services components for the metadata, data, content, master data, and analytical data domain.

- The gray boxes represent information service-related components such as the EII Component, the Mashup Hub Component, and IT Service & Compliance Management Services Component.

- The light gray boxes are components that are not part of the previous two categories and are typically found in a solution based on the EIA.

5.3 Component Description

Those key functional components are described using the following structure (depending on concrete project needs, a more enriched structure might be needed):

- **ID**—For easy identification
- **Name**—Applying intuitive naming convention

- **High-level description**—Short paragraph for quick understanding
- **Service description**—Focus on service, including service patterns
- **Interfaces**—Component interactions and interface standards (such as XML)

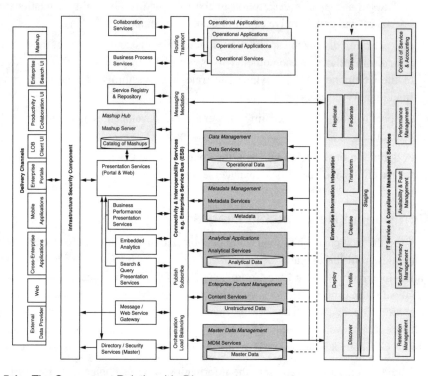

Figure 5.1   The Component Relationship Diagram

5.3.1 Delivery Channels and External Data Providers

The next generation EIA enables unconstrained access within the user's familiar environment. This is established through a versatile system access layer. This access layer, with its multiple information delivery channels, provides the mechanism for end users, applications, business processes, or external systems to interact with system components. It is supported by an enterprise platform that delivers a consistent view of trusted information to clients at the right time, in the right format and language, and within the required business context. This interaction might be human or automated (through a web service, for example).

We differentiate between two different categories:

- **Internal**—The access is provided to internal users or systems.
- **External**—Serves external clients or data providers.

Note that some delivery channels can also appear in both categories. In these cases, we noted it in the description to avoid redundancy. Following is a description of the key *internal* components of the information delivery channels:

- **Mobile applications**—Many mobile and handheld devices, such as notebook PCs, smart phones, Personal Digital Assistants (PDAs), pagers, Windows® clients, GPS devices, and so on are used online or disconnected from the network. These mobile devices are not only used to access information; they might also be used for local, disconnected processing.

- **Enterprise portals**[1]—Portals are used as a framework for integrating people, processes, and information within an enterprise or even across enterprise boundaries. Portals provide a secure unified access point, often in the form of a web-based user interface. They allow for information subscription, aggregation, and personalization through application-specific portlets and portlet wiring. This channel can also be an external channel.

- **LOB Client User Interface (UI)**—These are the UIs of traditional LOB applications, including packaged applications such as SAP ERP, SAP CRM, or Independent Software Vendor (ISV) applications. These applications can be horizontal or vertical in nature, and they can be enterprise-wide or serving a department or smaller organizational needs.

- **Productivity/Collaboration UI**—Various productivity and collaboration UIs serve applications and systems such as e-mail systems, word processing, presentations, spreadsheets, wikis, and blogs.[2] One of the objectives is to facilitate collaboration in the enterprise, but also beyond enterprise boundaries.

- **Enterprise search UI**—Enterprise search is the practice of identifying and enabling specific content across the enterprise to be indexed, searched, and displayed to authorized users. This helps get the right information to the right people at the right time. A key challenge is the need to index documents from a variety of sources such as the intranet, file systems, document management systems, e-mail systems, and relational databases. Then, you must assemble and present a consolidated list of prioritized documents to the requesting client.

- **Mashup**—Mashup is the remix or blending of existing information content to derive a single, integrated, new information content. The term mashup implies easy and fast integration, frequently based on open APIs and data source interfaces. Mashups achieve results that were not the original reason for producing the raw source data. Contrary to

---

[1] Enterprise portals are also known as Enterprise Information Portals (EIPs) or corporate portals.

[2] The term *blog* is actually a shorter version of the word weblog. A blog (for more details, see [1]) is usually a website where a user regularly posts content such as diary entries, pictures, videos, and comments on certain events. Used as a verb, *to blog* means writing and maintaining a blog. It is common for readers of blogs to also post comments. The entries within a blog usually appear in reverse-chronological order. A collection of blogs is known as a *blogosphere*, and there are dedicated blog search engines such as Technorati (see [2] for more details) that search the blogosphere.

traditional portals, where aggregated content is presented next to each other, mashups of individual content can be combined in any manner, resulting in arbitrarily structured information content, which enables new insight. Info 2.0[3] has the information-centric capabilities that are needed for Web 2.0 implementations. The information fabric delivered with Info 2.0 enables IT and business users alike through intuitive and easy-to-use tools to assemble and access information into mashups from heterogeneous sources such as spreadsheets, packaged applications, and databases. New standards supporting new ways of delivering data (for example, Asynchronous JavaScript™ and XML [AJAX], DOJO,[4] Really Simple Syndication [RSS], and JavaScript Object Notation [JSON]) enhance Web 2.0 from an information-centric perspective. Note that this channel can also be an external channel.

Following are the *external* components:

- **External data provider**—Obviously, there are numerous external data providers or business partners. The exchange of data between external data providers and consumers is often driven by standards and networks such as the GDSN and EPCglobal network[5] (mainly in the retail and manufacturing industries) and ACORD[6] (in the insurance industry).

- **Web**—The Web allows for browser-based thin clients, browser extensions, and browser clients to be used. The Semantic Web provides a common framework that enables data to be shared and reused across applications, enterprises, and community boundaries.

- **Cross-enterprise applications**—These types of applications are becoming more popular. They are driven by the need for enterprises to collaborate in real-time for a variety of different business processes, where data and information need to be exchanged on demand.

5.3.2 Infrastructure Security Component

The Infrastructure Security Component represents a De-Militarized Zone (DMZ). A *DMZ* provides secure and authorized access to trusted and controlled network areas. For a DMZ, different implementation patterns exist.[7]

---

[3] The term Info 2.0 became popular in 2007; one of the first places it is mentioned officially is at [3].

[4] DOJO is the Open Source JavaScript Toolkit for constructing dynamic web user interfaces. It offers widgets, utilities, higher IO (AJAX) abstraction, and so on.

[5] The GDSN and EPCglobal are industry bodies defining a set of standards enabling data synchronization. More details for both can be found at [4] and [5].

[6] ACORD is the abbreviation for Association for Cooperative Operations Research and Development. (See [6] for more details.)

[7] There are variations of the Reverse Proxy Patterns; several examples can be found in [7]. Typical technologies for implementation can be found in [8].

The firewalls are used to control access from external and internal networks that are less trusted than internal network areas with a higher trust level. These firewalls can apply protocol and content filtering techniques and redirection techniques. The Reverse Proxy manages the IP traffic by applying caching and security techniques (including encryption) to monitor access to the presentation services. The Reverse Proxy uses a replica for authentication of the Directory Services that represents a slave of the Directory Services Master. Through the Reverse Proxy, a gateway can be used to route web services and messages to the internal ESB where the Reverse Proxy applies necessary security measures. Finally, load balancing in the DMZ improves server and network performance by applying workload distribution techniques.

5.3.3 Presentation Services

In this section, we describe the following presentation services:

- **Business Performance Presentation Services**—To enable and visualize corporate business insight to further optimize and streamline business planning and operations

- **Embedded Analytics**—To better exploit BI analytical systems by integrating analytical insight into operational transactions

- **Search and Query Presentation Services**—To search for data within and beyond enterprise boundaries and to visualize and make results available to users and applications

5.3.3.1 Business Performance Presentation Services

Business Performance Management (BPM) is about monitoring and managing the attainment of business performance and achievement of business goals. This enables businesses to become more proactive, responsive, and better able to rely on information for a cohesive and comprehensive view of their enterprises. BPM requires an integrated business and technical environment that can support the many tasks associated with Performance Management (PM). These tasks include strategic planning and budgeting, predicting and modeling, monitoring and reporting, analysis and alerting, and so on.[8] In the case of strategic planning and forecasting—often done at the same time and done annually based on the prior year's results—success is measured against previously defined business drivers or a set of Key Performance Indicators (KPIs).

Business Performance Presentation Services are the underlying set of presentation services that enables and visualizes the comprehensive corporate business insight. As you saw in Figure 5.1, these reporting services can be requested by any component of the delivery channel through the Presentation Services Component. The Business Performance Presentation Services are not only requested occasionally in a scheduled, periodic fashion; quite the opposite is true. Business decision makers need to rely on an IT infrastructure that delivers business insight and

---

[8] See [9] and [10] for a discussion of relevant concepts, and see [11] for a software product useful for implementation.

performance on demand. This requires interfaces to the operational systems and to the other components of the Component Model as follows:

- **Metadata Management**—Exploitation of enterprise-wide Metadata and corresponding Metadata Services are used, for instance, for transparent reports, further insight, and visualization purposes.

- **Master Data Management**—Relying on a single version of the truth is a key enabler to establishing a trusted information layer as a foundation for reliable performance reporting.

- **Data Management**—PM reporting is mainly based on structured data (relational or hierarchical) and also semistructured data (such as XML) sources.

- **Enterprise Content Management**—Unstructured Data is increasingly exploited to gain further insight and adequately incorporate corporate performance reporting.

- **Analytical Applications**—Gaining insight, for instance, into fraud requires interfacing with analytical applications, such as an Anti-Money Laundry (AML) application or other fraud detection modules.

The trusted information layer with the key information integration services enables the required integration and synchronization among the previous systems, including operational systems.

5.3.3.2 Search and Query Presentation Services

Information today resides on file systems, in content management systems, in Relational Database Management Systems (RDBMS), in emails or wikis, in blogs, and on websites. For searching the Web, a Web browser and an Internet search engine such as Google can be used. The Search and Query Presentation Services have a different scope; they focus on the intranet search limited to the information resources within the enterprise. These services provide access through search queries based on information resources hosted within enterprise boundaries. These can be files on network file systems and in content management systems, relational and XML data in databases, emails in email archives, and information contained in blogs and wikis. Search queries are created and submitted by users to satisfy their information needs.

Queries operating on relational data are Structured Query Language (SQL)-based programs for the retrieval and management of relational data in a database. They are used for querying and modifying data and managing databases and related objects. SQL enables the retrieval, insertion, updating, and deletion of data.[9]

---

[9] See [12] for more details.

In addition to plain SQL queries, there are numerous additional standards. For instance, IBM's DB2 9.5[10] is a hybrid data server that contains an innovative capability that supports queries across XML and relational data. Following are a few additional popular query standards:

- SQL/XML is an ANSI and ISO[11] standard that provides support for using XML in the context of a SQL database system. SQL/XML makes it possible to store XML documents in a SQL database, to query those documents using XPath and XQuery, and to "publish" existing SQL data in the form of XML documents.

- XQuery is an XML query and functional programming language that is designed to query collections of XML data. XQuery uses XPath expression syntax to address specific parts of an XML document. The language also provides syntax for new XML documents to be constructed.

Searching through unstructured information is often implemented with search capabilities based on the Unstructured Information Management Applications (UIMA) standard.

The UI capabilities required to seamlessly create and submit queries and then review the results across all data domains supporting the relevant standards is the task of the Search and Query Presentation Services.

5.3.3.3 Embedded Analytics

Embedded Analytics is the capability to provide analytical insight for a specific step in a business process to optimize day-to-day business decisions. It is a key aspect of operational Business Intelligence (BI).[12] Compared to strategic BI, operational BI is characterized by a low latency that requires the delivery to happen intra-day, intra-hour, or even less—otherwise it is too late for decisions in the operational applications.

For example, a CRM application user processing a customer complaint must decide which action to take. A smart decision could be characterized by minimum effort achieving maximum business benefit, which is indicated by not losing highly profitable customers who might have complaints. The ability to make such a smart decision requires insight into the customer given by metrics such as revenue to date, future cross- and up-sell potential, and so on, all of which is analytical data. The capability to display this analytical insight "on demand," without any BI skill by the LOB user in the context of the application UI used, is the core of Embedded Analytics. The Embedded Analytics Component has the capability to detect the

---

[10] See [13] and [14] for more details.

[11] The American National Standards Institute (ANSI) and the International Organization for Standardization (ISO) are two well-known standardization bodies (see [15] and [16]).

[12] This is also sometimes called *BI for the masses* because the user group is not the small group of the executive management but all regular LOB employees.

context of the step performed by the operational application and apply appropriate enrichments for analytical data. The end user has the relevant analytical data available, improving decision making.

5.3.4 Service Registry and Repository

SOA Governance is a subset of IT Governance; it is specialized to govern the lifecycle of services. It continuously ensures the ongoing business value of the SOA implementation. A key component supporting SOA Governance in a service-oriented architecture is the Service Registry and Repository (SRR) Component. An SRR provides through its registry and repository answers to questions such as:

- What services are available?
- Where are these services located?
- How are the services used and how do they interact?
- Who is using these services and why?

Thus, the SRR enables business process vitality and agility, service reuse, connectivity, and the alignment of business and IT. From an information perspective, information services can be published to an SRR and discovered through the SRR by all consumers of services within the enterprise. A publication of an information service into the SRR includes Metadata artifacts such as the description of the service interface—in the case of Web services, that would be given through a Web Service Description Language (WSDL) file. The availability of information services through an SRR is a required step in making those information services a first-class SOA citizen. An SRR also provides capabilities such as service versioning, currency of service endpoints, Universal Description Discovery and Integration (UDDI)-based federation of SRRs, and policy management for services.

5.3.5 Business Process Services

The purpose of IT is to support the enterprise business needs. An enterprise decomposes the overall business into various business processes, supporting the overall business strategy. The Business Process Services Component provides the key capabilities for the modeling, deployment, orchestration, and execution of business processes. These business processes can be further decomposed into individual steps that can occur in parallel or in sequence, or any combination of both. Each step can be either a human task or an automated process carried out by an IT system.

The core of this component is a workflow engine that drives the business processes. The Business Process Execution Language (BPEL) is a standard that is often supported by an implementation of this component. In an SOA, this component orchestrates services for achieving an end-to-end business process with transaction integrity. Powerful support for human tasks and activity lists are also key capabilities.

From a lifecycle perspective, the Business Process Service Component has to provide monitoring for the business services executed. This is required to obtain a complete status and to control the overall enterprise business performance—at any given point in time.

5.3.6 Collaboration Services

The Collaboration Services Component enables employees of an enterprise or across enterprises to efficiently collaborate with each other. The foundation for collaboration in many companies today is e-mail, calendar, and instant messaging functions. Furthermore, teamrooms, blogs, activity management, threaded discussions (typically based on forums and wikis), and expertise location capabilities are used by many teams today in their daily operations to share documents, assign and follow up on action items, or find an expert for a specific task. This component also includes the capability to provide e-learning through web conferences and other means, wherein employees can share knowledge globally at any time.

5.3.7 Connectivity and Interoperability Services

The Connectivity and Interoperability Services Component represents the backbone used by all IT systems in the enterprise to communicate with each other. It can be extended to also allow connection to other components beyond the enterprise, for instance in Business-to-Business (B2B) scenarios. Historically,[13] there are several known major techniques to implement this component:

- Application Server-based where the application and integration logic is not separated and usually a hub-and-spoke approach is used.
- Message Oriented-Middleware (MOM) usually suffers from a lack of separation of application and integration logic but uses distributed integration techniques.
- Enterprise Application Integration (EAI) separates application from integration logic but still uses hub-and-spoke integration patterns.
- Enterprise Service Bus (ESB) separates application from integration logic and uses distributed integration techniques.

There are many integration patterns[14] available that can be used to implement the Connectivity and Interoperability Component. Because many enterprises today adapt an SOA[15] for their Enterprise Architecture, the use of an ESB is becoming more widespread. Thus, we briefly introduce a few key capabilities of the ESB. More details about the ESB and the other techniques can be found in the References section of this chapter.

5.3.7.1 ESB

The ESB is a communication backbone between applications and transport requests represented by messages (typically, with XML-based formats today) between service consumers and service

---

[13] This classification is simplified but aligned with the presentation in [17]. This is also a good introduction to the concept of an ESB.

[14] For examples, see [18] and [19].

[15] For an introduction to SOA, see [20].

providers. For this task, the ESB has to support many different transport protocols in a transparent manner. In addition, the ESB has to perform *mediations*. Typical tasks in mediations are transformations (for example, message format conversions using XPath to achieve XML-to-XML translation), content-based routing, logging, monitoring, metering, and policy enforcement. Service Level Agreement-based routing capabilities are delivered by an ESB leveraging the Quality of Services capabilities provided by the IT Services & Compliance Management Services Component. An ESB also has to deliver the required security capabilities for authentication, authorization, and access management, and the ESB has to be compatible with firewalls. Finally, the ESB has to support non-functional requirements regarding availability, performance, and reliability.

5.3.7.2 Message and Web Services Gateway

IT systems external to the enterprise can be connected to the Interoperability and Interconnectivity Component using the Message and Web Services Gateway as an additional component. This component uses key capabilities such as mediation and security of the Interoperability and Interconnectivity Component to implement tasks such as routing and management services. This component also hides the details of the internal services from the external participants.

5.3.8 Directory and Security Services

The Directory and Security Services Component is usually based on the Lightweight Directory Access Protocol (LDAP). This component maintains authentication credentials for users and security policies including rules and access control lists. Typical services include Authentication Services including Single-Sign On (SSO). SSO allows users to authenticate only once and then access a wide range of applications without further authentication needs. This component also delivers services such as Authorization Services, Identity Services, and Identity Provisioning Services. The OASIS Web Services Security WS-Trust standard defines a procedure to take a security token and its validation and is encountered when implementing identity and authentication services. The Service Provisioning Markup Language (SPML) and the WS-Provisioning standard from OASIS define a framework for the provisioning and management of identities within and between enterprises. For implementing security policies in a Web services world, WS-Policy and WS-SecurityPolicy define structures for descriptions of how service consumers and providers specify their requirements that need to be enforced. Web service calls based on Simple Object Access Protocol/HyperText Transfer Protocol (SOAP/HTTP) can have security policy assertions in the SOAP header related to authentication.

Chapter 6 shows how these capabilities are provided through the network and OS services in the Operational Model.

5.3.9 Operational Applications

This component has the name Operational Applications and the ID OA001. There are many different types of operational systems, some of which can be highly complex. In this section, we provide a high-level overview and mention the operational systems in the context of the EIA Component Model.

5.3.9.1 High-Level Description

We talked about operational systems and applications in previous chapters. So it's time to have a closer look at what we mean by these and what role they play in the EIA Component Model. An *operational system* is used to process the daily transactional load of an organization and is frequently called a transactional system. It is typically composed of two tiers: the application tier and the persistency tier. For example, an SAP CRM system runs the CRM application on one physical server and the persistency tier given by a database on another, separate physical server. The Operational Applications Component embodies the application tier. The persistency tier is reflected in the Component Model by the Data Management and Enterprise Content Management Components and the respective services used by operational applications to create, read, update, and delete structured and unstructured, operational data.

There are multiple design points that need to be addressed by operational applications, including the following:

- Concurrency in terms of addressing a high number of users who are concurrently using the system.
- Performance regarding transaction response time or end-user response time.
- Throughput regarding the transaction rate, meaning the number of transactions per time interval.
- Scalability to enable growth to be addressed in terms of allowing more users to interface with the operational system, for example.
- Continuous availability by implementing high availability and continuous operations to address unplanned and planned outages.
- Security, delivering data protection, authentication, and authorization either with built-in capabilities or by interfacing with external providers.

(This list of operational system characteristics is not complete—further discussion of these terms can be found in Chapter 6.)

These operational systems are designed to make the processing of the daily transactional workload efficient and to guarantee the required integrity of the transactional data. There are industry-specific and cross-industry operational systems. Table 5.1 lists a few examples of operational applications.

Table 5.1 Examples of Operational Applications

Industry	Examples of Operational Systems
Banking	Automatic Teller Machine (ATM) applications
	Electronic banking systems
	Core banking applications
	Credit/debit card processing systems

Table 5.1   Examples of Operational Applications

Industry	Examples of Operational Systems
Telecommunications	Call billing systems
	Operator services systems
Travel and Transportation	Airline and travel reservation systems
	Hotel reservation systems
Manufacturing	Just-in-time inventory control systems
Retail	Sales processing systems
	e-Commerce and e-Trading systems
Cross-Industry	Customer Relationship Management (CRM) systems
	Enterprise Resource Planning (ERP) systems
	Human Resource (HR) management systems

5.3.9.2 Interfaces

Using the Connectivity and Interoperability Services (such as the ESB), Operational Systems do interface with other systems. Here are a few examples:

- **MDM component**—The MDM component needs to synchronize core master information with some, if not all, operational systems.
- **Analytical Applications**—There are multiple different interface patterns, including:
  - **Traditional Warehousing**—Transactional data from operational applications will be transformed (using ETL) and loaded into traditional DW systems based on a static schedule.
  - **Dynamic Warehousing**—Updated or new transactional data needs to be captured and replicated from operational systems in near real time or real time and made available for on-demand reporting.
  - **Fraud Detection and Prevention**—Operational transactions (for instance, an "opening account" transaction) need to be linked and often even intertwined with BI and analytical capabilities to detect and prevent fraud.
- **Metadata Management**—Metadata needs to be consumed by operational systems to optimize the execution of key transactions.

5.3.10 Mashup Hub

This component has the name Mashup Hub and the ID MH001.

5.3.10.1 High-Level Description

This component is responsible for delivering the Info 2.0 promise using mashup and web syndication functions. Web syndication is a web feed that publishes new content on a website where feed readers[16] in web browsers can read and display them.

In some enterprises, strategic applications have long planning and deployment times and they are usually targeted at large user groups. However, there is an increasing demand for tactical applications—each of them intended for a smaller user group. Serving the need for tactical applications is the key responsibility for the Mashup Hub Component. A *mashup* is considered a lightweight web application created by combining information from a set of heterogeneous sources or other capabilities from various existing sources to deliver new insight. Mashups are built on a web-oriented architecture and leverage lightweight, simple integration techniques such as Representational State Transfer (REST), HTTP, AJAX, RSS, and JSON. Using these technologies, desktop-like web applications are created quickly and efficiently through the use of this component.

There is an important difference between web syndication and e-mail. Web syndication is pull-based, which means the user can decide from which source a feed is accepted whereas e-mail is push-based, which means the user has no control of who can send e-mails, and the best spam filters do not catch all spam. The capability to control what is received makes feeds attractive to users when mashups are built.

5.3.10.2 Service Description

The Mashup Hub Component provides the following key groups of services for unstructured information and is shown in Figure 5.2:

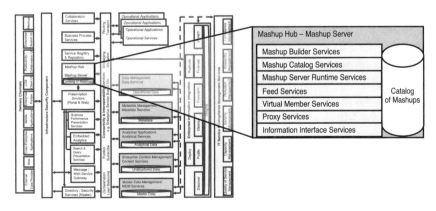

Figure 5.2   The Mashup Hub Component

---

[16] A widely used feed reader is the Google Reader, which can be used for free with registration.

- **Mashup Builder Services**—Mashup Builder Services cover two areas: (1) creating individual, reusable parts for a mashup that are persisted after they are created in the Mashup Catalog using the Mashup Catalog Services, and (2) discovering relevant parts from the Mashup Catalog and wiring them to a mashup application (which is persisted in the Mashup Catalog).

- **Mashup Catalog Services**—Create, Read, Update, and Delete (CRUD) access to parts of a mashup or entire mashup applications is provided by the Mashup Catalog Services. Versioning and Metadata management for parts or entire mashup applications are additional functions in this service group.

- **Mashup Server Runtime Services**—The runtime for a mashup is given through these services. They provide the deployment services and the runtime services for a mashup. They also interface where needed with services from the IT Services and Compliance Services Component where leveraging the availability of services is one example.

- **Virtual Member Services**—Authentication and authorization management for mashups is a functional need that this component needs to satisfy. Typically, this component interfaces with the Directory and Security Services Component (see section 4.3.7) through the Virtual Member Services to address these requirements.

- **Feed Services**—Feeds are created using Syndication Services. There are two widespread standards in use for feeds: RSS (in various versions) and ATOM.[17]

- **Proxy Services**—Mashup applications often include parts (for example, widgets) that do not run on the same Mashup Server runtime. To ensure security, "same origin" policies have to be enforced to avoid attacks based on malicious JavaScripts. The Proxy Services enable the Mashup Server Runtime Services infrastructure. It includes the capability to integrate parts into a mashup application that are executed on a remote system in a trusted manner. For more on security, see the forthcoming book on sMash.[18]

- **Information Interface Services**—These services are used whenever the information service to be consumed by the mashup does not have an easy-to-consume interface. For example, a federated query might need to be wrapped in a REST-based interface to be consumable within a mashup. Obviously, interface mappings are usually done by the Connectivity and Interoperability Component previously introduced; however, if the software selected for this component lacks a certain mapping capability, the Information Interface Services of the Mashup Hub Component must fill the gap.

---

[17] A good introduction to syndication, including a history and the relationship of the RSS and ATOM standards, can be found in Chapter 7 in the book *Enterprise 2.0 Implementation* (see [21]).

[18] See [22]. This book is scheduled for publication in 2010.

5.3.10.3 Interfaces

This component is invoked by the Mashup subcomponent of the Delivery Channels Component, as shown in Figure 5.1. Typical supported protocols are RSS and ATOM for the syndication services. The Mashup Hub Component often invokes information services through REST and Web Service protocols.

5.3.11 Metadata Management Component and Metadata Services

This component has the name Metadata Management and the ID MM001. *Metadata* is information that is usually embedded in data and describes its attributes such as where it originated, who owns the data, the semantics, where it originates, and how it can be used. The emphasis in this book is on the relevance of Metadata Management for the EIA Component Model. Also, when we elaborate on Metadata and Metadata Services, we limit the scope to information-centric and information management-related types of metadata. For instance, we focus on the following (this is not a complete list):

- Data about visualization rules of business information
- Data about transformation and aggregation logic
- Data about quality improvement rules
- Data about conceptual model mapping to physical data models
- Data about source data for data harmonization tasks

5.3.11.1 High-Level Description

Metadata Services provide a common set of functionalities and core services for enabling open communication, exchange and consumption of Metadata between systems that use different data formats—including storage and optimization models, data models, directories, EII functions—and core data management functions.

Not only does Metadata Management enable the communication between systems, but it also enables and facilitates a more effective and consistent collaboration between different roles and tasks. For instance, a business user expressing required improvements in the context of specific use case scenarios or business processes—using specific business terms—can communicate this to the IT organization much more efficiently through exploitation of Metadata Services.

One of the key capabilities of the Metadata Management Component is to enable exploitation and consumption of Metadata for interconnected tasks. More specifically, Metadata is generated as output by one task to serve as input for one or several subsequent tasks.

5.3.11.2 Service Description

The Metadata Management Component provides the following key groups of services and is shown in Figure 5.3:

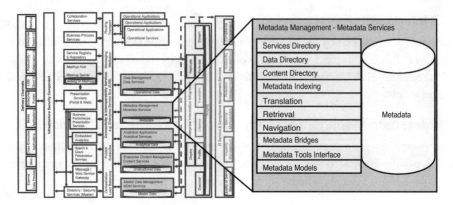

Figure 5.3   The Metadata Management Component

- **Services Directory Services**—This directory lists all actions on Metadata as it relates to the entire Metadata lifecycle, including the exploitation of metadata. This is a list of metadata-related functions, such as requesting a job or data lineage service, assigning a term to a selected Metadata asset or object, requesting an impact analysis service, and so on.

- **Data Directory Services**—Part of the Metadata is represented in relational format. For instance, a relational format might be a business term, the semantic of the term, or related IT objects such as database tables, indexes, and so on. Another example is the property of a data file or specifications of a BI report.

- **Content Directory Services**—Another part of the Metadata is represented in unstructured (content) format. For instance, a transformation job is described in terms of the property of the job, job design information, and images that depict the transformation job for a UI-based tool.

- **Metadata Indexing Services**—Performing simple or advanced searches of Metadata and identifying the right Metadata needs to be done in the context of a specific business or technical task. Indexing the Metadata is done to facilitate this search of the entire Metadata repository at a reasonable speed. These services enable the exploration of Metadata and the generation of graphical or report views of Metadata asset relationships.

- **Translation Services**—Generating or importing Metadata from a diverse set of sources and making this Metadata available for other services requires the translation of Metadata from proprietary formats to unified standardized Metadata formats, such as using the Common Warehouse Metamodel (CWM)[19] of the Object Management Group (OMG).

- **Retrieval Services**—These services enable you to browse and retrieve the contents and services of the Metadata Management Component and obtain information that can be

---

[19] For more details on the Common Warehouse Metamodel, see [23] and [24].

useful to you when transforming information, improving quality of source data, performing data modeling tasks, or developing applications.

- **Navigation Services**—Metadata Navigation Services are needed to understand available Metadata of a specific scope of interest or in the context of a specific use case scenario. They enable navigation through the diverse types of Metadata to fulfill a defined user need. For example, Metadata can be used to get the right search criteria for an enterprise-wide search definition.

- **Metadata Bridges Services**—These services enable the import and export of Metadata from heterogeneous sources such as physical database models from a heterogeneous set of databases or to export Metadata into Excel spreadsheets or PDF documents.

- **Metadata Tools Interface Services**—The Metadata Tools Interface Services enable Metadata modeling tools[20] to read, modify, and write data to the Metadata repository.

- **Metadata Models Services**—These services help establish Metadata models for a defined set of problems, tasks, use case scenarios, or business processes. These include the analysis, design, and build process to generate and make available Metadata models for exploitation of Metadata by other tools and tasks.

5.3.11.3 Interfaces

Depending on the scope of Metadata and Metadata Services, the Metadata Management Component mainly interfaces with the EII Component and the Analytical Applications Component. There might also be an interface to chosen operational systems, assuming that the Metadata is semantically rich enough to meet requirements of an operational application to leverage the Metadata.

5.3.12 Master Data Management Component and MDM Services

This component has the name Master Data Management and the ID MDM001.

5.3.12.1 High-Level Description

The management of master data throughout its lifecycle is the core task this component must perform. This component is the single, authoritative, enterprise-wide source of trusted master data and maintains it at a high level of quality.

The scope of the Master Data Management Component can be defined by three dimensions that make up the concept of Multi-Form MDM.

Domains of master data determine which master data business objects are managed. Typical master data domains include, but are not limited to, customer, product, account, location,

---

[20] Typical modeling tools include IBM InfoSphere Data Architect or CA Erwin Data Modeler.

and contract. Since 2008, we see an increasing shift toward multi-domain implementations, where this component also manages the relationships between master data domains such as customer-product relationships.

There are three methods of use: collaborative authoring,[21] operational, and analytical. Collaborative authoring refers to capabilities that support collaborative authoring of master data, including the creation, augmentation, and approval by different people who often have different roles. The collaboration method is usually encapsulated in workflows through which master data flows task by task, and each task can be either automated or manual. For example, the New Product Introduction workflow is a typical workflow in the product domain.

The operational method requires this component to act like an Online Transaction Processing (OLTP) system. This method is characterized by stateless services for many concurrent applications and users in a high-performance environment. The operational MDM Services provided by this component are often designed to seamlessly fit in an SOA. Typical examples are services to create a customer and to create an account in a New Account Opening business process.

The analytical method has three distinct capabilities. The first is to provide clean and consistent master data to BI systems, such as data warehouses (DW), for improvements in reporting. The second is analytics on the master data itself. An example is a report of how many new customers were created in a week or month with this component. The third capability is identity analytics. Identity analytics is an analytical capability of the Analytical Services component and is reused here.

This component supports three implementation styles:[22] the Registry Implementation Style, Coexistence Implementation Style, and the Transactional Hub Implementation Style. These are explained and compared to each other in more detail in Chapter 11. Note that at any given point in time, more than one style can be deployed. For example, for the product domain, the component provides a Coexistence Implementation Style deployment, whereas for the customer domain, it provides a Transactional Hub Implementation Style deployment.

Depending on the domains, methods of use, and the implementation styles, a selection and scope of the needed services representing the key capabilities of this component are done. For example, in a pure Customer Data Integration (CDI) deployment, the check-in and check-out workflow capabilities that are part of the authoring services might not be instantiated in a concrete deployment.

5.3.12.2 Service Description

The key services provided by this component are shown in Figure 5.4 and are as follows:

- **Interface Services**—This service group is the only interface the Master Data Management Component has to other components. It is the only consistent entry point to request a function from this component. Providing a rich set of MDM support, it enables seamless

---

[21] We sometimes use the term "collaborative" and mean "collaborative authoring."

[22] Further details on the master data domains, the methods of use, and the implementation styles can be found in [25].

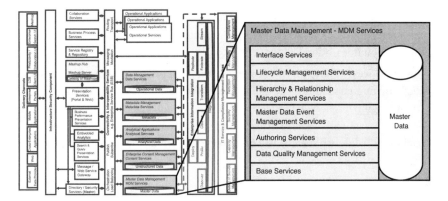

Figure 5.4 The Master Data Management Component

consumption of this Master Data Management Component. (See section 5.3.12.4 for further details.) Note that these services are used to separate the business functions provided by the Master Data Management Component from the means of invocation.

- **Lifecycle Management Services**—These services manage the lifecycle of master data and provide CRUD operations on it. These services also apply relevant business logic and invoke Data Quality Management Services and Master Data Event Management Services.

- **Hierarchy and Relationship Management Services**—Hierarchies (such as product hierarchies or organization hierarchies), groupings, and relationships (such as customer-product relationships or household relationships) are managed by this services group. If there is a business need, Identity Analytics Services from the Analytical Services Component can be called by these services to discover nonobvious relationships that are then persisted as part of the master data.

- **Master Data Management Event Management Services**—Actionable master data is the key objective of the services in this group. Events can be defined based on business rules, time scheduled, or governance policies. An example is an event based on a contract for a fixed term deposit that expires in four weeks. The bank clerk receives a notification due to this event to call the customer to discuss which other financial product would be the right fit for a reinvestment after the money becomes available, optimizing business results for the bank.

- **Authoring Services**—Support for the Collaborative method of use is enabled by the Authoring Services. They provide capabilities to author, augment, and approve the definition of master data in collaborative workflows.

- **Data Quality Management Services**—Data quality rules are validated and enforced by the Data Quality Management Services. Examples include name and address standardization, cross referencing, and master data reconciliation tasks. Reconciliation covers deterministic and probabilistic matching, collapse and split, conflict resolution, and self-correcting capabilities. These services might leverage appropriate services from the Information Integration Component.

- **Base Services**—These services cover security and privacy aspects such as authorization, audit logging capabilities on the service, data, event level, and workflow capabilities. Audit logging might be integrated with an end-to-end audit logging infrastructure as part of the Operational Model. Furthermore, search functions such as exact match, partial match, and wild card search, as well as predefined and ad-hoc queries, are supported.

5.3.12.3 Interfaces

The interfaces of this component are encapsulated in the interface services group. Thus, MDM Services are available through a variety of technology bindings supported by the interface services. Typical examples include Java™ Messaging Service (JMS), Web services, remote method invocation, and batch mechanisms.

5.3.13 Data Management Component and Data Services

This component has the name Data Management Component and the ID DM001.

5.3.13.1 High-Level Description

Data Management has been around as long as computers have. Actually, the importance of data for the business and its need to process and manage data are the core domains of Data Management. It provides a common set of functionality and core services to access and manage data stored in a heterogeneous set of repositories. A typical example for the use of this component is a two-tier solution like SAP CRM, consisting of the application tier (an instance of the previously discussed Operational Application Component) and an instance of this component as a data tier. The Data Management Component typically delivers the persistency for operational data for the instances of operational applications given by the Operational Applications Component.

These services also enable an open communication and exchange of information between systems that use different data formats, data access methods, and programming models. It includes data storage and performance optimization models, data security schemas, and core data management functions. This requires core management and administrative services and query and programming services. There are also quite a number of non-functional aspects that need to be delivered by Data Services, such as continuous availability services including high availability and continuous operation services to address unplanned and planned outages, respectively. The non-functional requirements are addressed by the Data Services by leveraging appropriate services from the IT Service & Compliance Management Services Component, which is discussed in detail in section 5.3.17.

5.3.13.2 Service Description

The Data Management Component provides the following key groups of services for structured information and is shown in Figure 5.5:

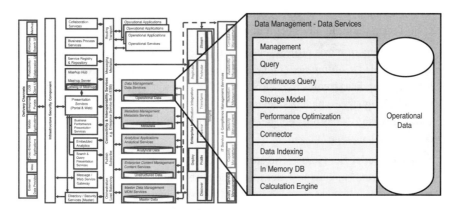

Figure 5.5   The Data Management Component

- **Management Services**—There are a number of basic Data Services, such as database administration and data maintenance. In addition, data modeling also sits within this service. Database administration includes maintenance of the database environment with recoverability, integrity, development, and testing support services. Data maintenance includes the adding, deleting, changing, and updating of data elements. Usually, data is edited and maintained at a slightly higher level of abstraction that takes into account the content of the data, such as text, images, and scientific or financial information. Data modeling involves the creation of data structures and conceptual, logical, and physical data models that adhere to concrete business requirements. It also enables the transformation of data among these models.

- **Query Services**—One of the basic services is to submit SQL queries against a database. SQL is a programming language for querying and modifying data and managing databases and database objects. In essence, SQL enables the retrieval, insertion, updating, and deletion of data stored in a relational DBMS.

- **Continuous Query Services**—Generically speaking, these services enable users to receive new results when available. One field of application is the Internet, where we are faced with large amounts of frequently updated data. These services are especially important to allow data streams to be managed effectively. A continuous query over those data streams is often called a streaming query. Following are some examples of key requirements that need to be addressed by the Continuous Query Services:

- Multiple data streams from different sources have to be continuously merged and aggregated.

- A rapidly changing aggregation hierarchy has to be maintained with corresponding drill-down and roll-up capabilities.

- Subscribers or observers require continuous publication of aggregations (for instance, multiple times per minute or once every second).

An interesting research project related to the SQL language enables management of data streams called *Continuous Query Language (CQL)*. CQL is an emerging declarative language for data streams in Data Stream Management Systems. It is an enhancement of the SQL language, which has been the focus of the STREAM[23] research project at Stanford University. It has not been determined if CQL will be established as an official standard query language.

- **Storage Model Services**—The storage model describes the relationship between key DBMS objects, such as instances and databases, table spaces and tables, containers or storage paths, physical machine memory, and physical disks associated to the machine. One of the aspects of the storage model is to describe the mapping of logical DBMS objects, such as a table to the physical disks. Modern relational DBMS systems also contain automatic storage mechanisms that would, for instance, allow for space allocation to grow automatically. Another key capability of the storage model is to support a variety of different data types and data structures, such as native support for XML type documents. The storage model needs to support functionality such as storing, querying, and modifying the XML data with required performance characteristics.[24]

- **Performance Optimization Services**—Driving, monitoring, and optimizing for performance are requirements to be addressed by the Data Management Component. This relates to performance requirements in terms of accommodating a high number of users, throughput (number of transactions per second), query response times, and so on. In addition, performance optimization needs to include capabilities to optimize for a mixed workload such as Online Transactional Processing (OLTP)[25] and decision support applications.

- **Connector Services**—These are essentially data access services. Data access typically refers to capabilities related to storing, retrieving, or acting on data that is stored in a database or other repository. Historically, different access methods and programming

---

[23] STREAM is short for STanford stREam datA Manager; more details can be found at [26].

[24] A good example is the pureXML Storage Engine, which is available with IBM's DB2 9.

[25] The key concepts for OLTP can be found in [27]; IBM's DB2 9 for z/OS has superb OLTP performance capabilities [28].

languages were required for every repository, different DBMSs, or file systems, where many of these repositories stored their content in different and incompatible formats. Standardized languages, access methods, and formats have been created to serve as interfaces for the often proprietary systems. Well-established standards include SQL, Object DataBase Connectivity (ODBC), Java Database Connectivity (JDBC), ActiveX® Data Object.NET (ADO.NET), XML, XQuery, and XPath. Brand-new[26] connector service standards support JMS, Web services using SOAP/HTTP, RSS, JSON, and REST, making operational data consumption for Mashup applications, lightweight Web applications, or other systems using these new protocols seamless.

- **Data Indexing Services**—Simply speaking, a data index is a data structure that is added to a table to provide faster access to the data. This is achieved by reducing the number of blocks that the DBMS has to retrieve and check. In addition to performance improvements (faster data access), another objective is also to ensure uniqueness of data values in a table. Furthermore, data indexing services need to address the needs of different application types, such as streaming applications, enterprise search, intelligent mining, and so on.

- **In-Memory DB Services**—An in-memory database management system primarily relies on main memory for computer data storage, contrary to traditional DBMS systems that employ a disk storage mechanism. Naturally, in-memory databases can be significantly faster than disk-optimized databases because the internal optimization algorithms are more straightforward, and data records don't have to be transferred from disk to memory.

- **Calculation Engine Services**—These are the basic calculation services that are inherent in the DBMS system. For example, they allow aggregations by grouping and ordering of result sets and can calculate average figures or statistical samples. More complex calculations—for instance aggregations in cubes—are typically delivered through DW capabilities that are part of the Analytical Applications Component discussed in section 5.3.15.

5.3.13.3 Interfaces

Due to the importance of the Data Management Component as one of the key elements of the enterprise information foundation, the Data Services can be found in almost all possible deployment scenarios. As a consequence, there are interfaces through the Connectivity and Interoperability Component to almost all other EIA components. In most deployment scenarios, some of the Data Services might even play in concert with other information services that are delivered through other EIA components.

---

[26] An article on these new connectivity services is located at [29].

5.3.13.4 Cloud Computing Delivery Model for Data Services

In this section, we show by example that the Data Services for the Cloud Computing delivery model
have impact on the functional components in the Component Model of the EIA Reference Architecture. More details on the Cloud Computing delivery model are covered in Chapters 6 and 7.

Figure 5.6 shows one example of a Multi-Tenancy scenario. Three tenants—T1, T2, and
T3—subscribe to the same application (which is multi-tenancy enabled) and thus share it. The
application uses a single database as persistency. The data separation in the shown scenario is only
logically, which means the database provides for each tenant separation of data by using a schema
per tenant: schema T1 for tenant T1, schema T2 for tenant T2, and schema T3 for tenant T3.

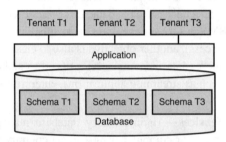

Figure 5.6   Data Services—Sample Multi-Tenancy Scenario

For this Cloud Computing environment, the database services would need the following
operations in a transparent manner:

- Schema-level backup and restore (backup and restore are administration functionalities
  that belong to the Management Services)
- Schema-level creation and deletion of objects such as tables and indices
- Schema-level instrumentation of all services for metering and billing to enable billing
  per storage and CPU consumption

It is worthwhile to note that the schema-based operations supporting the tenant concept
transparently are either not available in commercial databases, have been recently introduced, or
are becoming available with next releases. For the IT Architect, mapping software to the Component and Operational Model, therefore, must consider the delivery model used for the solution
because functionality might be required that excludes certain products or certain delivery model
configurations.

The scenario shown is just one of several options for delivering data services in a Cloud
Computing environment. Depending on software selection in the Operational Model, some
commercial databases used for implementing the data services have some or all functions for
certain possible Cloud Computing scenarios. However, the key point is that to a certain
degree, the capabilities required for the Cloud Computing delivery model already surface in
the Component Model.

5.3.14 Enterprise Content Management Component and Content Services

This component has the name Enterprise Content Management Component and the ID ECM001.

5.3.14.1 High-Level Description

This component delivers all relevant capabilities for the management of Unstructured Data, which is often just called content. Examples of Unstructured Data are images, movies, audio files, all types of documents such as PDFs, PPTs, and variations of free text, such as e-mails. It also provides the necessary content-specific business process workflow capabilities.

The purpose of the Enterprise Content Management Component is to enable a broad variety of solutions such as:

- Contract management in the insurance industry
- E-mail archiving solutions applicable across industries
- Knowledge management
- Web content management

These solutions are enabled by the Enterprise Content Management Component that manages unstructured information across its lifecycle. Metadata is typically associated with unstructured information for further description and annotation purposes. Thus, the capability to tie together the Metadata for unstructured information with the unstructured information itself and its management represents another key capability of this component. Unstructured information often appears in business processes with a dedicated workflow, such as an insurance contract. Thus, the workflow and the collaboration of various business users are enabled by this component, too. In addition, this component is designed to enable content publishing, capturing, indexing, reporting, and monitoring.

5.3.14.2 Service Description

The Enterprise Content Management component provides the following key groups of services for unstructured information and is shown in Figure 5.7:

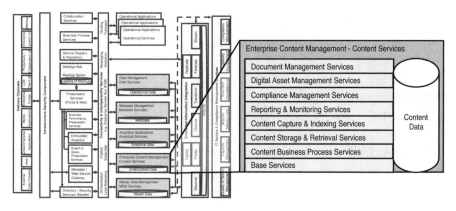

Figure 5.7   The Enterprise Content Management Component

- **Document Management Services**—Creating and authoring documents are the core functions provided by the Document Management Services. Furthermore, annotation of unstructured information with Metadata is provided by this service group.

- **Digital Asset Management Services**—This is a specialized group of services for the management of images, videos, animations, and audio files. They provide specialized functions to more efficiently work with JPEG, MPEG, GIF, WAV, MP3,[27] and other formats typically used to encode this type of information. These services often interface with specialized software used to create and maintain this type of information, such as digital imaging software used by graphic designers.

- **Compliance Management Services**—In many countries today, if companies have to settle legal issues in court, e-mail documents are considered relevant documents for assessing guilt or innocence. Thus, there are countries that have legal requirements to archive e-mail and make it accessible as evidence in court. Compliance Management Services provide the capability to implement compliance with legal requirements and with relevant audit functionality.

- **Reporting & Monitoring Services**—These provide the capability to report on the unstructured information managed by the Enterprise Content Management Component. Reports can be ad-hoc or scheduled. Monitoring Services provide the capability to define rules on which certain events and notifications must occur. For example, before a document is deleted due to a retention policy, a rule might have been implemented that a person needs to review the document and either confirms that deletion is okay or extends the timeframe for keeping it. In this case, the person who does the review is notified by the Monitoring Services that a certain event (the document approaching the end of its retention time) occurred. Note that the Monitoring Services in this component are not the Monitoring Services needed to administrate and debug system health indicators. These types of monitoring services are part of the Operational Model.

- **Content Capture & Indexing Services**—Capturing Services provide the capability to capture digital content with scanning technologies. A typical example would be capturing an image with a scanner. Other examples would be capturing an x-ray image digitally, a fax, or a syndicated RSS feed. Indexing services provide capabilities such as assigning unique identifiers to a digital document. More advanced indexing capabilities include the analysis of the Metadata of a content item to classify it. Smart indexing techniques are crucial for quick performance of Retrieval Services, and sometimes indexing capabilities include the capability to build topologies.

- **Content Storage & Retrieval Services**—These services provide the capability to implement hierarchical storage management for Unstructured Data interfacing with the Retention Services provided by the IT Services and Compliance Management Services

---

[27] These are typical and usually well-known formats of unstructured content; thus, we do not provide references.

Component. The movement of documents from fast, expensive storage to slower, cheaper storage based on policies and access patterns is enabled by these services. The Content Storage Services must also provide the capability for a long-term strategy on managing unstructured information with relevant format conversion capabilities. The Retrieval Services return requested documents. Their performance depends on the index structure created by the Indexing Services.

- **Content Business Processes Services**—Content-specific workflows are enabled by this services group. An example would be a workflow through which images and audio files need to go as part of a publishing procedure for a website. Content Business Process Services must support human tasks and automated tasks with check-out and check-in capabilities of documents from the content management system. Work lists are a common feature enabled by these services. Routing a document differently through the workflow based on rules must be supported, too. For example, depending on the amount covered by an insurance contract, the contract document must be routed to different approvers.

- **Base Services**—This group of services provides capabilities such as authorization, digital signing of a document, versioning, release management, and logging.

5.3.14.3 Interfaces

Due to the heterogeneous nature of Unstructured Data, there is no single way of interacting with this component. Even though there are some standards for the generalized exchange of information, any implementation of this component will support more than one way of accessing it. Examples include proprietary interfaces and open Web services interfaces to create, read, update, or delete unstructured information managed by this component.

The Content Business Process Services of this component often need to interface with the Business Process Services Component to drive end-to-end business processes.

5.3.15 Analytical Applications Component and Analytical Services

This component has the name Analytical Applications Component and the ID AA001. We discuss Dynamic Warehousing and BI topics at length later in Chapter 13; Analytical Services are covered briefly here.

5.3.15.1 High-Level Description

What do we mean by Analytical Applications? Analytical Applications are comprised of BI and PM services. They enable departments, organizations, and large enterprises to leverage information to acquire a better understanding of their commercial context and to better understand and optimize business performance.

This broader scope of Analytical Applications is sometimes called BI 2.0. The "2.0" aims for highlighting the proactive and participative aspects compared to the more reactive, traditional BI services. Data Warehousing is an underlying concept to enable BI and PM. For instance, most BI applications access data that is stored in a DW or a data mart. Dynamic Warehousing expresses the next generation of Data Warehousing. Dynamic Warehousing is the underlying principle to achieve BI and PM systems that are more dynamic, including a broader variety of information, and capable of delivering business-relevant results on demand. We show how to implement the near-real-time or real-time aspects of Dynamic Warehousing using replication in Chapter 8.

5.3.15.2 Service Description

The Analytical Applications Component provides the following key groups of services and is shown in Figure 5.8:

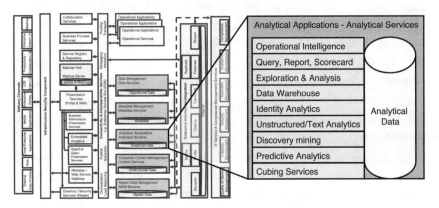

Figure 5.8   The Analytical Applications Component

- **Operational Intelligence Services**—These services focus on providing real-time monitoring and event-based analytics of business processes and activities. They assist in optimizing the business through improved process modeling and analysis of industry and even customer-specific scenarios.

- **Query, Report, Scorecard Services**—These are the basic services, such as business report generation, report versioning, traditional batch reports, and query planners, but also more sophisticated services to allow ad-hoc queries for supporting on-demand report generation.

- **Exploration & Analysis Services**—These are the core capabilities, such as OLAP and slicing and dicing services for performance optimization, trend, trend series analysis, and descriptive statistics. Sorting, filtering, and calculation services are also included.

- **Data Warehouse Services**—As stated previously, DW services technically underpin and enable BI and PM solutions through various services, such as different data partitioning capabilities, Materialized Query Tables (MQT),[28] and Multi-Dimensional Clustering (MDC) services.

- **Identity Analytics Services**—Relevant for fraud detection and prevention scenarios, these identity analytics services include identity verification and resolution, nonobvious relationship discovery, and name recognition in heterogeneous cultural environments.

- **Unstructured and Text Analytics Services**—These services provide analytics on Unstructured Data and text. Typical techniques include named entity recognition (detect names) and relationship detection (for example, a part causes a problem). Another technique is co-reference resolution; for example, *Martin* works for IBM. *He* is a coauthor of this book.

- **Discovery Mining Services**[29]—Finding patterns in data is the key capability delivered by Discovery Mining Services. Techniques applied cover association rules (to find products typically purchased together by customers), sequential patterns (to discover a typical series of events), and clustering (to group similar data records to detect fraud patterns).

- **Predictive Analytics Services**—Using known results to create models capable of predicting future values is the heart of Predictive Analytics. We describe an example in the healthcare industry in Chapter 14.

- **Cubing Services**[30]—Cubing Services depend on a cube model and typically have four stages within their lifecycle: design, test, deploy to production, and delete. They provide multidimensional views for data stored in a relational database. Cubing Services enable the creation, modification, and seamless deployment of cube models over the relational warehouse schema. Improving the performance of OLAP queries, a core component of DW and analytics, is another key capability of Cubing Services.

5.3.15.3 Interfaces

The Analytical Services are requested in a number of critical deployment scenarios, where the interfaces are utilized in both directions:

- Analytical Services are requested from other components. An example is the identity resolution or any other identity analytics service that might be requested from an operational system. For example, in a banking context, an operational system might require a

---

[28] See [32] for more details on MQTs and MDC.

[29] Note that data mining is a term typically used to address discovery and prediction mining techniques. We introduce these two techniques separately due to their importance.

[30] The term No Copy Analytics is sometimes used as a superset covering Unstructured and Text Analytics Services, Discovery Mining Services, Prediction Mining Services, and Cubing Services. This is because the data for these analytics typically remains in place.

service that attempts to verify the identity of a new customer in the scope of a New Account Opening business process.

- Analytical Services request services from other components. An example is the transformation and quality improvement of source data prior to storing data records in a DW or a data mart. These services are requested from the EII Component.

5.3.16 Enterprise Information Integration Component and EII Services

This component has the name EII Component and the ID EII001.

5.3.16.1 High-Level Description

The EII Component contains the key services to deliver and maintain trusted information. (Chapter 8 details the EII Component for all capabilities and with example scenarios.) It is a comprehensive, unified component of any EIA that needs to be capable of scaling to meet any information volume, performance, and deployment requirement so that companies can deliver business results faster and with trusted information.

These EII services are delivered through a set of tools and products that help enterprises derive more value from the complex, heterogeneous information spread across their systems. These services enable users to quickly understand, transform, and integrate large amounts of information stored within their enterprises. It helps business and IT personnel collaborate to understand the meaning, structure, and content of information across a wide variety of sources.

Furthermore, these services help to ensure high-quality information over time, delivering it on demand to any requesting person or application, other system components, or in the context of a defined business process.

5.3.16.2 Service Description

Following are the key services shown in Figure 5.9 that make up the EII Component.

These EII services are delivered by different business and technical users according to their respective roles and responsibilities:

- **Discovery Services**—Discovery Services is a critical first step in any information integration project; it can help you automatically discover data structures, and most importantly, the relationships of objects such as tables in a database schema or table column relationships of various tables in different database schemas. These discovery services need to be implemented through tools to improve productivity through automation and to define and apply discovery rules for consistency purposes throughout any information integration project.

- **Profiling Services**—These services include the analysis, definition, and modeling of data and information content and structure, and also their meaning and relationships. Analysis services can automatically scan a suitable sample of your data to determine quality and

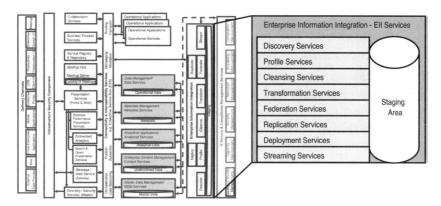

Figure 5.9   The Enterprise Information Integration (EII) Component

structure. Profiling services enable you to discover data quality problems that require correction with structure or validity before they affect your project, reducing project risks. Profile services must address the following objects: the data, values, structures, and relationship of those objects, and last but not least, rules that are best understood by business users that can facilitate the dialogue between business and technical roles and responsibilities. The initial profiling of data and other information-related objects needs to be followed by an ongoing data analysis as part of an organizational or enterprise-wide data governance strategy to ensure trusted information is delivered over time. In other words, information-profiling services are part of a monitoring and auditing process that ensures validity and accuracy, adherence with business rules, and compliance with internal standards and industry regulations. (There is a link to IT Service & Compliance Management Services. We elaborate on them as part of the Operational Model in Chapter 6.)

- **Cleansing Services**—Improving and maintaining a high quality of data is another essential part of the Information Integration Component. Cleansing Services help to reduce the time and cost to implement CRM, ERP, BI, DWs, and other strategic customer-related IT initiatives. Cleansing Services support the required information quality and consistency by standardizing, validating, matching, and merging data. Cleansing services provide a set of integrated components for accomplishing data quality improvement and restructuring tasks. A cleansing routine is executed step-by-step as follows:

    1. **Investigation Step**—This step is delivered through the Discovery and Profiling services and is related to understanding the quality aspects of the source data records.

    2. **Standardization Step**—This step conditions the data records further and standardizes these records according to structures of the source data and quality improvement rules. This is a typical Cleansing Service functionality.

3. **Matching Step**—During this step, matches are determined through deterministic or more sophisticated probabilistic matching capabilities. Matching Services are another common task delivered through Cleansing Services.

4. **Determination Step**—The final step includes the decision about which data records will survive and which ones will be discarded. This step enables a single record to survive from the best information across specified data sources for each unique entity. This is based on survivorship rules at the record or attribute level. Survivorship functions are also part of Cleansing Services.

   Executing the quality services step-by-step can help you create a single, comprehensive, and accurate view of trusted information across heterogeneous data sources.

- **Transformation Services**—These services transform and enrich information to ensure that it is in the proper context for new usage scenarios. This includes restructuring and aggregating information along with high-speed joins and sorts of heterogeneous data. Furthermore, these transformation services provide high-volume, complex data transformation and movement functionality that can be used for standalone ETL scenarios, or as a real-time data processing engine for applications or processes.

- **Federation Services**—These services hide the complexity and diversity of the underlying heterogeneous data landscape. Applications need to access data that resides in different data repositories, managed by DB2, Oracle, Sybase, or MS SQL Server DBMS systems. Federation services provide a level of transparency between the application and the underlying data landscape, so that the application doesn't have to be aware of this level of complexity and diversity.

- **Replication Services**—The objective of Replication Services is to ensure consistency between redundant resources. Change Data Capture (CDC) techniques (trigger-based or based on reading the transactional logs) are used to identify the changes that need to be replicated from the source to one or multiple targets. Depending on the requirements and use case scenarios, Replication Services can be delivered with a wide variety of different attributes such as:[31]

  - **Replication direction**—Uni- or bi-directional

  - **Replication frequency**—Daily, hourly, on demand

  - **Data volume**—Few records, high-volume

  - **Latency**—Delay in data replication

- **Deployment Services**—These services provide an integrated environment that enables the user to rapidly deploy other EII capabilities as services to a user or an application.

---

[31] Note that this list shows only a subset of attributes relevant for replication.

Deployment Services should also leverage other EII services for understanding, cleansing, transforming, and federating information. Deployment Services deploy those integration tasks as consistent and reusable information services. After an EII service has been built and is enabled for deployment, any enterprise application or enterprise integration software can invoke the service by using a binding protocol such as Web services.

- **Streaming Services**—These services provide the capability to perform real-time analytics while the data is in motion. With real-time analytics, response times in micro-seconds are required on large volumes of data. IBM InfoSphere Streams is the first product delivering such capabilities. In Chapters 8 and 14, we describe in more detail the capabilities and typical use case scenarios.

5.3.16.3 Interfaces

Let's look at how this component interacts with other components of the EIA. Before we do, we need to consider the business context in which EII services are deployed. As these EII services help you access and use data in new ways to deliver trusted information and to drive innovation, the EII Component will support a number of business initiatives, as follows:

- **BI**—The EII Component makes it easier to develop a unified view of the business for better decisions. It helps you understand existing data sources, cleanse, correct, and standardize information, and load analytical views that can be reused throughout the enterprise.

- **Master Data Management**—The EII Component simplifies the development of authoritative master data by showing where and how information is stored across source systems. It also consolidates disparate data into a single, reliable record, cleanses and standardizes information, removes duplicates, and links records together across systems. This master record can be loaded into operational data stores, DWs, or a master data management system. The record can also be completely or partially assembled in an on-demand fashion.

- **Infrastructure Rationalization**—The EII Component aids in reducing operating costs by showing relationships between systems and by defining migration rules to consolidate instances or move data from obsolete systems. Data cleansing and matching ensure high-quality data in the new system.

- **Business Transformation**—The EII Component can speed up development and increase business agility by providing reusable information services that can be plugged into applications, business processes, and portals. These standards-based information services are maintained centrally by information specialists, but they are widely accessible throughout the enterprise.

- **Risk and Compliance**—The EII Component helps improve visibility and data governance by enabling complete, authoritative views of information with proof of data lineage and quality. These views can be made widely available and reusable as shared services, while the rules inherent in them are maintained centrally.

With this business context in mind, you can see that the EII services can be requested from many of the other components of the EIA Component Model and must therefore support many different interface standards and protocols to support the previous use cases.

5.3.17 IT Service & Compliance Management Services

The IT Service & Compliance Management Services Component is responsible for delivering the non-functional requirements for the EIA Reference Architecture. This component is a key link into the operational model. We limit the scope to the services provided through this component, which are especially relevant for delivering the information-related capabilities of the EIA.

The following key services are provided by this component as shown earlier in Figure 5.1:

- **Compliance Management Services**—The services of this group are used to verify compliance with requirements that manage operational risk and retention policies. Compliance with business SLAs or legal requirements from a functional perspective is not the responsibility and not a capability of this services group.

- **Availability Management Services**—Availability is the measurement of the readiness to use an IT system. This component has the inherent measure of reliability that is defined as the probability that an IT system delivers the desired functions under stated conditions for a given period of time. Obviously, if the reliability is low, the availability cannot be high. Thus, high availability implies high reliability. For availability, critical metrics are the Mean Time To Recovery (MTTR), Mean Time To Failure (MTTF), and Mean Time Between Failures (MTBF). The MTTR defines how long it might take in the worst case until a system is available again, and thus, it provides insight into performance requirements for operations such as the restoration of a database backup in a disaster recovery case. If a capability relies on multiple components, then the availability for this capability is given by the product of the availability measures for all involved components. Availability can be improved through redundancy, which means the same component is deployed multiple times in a redundant fashion in conjunction with load balancing techniques. This approach ensures that the overall availability is higher than the availability of each of its redundant components. The Availability Management Services address these needs by providing appropriate availability for the services of the functional components including load balancing and backup and restore services.

- **Retention Management Services**—The amount of structured and unstructured information grows at a constantly increasing pace.[32] For companies, it is more important from

---

[32] For more details on the increase in the growth rate of the information volume, see [33].

a storage cost perspective to determine how long an information asset should be kept. In some areas, there might be legal requirements about the minimum or maximum retention time of an information asset. In addition, access patterns need to be considered: Is the information asset retrieved frequently and the anticipated retrieval time required short, or, is it retrieved rarely and a longer retrieval time is acceptable? If it's the latter, the storage costs can be reduced by offloading information assets with this characteristic to slower and cheaper storage. Retention Management Services address these needs by providing the capability to specify and enforce policies regarding the retention of an information asset. These services are essential to implement hierarchical storage management for the enterprise Content Services or for storage cost reduction in a DW environment where older data that is less often queried is placed on cheaper and slower storage to reduce operational costs.

- **Security Management Services**—First, Security Management Services must prevent information leaks. Second, these services must secure, for instance, archived data through proper encryption techniques on various storage types such as disks or tapes in a multi-tier environment. Encryption and decryption before and after transmission of data is the third responsibility for these services. Intrusion detection, identity management, and related key lifecycle management complete the Security Management Services.

- **Capacity Management Services**—These services assure proper capacity for a component to achieve expected throughput and performance.

- **Quality of Services Management**—Service qualities cover functional, operational, security, and maintainability aspects. Selecting the quality of services and being able to dynamically deploy them is critical to offer software as a service and cloud capabilities for information services.

5.4 Component Interaction Diagrams—A Deployment Scenario

IT architects typically use multiple Component Interaction Diagrams to validate a Component Model. In this chapter, we include only one because Chapters 7 through 14 show additional Component Interaction Diagrams. The example is an information-centric application. With this example, we show how the components interact with each other for a specific use case scenario. The objective is to illustrate the use of the Component Model for application and industry-specific needs, validating the relevance and interrelationship of some of the components for this use case scenario.

5.4.1 Business Context

In saturated markets in a globally competitive environment, the ability to create a new business model is what gives companies an advantage against their competitors. Leveraging information and gaining business insight through information-centric applications has become an increasingly important differentiator in the market.

Consider an example of a new information-centric application, the Nike community website. This site is for a community of people who run with certain types of Nike shoes in combination with equipment such as an Apple iPod. With this setup, Nike achieves the following:

- Nike takes a consumer product—running shoes—and looks at them from an information perspective, realizing the value of the information the shoes can collect to create a unique value proposition for potential buyers.

- This information (average speed, the route that was run, and so on) is unlocked by adding a sensor to the shoe that communicates with a carrying device, the Apple iPod. This information can be made available to laptops and desktop PCs.

- The combination of the shoes and the iPod (carried by many runners who listen to music while working out) makes this unlocking of information particularly enticing. It doesn't create the need to buy a new device that needs to be carried. Instead, it seamlessly integrates with a known device already carried by the runner.

- Nike created an online community for the customers who bought a pair of Nike shoes. The online community is not new, but applying it the way Nike did to create value from the information unlocked from its shoes by centering it around information the shoes collect makes this an innovative, information-centric application. In this community, a *runner* can manage his personal profile, training schedule, and favorite routes (plotted by a third-party service from Google). He can check for current running competitions, become a member of a running team, or join a distance club among other things. This is an innovative way to help lock the runner into Nike products.

With the now information-enabled shoe that has been a consumer product without any relation to IT previously, Nike created a completely new business model with strong support from the running community.

This example is an information-centric application that does the following:

- Unlocks operational data (route taken, average speed, and so on) from an unexpected source such as a consumer product of daily life

- Integrates the operational data with master data (the customer, the product[s]) and Unstructured Data (music, maps, and so on)

- Makes available the information on a community platform to create customer retention by providing added value.

In addition to establishing better customer retention, Nike also has the additional benefit of getting deeper insight into their end customers. Before, if a pair of running shoes was bought in a store, Nike didn't know who the end customer was and how the product was used. Now, to participate in the community, customers have to register. With the registration process, Nike learns who the customers are and what products they have acquired, where they live, how often they run (at least the published trainings), and so on. This gives Nike better insight into their customers and into how the running shoes are used, enabling the possibility to promote new products or product upgrades on the community platform. All of this contributes to improved business results.

5.4.2 Component Interaction Diagram

In this section, we look at an example of a Component Interaction Diagram that supports an information-centric application. This is not based on a concrete implementation; it represents key flows through the EIA to show that the proposed Component Model supports a use case. We describe the Registration and Upload/Download personal data sub-scenarios.

Each step in a scenario is indicated with a number in Figure 5.10. We now begin with the first scenario. Here we assume the user (a customer) bought a consumer product (e.g. shoes, mobile phone, PDA, and so on) in a store.

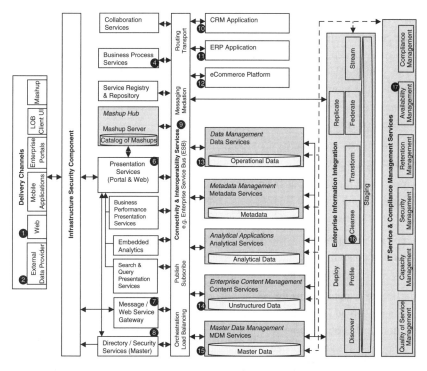

Figure 5.10   Walkthrough for the information-centric application deployment scenario

1. The customer opens a browser on a computing device (a laptop, desktop or PC, for example) with Internet connectivity and requests the company community website (1) for registration through a web browser.

2. Additional information may be provided through an external data provider (2).

3. The request for the website (typically an HTTP request) is received by the Infrastructure Security Component (3) where load balancing and security-related tasks are completed.

4. The Infrastructure Security Component (3) then invokes the Presentation Services Component (6).

5. The Presentation Services Component (6) invokes the Business Process Services Component (4) through the Connectivity and Interoperability Component (9) to start the registration process. The Business Process Services Component opens a two-phase commit transaction and becomes stateful waiting for the input from the user. A threshold for a timeout is set to avoid blocking resources for too long; thus, if the user doesn't complete the required step in a certain amount of time, the process has to start over.

6. The Presentation Services Component (6) then returns the registration website to the customer for rendering in the web browser (1) through the Infrastructure Security Component (3).

7. The customer fills in fields such as name, address, email address, products acquired, user name, the password for the community, and relevant fields related to the product. (The profile-related fields in a community website will vary based on the product because the interest will be different; think about different products such as a smart phone versus a pair of shoes.) The customer then clicks to complete submission of the registration form.

8. The Infrastructure Security Component (3) processes the request for security and load balancing aspects, and then routes it to the Presentation Services Component (6).

9. Upon receiving the input from the customer, the Presentation Services Component (6) interacts again with the Business Process Services Component (4) through the Connectivity and Interoperability Component (9).

10. Upon receiving the input, the Business Process Services Component (4) executes a workflow that contains the following steps. These three service calls must complete successfully; otherwise, a rollback across all involved components is issued.

    a. Invoke a data-cleansing service from the EII Component (16) to standardize the name and address information. In addition, if needed and available, address validation and Global Name Recognition for name transliteration into a unified code set can be part of this service.

    b. At the next step, the Directory and Security Services Component (8) is invoked through the Connectivity and Interoperability Component (9) to create a user ID and a password by invoking an appropriate Identity Provisioning Service of that component.

    c. Then, the customer and the customer-product relationships are created via an appropriate master data services from the MDM Component (15). Note that, physically, there might be more than one master data repository where the master data services provide an abstraction across them. Also note that the MDM Component (15) uses availability services (17) from the IT Service & Compliance Management Services Component.

11. Assuming the registration process succeeds, the Presentation Services Component (6) returns through the Infrastructure Security Component (3) the corresponding website to the user (1) who can then log in to the community website.

The next scenario is related to the ability to upload or download data to the community website. As outlined in section 5.4.1 in the Nike scenario, this could, for example, mean uploading the routes the runner has taken to create maps or downloading routes from other runners. In another use case, this might mean downloading a software upgrade to the smart phone from a smart phone gaming community. This scenario requires completion of the previous registration scenario.

In order to upload or download data to the community website, the following steps need to be performed:

1. The user requests the login web page through a browser (1), which is delivered by the Presentation Services Component (6) to the community platform and enters the credentials created in the registration process and submits the credentials.

2. The Infrastructure Security Component (3) performs authentication verification, and assuming success, routes the request for the community platform to the Presentation Services Component (6), which returns the start page.

3. The user then selects to upload information to the community platform. Depending on the information types involved in the task, structured information might be entered into input fields on the web page, and unstructured information might be attached on a file-by-file basis for the upload. After the information is entered, attached, or a combination of both, the user triggers the upload procedure. Depending on the implementation, various protocols and mechanisms are involved in the upload transfer.

4. The Presentation Services Component (6) receives the request for upload through the Infrastructure Security Component (3). Depending on whether the information is structured, unstructured, or both, information services are called through the Connectivity and Interoperability Component (9) from the Data Management Component (13) or the Content Management Component (14).

5. After the information service completes, the Presentation Services Component (6) returns a success screen update to the user (1) through the Infrastructure Security Component (3).

The download scenario works in the opposite direction where structured or unstructured information is downloaded to a device such as a PDA, Apple iPod, laptop, or desktop computer for further use.

5.4.3 Alternatives and Extensions

If the implementation of the community website is not based on web and portal technology only, then the Mashup Hub Component (5) might be used to deliver certain aspects of the community website. Examples are feeds based on web syndication, chat services from the Collaboration Services Component embedded in a mashup, and so on.

A natural extension of the community website is the inclusion of an Operational Application Component serving as an eCommerce Platform (12) that enables participants in the community to easily order upgrades and new products. The order is fulfilled through an Operational Application Component that provides fulfillment capabilities such as an ERP (11) system. This is a component used as a complement to the CRM solution (10) used to deliver marketing events to the community platform. The ERP and CRM application functions are often delivered through standard prepackaged applications such as a SAP NetWeaver ERP system or a Siebel CRM system.

Alternatively, part of the cleanse service invocation from the EII Component (16) can be invoked from a third-party provider. In this case, this service would be routed through the Connectivity and Interoperability Component (9) to the Message and Web Service Gateway (7), and then to the External Data Provider (2).

5.5 Conclusion

In this chapter, we introduced the Component Model of the EIA Reference Architecture. We defined all relevant information-centric components and their services. Using a Component Interaction Diagram, we demonstrated the viability of the Component Model. Component Interaction Diagrams in Chapters 7 through 14 will prove its structure and deepen your understanding.

In the next chapter, we introduce key aspects of the Operational Model.

5.6 References

[1] Bruns, A., Jacobs, J. (Editors). *Uses of Blogs*. Peter Lang Publishing, 2006.

[2] Technorati. *The Technorati Blogosphere Search Engine*. http://technorati.com/ (accessed December 15, 2009).

[3] IBM Press Announcement. 2007. *Web 2.0 Goes to Work*. http://www-03.ibm.com/press/us/en/pressrelease/21748. wss (accessed December 15, 2009).

[4] The Global Data Synchronization Network (GDSN). http://www.gs1.org/productssolutions/gdsn/ (accessed December 15, 2009).

[5] The EPCglobal Network. http://www.epcglobalinc.org/home (accessed December 15, 2009).

[6] Association for Cooperative Operations Research and Development (ACORD). http://www.acord.org/home (accessed December 15, 2009).

[7] Sommerlad, P. 2003. *Reverse Proxy Patterns*. http://www.modsecurity.org/archive/ReverseProxy-book-1.pdf (accessed December 15, 2009).

[8] Buecker, A., Carreno, V., A., Field, N., Hockings, C., Kawer, D., Mohanty, S., Monteiro, G. *Enterprise Security Architecture Using IBM Tivoli Security Solutions*, http://www.redbooks.ibm.com/pubs/pdfs/redbooks/sg246014. pdf (accessed December 15, 2009), IBM Redbook, 2007.

[9] Neely, A. (Editor). *Business Performance Measurement: Unifying Theory and Integrating Practice*, Second Edition. New York, NY: Cambridge University Press, 2007.

[10] Eckerson, W. W. *Performance Dashboards: Measuring, Monitoring, and Mapping Your Business.* Hoboken, New Jersey: John Wiley & Sons, Inc. 2006.

[11] Volitich, D. *IBM Cognos 8 Business Intelligence: The Official Guide. Based on IBM Cognos 8 Business Intelligence Version 8.3.* City, State: McGraw-Hill, 2008.

[12] Van der Lans, R. F. *Introduction to SQL: Mastering the Relational Database Language,* Fourth Edition. City, State: Addison-Wesley Professional, 2006.

[13] IBM. 2009. *DB2 for Linux, Unix and Windows—pureXML™ and Storage Compression.* http://www-01.ibm.com/software/data/db2/9/ (accessed December 15, 2009).

[14] Zikopoulos, P. C., Eaton, C. L., Baklarz, G., Katsnelson, L.D. *IBM DB2 Version 9 New Features.* New York, NY: McGraw-Hill, 2007.

[15] American National Standard Institute (ANSI). http://www.ansi.org/ (accessed December 15, 2009).

[16] International Standard Organization (ISO). http://www.iso.org/iso/home.htm (accessed December 15, 2009).

[17] Chappell, D. *Enterprise Service Bus.* Sebastopol, CA: O'Reilly, 2004.

[18] Fowler, M. *Patterns of Enterprise Application Integration,* Boston, MA: Addison-Wesley, 2003.

[19] Hohpe, G., Woolf, B. *Enterprise Integration Patterns,* Boston, MA: Addison-Wesley, 2004.

[20] Bieberstein, N., et al. *Service-Oriented Architecture (SOA) Compass,* Upper Saddle River, New Jersey: Pearson Education, 2006.

[21] Newman, A. C., Thomas, J. G. *Enterprise 2.0 Implementation.* New York, NY: McGraw-Hill, 2009.

[22] Lynn, R., Bishop, K., King, B. *Getting Started with IBM WebSphere sMash.* Indianapolis, IN: IBM Press, forthcoming (2010).

[23] Funke, K. *Metadaten-Management für Data-Warehouse-Systeme: Grundlagen, Nutzenpotentiale und Standardisierung mit dem Common Warehouse Metamodel.* Vdm Verlag Dr. Müller, 2008.

[24] Poole, J., Chang, D., Tolbert, D., Mellor, D. *Common Warehouse Metamodel: An Introduction to the Standard for Data Warehouse Integration.* New York, NY: John Wiley & Sons, 2001.

[25] Dreibelbis, A., Hechler, E., Milman, I., Oberhofer, M., van Run, P., Wolfson, D. *Enterprise Master Data Management—An SOA Approach to Managing Core Information.* Indianapolis, IN: IBM Press, 2008.

[26] Arasu, A., Babcock, B., Babu, S., Cieslewicz, J., Datar, M., Ito, K., Motwani, R., Srivastava, U., Widom, J. 2004. STREAM: *The Stanford Data Stream Management System.* Technical Report. Department of Computer Science, Stanford University. http://ilpubs.stanford.edu:8090/641/ (accessed December 15, 2009).

[27] Inmon, W. H. *Building the Operational Data Store.* New York: John Wiley & Sons, 1999.

[28] Bruni, P., Harrison, K., Oldham, G., Pedersen, L., Tino, G. 2007. *DB2 9 for z/OS Performance Topics.* IBM Redbook. http://www.redbooks.ibm.com/redbooks/pdfs/sg247473.pdf (accessed December 15, 2009).

[29] Zikopolous, P. 2008. *Transforming Business Logic into Web Services Using DB2 9.5 and IBM Data Studio.* http://www.databasejournal.com/features/db2/article.php/3784896/Transforming-Business-Logic-into-Web-Services-Using- DB2-95-and-IBM-Data-Studio.htm (accessed December 15, 2009).

[30] Kimball, R., Ross, M. *The Data Warehouse Toolkit: The Complete Guide to Dimensional Modeling* (Second Edition). City, State: John Wiley & Sons, 2002.

[31] IBM Dynamic Warehousing homepage. http://www-01.ibm.com/software/data/infosphere/data-warehousing/ (accessed December 15, 2009).

[32] Chen, W.-J., Fisher, A., Lalla, A., McLauchlan, A. D., Agnew, D. 2007. *Database Partitioning, Table Partitioning, and MDC for DB2 9.* IBM Redbooks.

[33] Gantz, J. F. et al. 2008. *The Diverse and Exploding Digital Universe—An Updated Forecast of Worldwide Information Growth Through 2011.* An IDC White Paper, sponsored by EMC. http://www.emc.com/collateral/analyst-reports/diverse-exploding-digital-universe.pdf (accessed December 15, 2009).

CHAPTER 6

Enterprise Information Architecture: Operational Model

In this chapter, we describe the operational characteristics of the Enterprise Information Architecture (EIA). This chapter should help you understand the definition and distribution of an IT system's components onto geographically distributed nodes,[1] also known as the Operational Model. We focus on the Information Services components in the EIA Reference Architecture. This chapter is predominately targeted at enterprise architects, information architects, and system architects; however, it can also be used as a reference for IT experts from different skill domains.

We start by introducing some definitions and terms of operational modeling that reflect the various layers of Enterprise Information Services (EIS). The key concepts of operational modeling provide an understanding of how physical nodes can be derived from logical components of the Component Model. We also look at related deployment scenarios to examine how delivery models such as Cloud Computing—which is also discussed in Chapter 7—or Software as a Service (SaaS)[2] are related to the Operational Model. We also describe operational patterns to show how parts of the overall Information Service can be constructed. Finally, we introduce a framework to aggregate operational patterns categorized by particular scopes of integration and give examples of how to apply the architectural patterns to specific business scenarios.

6.1 Terminology and Definitions

According to the IBM Architecture Description Standard (ADS),[3] the Enterprise Architecture can be presented at different levels. One of the principles that guides the development of an ADS is

---

[1] The distribution of components does not necessarily mean deployment on distributed nodes. Operational requirement will decide to have components, deployed on one local IT resource such as a server or on various IT resources, such as a clustered environment.

[2] More details on the SaaS delivery model can be found in [1].

[3] Detailed definitions, architecture building blocks (ABBs), and relationship diagrams can be found in [2].

147

the recognition that infrastructure design is a specialized skill and that its exponents deal with concepts, entities, and methods that are different from those known in the area of application development. This recognition led to the division of the EIA Reference Architecture into three parts: a Conceptual Level, a Logical Level, and a Physical Level (see also Chapter 2).

At the Physical Level, the Operational Model defines and documents the distribution of an IT system's components onto geographically distributed nodes—together with the connections necessary to support the required component interactions—to achieve the IT system's functional and non-functional requirements (NFR). Thus, the Operational Model is focused specifically on the aspects of architecture necessary for the infrastructure designer to perform the job. The focus of the operational aspect is to describe the operation of the IT system. It is also primarily concerned with representing the network organization (hardware platforms, connections, locations, topology, and so on), where software and data components are "placed" on the network, how service-level requirements (performance, availability, security, and so on) are satisfied, and the management and operation of the whole system (capacity planning, software distribution, backup, and recovery).

6.1.1 Definition of Operational Model Levels

An Operational Model itself can be presented at different levels of granularity:

- Logical Operational Model (LOM)
- Physical Operational Model (POM)

The LOM identifies the required technical services, develops the connections, and refines the technical specifications. It describes:

- Placement of specified components onto specified nodes
- Specified connections between those nodes necessary to support the interactions between specified components
- Non-functional characteristics of those nodes and connections, acquired from the placed specified components and their interactions

At the POM level, the hardware and software technologies needed to deliver the Operational Model's characteristics and capabilities are identified and configured. It documents the overall configuration of the technologies and products necessary to deliver the functional requirements and NFRs of the IT system. In particular, it describes:

- Hardware and software technology and product selection for computers and networks
- Hardware specifications, such as processor speed and disk configuration, or network bandwidth and latency
- Overall hardware configurations, such as "fail-over" or "scalable" arrangements
- Software product specifications (such as version) and detailed configuration, such as the need for multiple instances of a software product (operating system, middleware, and communication element or application system) on a computer

6.1.2 Terms of Operational Aspect

This section introduces the concepts and notations used in the Operational Model. The central concept is the node. A *node* is a platform on which software executes. During early stages of the design process, a node represents a potential platform, before decisions have been made about how to map it to actual platforms. Each node has a name and optionally the number of instances. *Connections* represent physical data paths between nodes and show the shape of the network.

Deployment units (DU)[4] are placed on the nodes. A *deployment unit* is the smallest unit of software or data for which an architect makes a placement decision. Deployment units are shown as named items on each node. A deployment unit consists of one or more components. In the context of the EIA, the data aspect of a component, which is discussed later in this chapter, is referred to as data deployment units (DDU), complemented by execution deployment units (EDU) that represent the installation and execution of components.

Nodes are grouped together in locations. A *location* is a geographical entity (such as a zone[5] or building type) and is shown by pictorial elements around one or more nodes.

6.1.3 Key Design Concepts within Operational Modeling

When implementing Information Services, various design and development tasks must meet the operational requirements of the IT system. The major conceptual work items are:

- The placement and grouping of components into deployment units
- The application of walkthroughs confirming operational aspects[6]
- The consideration of constraints and quality requirements
- The physical configuration for a set of technologies

Placement of components determines how to group them into DUs and on which nodes to place them. This is influenced mainly by what data the users are operating on and what activities the users perform. Another factor in the decision process is the consideration of NFRs.

Performing end-to-end walkthroughs is another means of augmenting the design work with the objective of confirming operational aspects of a system as feasible and acceptable. A walkthrough is used to assess the operational behavior of the system, specifically whether the system will be able to satisfy particular SLAs.

---

[4] Aspects such as executable code or the data of each component are usually mapped onto deployment units (DU), which might also be used to represent grouped or split components, depending on the functional and non-functional characteristics.

[5] A zone represents an area for which a common set of NFRs can be defined. In this context, we consider the area as a set of maintenance capabilities such as to restore a system to a working state after a failure.

[6] The walkthroughs build on the Component Model deployment scenarios.

SLAs represent specific types of quality requirements or constraints that an IT system must satisfy. These requirements are also known as NFRs, which might include availability or system performance. The placement of components is highly influenced by the consideration of NFRs.

Finally, the selection and configuration of a set of technologies are drawn up to achieve a set of requirements (usually non-functional) as defined by a corresponding functional aspect. How to use a "fail over" or clustering technology would fall into this category.

The Operational Model can be a large and complex work product. Therefore, it is important to understand how it is used and presented in the context of the EIA Reference Architecture. We took the characteristics from the LOM and generalized some views of the POM. Technologies and products, including detailed configurations, are not in the scope of this book. However, to demonstrate typical configurations for a set of technologies, we introduce topology views and sample configurations from the POM for a range of requirements.

6.2 Context of Operational Model Design Techniques

Now that we have described the terminology and definitions of the Operational Model, we describe the context and integration of operational aspects within the EIA Reference Architecture. We focus on the integration of the functional design with the infrastructure design. The success of major solution development projects often critically depends on the integrated design of operational aspects.

Figure 6.1 depicts how the Operational Model derives from the Component Model and it details functional component interactions and deployment scenarios. The process of operational modeling means the partitioning and aggregation of logical components to DUs. We discuss the placement of DUs on physical nodes, the related locations and zoning capabilities, we specify the node-to-node connections, and we analyze the supported range of NFRs, the selected delivery model, and the scope of integration needed to meet the business context and related use cases.

Because we cannot provide a fully detailed, sized configuration of all kinds of EIA deployment scenarios, we focus on generalized LOM and partial POM views of the Operational Model. In this case, both views are usually incomplete in some well-defined way, requiring tailoring and integration with fully outlined configuration aspects before completion.

However, the generalized Operational Model allows us to select, customize, and integrate predeveloped architectural patterns for our needs. For this reason, we provide a collection of pre-defined node types, connection types, location types, and DU placements. Furthermore, we have selected relevant IT service management node types, specified technical components, and topology patterns.[7] We also provide inter-location border types and interrelationships of specified nodes for the most common distribution scenarios of logical components.

---

[7] Topology patterns are variations of the node-to-node connections in a specific runtime environment and describe topological relationships such as point-point connections.

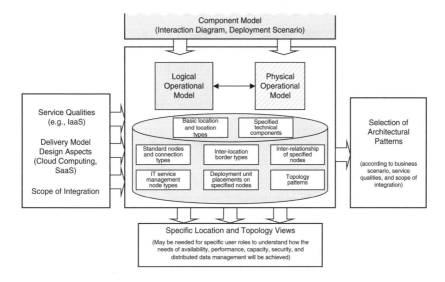

Figure 6.1   Selection of architectural patterns from generalized Operational Models

With these operational design techniques, we can maximize the reuse of robust solution outlines by selectable architectural patterns in the context of the EIA Reference Architecture. An important aspect of the operational design is the chosen delivery model of Information Services. We have scoped a variety of delivery models to the most popular ones, which are the emerging Cloud Computing and the SaaS[8] delivery model. For example, it is common for both delivery models that multiple customers are hosted within one environment. This requires the solution to provide exceptionally effective network isolation and security. For similar wants and needs concerning security, availability, performance, capacity, and how distributed data management will be achieved, we provide specific location and topology views.

For operational modeling purposes, it is important to understand that NFRs can be derived from affected data domains such as Operational or Analytical Data. For example, service availability and transaction throughput has different relevance for the data domains. Thus, we elaborate on the types and impact of NFRs that from now on we refer to as service qualities.

---

[8] The SOA-oriented Information as a Service (IaaS) model has already been discussed in Chapter 2. In this chapter, we focus on the challenges and solution aspects associated with exposing information with an SOA service interface. The SaaS delivery model in the context of EIA is considered an extended concept to deliver subscription-based Information Services that are managed and maintained by an external service provider.

6.3 Service Qualities

In accordance with the taxonomy of The Open Group Architecture Framework (TOGAF),[9] we introduce the notion of service qualities that represent a set of requirements, also known as NFRs, and are applicable across the components and nodes in the EIA. For the purpose of managing the effectiveness, reliability, and efficiency of the Information Services, we categorized the variety of service qualities in four dimensions. This applies to all instantiations of the service qualities, for instance to IaaS:[10]

- **Functional service qualities**—These are functional attributes applied to NFRs such as portability of data and components, the ability to change and adapt quickly to new use cases and workflow behaviors, the request driven provisioning of new functions and information objects, but also required data flows due to compliance and regulatory reasons.

- **Operational service qualities**—These attributes include service availability, scalability, performance indicators measured by transaction throughput or minimum transaction capacity, the capability of components to grow or shrink in capacity according to the demands of the environment, and the minimum of free storage on nodes in a certain time period.

- **Security management qualities**—These attributes are usually demanded across the business and technology domain. They include the protection of information from unauthorized access, identity control and management services, authentication services, policy enforcement, reconciliation services and so on.

- **Maintainability qualities**—These attributes include the capability to remotely access relevant components, identify problems and take corrective action, repair or upgrade a component in a running system, find a system when necessary, restore a system to a working state after a failure, and so on.

6.3.1 Example of Operational Service Qualities

Examples of operational service qualities are outlined in Table 6.1. The application of operational service qualities is typically applied to specified nodes. The comments describe the parameters and their meanings in more detail.

---

[9] The Open Group Architecture Framework (TOGAF) Version 9 can be found in [3].

[10] As explained in Chapter 2, an IaaS can provide the full or partial implementation of service components. This implementation typically requires functional requirements, such as reusability, and operational requirements, such as scalability in a shared environment.

Table 6.1 Sample Operational Service Qualities

Operational Service Quality	Specified Node 1	Specified Node 2	Specified Node 3	Specified Node 4	Comments
Service availability	99.9%	99%	99%	99.9%	99% = 5,256 minutes of downtime per year 99.9% = 526 minutes of downtime per year
Average transaction throughput of the node	214,000 / hour	4 files /hour	107,000 / hour	107,000 / hour	A day = 14 hours End-of-day processing takes two hours.
Maximum estimated CPU utilization by the node	80%	50%	80%	80%	CPU utilization is important because the higher the percentage of the CPU used, the less power the CPU can devote to other tasks.
Average service time	0.00022 min	7.5 min	0.00045 min	0.00045 min	Average time available to service each transaction
Minimum transaction capacity of the node	4,545 trans/min	0.13 files/min	2,222 trans/min	2,222 trans/min	The inverse of average service time

Table 6.1   Sample Operational Service Qualities

Operational Service Quality	Specified Node 1	Specified Node 2	Specified Node 3	Specified Node 4	Comments
Minimum file system I/O rate of the node	18,180 /min	1 /min	4,444 /min	4,444 /min	Node-1 = 4 I/O operations per transaction Node-2 = 2 I/O operations per transaction Node-3 = 2 I/O operations per file Node-4 = 2 I/O operations per transaction
Minimum free storage on the node (to store one day's load)	50.25 GB	47.25 GB	—	100 GB	Assuming circular logging, 100 primary log files, 50 secondary log files, log file size of 2,048 Kb, persistent messaging, and X86 platform

6.3.2 Relevance of Service Qualities per Data Domain

As already mentioned in section 6.2, service qualities can be derived from affected data domains. According to the EIA Reference Architecture, there are five data domains (for more explanation, see Chapter 3) which are Metadata, Unstructured Data, Operational Data, Master Data, and Analytical Data. Typically, the involvement of certain data domains in the solution design is an indicator of how relevant particular service qualities are and how they should be treated. This is true even if the related NFRs are not explicitly specified. In Table 6.2 on the next page, we collected the relevant service qualities per data domain involved. This table is not an exhaustive list of all conceivable requirements per data domain. Instead, we point out the most relevant dimensions of service qualities based on recurring demands from various real solutions.

6.4 Standards Used for the Operational Model Relationship Diagram

Now that you understand the Operational Model design techniques and service qualities needed to satisfy a certain business scenario, we can introduce the Operational Model relationship diagram. The Operational Model relationship diagram is a depiction of nodes, locations, and correlating connections separately documented as the design proceeds. The relationship of those elements is developed to verify the way in which the Operational Model supports crucial use case scenarios. We introduce the generalized level of the LOM and POM to convey the application of patterns and reuse. Generalization means we provide a collection of standard node types, pre-defined connection types, location types, and deployment unit placements for specific business scenarios.

It is important to recognize that the standards provided are a representation of typical IT landscapes over which the system is distributed. They represent the "design building blocks" that will be used when deciding upon the detailed physical configuration for a set of technologies.

6.4.1 Basic Location Types

Business applications and Information Services are typically distributed throughout the enterprise. Data flows between physical nodes deployed in one location to nodes in another location. The location can be considered an environment that determines certain service-level characteristics. For the purpose of general use of architectural patterns, we introduce basic location types that we refer to throughout the book:

- **External Business Partners Location**—Represents external organizations that provide complementary services to the client. These organizations can include insurers, credit/debit payment processors, or third-party application vendors.

- **Public Service Providers Location**—Represents organizations that provide the network and communication services necessary for the client to connect to its external business partners. Branch systems can access public service providers through a certain type of communication infrastructure.

- **Disaster Recovery Site Location**—Represents a zone or site that provides for protection against unplanned outages such as disasters. There are data mirroring concepts and

(continued after Table 6.2)

Table 6.2   Relevance of Service Qualities per Data Domain*

Data Domain / Quality Dimension	Functional Service Quality	Operational Service Quality	Security Management Quality	Maintainability Quality	Comments
Analytical Data	Near-real-time provisioning of staged data (H), and data flow throughput for the purpose of compliance (M)	File transfer or data replication throughput (M)	—	—	The relevance of functional service qualities is heavily dependent on the type of Analytical Data.
Operational Data	—	Service availability (H), transaction throughput (H), and minimum I/O rate of node (H)	Authentication and Authorization Services (H)	Recoverability with specified service levels (recovery time objective, recovery point objective) (H)	Service qualities of Operational Data can vary according to the method of use in particular business scenarios.
Master Data	—	Service availability (H), transaction throughput (H), and data quality indicators and de-duplication services (H)	Access restriction of this core information (M)	Recoverability with specified service levels (recovery time objective and recovery point objective) (H)	The recoverability of Master Data is of even higher relevance than Operational Data due to the sharing of authoritative sources.

*H: High Relevance; M: Moderate Relevance; L: Low Relevance (Not Covered)

Table 6.2 Relevance of Service Qualities per Data Domain*

Data Domain / Quality Dimension	Functional Service Quality	Operational Service Quality	Security Management Quality	Maintainability Quality	Comments
Unstructured Data	—	Enforcement of retention policies (M)	Protection from unauthorized access (H), self encryption services (M)	—	Most of a company's digitized data is Unstructured Data, including rich media streaming, website content, e-mail, and so on. Trusted access to such information is critical; so is its retention period due to compliance reasons.
Metadata	Extensibility of descriptive information elements (M)	Service availability for end-to-end exploitation purposes (H)	Authentication and Authorization Services (M)	Access to relevant components of descriptive information (DBMS catalog and XML schema) (H)	Metadata forms the basis for many of the queries run to identify content. This fact demands high availability and remote access to these information resources.

*H: High Relevance; M: Moderate Relevance; L: Low Relevance (Not Covered)

management systems in place to enable the shift of business system workload to this site and to enable a recovery from secondary storage systems in case of an unplanned outage.

- **Branch Systems Location**—Represents systems within branches of the enterprise. These systems can provide business functions such as retailing, inventory control, customer relationship management, or in-branch integration.

- **Head Office Systems Location**—Represents corporate systems located at the enterprise's head office. These systems can handle enterprise relevant processes, DW, EII, and connectivity to external business partners.

6.4.2 Inter-Location Border Types

The placement of application functionality and business data heavily depends on the networking capabilities within and between the various location types. The illustration of all these inter-connections is depicted via the use of a convenient line notation for the defined inter-location border types, which are:

- **Corporate WAN**—Corporate wide area network
- **Branch LAN**—Internal local area network (LAN within a branch)
- **Head Office LAN**—Internal local area network (within head office)
- **Internet Link**—Internet link and access to the external business partner's organization

6.4.3 Access Mechanisms

In addition to describing how the component model is implemented across IT systems, the Operational Model documents the access mechanisms used by all users of the system. In operational terms, people (and systems) can use and access the system components in a variety of access mechanisms according to the defined use cases. Well-known standard access mechanisms include:

- System Support and Management
- File Download (from file producers)
- File Upload (to file consumers)
- Message Receipt (from message producers)
- Message Sending (to message consumers)
- Socket Request (from socket requestors)
- Socket Response (from socket responders)

6.4.4 Standards of Specified Nodes

Specified nodes do not represent actual computing resources. Rather, they provide a formal mechanism for enabling the specification of the location for the solution's application and underlying technical components across the geographic landscape. Using standard specified nodes for the EIA

Reference Architecture, we examine the patterns of how Information Services can be constructed and instantiated. We also build node relationships, further elaborating on node-to-node connections and fleshing out exemplary topology views to meet particular service-level characteristics. As first input to the design of node relationships, including confirmation that the business problem is well articulated, we introduce the categorization of common capabilities in layers. The classification is done in four layers: Information Services, Application Platform Layer for Information Services, Technology Layer for Information Services,[11] and IT Service & Compliance Management Services. In Figure 6.2, you can see an overview of the mapping of node types and capabilities into the various layers.[12]

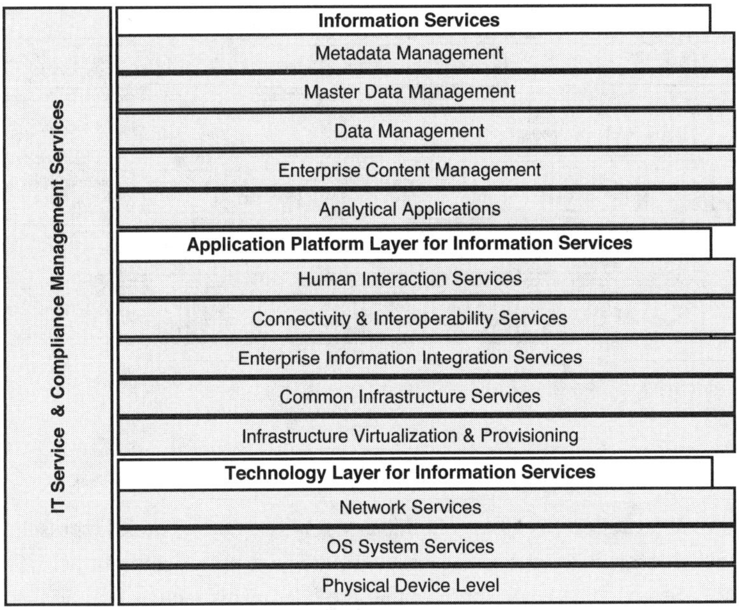

Figure 6.2   Standard node types and their categorization in layers

The node representation of Information Services with components covering Metadata Management, Master Data Management, Data Management, Enterprise Content Management, and Analytical Applications are already described in detail (see Chapters 4 and 5) and not

---

[11] With the categorization of components in the Application Platform Layer and Technology Layer, we present a view that has a context to the meta-model objects described in TOGAF V9; see [3]. The Application Platform Layer corresponds to TOGAF Logical Technology Components that provide an encapsulation of technology infrastructure. The Technology Layer corresponds to TOGAF Platform Service that describes technical capabilities required to support the delivery of applications.

[12] Due to space, we do not include all subcomponents of each of the five Information Services in the layer. Any services group introduced in Chapter 5 is on the layer specified even if it is not shown. Also note that we abbreviated some names previously introduced.

explored in this section. However we do describe the nodes further as this discussion allows for the realization of specific business scenario implementations. In Figure 6.3, you can see the Information Services in the framework of standard node types.

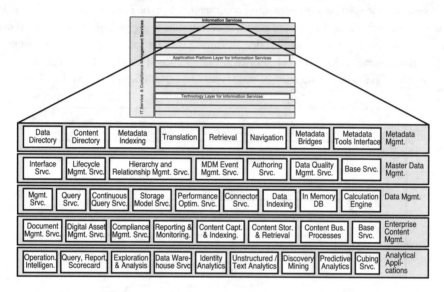

Figure 6.3   Information Services Layer

The Application Platform Layer for Information Services consists of the following categories:

- **Human Interaction Services**—In this category, we outline nodes representing Presentation and Personalization Services often found in a portal environment. This layer also includes Search and Query Services that provide for interactive selection, extraction, and formatting of stored information from information resources. Mashup Services representing lightweight web front-end applications that combine information or capabilities from existing information sources are included. Embedded Analytics are also categorized in Human Interaction Services because with those capabilities, you can extract elements in the text of a presentation interface for which analytical enrichment should happen. We also consider Business Performance Services, implementing the monitoring of business processes and the establishment of key threshold values for comparison. Finally, to display associated real-time, data we include interactive Dashboard Services.

- **Connectivity and Interoperability Services**—In this category, we outline services that are usually implemented by an Enterprise Service Bus (ESB).[13] These are ESB Connector Services relevant to decouple application systems from underlying information resources. Formatting and Routing components are required to provide a

---

[13] See also the detailed descriptions and deployment scenarios of ESB services in [4].

centralized capability for dealing with message formats coherently by the appropriate target systems and for managing the message routing paths and alternative channels. With Service Broker and Registry Services, dynamic look-up mechanisms are provided for information about service endpoints and messages. This means that when changes occur in the service endpoint environment, the associated ESB Messaging and Mediation Services (which are also included in this layer) don't have to change. For data integration and data exchange purposes, we introduce the Orchestration Services that act as an intermediary service for the data transaction. It provides functions such as service aggregation and orchestration controlling the data flow between the data systems. Likewise, Publish and Subscribe Services can help to simplify the task of getting business messages and transactions to a wide, dynamic, and potentially large audience in a timely manner. With Queue Manager Services, we provide a collection of capabilities particularly for the clustering of message queues and related areas of workload balancing.

- **Enterprise Information Integration Services**—This type of service (see also more details in Chapter 8) includes Deployment Services, Discovery Services, Profiling Services, Cleansing Services, Transformation Services, Replication Services, Federation Services, and Streaming Services. With information virtualization, we point out the difference between virtualization on the information level versus the infrastructure level. In the context of information virtualization, we consider design aspects such as data federation that virtualizes data from multiple disparate information sources. This type of virtualization creates an integrated view into distributed information without creating data redundancy while federating both Structured and Unstructured Data. Data and Information Integration is a widely used business scenario that includes new requirements such as management and scale-out capabilities in a near-real-time environment.

- **Common Infrastructure Services**—Within the scope of EIA, we focus on Directory and Security Services, Message and Web Service Gateway Services, Business Process Services, e-mail Services, Instant Messaging Services, and Data Masking Services. Instant messaging as part of Collaboration Services is considered as the exchange of text messages through a software application in real-time. Generally included as an instant messaging capability is the ability to easily see whether a chosen friend, co-worker, or "buddy" is online and connected through the selected service. Instant messaging differs from e-mail services in the immediacy of the message exchange. Concerning e-mail services regulatory compliance, legal discovery and storage management requirements drive more organizations to consider advanced service qualities such as e-mail archiving. We include Remote Copy Services, which we discuss in the context of business resiliency and service qualities in the recoverability domain. Remote Copy Services include peer-to-peer remote copy (PPRC), extended remote copy (XRC), FlashCopy,[14]

---

[14] FlashCopy is an IBM feature supported on various IBM storage devices that enables you to make nearly instantaneous copies of entire logical volumes or data sets.

and concurrent copy. Data Masking Services are needed to protect sensitive data while used during development and testing of data transformation services. This is required to use real data, which is masked to ensure privacy. Data masking techniques translate the original values of the real data to new values while maintaining patterns and value distribution of the real data. In general, Data Masking Services[15] help to comply with privacy and security requirements and support Information Governance.

- **Infrastructure Virtualization and Provisioning Services**—We have focused on storage virtualization services and related provisioning capabilities. Storage virtualization services simplify storage infrastructure by combining the physical capacity from multiple disk and tape storage systems into a single logical storage pool, which can be centrally managed. With the use of Resource Mapping and Configuration Support Services, changes to the storage infrastructure can be automatically administered. We include the Scheduling Services, representing node types that trigger batch jobs and job stream execution based on real-time events. They notify users when unusual conditions happen in the infrastructure or batch scheduling activities such as the provisioning of additional storage resources. The Provisioning Services provide for an automation capability to provision capacity from a single point of control including the management of LUNs[16] or copy services across the storage environment. The Workload Management Services are capabilities that can be used to manage exceptions when existing infrastructure resources cannot cope with the required SLAs.

In Figure 6.4, you can see the Application Platform Layer for Information Services in the framework of standard node types.

The Technology Layer for Information Services consists of the following elements:

- **Network Services**—This category of components includes Transport and Semantic Services that provide interfaces and protocols for reliable, transparent, end-to-end data transmission across communication networks. Socket Connection Services are provided to support distributed end-points for communications using the TCP/IP protocol. In the context of highly scalable, multi-threaded communication types, we introduce those services that also represent message queue interfaces and listener programming code. In addition, Distributed File and Name Services provide transparent remote file access and mechanisms for unique identification of resources within a distributed system environment. The Routing and Switching Services are used in the context of storage area networks that encompass capabilities of inspecting data packets as they are received, determining the source and destination device of each packet, and forwarding them appropriately. We also introduce Load Balancing Services to route transaction or data

---

[15] The recent Forrester report (see [5]) outlines why Data Masking Services should be part of the EIA.

[16] LUN is the logical unit number assigned to a SCSI protocol entity, the only one that might be addressed by the actual input/output (I/O) operations.

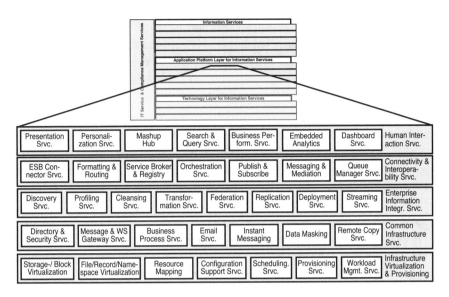

Figure 6.4 Application Platform Layer for Information Services

requests to different infrastructure resources, often in a round-robin fashion.[17] Because load balancing requires multiple nodes, it is usually combined with failover and backup services. The Reverse Proxy Services, typically used as part of an authentication mechanism, is a major node type for data protection services (see also Chapter 5).

- **Operating System Services**—Within this level, the Batch Processing component supports the capability to queue jobs and manage the sequencing of job processing based on job control commands and lists of data. In addition, File System Services allow the management and transfer of local or remote files. File and Directory Synchronization Services refer to the coordination of simultaneous threads or processes to complete file operations or the process of synchronizing directory information. Command Utilities allow the execution of command scripts and provide for editing files and moving files in the file system. The Domain or Protocol Firewall node type is often deployed to a specially designated computer that is separate from the rest of the network so that no incoming request can get to private network resources. There are a number of firewall screening methods, such as the domain or protocol-oriented methods. In these cases, the firewall screens requests to make sure they come from acceptable domain names or Internet Protocol addresses. Encryption is another service that provides for encoding data so that it can be read only by someone who possesses an appropriate key or some

---

[17] Round-robin algorithm means that you spend a fixed amount of time per requestor. Other algorithms exist, such as priority-based algorithms (most important requestors first) or first-come-first-serve algorithms.

other piece of identifying information. We include Caching Services as important components for high-performance requirements. For instance, caching can be implemented as part of database management systems. In environments with high demand on performance, work files that might be scanned many times can be cached in dedicated virtual memory pools, which in turn are immediately available for joined operations.

- **Physical Device Level**—This level includes all components in the networked storage environment[18] that handle the physical aspects of storage systems, disk arrays, or other types of block subsystems.[19] This type of node handles functionality that is not exposed to other elements in the networked storage environment. The File and Record Subsystem represents the interface between upper-layer applications and the storage resources. Database applications such as Microsoft SQL Server and IBM DB2 use a record format as processing units, whereas most other applications expect to process files. For the purpose of elaborating business resiliency patterns, we introduce the Secondary Storage Device node type. We use this node type as backup storage intended as a copy of the storage that is actively in use so that, if the primary storage medium such as a hard disk fails and data is lost on that medium, it can be recovered from the copy. The System Interface Module represents host attachment capabilities that address key aspects of particular types of connections such as Fibre Channel (FC) and Internet Small Computer System Interface (iSCSI) protocols. We include the Remote Management Interface node type to provide for remote access to infrastructure components. Services such as storage management services might be outsourced to an external service provider that oversees the company's storage and information systems. Outsourcing demands secure interfaces in the management environment. Functions of a managed storage management service include round-the-clock monitoring and management of storage systems, overseeing patch management, and storage assignments.

Clustering is another node type that can be implemented purely on a device level (in-box clustering) and is based on fail-over technique0s in the networked storage environment. A storage cluster is two or more devices (computers, controllers, Network-Attached Storage [NAS][20] appliances, and so on) that work together to provide access to a common pool of storage. Clusters can be active/active, where both nodes process data all the time, or they can be active/passive with primary nodes that process requests under normal conditions and standby nodes that deal with requests only when the primary fails. Also in scope are Partitioning Services of database management systems that are either

---

[18] See more details in the Storage Networking Industry Association (SNIA) documentation in [6].

[19] According to SNIA [6], information is ultimately stored on disk or tape as contiguous bytes of data known as blocks. Blocks are written to or read from physical storage, represented as a block subsystem in the Shared Storage Model.

[20] NAS represents a centrally managed pool of network-attached storage devices.

in a single node or across multiple nodes. Using a partitioned database enables administrators to maximize the scalability and capacity of database management systems such as IBM DB2. Although the Database Partitioning Feature (DPF) of IBM DB2 is actually just a license and does not require any additional products, we use this feature as node type to flesh out operational scenarios in the area of near real-time BI.

In Figure 6.5, you can see the Technology Layer for Information Services in the framework of standard node types.

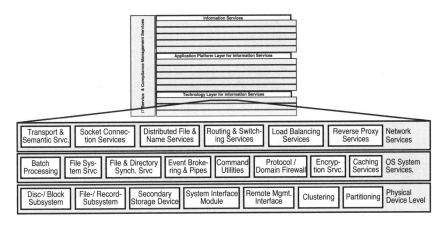

Figure 6.5 Technology Layer for Information Services

The IT Service & Compliance Management Services consist of the following elements:

- **Compliance Management Services**—These services include policy-based data management capabilities, regulations for nonerasable, nonrewritable (NENR) retention, requiring that the data not be changed, deleted, or disposed. Also included are capabilities for policy enforcement and lifecycle management, monitoring, analysis, simulation, and reporting for legal and operational purposes. They are complemented by the dependency management of storage resources.

- **Availability Management Services**—These services include redundant and hot-swappable components, Redundant Array of Independent Disks (RAID) protection, I/O path failover, self-healing disk rebuild, and automatic self-tuning procedures. To ensure appropriate fault management, proactive and reactive call home procedures and nondisruptive data migration mechanisms are included to allow for mitigation of potential availability exposures.

- **Retention Management Services**—These services include policy-based archiving that enables administrators to define rules that identify which content should be moved to what type of storage and how long that content should be kept. Also included is the migration of content on alternate storage tiers and the management of data placement across storage tiers to match service levels. For optimization purposes for storage usage, data can be moved from disk to tape and from generation to generation while maintaining data as NENR until deletion is permitted by applied retention policies.

- **Security Management Services**—These services include all capabilities to secure the company from information leaks and to provide secure access for information through encryption on either disk, tape, or both in a tiered environment. Also included are data encryption services before data is transmitted over the network or when saved to disk or tape, providing a safe and secure place to keep track of digital keys. Encryption services handle both application-managed capabilities (storage management technologies, such as Tivoli® Storage Manager [TSM]), system-managed capabilities (such as Data Facility Storage Management Subsystem [DFSMS][21]), and library-managed encryption. Intrusion detection, identity management, and related key lifecycle management complete the Security Management Services. Complementary components to Security Management Services are authentication, authorization, access control, Single Sign-On (SSO), digital signature, firewalls, and reverse proxy server, which we described in Chapter 5.

- **Capacity Management Services**—These services include the capacity management disciplines such as analyzing current and historic performance capacity, and workload management tasks to identify and understand applications that use the system. These also include capacity planning activities that are used to plan required infrastructure resources for the future.

- **Quality of Service Management Services**—These services include administration, configuration, and identification and specification of all component resources. In the scope of these Management Services are also registration services, utilities for the control of service billing, service triggering, account management, as well as health-monitoring and system-monitoring utilities. For Cloud Computing and the SaaS delivery model, the metering, monitoring, pricing, and billing services are described as separate components due to their particular importance in these delivery models. For all other scenarios, we condense them into this subcomponent.

In Figure 6.6, you can see the IT Service & Compliance Management Services within the framework of standard node types.

---

[21] DFSMS is a software suite that automatically manages data from creation to expiration on IBM mainframes. DFSMS provides allocation control for availability and performance, backup/recovery and disaster recovery services, space management, and tape management.

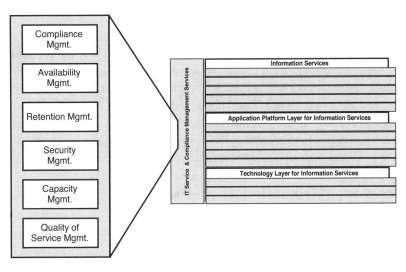

Figure 6.6 IT Service and Compliance Management Services

6.4.5 Logical Operational Model Relationship Diagram

Populated LOM relationship diagrams describe the placement of the solution's technical and application-level components across the geographic landscape. Details of the solution components with their specified nodes, locations, and access mechanisms are documented and can be analyzed for further elaboration. In Figure 6.7, we present an example of a populated LOM.

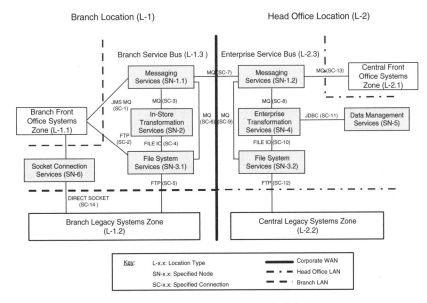

Figure 6.7 Example of a populated Logical Operational Model

The example originates in the retail industry. It represents a store integration system that should provide optimum balance between high performance and manageability of the services implemented. The LOM relationship diagram depicts how in-store integration is implemented in one internal branch location. This prevents unnecessary loading of the corporate WAN with store-only traffic and boosts overall performance. On the other hand, all enterprise-wide integration services are concentrated in one central place, namely the head office location, providing for easier manageability and scalability. In this example, you will find File System Services is one standard node type of the Technology Layer for Information Services, whereas Data Management Services can be found in the Data Services category of the Information Services.

6.5 Framework of Operational Patterns

To outline better solutions, it is good practice to capture and reuse the experience of past engagements. You do this by taking experiences and using them to build a repository of elements that become a framework from which architects can build future solutions. This repository of recurring solution elements is called the framework of operational patterns.[22] From the lessons learned applying Information Services, you can consider the "scope of integration" which is determined by typical deployment scenarios of these services. The scope of integration impacts the requirements for availability, resiliency, security, and, to a certain extent, scalability. The scope of integration can be categorized in three ways:

- **Discrete solution scope**—Predominately applies to the use of services in a single LOB
- **Integrated solution scope**—Typically signifies the use of services as shared services across the enterprise
- **Cross-domain solution scope**—Applies to the use of services in a multi-enterprise context, typically through the interconnection with partners or third-party providers

Figure 6.8 depicts a matrix of the node types in the Information Services and Application Platform Layer against their scopes of integration. The figure denotes typical integration scenarios (indicated by Yes) across the node types within the operational component layers. Note that the node types of the Technology Layer for Information Services are not illustrated; this is because their implementation depends heavily on the enterprise strategy for a shared IT environment.

Next, we elaborate on the implementation requirements for typical service qualities that drive the application of specific operational patterns.

6.5.1 The Context of Operational Patterns

In Section 6.3, we discussed the relevance of service qualities per data domain. The knowledge of typical data domain behavior within and across enterprises enables us to create reusable solution building blocks that shape the operational patterns. As introduced in the previous section, the scope of integration determines the requirements: availability, resiliency, security, and scalability. This is why we capture additional requirements according to the scope of integration.

---

[22] For easy reference to architecture patterns that can be considered a superset of operational patterns, see [7].

Operational Component Layer	Node Types within Operational Component Layers	Discrete (Single LoB)	Integrated (Enterprise)	Cross-Domain (Multi-Enterprise)
Information Services	Metadata Management	Yes	Yes	Yes
Information Services	Master Data Management		Yes	
Information Services	Data Management	Yes	Yes	
Information Services	Enterprise Content Management	Yes	Yes	
Information Services	Analytical Applications	Yes	Yes	
Application Platform Layer	Human Interaction Services	Yes		
Application Platform Layer	Connectivity & Interoperability Services		Yes	Yes
Application Platform Layer	Enterprise Information Integration Services	Yes	Yes	Yes
Application Platform Layer	Common Infrastructure Services		Yes	
Application Platform Layer	Infrastructure Virtualization & Provisioning	Yes	Yes	Yes

Scope of Integration

Figure 6.8   Determination of operational patterns by scope of integration

In Table 6.3, we collected all the relevant service qualities per data domain and the most applicable operational patterns. This table is not intended to be an exhaustive list of considerable runtime configuration. However, it is a good representation of operational considerations that apply the EIA Reference Architecture in the enterprise.

6.5.2 Near-Real-Time Business Intelligence Pattern

Near-real-time BI means you have access to information about business actions as soon after the fact as is justifiable based on the requirements. The implementation of near-real-time BI[23] involves the integration of a number of activities required in any DW or BI implementation; however, the importance of time is elevated. The Near-Real-Time Business Intelligence pattern, as shown in Figure 6.9, is comprised of the following:

- **Capturing data from operational systems as data are created or changed**—On the Application Server Node, transactional programs write system logs or archive the changes that occur to the data. The information from those logs or archives are captured. A transaction executes, picks up the data changes from the log, and provides them to the message queues of the Messaging Hub Node. In the case of the DB Server Nodes, database triggers or database change data capture mechanisms (see more details in Chapter 8) are used to provide the message hub with the data changes that occur.

- **Parallel Extract-Transform-Load (ETL) engines (Transformation Service)**—Before data can be placed in the DW, it must be extracted from the operational environment, cleansed, and transformed. This makes it usable for improved query processing and analysis. ETL processes have historically been batch-oriented. They are altered to run on a

---

[23] To learn how to implement IBM DB2 as a near real-time BI solution, see [8].

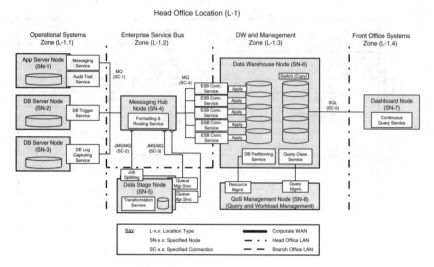

Figure 6.9   Near-Real-Time Business Intelligence operational pattern

continuous or near-continuous basis. Additionally, ETL processes are deployed as a service, which can be requested when it is needed. Running multiple Transformation Service processes in parallel (Data Stage Nodes) is the mechanism for getting data into the DW as quickly as possible. Parallel technology operates to split the largest integration jobs into subsets (partition parallelism) and links these subsets concurrently across all available processors (pipeline parallelism). This combination of pipeline and partition parallelism can deliver linear scalability (defined as an increase in performance proportional to the number of processors) and makes hardware the only mitigating factor to performance.

- **Data buffer between Transformation Services and Apply Services**—The Message Hub Node acts as a data buffer and feeds the Apply Services in an independent way. By keeping the Apply Services independent from the Transformation Services, you have more control of what techniques are used to accomplish the balance between updating and querying.

- **Partitions of the target DW table**—For each partition of the DW, there is a message queue that provides input messages to the Apply Services. The Apply Services then take the messages and update the appropriate database partition.

- **Managing the concurrency of Update and Query Services**—Resource and workload management (QoS Management Node) becomes even more important in a near real-time environment. The Operational Model must be able to manage task execution and control priorities to assure appropriate service levels. The capabilities of query management enable you to regulate your database's query workload so that small queries and high-priority queries can run promptly, and your system resources are used efficiently. On the

(continued following Table 6.3)

Table 6.3 Deduction of Operational Patterns per Data Domain

Data Domain	Specific Requirements According to Scope of Integration	Derived Operational Patterns (Selection and Reuse)	Comment
Analytical Data	**Discrete and Integrated:** Change, flexibility, and speed are key requirements for staying in business. For instance, strategic decisions are made from historical data, which might be contained in a DW. Thus, the emerging requirement is the capability to provide current information to stakeholders, also called dynamic warehousing. That means that you have to get the data into the DW in a much timelier manner, also known as near-real-time BI. **Integrated:** Capture, Deliver, Transform, and Apply functions are part of the DW process flow. For a near-real-time scenario, many techniques can be employed to capture data as it is created. Maximum throughput and scalability are often the requirements for the entire process flow, including integration and aggregation of data. To allow independent processing through the DW flow, you can also utilize asynchronous messaging middleware (such as ESB). In this case, the ESB has to take care of reliably delivering the message to the DW. The messaging hub is responsible for routing the messages, in most cases, to highly scalable destination queues at multiple locations and perhaps even for reformatting the messages with a high throughput.	*Near-Real-Time Business Intelligence pattern* *Data Integration and Aggregation Runtime pattern* *ESB Runtime for Guaranteed Data Delivery pattern* *Real-Time Data Streams Advanced Analytics pattern* (This pattern is introduced and used in Chapter 14)	Typically, DW processes are batch, rather than near real time. They follow a fairly standard ETL scenario. The batch update window for most companies, particularly in a global economy, is shrinking. This is just one more requirement that fuels the move toward near real time. DWs must begin to support continuous updating to make available the most current data and enable continuous user access, all requirements for near-real-time BI.

Table 6.3   Deduction of Operational Patterns per Data Domain

Data Domain	Specific Requirements According to Scope of Integration	Derived Operational Patterns (Selection and Reuse)	Comment
Operational Data	**Discrete and Integrated:** Along with data volumes, there is a growing need for 24-hour-a-day, 7-day-a-week access to the data. For transactional systems handling Operational Data, these are typical requirements for high availability and disaster recovery. This requires capabilities such as providing additional hardware and software resources that will improve the length of time it takes to recover from an error situation. **Integrated:** For integrated operational systems, there are even more requirements for high availability and disaster recovery because more systems and operational data depend on each other.	*Continuous Availability and Resiliency pattern*	When a site fails, it can remain nonoperational for any length of time. With proper planning, you can resume the operation of information systems handling Operational Data elsewhere. Although a site cannot be made 100 percent failure-proof, the information such as data in the database can be saved, and operations using the same data can be resumed at another site that uses specific disaster recovery scenarios.
Master Data	**Integrated:** When the MDM system is deployed as a Registry Hub Master Data model, the data is mainly stored in legacy systems and can be consistently viewed only by a federated query for key attributes in the connected systems. This fact requires high availability across all affected tiers in the system.	*Multi-Tier High Availability for Critical Data pattern*	Load balancing techniques and high-availability services implemented as database replication capabilities provide for high availability for Master Data deployed in any style.

Table 6.3 Deduction of Operational Patterns per Data Domain

Data Domain	Specific Requirements According to Scope of Integration	Derived Operational Patterns (Selection and Reuse)	Comment
Unstructured Data	**Discrete and Integrated:** Resource management services such as Document Resource Manager components are critical resources because the content and its metadata are the most vulnerable data in the solution. Typically multinode high availability is needed to secure Unstructured Data.	*Content Resource Manager Service Availability pattern*	Much of a company's digitized information is Unstructured Data, including rich media streaming, website content, facsimiles, and computer output. Access is critical to enable a complete view of the entire information available to solve a business need.
Metadata	**Discrete and Integrated:** The Metadata Federation Services provide a set of capabilities for sourcing, sharing, storing, and reconciling a comprehensive spectrum of metadata including business metadata and technical metadata. For these capabilities, a secure and continuous access to this data is required. **Cross-Domain:** For cross domain Metadata there are even more requirements for continuous access.	*Federated Metadata pattern*	Metadata-driven connectivity is typically shared across system resources, and connection objects are reusable across functions. This is the reason why access to dynamic metadata during runtime is vital; in addition, error handling and high-performance data access are important service-level characteristics.
Specific Application Platform Services—Mashup Hub	**Discrete:** Mashup services do not have comprehensive availability requirements because they are typically built for temporary purposes or for specific LOB functions. However, connectivity and security play a vital role, predominately because these services require proxy services for external feeds.	*Mashup Runtime and Security pattern*	Usually widgets run in the browser and access domains other than the one from which the mashup application was loaded. This requires the application of specific security patterns.

Table 6.3   Deduction of Operational Patterns per Data Domain

Data Domain	Specific Requirements According to Scope of Integration	Derived Operational Patterns (Selection and Reuse)	Comment
Other Application Platform and IT Service & Compliance Management Services	**Discrete and Integrated:** In the enterprise, data protection requirements are driven by a variety of reasons such as greater data security, integrity, retention, audit capability, and privacy. There are also requirements for the ongoing discovery of end-to-end relationships of system components to control the dependencies between software applications and physical components. Information lifecycle management and retention management are also required for regulatory compliance. It involves not only data movement, but also encompasses scheduled deletion. **Cross-Domain:** In the inter-enterprise context, private and public clouds are an evolving delivery model. In that context, requirements for virtualization of storage, file systems, and information resources are mandatory. In addition, automated service lifecycle management is common for an efficiently managed Cloud Computing delivery model.	*Compliance and Dependency Management for Operational Risk pattern* *Retention Management pattern* *Encryption and Data Protection pattern* *File System Virtualization pattern* *Storage Pool Virtualization pattern* *Automated Capacity and Provisioning Management pattern*	Along with virtualization techniques across system resources, the IT Service & Compliance Management Services in the Component and Operational Model encompass most of the required capabilities.

other hand, the resource management capabilities can monitor the behavior of transactions that run against the DW and indicate when transactions use too much of a particular resource. Appropriate rules specify the action to take, such as to change the priority of the transactions. This can also be applied in a partitioned environment utilizing resource management daemons that can be started on each partition of a partitioned database.

- **Enterprise Service Bus queues**—The queues managed by the Messaging Hub Node are critical in a real-time environment. They are part of a messaging oriented infrastructure, which has the responsibility for guaranteed delivery of messages to their designated end points. This is a separate operational pattern which will be discussed later.

6.5.3 Data Integration and Aggregation Runtime Pattern

Data integration and aggregation build on the solid foundation of existing data management solutions. Data integration and aggregation provide solutions for transparently managing both the volume and diversity of data that exists in enterprises across the LOBs. Database federation[24] is one mechanism that can be considered for those cases in which data movement is not possible or ideal. Database federation enables queries to be processed that reference data in multiple databases. The integration and federation logic determine the optimal way to access the databases that are involved and to combine the results from the different sources to produce the final query result. Federation is a good alternative when data currency is critical; that is, when you need to see the data as it exists at any given moment. In addition, it provides a way to quickly enable ad-hoc queries across the enterprise and it enables updating.

The function of the Data Integration Node shown in Figure 6.10 is typically invoked by an Application Server Node, which is often implemented separately from the Data Integration functionality. The Data Integration Node processes the request by utilizing its metadata, which defines the data sources. Then, it passes the requests on to the appropriate data sources. The results that are returned from each individual data source must then be aggregated and normalized by the integration and federation logic so that the results appear to be from one "virtual" data source.

In some cases, you need specialized processing designed and optimized for reading and writing data from or to data stores and for transforming the data, often in sophisticated ways, as it streams over the network in a near-real-time mode. Multiple data sources might be involved in the process and reasonably sophisticated filtering, cleansing, and transformations (Data Stage Node) might occur along the way. For this reason, we have introduced another mechanism that is specialized for handling efficient throughput of large batches of records (from branch office data services) that require extensive transformation, or for fast throughput of individual records in near-real-time. The data from the branch office might be stored in files and accessed through file I/O routines (processed by the Application Server Node) or it might be stored in a database

---

[24] See more details about how to implement data integration with DB2 Information Integrator in [9].

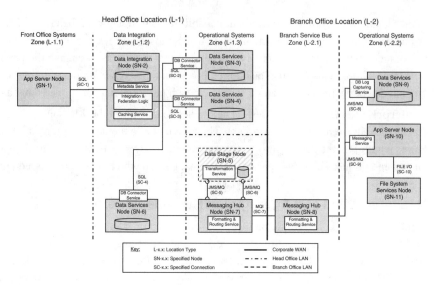

Figure 6.10   Data Integration and Aggregation operational pattern

with more structured and managed access methods (Data Services Node). In the case of Unstructured Data, the information is provided through file I/O routines, transformed to messages by the application server logic, and submitted to the Messaging Hub Node representing the ESB. In the case of integrating with Data Services Nodes, database triggers or change data capture mechanisms are used to provide the Messaging Hub Node with the data changes that occur.

The same mechanism can be used when access to the data is under the control of the owning applications, which limits the ways in which the user can access or change the underlying data. To ensure that users do not make unintended or unauthorized changes to critical business data, we recommend using the data integration and aggregation as replication scenario. Replication of data often demands two-way synchronization with additional capabilities to ensure that conflicting updates are not applied to either data store.

6.5.4 ESB Runtime for Guaranteed Data Delivery Pattern

We already explored the Near-Real-Time Business Intelligence pattern and why its input to business decision-making processes demands a move to a more timely fashion. This type of requirement involves the integration of various technologies such as message-based communication mechanisms, guaranteed delivery of messages over the network, assurance of once-only delivery of messages, different communications protocols, dynamically distributed workloads across available resources, and recovery procedures after message system and connectivity problems.

The ESB runtime environment enables you to support various messaging types including datagram, request/reply, and publish/subscribe. In the datagram paradigm, the messaging function sends or receives messages with no expectation of a reply being generated. With a request/reply, when a message is sent, you expect to receive a reply, and the messaging function uses a correlation identifier to associate a reply with its request when it arrives back. When publish/subscribe is used, the messaging function sends a message to a topic and interested parties subscribed to that topic receive the message.[25]

The core function of service management capabilities is to protect messages from loss. With asynchronous messaging, the producer, consumer, and the means of communication don't have to be available at the same time because the messaging hub can safely pass the message from one party to another when they are available. However, in the new world of near real-time environment messages are time-critical and need to be processed sooner rather than later, so the systems that process them must be highly available. This is the reason why the referred ESB Runtime for Guaranteed Data Delivery pattern, as shown in Figure 6.11, is different from previous considerations where overnight batch processing or spooling data were enough to

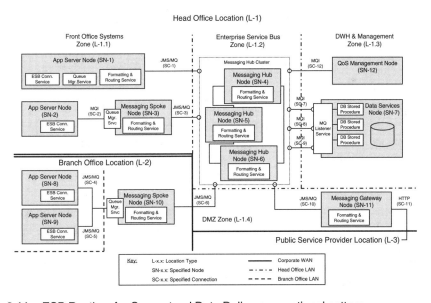

Figure 6.11   ESB Runtime for Guaranteed Data Delivery operational pattern

---

[25] See more details about how to apply hub and spoke design architectures that offer a combination of a centralized enterprise DW and a set of dependent data marts in [10].

satisfy the requirements. In summary, the pattern represents the combination of the following requirements:

- Messaging middleware must be continuously available and reliable.
- Queues must scale to the power required to handle the throughput.
- The system must be configurable for quality of service reasons, supporting tuning tasks to avoid contention and bottlenecks.

The ESB Runtime for Guaranteed Data Delivery pattern can be used in the context of message-based replication techniques; these are discussed in Chapter 8. It can also be used for Master Data synchronization from a MDM System, which is deployed using the Transactional Hub implementation style. The pattern is comprised of the following building blocks:

- **Messaging Hub clusters for high service availability**—To provide high availability, there is the capability of joining Message Hub Nodes together in a Messaging Hub cluster. Messaging Hub clusters allow multiple instances of the same service to be hosted through multiple Messaging Hubs. Applications such as the Data Services Node requesting a particular service can connect to any Messaging Hub in the cluster. When the Data Services Node makes requests for the service, the Messaging Hub to which they are connected automatically workload balances these requests across all available Messaging Hub Nodes that host an instance of that service. This allows a pool of machines to exist within the cluster.

- **Hub and Spoke mechanism for scalability and high throughput**—Connecting to a Messaging Hub Node from an application server has limitations. A network connection is placed between the application and the Messaging Hub, which has performance implications, especially over longer distances. This also requires that a network connection be available for the application to operate. This approach can be scaled, without alteration to the application, to include multiple Messaging Hub Nodes. Applications accessing a service can have a Messaging Hub hosted on the same node, providing a fast connection to the infrastructure, and gain asynchronous communication with the service hosted on another Messaging Hub. Alternatively, applications accessing a service can connect as clients (Messaging Spoke Node) over a fast network to a Messaging Hub Node, for example, all applications accessing a service in a branch office location. With this approach, the messaging environment can also provide an external interface by providing a Messaging Gateway Node for accessing services over the Internet.

- **Reliability**—Large proportions of the messages that flow through a message queuing infrastructure contain business-critical data. Therefore, it is important for a message queuing infrastructure to provide assurances that these messages are not lost. Messages containing business-critical data can be marked as persistent. In this case, the Messaging Hub assures exactly one delivery of persistent messages. This means that the

Messaging Hub does not discard a persistent message through network failures, delivery failures, or planned restarts of the queuing service. Each Messaging Hub keeps a failure-tolerant log, sometimes referred to as a journal, of all actions performed on persistent messages. This protects against unplanned abrupt failures, causing persistent messages to be lost.

- **Quality of Service Monitoring**—Quality of service monitoring (QoS Management Node), in the context of a message queuing infrastructure, involves measuring the number and duration of actions that occur when services access queues or when messages pass through queues on intermediate nodes. You can use this information to derive performance and capacity information from those services and the infrastructure that supports them. This can be helpful when provisioning resources for a service or when deciding whether additional resources are needed to scale the capabilities of a service. Monitoring quality of service can also be useful to identify any sudden or gradual changes in usage patterns to anticipate problems before they occur.

6.5.5 Continuous Availability and Resiliency Pattern

High availability and continuous availability are often confused. High availability is a component of continuous availability. High availability focuses on reducing the downtime for unplanned outages, and continuous operations focus on reducing the downtime for planned outages. The sum of high availability and continuous operations equals continuous availability, and enables "never stop" of a set of information systems. For example, the data services for managing the operational data created through an e-commerce operational application must be available 24 hours, 7 days a week because if someone wants to buy something online on a Saturday night, the online shop shouldn't be closed. Therefore, this Continuous Availability and Resiliency pattern, as shown in Figure 6.12, can be used to satisfy the most critical demands regarding availability and resiliency of Information Services.

Synchronous and asynchronous data transfer represents two methods to replicate data. Before selecting a data replication technology, one must understand the differences between the methods used and the business impact. When using synchronous data transfer such as Metro Mirror (PPRC),[26] the application writes are written to the primary Block Subsystem Node and then forwarded on to the secondary Block Subsystem Node. When the data has been committed to both the primary and secondary nodes, an acknowledgement that the write is complete is sent to the application. Because the application must wait until it receives the acknowledgement before executing its next task, there is a slight performance impact. Furthermore, as the distance between the primary and secondary nodes increases, the write I/O response time increases due to signal latency. The goals of synchronous replication are zero or near-zero loss of data and quick

---

[26] Metro Mirror (also known as Peer-to-Peer Remote Copy [PPRC]) is an IBM term for a synchronous long-distance copy option that constantly updates a secondary copy of a volume to match changes made to a source volume.

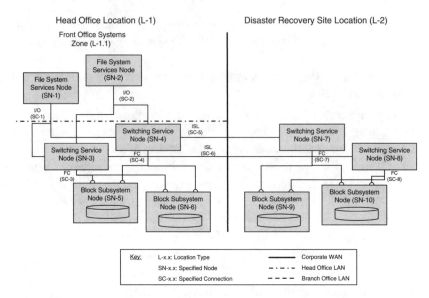

Figure 6.12   Continuous Availability and Resiliency operational pattern

recovery times from failures that occur at the primary site. In addition, synchronous replication can be costly because it requires high-bandwidth connectivity.

With asynchronous replication, for instance by Global Mirror (XRC),[27] the application writes to the primary Block Subsystem Node and receives an acknowledgement that the I/O is complete as soon as the write is committed on the primary node. The write to the secondary Block Subsystem Node is completed in the background. Because applications do not have to wait for the completion of the I/O to the secondary node, asynchronous solutions can be used at virtually unlimited distances with negligible impact to application performance. In addition, asynchronous solutions do not require as much bandwidth as the synchronous solutions and they tend to be less costly.

When selecting a remote copy solution, a business impact analysis should be performed to determine which solution meets the businesses requirements while ensuring your service delivery objectives continue to be met. The maximum amount of transaction loss that is acceptable to the business (RPO)[28] is one measurement used to determine which remote copy technology

---

[27] Extended Remote Copy (XRC), also known as zSeries Global Mirror, is IBM's high-end solution for asynchronous copy services.

[28] The recovery point objective (RPO) and the recovery time objective (RTO) are two specific parameters that are closely associated with recovery. RPO dictates the allowable data loss, and RTO indicates how long you can go without a specific application.

should be deployed. If the business is capable of tolerating a loss of committed transactions, an asynchronous solution provides the most cost-effective solution. When no loss of committed transactions is the objective, a synchronous remote copy must be deployed. In this case, the distance between the primary and secondary Block Subsystem Nodes and the application's capability to tolerate the increased response times must be factored into the decision process.

6.5.6 Multi-Tier High Availability for Critical Data Pattern

Redundancy is a critical and well understood means of achieving high availability. This includes redundant components, redundant systems, and redundant data. Hardware components can fail, and software quality varies from release to release, making other techniques for high availability equally important. The Multi-Tier High Availability for Critical Data pattern shown in Figure 6.13 represents data access to the MDM Node in a highly available fashion. In this example, the MDM system is deployed as Registry Hub, which means that Master Data is stored in legacy systems (represented by downstream Data Services Nodes), and can be consistently viewed only with a federated query for key attributes in the MDM Node and other Master Data from the Data Services Node.

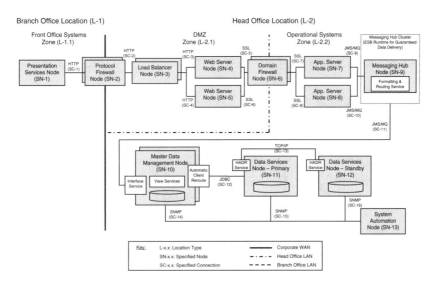

Figure 6.13   Multi-Tier High Availability for Critical Data operational pattern

The Multi-Tier High Availability for Critical Data pattern incorporates two redundancy modes for achieving high availability:

- **Active/active mode**—Two services reside in two nodes (for example, Web Server Node on SN-4 and Web Server Node on system SN-5) that are configured as a horizontal cluster. Horizontal clustering exists when multiple instances of an application are located across multiple physical nodes. In this pattern, the Web Server Node (HTTP server) distributes requests to the cluster of Application Server Nodes. This clustering technique enable the overall system to service a higher application load than provided by a single node configuration because the number of Application Server Nodes can load balance the transactions across the cluster in conjunction with the Web Server Nodes.

- **Active/standby mode**—One node is configured as the primary to run the full software stack, and the other node is configured as a hot standby (for example, Data Services Node SN-11 as primary system and Data Service Node SN-12 as standby system). The active/standby mode is also known as fail-over platform clustering technique. In this example, we use a High Availability Disaster Recovery (HADR) service[29] acting as database replication capability that provides a high availability solution for the referenced Master Data. The Data Services Node can fail from any number of factors: environmental (power/temperature), hardware, network connectivity, software, or human intervention. The HADR service protects against data loss by continually replicating data changes from the source database, called the primary, to a target database, called the standby. The replication is done by transmitting the log records from the primary Data Services Node to the Standby Node. The Data Services Standby Node replays all the log records to its copy of the database, keeping it synchronized with the Primary Node. The Standby Node is in a continuous roll-forward mode and is always in a state of near-readiness, so the takeover to the Standby Node is fast. We also outlined how to seamlessly redirect the federated query from the MDM Node by using Automatic Client Reroute services[30] and retrying logic in the application.

In summary, the configuration for both modes is similar. The advantage of the active/active mode configuration is lower hardware costs; the disadvantage is that the service performance is reduced when a failover occurs. The advantage of the active/standby mode configuration is steady performance; the disadvantage is that redundant hardware is needed.

You can consider additional component redundancy in the Multi-Tier Availability for Critical Data pattern:

- **Load Balancer Node**—The pattern outlines a high availability implementation with a primary and backup load balancer (shadow node, not explicitly specified). The backup would be a similarly configured load balancer that has a heartbeat with the primary. If

---

[29] IBM's DB2 database has a HADR feature that provides a high availability solution for both partial and complete site failures. HADR protects against data loss by replicating data changes from a source database to a target database. Oracle has a comparable feature that is called Real Application Cluster (RAC).

[30] Automatic Client Reroute is a feature of DB2 HADR that enables the client application to reconnect to the server after a loss of communication.

the primary load balancer fails, the backup initiates a takeover function. This feature is available in most load balancers. It is a software-based solution that provides dynamic load balancing across multiple server nodes, groups of servers, and geographic locations in a highly scalable, highly available fashion.

- **Firewall Services**—The pattern outlines the redundant use of firewalls to provide for load balancing and availability benefits (shadow node, not explicitly specified). The Protocol Firewall Node is typically implemented as an IP router and is basically configured with filters. It protects from access to unauthorized services in the DMZ zone and can also avoid inadequate LAN bandwidth usage. The Domain Firewall Node prevents unauthorized access to servers on the internal network by limiting incoming requests to a tightly controlled list of trusted servers in the DMZ.

- **Web Server Node**—As already mentioned, the Web Server Nodes are implemented as redundant server nodes in a horizontal cluster configuration and load balanced with a load balancer (IP sprayer) to give greater availability and throughput. Each Web Server Node should be able to handle any request identically.

- **Application Server Node**—This node appears as a group of independent nodes interconnected and working together as a single system. A load-balancing mechanism, such as an IP spraying, as previously discussed, can be used to intercept the HTTP requests and redirect them to the appropriate node on the cluster through an HTTP plug-in, providing scalability, load balancing, and failover as part of the Web application server of choice.

- **Messaging Hub Node (Cluster)**—Queues managed by the Messaging Hub Node are part of the messaging-oriented infrastructure, which has the responsibility for guaranteed delivery of messages to their designated end points. See section 6.5.4 for details of this operational pattern.

- **Master Data Management Node and Data Services Node (representing critical data in the registry style of MDM)**—The MDM Node is deployed as a Registry Hub, which means that a thin slice of core data is stored in the data repository of the MDM Node. In addition, there is a store of cross-referencing keys that indicates which Data Services Node is the source for other attributes of Master Data. The access to particular Master Data is implemented as a composite Master Data service representing a federated query of key attributes from the MDM Node and other Master Data attributes from the Data Services Node. The operational pattern illustrates the fail-over platform clustering technique using HADR database replication capabilities and automated rerouting services implemented on the Registry Hub.

- **System Automation Node**—The System Automation Node provides high availability for any resource group that it manages by restarting all of its resources if it fails. For example, both the Data Services Node and the file system that are used by the database have start, stop, and monitor commands. Therefore, system automation policies can be implemented to manage these resources automatically.

6.5.7 Content Resource Manager Service Availability Pattern

ECM systems with multi-tiered infrastructure can inherently contribute to availability by segregating functions and can enable increased redundancy, increased scalability, and simplified management among components. In an ECM system, there are several components within the tiers that need to be taken into consideration when designing an end-to-end, high-availability system. We already discussed the Multi-Tier High Availability for Critical Data operational pattern, which covers the client tier, the presentation tier, and the data access tier (load balancing node, web server node, and application server node). This is also true for deployment scenarios of Content Management environments, particularly if you want to focus on Document Resource Manager components[31] that are critical because the content is the most vulnerable data within the solution. With database content, it is recommended that all databases are in a roll-forward recovery mode in case there is a database or file system failure. This enables you to restore a backup copy of the database and then apply the database logs, restoring to the point of failure or the last committed transaction and ensuring the data integrity of the system at the database level. With file system content, there are no roll-forward logs, thus replication of the content adds an additional level of protection in the event of disk or file system failure.

Multiple node configurations are common in Content Management environments. Typical layouts include a Document Library Node and a Document Resource Manager Node on different physical nodes as shown in Figure 6.14:

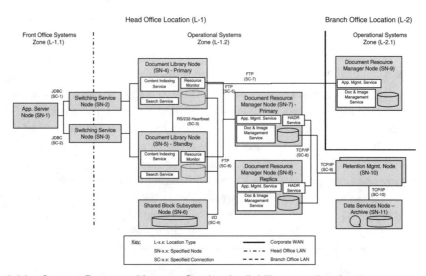

Figure 6.14   Content Resource Manager Service Availability operational pattern

---

[31] For example, IBM Content Manager has resource manager components that are specialized repositories that are optimized to manage the storage, archiving, retrieval, and delivery of enterprise content. See more details in [11].

- **Document Library Node**—This node manages the content metadata and is responsible for access control to all content. It maintains the indexing information for all multimedia content held in a Document Resource Manager Node. Users submit requests through the Document Library Node. The Document Library Node validates the access rights of the requesting client and then authorizes the client to directly access the object in the designated Document Resource Manager Node. The Document Library Node also maintains referential integrity between the indexing information and the objects themselves.

- **Document Resource Manager Node**—This node represents the repositories that contain the digitized content and manages the storage and retrieval of objects. The Document Resource Manager Node supports caching, replication, and hierarchical storage management when used in conjunction with Retention Management Nodes.[32]

- **Retention Management Node**—With this node, you can make copies of the data stored on storage pool volumes to other storage pool volumes. This is useful to safeguard the data on tape or optical volumes in case of corrupted data. For ECM environments, it is also common for Shared Block Subsystem Nodes to be used for sharing database logs and critical components that need to be installed and accessible on a shared disk technology. Typically, there are additional requirements when optical or tape libraries are involved; for example, a SCSI, SAN switch, or twin-tail connection will be needed for both the primary and backup machines to have physical connectivity in the event of a host failure.

6.5.8 Federated Metadata Pattern

Federation, in contrast to synchronization, leaves the data in its source. No data is imported into the target system when using the federation approach. Wrapper services, as shown in Figure 6.15, are used by the Metadata Federation Services Node to communicate with and retrieve data from remote data sources. They abstract the communication protocol and access mechanism of the remote data source to the Metadata Federation Services Node.

If the attribute is something that exists in an external Data Services Node and you wish to simply make it available for displaying additional detail about a Metadata object, then it would be best to make the data available by configuring it as a federated attribute.

The Metadata Federation Services Node usually provides a variety of services to other components of the system environment such as metadata access, metadata integration, metadata import and export, impact analysis, and search and query services. The Metadata Federation Services Node provides a common repository with facilities that are capable of sourcing, sharing, storing, and reconciling a comprehensive spectrum of metadata including Business Metadata and Technical Metadata.

Metadata-driven connectivity is shared across the nodes, and connection objects are reusable across functions. Connectors provide design-time importing of metadata, data browsing

---

[32] For instance, the IBM Tivoli Storage Manager is a physical representation of the Retention Management Node.

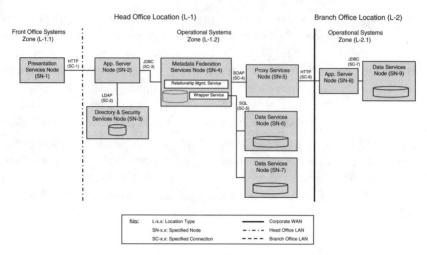

Figure 6.15   Federated Metadata operational pattern

and sampling, runtime dynamic metadata access, error handling, high functionality, and high performance runtime data access.

6.5.9 Mashup Runtime and Security Pattern

Various nodes represent the Mashup Runtime and Security operational pattern, as shown in Figure 6.16:

- **Presentation Services Node**—This node represents the Mashup runtime typically provided by a Web browser. The Web browser provides a JavaScript framework for rendering the Mashup user interface that consists of widgets. The Java script framework also allows for managing the interactions and linkage between the widgets, data sources (enterprise or public), and services acquired from other vendors.

- **Mashup Server**[33]—The Mashup Server component provides the runtime infrastructure for deploying and hosting Mashup applications. Three major components deployed on Mashup Builder Node, Mashup Catalog Service Node, and Mashup Widget Service Node provide an information management environment for IT and business professionals to unlock and share enterprise data, including Web, departmental, personal, and enterprise information. The Mashup Builder Node interfaces with these data sources to create Atom feeds. Similarly, the node can aggregate, transform (that is, apply operators and functions to filter or reconstruct), or sort data from one or more of the data sources to create a consolidated Atom feed, which is referred to as a *feed mashup*.

---

[33] For instance, a mashup server can be realized through the IBM Lotus Mashups lightweight mashup server. For an example using this pattern, see Chapter 12.

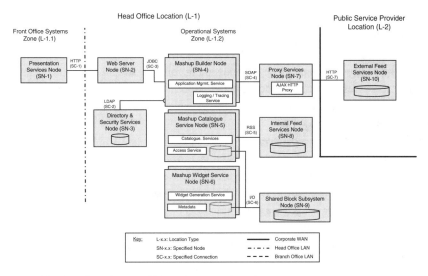

Figure 6.16   Mashup Runtime and Security operational pattern

- **Proxy Services Node**—This node enables widgets running in the browser Mashup Runtime component to access domains other than the one from which the Mashup application was loaded. Browsers enforce a "same origin" policy that prevents client-side scripts such as JavaScript (which widgets are based on) from loading content from an origin that has a different protocol, domain name, or port.

- **Internal Feed Services Node**—An internal system that provides XML data that supports Really Simple Syndication (RSS)[34] or Atom formats is considered an Internal Feed Services component. The formats and associated protocols are used to syndicate content that is updated frequently.

- **External Feed Services Node**—This node provides feed services from external resources.

6.5.10 Compliance and Dependency Management for Operational Risk Pattern

With today's renewed focus on ensuring business performance while protecting investors and the corporate brand, executives are prompted to reprioritize the importance of operational risk management within their organizations. Adding another layer of complexity to this problem is the

---

[34] RSS is a format for delivering regularly changing web content. Many news-related sites, weblogs, and other online publishers syndicate their content as an RSS feed to whoever wants it.

increasing demand for regulatory compliance. The Sarbanes-Oxley Act (SOX),[35] and Basel II[36] are examples of the international regulations, standards, and governing bodies that outline requirements for security and risk management.

The Compliance and Dependency Management for Operational Risk pattern, as shown in Figure 6.17, addresses formal and documented dependency and configuration management procedures, inter-relationships of information resources, and the impact of a single-configuration change on business applications and infrastructure services. For instance, questions such as, "What are the interdependences between business applications, software applications, and physical components?" or "Which storage resources are connected to particular application resources?" serve a number of important uses. They derive business-driven information lifecycle management policies involving data, improving accuracy of root-cause analysis in case of failures, accounting for storage usage on a per application basis, and reasoning about data and application availability and reliability. This kind of application and system relationships should be enabled through metadata exploitation and instantiation of specific nodes and services:

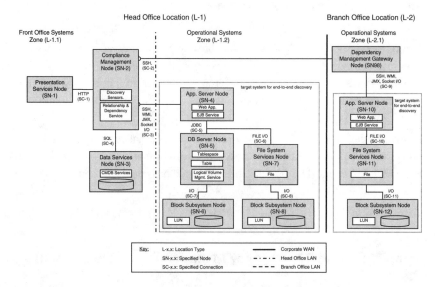

Figure 6.17   Compliance and Dependency Management for Operational Risk pattern

---

[35] The Sarbanes-Oxley Act of 2002 (often shortened to SOX and named for its sponsors Senator Paul Sarbanes and Representative Michael G. Oxley) is a law that was passed in response to financial scandals. See more details in [12].

[36] Basel II is the second of the Basel Accords, which are recommendations on banking laws and regulations issued by the Basel Committee on Banking Supervision.

- **Compliance Management Node**—Discovery is based on the scheduled execution of a discovery profile that defines what to discover and the depth of discovery. Core to the discovery process are light-weight discovery sensors that discover the infrastructure components, their configurations, and their dependencies. Discovery sensors are implementations for numerous kinds of target systems, middleware, and application components, and they use open and secure protocols and access mechanisms to discover the target systems. The discovery metadata is typically stored in the Configuration Management Database (CMDB)[37] and represented by the Data Services Node.

- **Relationship and Dependency Services**—To gather and analyze the data, a relationship and dependency service scans computers and other devices connected to a network and records information about their installed hardware and software. In addition, it examines the ways that middleware are configured to serve a particular application and the reliability of the underlying infrastructure as it relates to that application. The relationship and dependency service combines its discovered end-to-end application structure, infrastructure resources, and data relationships to construct an application-specific, end-to-end reliability assessment that can be used to indicate potential weaknesses in the enterprise infrastructure.

- **Dependency Management Gateway Node**—The management environment itself is targeted to discover the distributed systems across all domains and locations of the enterprise. This usually requires that the discovery requests need to cross firewalls to get to the target system. The Dependency Management Gateway Node provides an entity that helps discover those systems inside a firewall-protected zone so that you just have to open one port from the central Compliance Management Node to the Dependency Management Gateway Node (typically connected with SSH[38]).

6.5.11 Retention Management Pattern

Retention Management is about retaining corporate records for the minimum appropriate retention period to meet business and regulatory requirements (laws, policies, and regulations on the business). Most companies have some form of retention management or a set of retention rules according to various requirements such as:

- Compliance, industry regulations, and government regulations often impose different retention requirements for information systems and records.

- Fiscal requirements on record keeping.

---

[37] IBM Tivoli Application Dependency Discovery Manager represents a product mapping of this pattern. See more details in [13].

[38] SSH (Secure Shell) is a protocol for creating a secure connection between two computers.

- Business requirements, which can include auditing, the company's retention policy, a legal counsel opinion, or business continuity reasons.

- Other needs for administration of data.

Four major elements can be addressed by the Retention Management pattern, as shown in Figure 6.18, on the operational level:

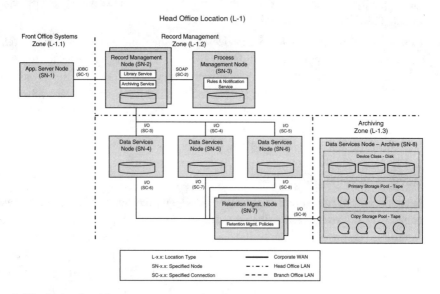

Figure 6.18   Retention Management operational pattern

- **Tiered storage management**—A tiered storage environment is designed to reduce the total cost of ownership of managing information. It can help with optimizing data costs and management and freeing expensive disk storage for the most valuable information.

- **Long-term data retention**—Not only are there numerous state and governmental regulations that must be met for data storage, but there are also industry-specific and company-specific ones. This pattern enables organizations to ensure that the correct information is kept for the correct period of time and is readily accessible whenever regulators or auditors request it.

- **Information lifecycle management (ILM)**—The underlying ILM involves more than just data movement; it encompasses scheduled deletion and regulatory compliance, too. Because decisions about moving, retaining, and deleting data are closely tied to application use of data, ILM is usually closely tied to application usage in a given business context.

- **Policy-based archive management**—Growth of information in corporate databases such as ERP systems and e-mail systems can make IT planners and administrators think about moving unused data off the high-cost disks. The pattern identifies database data that is no longer regularly accessed and moves it to an archive where it remains available. On the other hand, it defines and manages what to archive, when to archive, and how to archive to the back-end archive management system.

Multiple node configurations are common for retention management purposes. Typical layouts include Records Management Nodes that provide classification of business objects and Retention Management Nodes that provide data management in a storage hierarchy. The functionalities and responsibilities distributed to the various nodes are outlined as follows:

- **Application Server Node**—Provides a comprehensive user interface and user access to documents and other business objects and access to any associated record management processes.

- **Records Management Node**—Provides the core definitions for business objects such as record classes, record folders, and disposition schedules upon which the records management system is built. Records management security capabilities that are built on the underlying security model coupled with default security roles that determine functional user access.

- **Retention Management Node**—Hierarchical storage management (HSM) refers to the core function of the Retention Management Node that automatically distributes and manages data on disk, tape, or both by regarding devices of these types and potentially others as levels in a storage hierarchy.

- **Process Management Node**—Provides process services, supports business rules for processes, and provides e-mail notification capability. Typically, there are additional capabilities, such as process simulation and orchestration applications for monitoring and tuning the business processes.

- **Data Services Node**—The devices in this storage hierarchy range from fast, expensive devices to slower, cheaper, and possibly removable devices. The objectives are to minimize access time to data and maximize available media capacity. The Retention Management Node stores data objects on disk volumes and tape media that it groups into storage pools.

6.5.12 Encryption and Data Protection Pattern

In addition to regulatory requirements, there is a need for greater data security, integrity, retention, auditability, and privacy. Important and sensitive data can be protected in many ways. Data can be encrypted by means of special software programs, hardware adapters, facilities, or outside of the device where the data is stored. Encrypting data with software programs takes away processor power, and encrypting data with hardware requires additional investment in hardware for the computers.

The Encryption and Data Protection pattern shown in Figure 6.19 represents the encryption of data at a tape drive level. When the drive can offer efficient data compression, the drive first compresses the data, and then encrypts it, providing more efficient data storage and media usage. Encrypting in the drive also eliminates the need for any additional machines or appliances in the environment by offloading the encryption processing overhead on the drive. Because the drive might also process unencrypted workloads, the IT environment is further simplified, eliminating the need for separate drives to process data that does not need to be encrypted.

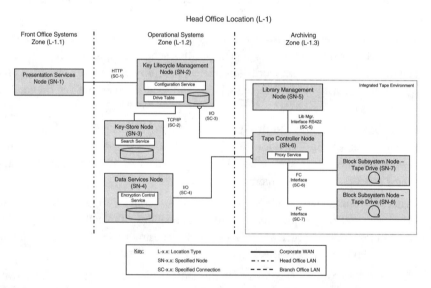

Figure 6.19   Encryption and Data Protection operational pattern

Technology has enabled increasingly sophisticated encryption algorithms. Today, there are several widely used encryption algorithms, including Triple DES (TDES)[39] and Advanced

---

[39] The Data Encryption Standard (DES) was developed by an IBM team around 1974 and adopted as a national standard in 1977. Triple DES is a minor variation of this standard and is three times slower than regular DES but can be billions of times more secure if used properly.

Encryption Standard (AES).[40] The Encryption and Data Protection pattern is comprised of the following building blocks:

- **Key Lifecycle Management Node**—For implementing the Encryption and Data Protection pattern, the Key Lifecycle Management Node is required to provide and manage keys. Key provisioning and key management can also be handled by the node. However, in the outlined pattern, system-managed implementation of encryption services are used. The tape drive table is used by the Key Lifecycle Management Node to track the tape devices that it supports. The tape drive table contains the list of drives that can communicate with the Key Lifecycle Management Node. The Key Lifecycle Management Node acts as a process awaiting key generation or key retrieval requests sent to it through a TCP/IP communication path.

- **Key-Store Node**—The Key-Store Node holds the certificates and keys (or pointers to the certificates and keys) used by the Key Lifecycle Management Node to perform cryptographic operations. Usually two types of encryption algorithms can be used: symmetric algorithms and asymmetric algorithms.[41] Symmetric keys such as 256-bit AES keys use a single key for both encryption and decryption. Symmetric key encryption is generally used for encrypting large amounts of data in an efficient manner. Asymmetric, or public/private encryption, uses a pair of keys. Data encrypted using one key can be decrypted using only the other key in the public/private key pair. When an asymmetric key pair is generated, the public key is typically used to encrypt, and the private key is typically used to decrypt.

- **Tape Encryption Management**—There are various options for implementing encryption management. With library-managed encryption, the *Library Management Node* controls whether a specific cartridge is encrypted. With system-managed encryption, the mechanism of encryption is determined at the tape drive level (Block Subsystem Node). For instance, when a read request is received by the Block Subsystem Node (tape drive), the drive sends the encrypted data key via the Tape Controller Node to the Key Lifecycle Management Node. This node verifies the tape device against the drive table entries. The Key Lifecycle Management Node fetches the corresponding private key from the Key-Store Node. Then the Key Lifecycle Management Node recovers the data key, which is then sent to the tape drive in a secure manner. The tape drive uses the data key to decrypt the data or to append more data to the tape.

---

[40] For more details on Advanced Encryption Standard (AES), see [14].

[41] More details on cryptography and encryption algorithms can be found in [15].

6.5.13 File System Virtualization Pattern

With the File System Virtualization pattern shown in Figure 6.20, you approach file virtualization through the use of a Distributed File System Services Clustered Node such as IBM General Parallel File System (GPFS).[42] The following relevant nodes represent the File System Virtualization pattern:

- **Distributed File System Services Clustered Node**—This node represents a high-performance, shared-disk cluster file system. It provides concurrent high-speed file access to applications executing on multiple nodes. GPFS services provide a single-system view of the file system across the Block Subsystem Nodes of the cluster. GPFS is based on the shared-disk model. This means that all nodes share read and write access to a group of block devices. All of the Block Subsystem Nodes in the grid export all files of all file systems simultaneously. This is a different approach from other clustered NAS solutions,[43] which pin individual files to a single node or pair of nodes, limiting the single file performance dramatically.

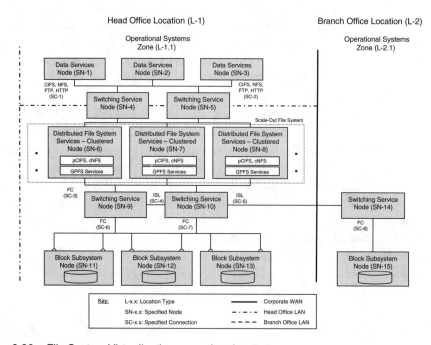

Figure 6.20   File System Virtualization operational pattern

---

[42] See more details about IBM GPFS as a shared-disk file system for large computing clusters in [16].

[43] See an instantiation of the file system virtualization pattern with IBM Scale out File Services in [17].

- **Block Subsystem Node**—File system virtualization is built from a collection of Block Subsystem Nodes, such as disks that contain the file system data and metadata. A file system can be built from a single disk or contain thousands of disks. The Distributed File System Services Clustered Node provides file-level virtualization through a rule-based policy engine. Data from files in a single directory can reside in one or across several storage pools. Determination of which storage pool the file data is initially written to and how it is migrated, mirrored, or deleted over its life span is based on a set of business rules in an administrator-defined policy.

6.5.14 Storage Pool Virtualization Pattern

Storage virtualization addresses the increasing cost and complexity in data storage management. It addresses this increased complexity by shifting storage management intelligence from individual SAN disk subsystem controllers into the network through a virtualization cluster of nodes. The Block Subsystem Virtualization Node shown in Figure 6.21, such as IBM SAN Volume Controller (SVC),[44] provides block aggregation and volume management for disk storage in the SAN. In simpler terms, this means that the Block Subsystem Virtualization Node manages a number of back-end disk subsystem controllers and maps the physical storage within those controllers to logical disk images that can be seen by Data Services Nodes, such as application servers and workstations in the SAN.

The Block Subsystem Virtualization Nodes are processing units, which provide Virtual Disk Services, including caching and copy services for the SAN. These nodes are usually deployed in pairs called I/O groups. One node in the cluster is the designated configuration node, but each node in the cluster holds a copy of the cluster state information.

6.5.15 Automated Capacity and Provisioning Management Pattern

Usually in a Cloud Computing or SaaS delivery model, the underlying services are dynamic. With the Automated Capacity and Provisioning Management pattern, you are able to control lifecycle, starting, stopping, and provisioning of services automatically. For Cloud Computing and SaaS, the services should be replicated or cloned automatically; multiple instances of the same service can be running to support scalability, for instance.

The Automated Capacity and Provisioning Management pattern as shown in Figure 6.22 is about masking the placement and execution of Information Services or applications across

---

[44] The IBM virtualization technology with SAN Volume Controller (SVC) improves management of information at the block level in a network, enabling applications and servers to share storage devices on a network. More SVC implementation scenarios can be found in [18].

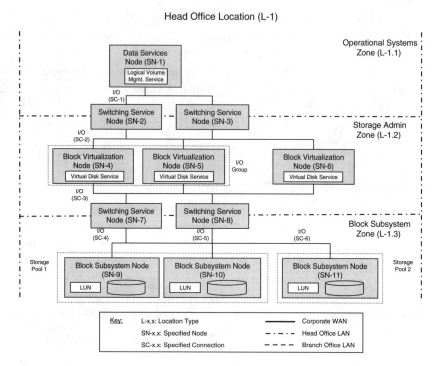

Figure 6.21   Storage Pool Virtualization operational pattern

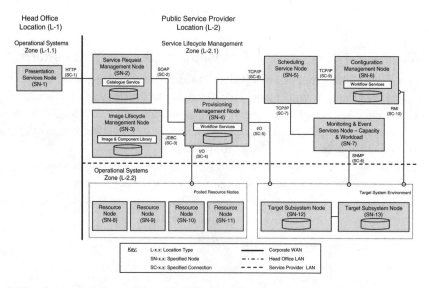

Figure 6.22   Automated Capacity and Provisioning Management operational pattern

the distributed environment. If you consider a scale-out computing environment, you don't know or care where things will or should run; you just want them to run. There is the need to specify the resource requirement, what the work needs, what the executable type is, how much memory the work might require, and when it needs to be completed. You also have to describe the sequencing of work or the workflow dependencies. Then, it is the interaction of job schedulers, workload, capacity management functionality and provisioning management capabilities that have to interact to deliver workload execution and Information Services delivery in a highly automated way. Automation is provided by the orchestration of the following operational nodes:

- **Service Request Management Node**—For the initial provisioning of particular infrastructure resources or Information Services, the Service Request Management Node handles user requests demanding certain Cloud services. Service templates are registered to the service catalog where they are associated with certain service-level attributes, terms, conditions, and configuration parameters. Based on these criteria, the instantiation of the Cloud service is executed by calling the Provisioning Management Node.

- **Provisioning Management Node**—With the help of pre-defined workflow activities, the required resources are selected out of pools of Resource Nodes, they are set up and configured according to the parameters selected by the requestor, appropriate images are copied and instantiated by the Image Lifecycle Management Node, and after the Cloud service instance (Target Subsystem Node) creation is finally completed, the Cloud service is made accessible to the service requestor.

- **Monitoring and Event Services Node—Capacity and Workload Management**—While a Cloud service runs, it must be managed from various perspectives. Concerning the requested service-level attributes, it is important to ensure the service levels are met, which have been selected by means of the Service Request Management Node. With this node, a set of management actions are provided and can be executed based on recommendations and rules.

- **Scheduling Service Node**—It is important to note that all of these management actions are executed for the Cloud service to ensure its overall consistency and to keep track of all changes applied to it. The Scheduling Service Node triggers the appropriate jobs, such as adding resources or changing configuration parameters maintained by the Configuration Management Node. When additional infrastructure resources have to be provisioned, the Provisioning Management Node is called and its workflow activities provide required resources that are selected out of pools of Resource Nodes.

6.6 Conclusion

In this chapter, we introduced the Operational Model of the EIA Reference Architecture. You saw how physical nodes can be derived from logical components of the Component Model and related deployment scenarios. We examined service qualities and elaborated on how the scope of integration determines the requirements for availability, resiliency, security, and scalability. With Operational Model relationship diagrams, we outlined how the inter-relationship of operational nodes, locations, and correlating connections can be documented as the design proceeds.

We introduced operational patterns that enable the architect to improve the reuse of the implementation design of Information Services. This chapter's discussion of the major operational considerations can now be applied easily to various business scenarios.

6.7 References

[1] Mitchell, D. 2007. *Dave Mitchell on Software as a Service and IBM*. Podcast and transcript. http://www.ibm.com/developerworks/podcast/dwi/cm-int080707txt.html (accessed December 15, 2009).

[2] R. Youngs, D. Redmond-Pyle, P. Spaas, and E. Kahan. *IBM Systems Journal* Vol. 38, No. 1, *A Standard for Architecture Description*, 1999.

[3] The Open Group homepage: *The Open Group Architecture Framework TOGAF—Version 9 "Enterprise Edition."* http://www.opengroup.org/togaf/ (accessed December 15, 2009).

[4] Chappell, D. *Enterprise Service Bus*. Sebastopol, CA: O'Reilly, 2004.

[5] Yuhanna, N. 2009. *Why Data Masking Should Be Part Of Your Enterprise Data Security Practice*. Forrester Research. http://www.alacrastore.com/research/forrester-Why_Data_Masking_Should_Be_Part_Of_Your_Enterprise_Data_Security_Practice-54927 (accessed December 15, 2009).

[6] Storage Networking Industry Association (SNIA): Storage Management Initiative Specification (SMI-S). http://www.snia.org/tech_activities/standards/curr_standards/smi/SMISv1_3_Overview.book.pdf (accessed December 15, 2009).

[7] IBM homepage: IBM Patterns for e-Business. http://www.ibm.com/developerWorks/patterns/ (accessed December 15, 2009).

[8] C. Ballard, R. MS, O. Mueller, Z. Y. Pan, A. Perkins, and P. J. Suresh. *Preparing for DB2 Near Real-Time Business Intelligence*. San Jose, CA: IBM Redbook, 2004.

[9] N. Alur, Y. Chang, B. Devlin, B. Matthews, S. Potukuchi, U. S. Kumar, and R. Datta. *Patterns: Information Aggregation and Data Integration with DB2 Information Integrator*. San Jose, CA: IBM Redbook, 2004.

[10] Theissen, M. *Hub-And-Spoke. Getting the Data Warehouse Wheel Rolling*. 2008. http://www.datallegro.com/pdf/white_papers/wp_hub_and_spoke.pdf (accessed December 15, 2009).

[11] W.D. Zhu, J. Cerruti, A. Genta, H. Koenig, H. Schiavi, and T. Talone. *Content Manager Backup/Recovery and High Availability: Strategies, Options, and Procedures*. San Jose, CA: IBM Redbook, 2004.

[12] SOX-online: *The Vendor-Neutral Sarbanes-Oxley Site*. http://www.sox-online.com/act.html (accessed December 15, 2009).

[13] B. Jacob, B. Adhia, K. Badr, Q. C. Huang, C. S. Lawrence, M. Marino, and P Unglaub-Lloyd. *IBM Tivoli Application Dependency Discovery Manager Capabilities and Best Practices*. Poughkeepsie, NY: IBM Redbook, 2008.

[14] Advanced Encryption Standard (AES) Announcement through the Federal Information Processing Standards Publication 197. 2001. *Advanced Encryption Standard*. http://csrc.nist.gov/publications/fips/fips197/fips-197.pdf (accessed December 15, 2009).

[15] Schneier, B. 1996. *Applied Cryptography. Protocols, Algorithms and Source Code in C.* New York, NY: John Wiley & Sons, 1996.

[16] F. Schmuck and R. Haskin, 2002. *GPFS: A Shared-Disk File System for Large Computing Clusters.* http://www. almaden.ibm.com/StorageSystems/projects/gpfs/Fast02.pdf (accessed December 15, 2009).

[17] S. Oehme, J. Deicke, J.-P. Akelbein, R. Sahlberg, A. Tridgell, and R. L. Haskin. 2008. *IBM Systems Journal* Vol. 52, No. 4/5, *IBM Scale out File Services: Reinventing Network-Attached Storage.*

[18] Dhulekar, S., Hossli, J., Koeck, D., Musovich, S., and J. Tate. *Implementing the IBM System Storage SAN Volume Controller V4.3.* Poughkeepsie, NY: IBM Redbook, 2008.

New Delivery Models: Cloud Computing

In this chapter, we describe the emerging delivery model of Cloud Computing in the context of the Enterprise Information Architecture (EIA) Reference Architecture. This chapter should help you understand the definition and application of Cloud Computing models within the context of Enterprise Information Services (EIS) Components across the enterprise.

The purpose of this chapter is to introduce definitions and terms related to Cloud Computing models and their different shapes and layers across the IT stack. We provide a holistic view of how the deployment model of EIS changes with Cloud Computing in place, and we also examine the impact of the new delivery models on operational service qualities.

In addition, we explore the impact of the deployment model of EIS when Cloud Computing services work with existing applications. In this case, we discuss the basic requirements that are needed to build information-centric cloud services such as flexible service composition and orchestration across clouds, the open and interoperable standards with a Service-Oriented Architecture (SOA), and Information as a Service (IaaS) implementation guidelines.

7.1 Definitions and Terms

Cloud Computing is considered a new paradigm in the way IT is delivered to serve business needs. At the time this book was written, Cloud Computing was considered a hot theme; the term Cloud Computing meant different things to different people, and contemporary discussions[1] summarized a broad range of capabilities under the umbrella of Cloud Computing. Among companies leading the way are a mix of expected and unexpected players such as Amazon, AppNexus, IBM, and Google. The cloud offerings these companies provide vary.[2]

---

[1] Examples for these discussions are located in [1] and [2].

[2] A hands-on comparison that includes interesting experiences as a guided tour is located in [3]; more use case examples are located in [4] and [5].

However, there still isn't an agreeable definition of Cloud Computing because it is considered both a new IT delivery model and a management methodology. As a new delivery model, Cloud Computing is the composition and orchestration of IT services from the user's perspective at anytime from anywhere delivered over the network. It has flexible pricing models provided by the cloud service provider. In this context, "the Cloud" is considered both a consumption and delivery model motivated from an Internet services consumer's point of view. As a new management methodology, the cloud services consumed are dynamically deployed and scaled up by a virtualized, elastic (see section 4.2.13.5 in Chapter 4 for an introduction of this term) IT environment that implements automation, business workflows, and resource abstraction. The Cloud provides a user interface that enables the consumers to browse a catalog of IT services, add them to a shopping cart, and submit the service request. Behind the scenes, automated tasks are initiated to manage the provisioning of resources through the lifecycle of the service request, including steps such as selecting hardware from pooled resources; allocating floor space and sufficient power and cooling; installing Operating Systems (OS), Middleware (MW), and software; provisioning the network; and securing the environment.

In this book, we shape the definition and nature of the Cloud Computing delivery model in terms of the EIA Reference Architecture. In an information-centric world, Cloud Computing means the provisioning, composition, and orchestration of EIS resources including the automated lifecycle management of information and data. With Cloud Computing, EIS resources are deeply integrated and optimized, providing a ready-to-use solution that can quickly turn information into insight. By leveraging a flexible infrastructure of software, servers, and storage, information-centric[3] clouds provide flexibility and simplicity in deployment to ensure you can adjust and grow the EIS solution to fit the ever-evolving business needs. Thus, information-centric clouds provide:

- A highly reliable and secure system platform that includes scalable server and storage resources

- An automated installation service and single point-of-service lifecycle management

- A trusted information platform that offers a high-performance Data Warehouse (DW) management and storage optimization

- An analytics platform that provides data mining, analytics of Structured and Unstructured Data, intuitive Business Intelligence (BI) reporting, and dashboard services

7.2 Cloud Computing as Convergence of IT Principles

Cloud Computing didn't appear over night. Cloud Computing is more the next logical step along an evolution of certain computing capabilities. Thus, before we drill down to basic requirements

---

[3] See [6] for an example of Business Analytics running in a cloud environment.

and relevant services of Cloud Computing we set the stage with major key drivers and evolutionary steps toward Cloud Computing.

7.2.1 Key Drivers to Cloud Computing

One of the key drivers to Cloud Computing is the concept of virtualization, which was gradually expanded beyond virtual servers to higher levels of abstraction. First, the IT industry adopted the abstraction of virtual platforms, including storage and network resources, and subsequently, the virtual application abstracted from the underlying infrastructure by the SOA paradigm.

7.2.1.1 Dynamic and Virtualized IT Resources

As mentioned previously, the evolution and adoption of virtualization and management techniques are key drivers that improve the efficiency and flexibility of computing environments and data centers in Cloud Computing. Thus, computing capacity could be managed more granularly as needed by the consumers. Computing environments can be dynamically created, expanded, shrunk, or moved as demand varies. Virtualization and the concept of "elastic" computing are well suited to a dynamic cloud infrastructure because they provide important advantages in sharing, manageability, and isolation.

7.2.1.2 Application Abstraction by Service-Oriented Architecture (SOA) Paradigm

In addition to virtualization beyond traditional infrastructure resources, the abstraction of applications and business processes was driven by the SOA paradigm. As a key concept of SOA, the Separations of Concerns (SOC) implies the separation of information from applications and processes for various reasons. First, it is important to understand that the same information usually needs to be accessed by many applications, not just a single one. Therefore, the need to reuse information in a controlled manner is a valid driver to abstract information services in the enterprise so that a single application can seamlessly consume data, not just from its own database, but from a variety of sources. Enterprises need to provide those applications with effective mechanisms to transform and integrate distributed data and content. Additionally, in many situations where data is distributed, enterprises find a lack of trusted information and conflicting data. They need to establish the single version of the truth that the application can access. In this context, MDM is a lighthouse example of the separation of information and application leading to a trusted information service provider in an SOA, leveraging the previously introduced Information as a Service concept.

According to the SOA paradigm, service components abstracted from the underlying infrastructure provide the implementation concept for IT services previously discussed. From the bottom-up, the service layer exposes interfaces from the service components which are, of course, part of the Metadata model associated with the overall architecture. Thus, Information Services as an instantiation of the SOA paradigm are also a key driver to Cloud Computing. Those Information Services are physically stored in some form of a service registry or repository to ensure consumers can search, find, understand, and reuse such services.

7.2.2 Evolution to Cloud Computing

If you start reviewing the history of Cloud Computing, you might recognize that it is not a revolutionary new development, but an evolution that has taken place over several decades.

7.2.2.1 Grid Computing

The trend toward Cloud Computing started with the concept of Grid Computing when a large number of systems were applied to a single problem, and when an exceptionally high level of parallel computation was needed. In Grid Computing, the focus is on moving a workload to the location of the needed computing resources and leveraging several computers in parallel to run a specific application. That said, a grid is usually a cluster of servers, on which a large task can be divided into smaller tasks to run in parallel. This concept requires applications or workloads to conform to the grid software interfaces. Additionally, open standards make Grid Computing work, and the Open Grid Forum[4] is one industry body driving standardization. In contrast to that, Cloud Computing is the concept that dynamically shapes and carves out computing and extended IT resources from the underlying infrastructure to make them available to deliver a specific service to the end user.

7.2.2.2 Utility Computing

As a next evolutionary step, Utility Computing expanded the concept of virtualization to higher levels of abstraction. First, it introduced virtual platforms, which make the storage and computing layer completely transparent to the consuming application. Subsequently, Utility Computing expanded the model of virtualization to the MW and application stack and developed appropriate metering and billing services for measuring resource consumption. Thus, Utility Computing is in essence the offering of computing resources as a metered service. This type of service was often used for web hosting scenarios driving out cost of local infrastructure. Otherwise, a lot of in-house hardware resources would have been required for very rare peaks in the load, for example, around Christmas or similar shopping events if the hosted website was an online store. The hardware required to absorb these peak loads was previously sitting around idle for the majority of the year. In fact, Cloud Computing has a lot in common with Utility Computing concerning the allocation of dynamic IT resources and offering a metered business model through the introduction of a management technique to improve the efficiency and flexibility of data centers and other computing environments.

7.2.2.3 Software as a Service (SaaS)

After packaged application vendors, such as SAP, Siebel, or JD Edwards, automated business processes, companies realized that running them in house was costly and required dedicated hardware, software licenses, and well-trained staff to install and maintain them. Furthermore, increasing

---

[4] More information on the Open Grid Forum can be found at [7].

demands for new hardware and additional software licenses couldn't be immediately satisfied and required a time-consuming and error-prone manual installation procedure. Thus, the next logical step in the evolution was the birth of SaaS, which enables the delivery of standardized application packages over the Internet as a service. This step was enabled when broadband Internet become ubiquitous during the last couple years because there was no performance difference for the end user using a local user interface if the application backend was hosted by in-house IT or by a service provider over the Internet. SaaS enables customers to subscribe to an offering through a subscription model—typically per user per month. The switch in paradigm is that the software is not purchased anymore. Thus, SaaS is a new business model where subscribers to applications or information services are charged not by the resources consumed but by the value of the subscribed service.

This subscription model was applied to standardized application packages such as Customer Relationship Management (CRM), and Salesforce.com is among the most well-known examples that spearheaded this model. In addition to packaged applications, business process platforms are now available through SaaS.[5] Again, Cloud Computing has a lot in common with the SaaS model by creating a network-subscription based application model, thus driving out cost of the in-house IT by consuming Software as a Service from an external provider.

In summary, Cloud Computing has evolved from the concepts of Grid, Utility, and SaaS. It is an emerging model through which users can gain access to their applications from anywhere, at any time, through their connected devices. These applications reside in scalable data centers where compute resources can be dynamically provisioned and shared to achieve significant economies of scale.

7.3 Cloud Computing as a New Paradigm

The paradigm of Cloud Computing pushes out the boundaries of IT beyond the SaaS concept. This section discusses the typical service layers encompassing Cloud Computing and explores the nature of public and private clouds and the basic requirements of Cloud Computing environments.

7.3.1 Typical Service Layers in Cloud Computing

The IT services delivered through Cloud Computing span the full stack of capabilities as shown in Figure 7.1. The stack of capabilities can be divided in layers such as Infrastructure as a Service, Platform as a Service, and Software as a Service. All layers have in common that cloud services are based on the assumption that data and related applications reside in massively scalable data centers where IT resources can be dynamically provisioned and shared to achieve significant economies of scale. Consequently, the automation of the lifecycle of the underlying services plays a crucial role. The cloud service provider benefits from Cloud Computing by economies of scale and improved resource utilization, whereas the service provider acting as intermediary can integrate cloud services with existing applications and make them available to the consumer.

---

[5] One vendor doing this, for example, is located at [8].

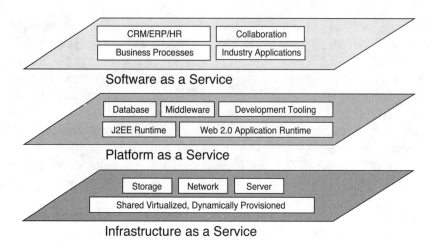

Figure 7.1   IT as a service

7.3.1.1 Infrastructure as a Service

Infrastructure as a service delivers basic storage and computes capabilities as standardized services over the network. Servers, storage systems, switches, routers, and other systems are virtualized, shared, dynamically provisioned to the needed capacity, and made available to handle specific workloads.

7.3.1.2 Platform as a Service

Platform as a Service (PaaS) encapsulates a layer of software and provides it as a service that can be used to build higher-level services. There are various perspectives on PaaS depending on the perspective of the producer or consumer of the services. One perspective of PaaS is to consider it a virtualized platform with an integration of OS and specific instances of MW and application software. Concerning the scope of EIS, database instances for testing purposes can be one characteristic that can be adopted from Amazon Web Services. Another perspective of PaaS is the encompassing stack of a Web 2.0 application runtime environment or a development environment including an integrated development tooling and support for additional programming languages. These offerings can provide for every phase of software development and testing, or they can be specialized around a particular area such as content management.

In summary, PaaS provides a powerful basis on which to deploy applications; however, they may be constrained by the capabilities that the cloud provider chooses to deliver.

7.3.1.3 Software as a Service

SaaS was already introduced as an evolutionary step to Cloud Computing. It features a complete industry application or business process offered as a service on demand. A single instance of the software runs on the cloud and services multiple end users or client organizations. There are many SaaS offerings available today including, for example, the IBM LotusLive[6] offering of basic business services including e-mail and collaboration services.

7.3.2 The Nature of Cloud Computing Environments

Now let's turn our attention to the nature and context of Cloud Computing as a new delivery model within the EIA Reference Architecture. We focus on the basic requirements of an efficient delivery model and the differentiation of public and private clouds.

7.3.2.1 Basic Requirements for Cloud Computing

We already discussed the key drivers to Cloud Computing that, in the past, required two major technological advancements. The first one was mainly driven by the virtualization of server and storage infrastructure. The second one was the standardization driven with the rise of SOA. Flexible service composition and orchestration of cloud services from the same or across clouds is, in our opinion, unthinkable without the notion of an SOA that is based on open, interoperable standards. This is also the reason why IaaS is a prerequisite before information-centric cloud services can be built. At the time this book was written, cloud offerings that represent new ways to manage data are already available (Greenplum Database and Amazon SimpleDB). Both vendor offerings are delivered as a cloud service with multi-tenancy support.

Emerging New Workloads Drive IT Re-Organization: Cloud Computing is fit for purpose, which means different types of workloads require different types of clouds. Even though many workloads can be delivered through Cloud Computing, there are workloads that do not fit into that delivery model. For instance, straight through processing with critical transaction throughput cannot be delivered by public clouds today. Thus, it's important to be aware of the variety of delivery options, especially while considering security, control, level of flexibility, and so on. Enterprise customers are wary of public clouds due to issues with security and privacy, whereas private clouds are client-owned managed environments, in which we re-engineer their existing resources to make them act more like the Internet—massively scalable and with extreme availability. Because this cloud physically sits behind the client's firewall, security and access are well within the company's control. Some workloads simply always remain in house, because public clouds aren't the answer to all the data center challenges.

Standardization of Services Is Key to Progress: The IT industry spent much of its first few decades developing the basic components of computing. Now that these can be standardized, traditional data centers can become factories for business and consumer services on an industrial scale. The key is to bring discipline and simplicity to the most complex corners of big businesses. Self-service drives standardization. Think of the ATM in banking: It started as a cash-dispensing

---

[6] See [9] for details.

function and drove international standardization to a commonly agreed level. However, as networks got connected, it forced standards for networking and security across the entire banking industry, especially if a consumer wanted to obtain cash from another bank's ATM.

Service Management Is the OS of the Twenty-First Century: Complex, distributed, mobile, hybrid systems require new levels of orchestration. Furthermore, evolving IT structures separated user experience and resources. As a result, we now need full automation of the build and management plans for the runtime environment. Service management is the intelligence in the system that automates access, security, new capabilities, and performance in a world where systems need to handle billions or trillions of transactions.

7.3.2.2 Public and Private Clouds

A cloud environment can be either a public cloud or a private cloud. A cloud service provider external to the enterprise provides a public cloud. A private cloud is an in-house cloud environment. There is a major difference between a public cloud and a private cloud; many of these differences are related to legal compliance, security, and trust:

- **Privacy**—Imagine you place your customer information as part of a CRM system in a cloud environment where you don't know where the servers and storage systems are physically located, and by the nature of the cloud, you need to assume that the data and application is dynamically moved and placed for an optimized utilization of the cloud environment across virtualized hardware infrastructure. Therefore, it is difficult to be sure if the customer information used by the CRM application in the cloud complies with privacy legislation. Some countries in Europe have stricter privacy legislations. For example, Amazon introduced the notion of regions for the Elastic Compute Cloud (EC2) Service with a region for Europe. The infrastructure supporting the EC2 Service is physically located in Europe if this region is selected as part of the Service Level Agreement (SLA). Addressing privacy legislation concerns with a private cloud is sometimes preferable if you need to be certain about compliance. In a private cloud you control data and hardware placement supporting the cloud services.

- **Security**—Another aspect in which public and private clouds differ is security. In a private cloud, total control of the security infrastructure, processes, and skill level of the staff is available and security concerns can be addressed as seen fit. In a public cloud, insight into the security infrastructure, security processes, and training and education levels of the staff operating the cloud environment of the cloud service provider is less transparent and cannot be influenced as easily as in an in-house infrastructure.

- **Customization**—Another important difference between public and private clouds is the mode of customization. For instance, a private cloud can be structured much better to the needs of the respective targeted consumers compared to a public cloud provider with mass-customization requirements in mind.

- **Trust**—The last differentiator between a public cloud and a private cloud environment is trust. Just consider some scenarios: If the cloud service provider has to file bankruptcy, can you retrieve the data from the cloud service provider systems? Which information assets are you willing to place into cloud services offered in a public cloud if your fiercest competitor might buy the cloud service provider? Can you afford a significant increase in cloud service costs if the cloud service provider is going through a hard time making the extraction of the data from the cloud environment expensive? The trust factor is a critical factor when choosing between public or private cloud environments.

7.4 Implication of Cloud Computing to Enterprise Information Services

In the previous section, we discussed the nature of Cloud Computing environments. Now we discuss the implication of Cloud Computing to EIS. We explore the important aspect of multi-tenancy and relevant capabilities of EIS in a cloud environment.

7.4.1 Multi-Tenancy

The purpose of this section is to explore the topic of multi-tenancy and show that it's a multi-facet concept offering many choices, but also requiring some thought on cloud service provider selection. However, let's start with an observation by looking at Figure 7.2.

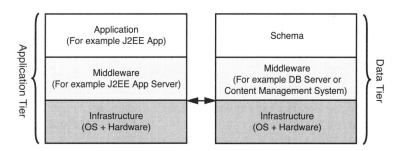

Figure 7.2 Typical application architecture

Typical, packaged applications such as SAP applications and numerous, custom-built applications are architected, as shown in Figure 7.2, with three distinct layers for the application tier:

- Application layer
- Middleware layer (often considered the deployment layer)
- Infrastructure layer

The data tier consists of the following layers:

- Schema layer

- Middleware layer (typically a database server or content management system)
- Infrastructure layer

The schema is a concept offered by many database and content management systems today to logically group information by an application instance that serves a tenant (keep in mind that a tenant can subscribe a service for one or multiple users).

The idea of multi-tenancy is to share resources to improve cost efficiency, and it can be applied to each of the identified layers. In section 7.4.1.1, we apply the multi-tenancy concept to the application tier, and in section 7.4.1.2, we apply it to the data tier. Because a typical application consists of the application tier and the data tier, the matrix of possibilities includes the combination of all multi-tenancy options of both tiers.

7.4.1.1 Multi-Tenancy for the Application Tier

As discussed, the application tier has three layers. Let's go top-to-bottom through the layers and explore the options for multi-tenancy step by step on each layer. As shown in Figure 7.3, there are three options for multi-tenancy on the application layer:

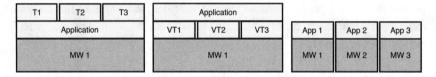

Figure 7.3   Multi-tenancy for application layer in application tier

- The first option is a fully multi-tenancy enabled application (shown on the left of Figure 7.3) that serves multiple tenants T1 to T3. The application itself resides on MW (denoted with MW1). This is a typical consideration for applications and services built from scratch or by re-engineering, where possible, existing applications. In such a scenario, the application has all needed capabilities to serve multiple tenants at the same time.

- Another option (shown in the middle of Figure 7.3) can be multi-tenancy enabled with virtualized tenants (denoted VT1 to VT3) through a smart feature of the underlying MW1. If the application is not enabled with multi-tenancy, but the MW has capabilities to deploy it virtually in a multi-tenancy fashion, this might provide the application multi-tenancy capabilities.

- The third option (shown on the right of Figure 7.3) is to instantiate an application instance (App1 to App3) and a corresponding MW instance (MW1 to MW3) per tenant. This might be the only option if neither the application nor the capabilities in the MW, as in the previous two options, allow multi-tenancy. In this case, the only multi-tenancy capabilities for optimizing resources can be achieved on the MW layer or the infrastructure layer—which we discuss next.

The next layer we explore is the MW layer. Again, there are three options:

- Each MW instance requires its own OS environment (shown on the left of Figure 7.4).

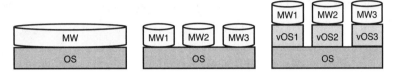

Figure 7.4   Multi-tenancy for MW layer in application tier

- The OS is capable of serving multiple instances of the MW (ranging from MW1 to MW3) (shown in the middle of Figure 7.4). This requires process-level and address space-level separation capabilities.
- The OS has virtualized OS capabilities with instances vOS1 to vOS3 (shown on the right of Figure 7.4). In this example, each MW instance runs in its own virtualized OS environment. Typical examples for this are techniques such as XEN[7] or VMware[8] as providers of virtualized OS environments.

We describe the infrastructure layer only once for the application tier. The multi-tenancy options presented here are the same for the data tier; therefore, we do not repeat this in section 7.4.1.2. On the infrastructure layer, there are two choices:

- A single OS instance per hardware instance
- Multiple OS instances OS1 to OS3 per hardware instance

7.4.1.2 Multi-Tenancy for the Data Tier

We limit the discussion in this subsection to database systems, but it applies conceptually in a similar way to other information management systems, such as content management systems or analytical systems such as DWs. Historically, usually each application had its own database system in the data tier. The downside of this approach is that there are multiple hardware instances with an OS each in addition to multiple database environments that need to be individually installed, configured, monitored, and managed over time. Additionally, each installation of database software creates redundancy in the installed software, wasting disk space. Technically, with the rise of the schema concept to group tables and other database objects logically, schemas can

---

[7] XEN provides virtualization capabilities on the Linux OS platform.

[8] VMware provides virtualization capabilities on the Windows OS platform.

be used to separate information for one application from information belonging to another application. Separation of information and other database objects might be required to satisfy customer needs for security (by enabling authorization privileges on a schema level enforcing who can see what) or to comply with legal regulations. For the discussion of multi-tenancy, the concept of schemas is a relevant concept and offers the following options:

- A fully multi-tenancy enabled application is self-sufficient within one schema (shown on the left of Figure 7.5). This choice is often available only for new applications, services, or reengineered applications (if possible). There is no logical separation for the multiple tenants sharing the single application instance. Thus, backup or restore operations per tenant are difficult.

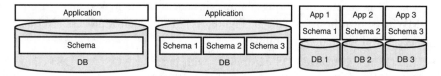

Figure 7.5   Multi-tenancy for schema layer in data tier

- The next option is one schema per tenant (shown in the middle of Figure 7.5 with Schema 1 to Schema 3). In this case, there is still just one application instance shared by multiple tenants, but the information is logically separated in the database with one schema per tenant. This is a precondition for something known as schema-based database operations. Some commercial databases allow maintenance services on a schema level, for example, to perform backup and restore operations on a schema level. This is a pre-condition to offer different SLAs for different tenants regarding backup and restore requirements in tenant-specific schemas. Schema-level operations are not yet available in all commercial databases for all required operations. Thus, the IT Architect designing or selecting this option must check for these capabilities during the software selection step in designing the Operational Model.

- If the application is not multi-tenancy enabled, the MW layer below the schema layer, in the data tier given by the database, must provide multi-tenancy (as shown on the right of Figure 7.5). This typically means a one-to-one relationship between application instance (one tenant per application instance) and schema and between schema and database. The benefit of this approach is that this configuration is well supported by database vendors today with maintenance operations (for example, backup and restore) on a database level.

From a conceptual level, the MW layer for the data tier (Figure 7.6) has exactly the same conceptual choices as for the application tier (Figure 7.4). The difference is that in the application tier, the discussion in the MW layer is applicable for application servers (such as J2EE application servers), whereas in the data tier, the MW is typically database or content management systems. The various MW options for the data tier:

- Each database instance requires its own OS environment (shown on the left of Figure 7.6). One OS per hardware instance (see the left part of Figure 7.6) combined with either the left or the right choice as shown in Figure 7.5, enables physical separation of information between tenants. Thus, if information security and data privacy are a concern, the combination just discussed is the maximum separation. At the same time, this also implies the least resource sharing and the least multi-tenancy setup.

- The OS is able to serve multiple instances of the database system (shown in the middle in Figure 7.6 shown as DB1 to DB3). This requires process-level and address space-level separation capabilities.

- The OS has virtualized OS capabilities (shown in the right of Figure 7.6 with vOS1 to vOS3). In this example, each database instance runs in its own virtualized OS environment using techniques such as XEN or VMware as providers of virtualized OS environments. For example, this can be an efficient mechanism to provide database systems for test purposes to various departments.

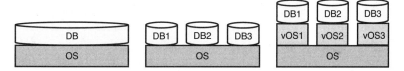

Figure 7.6   Multi-tenancy for MW layer in data tier

7.4.1.3 Combinations of the Various Layers

In this section, we discuss combinations of the previously introduced layers for the application and data tier. In Figure 7.3, the infrastructure layer has been omitted—purposely. We did this due to the following observations on the application tier:

- There are three options on the application layer (Figure 7.3).

- Each of them can be combined with options on the MW layer (Figure 7.4).

- The options on the MW layer can be combined with the options on the infrastructure layer.

The same observations apply to the data tier. In other words, there are many different deployment options in a combination of various layers within a tier and even more for the overall solution that consists of application and data tier. We couldn't conceive a single figure illustrating all possible options in a meaningful way. Thus, we give you one example for a combination. This should help you understand the many combination possibilities. For the application tier, each of the three options in Figure 7.3 can be combined with the various options for the MW in Figure 7.4. For example, the option in the middle for one application in Figure 7.3 can be combined with the right option in

Figure 7.4. This means the application shown in the middle in Figure 7.3 can run on MW1, and other applications on different MW instances (MW2 and MW3) can run on the same OS (OS) with virtualized OS instances (vOS1 to vOS3). For the OS shown in Figure 7.4, there are two deployment options on the infrastructure layer as previously discussed. With this example, you can see that there are multiple deployment options combining these layers.

7.4.2 Relevant Capabilities of EIS in a Cloud Environment

As introduced in Chapter 4, the relevant capabilities of EIS in a cloud environment are summarized in the following bulleted list:

- **Multi-Tenancy**—This must be supported on the application, information, and infrastructure layer.

- **A Self-Service UI**—This includes catalog management and request handling of changes according to predefined building blocks.

- **Full automation based on automated provisioning and Remote Deployment Management Services**—This includes the Reservation and Scheduling Services to accommodate the underlying computing resources with a status of the current and required capacity. The Provisioning and Deployment Services are discussed in Chapter 6.

- **Virtualization**—Virtualization on the hardware and storage layer enables a segregation of concerns. Storage layer virtualization includes a highly scalable, completely virtualized file system layer.[9] Virtualization techniques are introduced in the Operational Model.

- **Elastic capacity services**—This includes the monitoring of existing usage of shared physical resources and exception handling for peak workloads based on workload management characteristics to ensure compliance with SLAs. Elastic Capacity Management is discussed in Chapter 4.

- **Information Integration and Service Broker**—This integrates data from a variety of sources, determines how and where the data needs to be processed and routed, and sends each piece of data to its destination in a form that the target system can use.

- **Metadata Services**—These services along with transformation rules from Enterprise Service Bus (ESB) Connector Services, determines how the data is processed, routed, and integrated with data at the destination. The Metadata Services provide the configurable rules that each module uses to do its job.

- **Identity integration**—This facilitates identity integration in innovative ways, such as enabling the reuse of existing application-access policies to control access to SaaS applications.

---

[9] An example is the General Parallel File System (GPFS). More details can be found in [10].

- **Metering, Monitoring, Pricing, and Billing Services**—These ensure compliance with SLAs and enable the ability to accurately bill the cloud service consumers. Price models are defined at build time and measurement and analysis of utilization of resources can be done at run time. Billing, including chargeback mechanisms, are services invoked to produce a bill for the customer according to the agreed conditions, for example, on a weekly or monthly basis. The Metering, Monitoring, Pricing, and Billing Services are jointly providing the overall usage and accounting management for the Cloud Computing delivery model.

7.5 Cloud Computing—Architecture and Services Exploration

In this section, we explore the theme of Cloud Computing from an architecture perspective. We show how the Cloud Computing delivery model provides a certain view of the Operational Model introduced in the previous chapter.

The Cloud Computing delivery model affects the way an IT service is delivered to the service consumer. Thus, the Cloud Computing paradigm has the most significant impact from an architecture design perspective on the Operational Model. Figure 7.7 provides a conceptual overview of an Operational Model that is capable of delivering Cloud Computing. Figure 7.7 is in essence a certain perspective of Figures 6.3 to 6.7 in Chapter 6 to show the Cloud Computing angle. For example, the Storage- and Block-Virtualization subcomponent and the Filespace, Recordspace, and Namespace Virtualization subcomponent of the Infrastructure Virtualization and Provisioning Layer (introduced in Chapter 6) are used to provide the Virtualized Storage as shown in Figure 7.7. The only new components not yet explained in the previous chapter are the six grey-white shaded components; all other components have been explained in the Operational Model and are not explained again.

We now explain the new components. A tenant (subscriber of a service) uses a Self-Service UI to subscribe to one or more cloud services from the Cloud Services Catalog. The Cloud Services Catalog contains all available cloud services a subscriber can choose from. In case the tenant orders a cloud service, the Ordering Component creates and manages the order. After the order is placed, the cloud service gets deployed and managed through its lifecycle using appropriate Service Lifecycle Management and Operational Management Services.

The Problem and Error Resolution Component is needed in case a service subscriber has inquiries or reports problems that require an answer or a resolution. Ideally, embedded problem diagnostics and self-healing capabilities as close as possible to the source of the error within the Cloud Computing Infrastructure resolve most issues autonomically. However, there might be a subset of issues requiring event correlation and event forwarding to an administrator. In case an error causes an SLA violation, reporting must be able to correctly report this and assign it to the appropriate tenant. In a virtualized environment where cloud services might use third-party software, a component performing License Management is needed. The administration of the cloud environment is done by cloud administrators using a Cloud Admin UI.

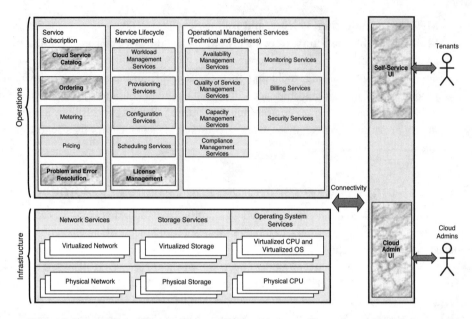

Figure 7.7   High-level Cloud Computing architecture from an Operational Model perspective

7.6 Business Scenario with Cloud Computing

In this section, we introduce a business scenario, followed by a Component Interaction Diagram showing how the Cloud Computing delivery model affects solution design.

7.6.1 Business Context

For this Cloud Computing scenario, we consider an insurance company based in the United States with the following demands:

- Ability to deliver appropriate customer relationship management at minimal costs
- Ability to accommodate peak loads when billing and similar periodic cyclic activities occur with minimal costs

The company analyzes the various options such as custom-built CRM applications, packaged CRM applications, and CRM as a Cloud Computing service. For flexibility and cost reasons, the company decides to subscribe to a CRM cloud service provider.

Because most of the insurance products offered by the company have monthly, quarterly, or yearly payment cycles, the creation of the bills is a batch process that requires significant processing cycles. It also measurably increases the amount of data in the ECM system, holding all unstructured information. Looking at current utilizations of in-house server and storage infrastructure, the company decides to reduce costs by not buying hardware for peak loads anymore, but by more intelligently leveraging the current assets in the context of an in-house private cloud environment.

Automated capacity management on virtualized infrastructure is a critical part of the more intelligent use of the existing assets.

7.6.2 Component Interaction Diagram

Figure 7.8 shows the key components for the solution that we now examine in more detail. Note that the Component Interaction Diagram is incomplete in the sense that we do not show all internal applications and their corresponding user interfaces. We focus only on the key areas.

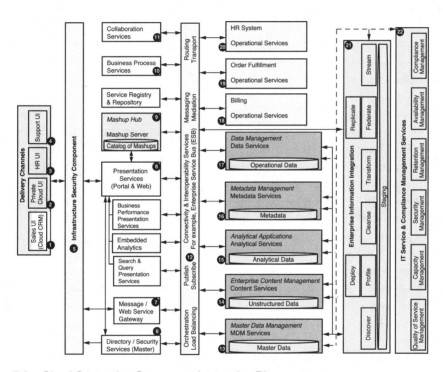

Figure 7.8 Cloud Computing Component Integration Diagram

Before we describe how certain components interact with each other, we first examine the components used. The Sales UI (1) is basically used by the insurance sales employees who are part of the user group using the CRM cloud service to which the insurance company is subscribed. The sales employees use the CRM cloud service focusing on the Opportunity-To-Order (OTO) business process. The sales employees can access this UI using their laptop and smart phone devices with a web browser. The Private Cloud UI (2) is a user interface that enables administrators to manage the internal private cloud infrastructure. The HR UI (3) is a rich-client user interface for the employees of the HR department. The Support UI (4) is an internal mashup-based

Web UI bringing together information from the CRM cloud services and relevant information from the internal Master Data Management (MDM), Enterprise Content Management (ECM), and fulfillment and billing systems. This enables all call center employees performing customer support to see all facets related to orders, bills, and contracts for customers across the relevant structured and unstructured information sources.

The Infrastructure Security Component (5) provides relevant Demilitarized Zone (DMZ) capabilities. For this scenario to work, the Directory and Security Services Component (6) needs to deliver federated identity management capabilities to enable a consistent security model regarding authentication and authorization for the public cloud service and the private cloud services. The Message and Web Services Gateway Component (7) is used to receive updates on customer and order information from the public cloud CRM Service in a secure manner. The Presentation Services Component (8) provides the Web UI infrastructure for the Private Cloud UI (2) and a unified delivery of Mashup UI Components provided by the Mashup Hub (9) in an enterprise portal environment.

The Business Process Services Component (10) and the Collaboration Services Component (11) deliver key capabilities such as service orchestration and e-mail capabilities to the enterprise. The Connectivity and Interoperability Services Component (12) connects all external and internal systems with each other and is instantiated with an ESB. The MDM Services Component (13) maintains the customer and contract master for the insurance across all systems. For the contracts, the MDM System manages the relational portion of the contract information and unique resource identifiers (URIs) to the unstructured contract information (the scanned contracts), which are managed by the ECM Services (14). The ECM Component (14) stores all scanned contracts and an electronic version of all bills sent to the customers. Thus, for example, this system must be able to accommodate peak loads when the Billing Component (18) produces a large number of new bills at the end of the month, quarter, or year in batch mode.

The Analytical Services (15) provide DW capabilities and fraud detection analytics. The DW also has peak loads at the end of a month, a quarter, and at year end when heavy analytical processing is performed to see how the business is doing. The Metadata Management Component (16) maintains metadata such as logical and physical data models. The Data Management Component (17) provides the relevant data services for the operational data (structured) created by the operational systems such as the Billing System (18), the Order Fulfillment System (19), and the HR System (20). In batch mode, the Billing System creates the bills sent out to clients. The EII Component (21) provides relevant information integration services such as Cleansing Services for name and address standardization that are used by the MDM System or replication services replicating order information from the order fulfillment system using trickle feed techniques to the DW. The IT Services and Compliance Management Services (22) provide necessary operational services, which we discuss after the Component Interaction Diagram walkthrough in more detail in this section.

The following steps walk you through the Component Interaction Diagram shown in Figure 7.8 and how a Customer Care Representative (CCR) working in the call center deals with a customer calling who received a wrong bill. We assume the CCR has already performed authentication to login into the Support UI (4):

1. When the customer calls, the CCR issues a lookup of the customer information using the Support UI (4) based on the customer number.

2. The lookup request of the customer information invokes through the Presentation Services Component (8) appropriate mashups provided by Mashup Hub (9).

3. The first mashup performs a lookup of the customer record invoking an MDM Service (13) through the ESB (11).

4. The second mashup retrieves the contracts using an ECM Service (14) invoked through the ESB (12) based on the URIs for the contract information returned by the MDM system alongside the customer information. In the mashup, links to the contracts are shown and when clicked, the relevant cached contract document could be shown through the browser.

5. The third mashup invokes the application CRM Service from the subscribed public cloud offering backend (1) to retrieve the latest opportunity information for that customer. This service invocation is routed through a mediation module in the ESB that first performs a lookup of the right authentication credentials from the Directory and Security Services Master Component (6) to retrieve the right credentials for the cloud service using a federated identity approach. In a second step, the mediation invokes the cloud service through the Message and Web Service Gateway (7) and the Infrastructure Security Component (5). The result is retrieved the same way and rendered in this mashup.

6. The fourth mashup uses the customer number to perform a lookup of the latest bills from the billing system (18) by calling an appropriate service through the ESB (12).

7. After all mashups receive their information by calling the appropriate Information Services, the Presentation Services using the mashup capabilities provide the results in a composite mashup UI to the CCR who then reviews the information.

8. Based on the problem with the latest bill, the CCR takes appropriate action. In this case, the CCR determines that the bill has been computed incorrectly because a discount for an insurance contract the customer was entitled to wasn't included due to an error in the customer information the sales representative entered in the contract. Thus, the CCR updates the customer record using the MDM Services (13) in the mashup, enabling the CCR to review and change the customer master information. After this is done, the CCR can close the phone call with the customer (if the customer has nothing else to discuss) because all remaining steps automatically happen.

9. The MDM Service used under the hood appropriates Cleansing Services from the Enterprise Information Integration Component (21) to update the customer information to ensure proper data quality. Upon completion of the MDM Service updating the customer record, a notification is placed into a queue of the ESB (12) for all subscribed consumers of the customer master data using a Publish/Subscribe pattern.

10. The update of the customer information triggers a content business process workflow—a subcomponent of the ECM Component (14). An employee responsible for contract management reviews the updated customer information and updates the contract accordingly based on a series of steps in this workflow. After the contract is updated, it is published on the ESB (12) and routed to the billing system (18).

11. The billing system (18) receives the updated contract information and creates a new, correct bill that is then sent to the customer.

As explained previously, a private cloud is established to optimize the use of internal server and storage resources and provide infrastructure cloud services. There is not yet much visible in the private cloud infrastructure because this delivery mode affects the Operational Model (see Chapter 6) and has a limited impact on the Component Model. Therefore, we provide insight into the Operational Model supporting the Component Interaction Diagram shown in Figure 7.8. For the EIS, there are two types of services that heavily benefit from a private cloud:

- **Analytical Services**—Namely the DW service subgroup benefits because the DW sometimes has large spikes of resource consumption where, for example, heavy sort operations demand more CPU cycles. Thus, virtualized, elastic CPU cycles increase efficiency, which makes them available while needed for the DW; otherwise, the resources are available to others. Completely virtualized storage simplifies operations for the database administrators, requiring less manual database reconfiguration when the growth of the DW demands new disk space.

- **ECM Services**—These services benefit from storage infrastructure cloud service because peaks created by the billing application can be accommodated easier.

If these services are deployed in a private cloud, the Cloud Computing architecture shown in Figure 7.7 provides you the list of required services to instantiate the information services through a Cloud Computing delivery model.

From the operational patterns introduced in Chapter 6, the Storage Pool Virtualization Pattern, the File System Virtualization Pattern, and the Automated Capacity and Provisioning Management Pattern are particularly useful for this scenario because they jointly deliver the infrastructure services of a completely virtualized storage and file system layer. These operational patterns leverage the following services as shown in Figure 6.5 (see Chapter 6):

- All services of the Physical Device Level Layer
- File System Services, File and Directory Synchronization Services, Caching Services, and Encryption Services from the OS System Services Layer
- Load Balancing Services from the Network Services Layer
- Storage- and Block-Virtualization Services; File-, Record, and Namespace-Virtualization Services, Resource Mapping Services, Configuration Support Services, Provisioning Services, and Workload Management Services from the Infrastructure Virtualization and Provisioning Layer (see Figure 6.4 in Chapter 6)

Finally, the IT Services and Compliance Management Services (22) with its six subcomponents provide the necessary services for operating the private cloud such as capacity management services, availability services, and Quality of Service (QoS) Management Services. Note that we focused on information-related aspects of the operational environment, which means that the relevant Virtualization Services for CPU and memory components of servers have not been shown. For the private cloud, these types of services are needed to deliver the overall infrastructure cloud service for the ECM and DW Services.

The in-house order fulfillment and HR system might be moved to cloud services. Also, the in-house e-mail services (part of the collaboration services in Figure 7.8) can be replaced by e-mail services in a public cloud, using cloud service offerings such as the LotusLive Notes.[10]

7.7 Conclusion

This chapter examined how the selection of a delivery model affects the functional requirements and the architecture, specifically on the level of the Operational Model and using Cloud Computing as an example. This discussion concludes the presentation of the Operational Model.

The next chapter provides an overview of the key information integration techniques that represent a vast set of tools for the Enterprise Information Architect.

7.8 References

[1] Gruman, G., Knorr, E. 2008. *What Cloud Computing Really Means*. http://www.infoworld.com/d/cloud-computing/what-cloud-computing-really-means-031?page=0,0 (accessed December 15, 2009).

[2] O'Neil, M. 2009. *Connecting to the Cloud, Part 1: Leverage the Cloud in Applications*. http://www.ibm.com/developerworks/webservices/library/x-cloudpt1/index.html (accessed December 15, 2009).

[3] Wayner, P. 2008. *Cloud Versus Cloud: A guided tour of Amazon, Google, AppNexus, and GoGrid*. http://www.infoworld.com/d/cloud-computing/cloud-versus-cloud-guided-tour-amazon-google-appnexus-and-gogrid-122?page=0,0 (accessed December 15, 2009).

[4] IBM Cloud Computing. 2009. *Seeding the Clouds: Key Infrastructure Elements for Cloud Computing*. ftp://ftp.software.ibm.com/common/ssi/sa/wh/n/oiw03022usen/OIW03022USEN.PDF (accessed December 15, 2009).

[5] O'Neil, M. 2009. *Connecting to the Cloud, Part 2: Realize the Hybrid Cloud Model*. http://www.ibm.com/developerworks/webservices/library/x-cloudpt2/index.html (accessed December 15, 2009).

[6] IBM Press Announcement (November 16, 2009): *IBM Builds Massive Business Analytics Cloud for 200,000 Employees and Unveils Version for Clients*. http://www-03.ibm.com/press/us/en/pressrelease/28823.wss (accessed December 15, 2009).

[7] The Open Grid Forum homepage: http://www.ogf.org/ (accessed December 15, 2009).

[8] Appian homepage for Business Process Management solution: http://www.appian.com/bpm-saas.jsp (accessed December 15, 2009).

[9] IBM LotusLive Cloud Computing offering homepage: *LotusLive*. https://www.lotuslive.com/ (accessed December 15, 2009).

[10] IBM General Parallel File System offering homepage: *General Parallel File System*. http://www-03.ibm.com/systems/clusters/software/gpfs/index.html (accessed December 15, 2009).

---

[10] For more information on LotusLive, please see [9] for details.

## CHAPTER 8

Enterprise Information Integration

This chapter provides an overview of the eight capabilities of the Enterprise Information Integration (EII) Component introduced in Chapter 5 as part of the Component Model. For each sub-component, we provide a use case scenario and a Component Interaction Diagram to show how the use case works. We highlight a few new scenarios of EII such as the streaming capability.

8.1 Enterprise Information Integration—Terms, History, and Scope

The fundamental nature of an EII framework for the design of an Enterprise Information Architecture (EIA) must support business-relevant themes, such as Master Data Management (MDM), Dynamic Warehousing, or Metadata Management, for the architecture to satisfy the demands of today's business environments.

Many of the subsequent chapters detail various aspects of the overall Enterprise Information Architecture (EIA) Reference Architecture and require a strong understanding of EII capabilities to enable them. We detail these capabilities in this chapter.

The area of EII is a wide and deep topic that covers all aspects of data movement and management from initial discovery and understanding of the data that resides within your business to the maintenance and management of that data from source to target destination.[1] Specifically, we cover the areas of discovery, profiling, cleansing, transformation, replication, federation, streaming, and deployment.

IT organizations are challenged when dealing with their own information integration efforts, and they have a large number of technologies from which to choose, including

---

[1] Chapter 4 defines EII as something that covers ETL, Federation, Replication, and EAI. Many in the industry previously defined EII as essentially just Federation Services.

Extract-Transform-Load (ETL), Enterprise Application Information (EAI), replication, federation, data profiling, data cleansing, and more. It can be difficult to understand which approach is suitable and how to map these offerings to business requirements and corporate standards. This chapter helps you understand which component to apply when first exploring the capabilities of each component described in Chapter 5. The chapter then explores a typical business scenario for how the components can be used.

In complex scenarios, the best solution is a combination of approaches. ETL and replication are more traditional ways to achieve data integration by means of physical movement of data, whereas federation achieves it in a virtual sense. EAI tools are meant to address application integration issues and are not often the first choice for data integration; however, they can be used as part of the solution to build real-time or near-real-time feeds into target information systems.

You must also consider an expanding area of data integration where Unstructured Data is added to Structured Data to enrich the information returned to an end user. An example of this is a sales or marketing application that retrieves product sales analytics, and then accesses any number of content stores to return competitor insights such as Profit/Loss (P/L) statements, annual reports, or advertising and market surveys. Enterprise Content Management (ECM) can manage the integration of documents, Web content, and other media such as voice or video. ECM builds a management layer over the top of a set of shared data stores with each managing differing content types. This layer is where metadata is created and managed and can be accessed to help integrate the content with Structured Data. The crucial point is that the metadata can be used by the differing integration styles to retrieve relevant content and aggregate it with Structured Data in the correct context and at the right time.

8.2 Discover

The discover stage enables a business to understand not just its existing data sources, but also the business rules and definitions associated with all data elements used within that environment.

8.2.1 Discover Capabilities

The Discover stage is preoccupied with analyzing various databases to better create a picture of and understand a business's metadata. Specific capabilities of this stage are:

- Discovering unspecified metadata including any relationships within and across a set of databases
- Reviewing and checking specified integrity rules within those databases for accuracy
- Potentially advising on issues and making recommendations regarding more appropriate data models

This stage does not look at the data stored within those data sources; profiling, the next stage, covers that. This stage focuses on the understanding of the data sources available across the enterprise. An additional challenge is to maintain this understanding in some suitable repository so it can be reused and maintained automatically on an ongoing basis. The latter is particularly important for the definition of an integrated data model over heterogeneous sources. This is essentially a metadata challenge and requires that different forms of metadata be brought together to present a complete and clear view of the status and context of your information system's static and in-motion information. Recall the two core types of metadata (see Chapters 3 and 10 for more details) that need to be managed in such scenarios:

- **Technical Metadata**—This refers to the location of the data sources, access protocol, physical schema of the data sources (data about data), and logical schema of data sources (for example, ER models or ontological models).

- **Business Metadata**—This includes the contextual information about the information retrieved such as business terms or business organizations. Business Metadata defines the information that defines business data and includes business attribute names, definitions, data quality, ownership, and business rules.

Without the creation of both forms of metadata, the maintenance and management of a discovery layer is difficult, if not impossible to do. What are the issues if we don't have a solution that can manage and maintain metadata? Consider the Discover stage; we cannot simply perform this process once and finish. This is not good enough; results must be stored with changes applied over time. This forms additional metadata to enhance the information about the systems under review for all those who create, use, and maintain those systems. Without this continual assessment,[2] the consequences of metadata becoming stale include the following:

- Changes that are made to source systems are difficult to manage and cannot match the pace of business change. Without metadata, every time a change is made, a separate review of the data being changed has to be made, including an impact analysis and change control that needs to be managed accordingly.

- Data cannot be analyzed across departments and processes or shared among products. Without meaningful metadata, data remains in silos and is of little use to the enterprise. This also means that deriving useful relationships across data domains might never be accomplished and data lineage is impossible.

- Without business-level definitions, Business Metadata users cannot understand the context for information, so they struggle to better understand and use the results they are given.

- Documentation can be out-of-date or incomplete, hampering change management and making it harder to train new users. Without metadata to help automate documentation, updates are difficult to complete.

---

[2] Good Information Governance (see Chapter 3) makes use of this metadata to help manage and control the usage, flow, accuracy, and quality of data around the enterprise.

- Efforts to establish an effective data stewardship program fail because of a lack of standardization and familiarity with the data. Without metadata to deliver standard reports on quality, standardization, survivorship, and several other topics to help Information Stewards govern their data, it is difficult to demonstrate this value.

- Establishing an audit trail for integration initiatives is virtually impossible. Without metadata that can be used to audit change at all points in the lifecycle and movement of data around the enterprise, a complete audit trail is hard to ensure.

- Governance and compliance aspects can be derived from complete metadata that ensures a business can identify all its data assets across the enterprise and clearly documents what purpose each asset serves.

What is required is a Metadata Repository from which all forms of metadata can be managed. This not only stores and maintains metadata definitions for the Discovery stage, but also links different forms of metadata together so that a true picture of end-to-end data lineage can be formed. Tooling is now available that allows enterprise information models and logical and physical data models to be combined. This tooling also allows additional links into metadata that describes technical changes made to the data as it flows through the various systems to track data lineage. We can create and use Business Metadata to allow end users to fully understand the meanings of terms in reports (linked to the other forms of metadata for data lineage). Also we need to understand linkage into repositories that allow services to be described. Analysts can then identify reusable services from that metadata to extend reuse where applicable in information integration scenarios. Such metadata models can be based around a single Metadata Repository or by a federation of metadata from various different engines.

Any metadata product needs Service Components that enable metadata interchange, integration, management, and analysis. For example:

- A data analyst might want to add business terms, definitions, and notes to data under analysis for use by a data modeler or architect. By using Metadata Services, the analyst can access the business description of the domain and any annotations that were added by other business users.

- A technical developer might want to find a function that performs a particular data conversion. By using Metadata Services, the technical developer can perform an advanced search for the function across the metadata and swiftly identify these by using tags or text searches within the metadata.

- A business analyst needs to better understand the business processes that are associated with a particular area of the business. The analyst wishes to decompose those processes down into finer-grained services that make the necessary calls to the underlying data domains to satisfy the users' requests. Metadata can hold information about the processes already in place.

Metadata becomes the critical glue that enables all the various information integration steps to be captured, used, and changed to ensure a 360-degree view of everything that happens to data as it passes through a business from its original creation to final deletion (or archive) to be fully understood and acted upon. See Chapter 10 for more information.

8.2.2 Discover Scenario

Understanding the end-to-end view of a business's information domains can be a daunting task. This scenario looks at how an Information Architect can gather all relevant metadata across the enterprise and hold it within a Metadata Repository. Without this enhanced level of understanding of systems and continual monitoring and revision of the metadata within them, governance is difficult to enable because the various staff employed to enable and run governance are hampered by the lack of information to help them do so.

It is useful for the Discover Component to be invoked on a regular basis as a service that is used to drive a regular auditing of the information systems that are in place. This can be accomplished by developing a set of discovery routines that build up an initial picture of the state of the existing systems and the relationships between them. The results from this can be stored in an analytical database for use later, or models can be captured and held in an appropriate modeling tool.

To ensure consistency of information and that changes are identified early and action taken as soon as possible, these routines can be rerun periodically by an analyst via a timed (or event-driven) business service to ensure appropriate checks are made and referenced back to previous result sets.

Contrast this with each Line of Business (LOB) having its own databases and systems with no knowledge shared between departments. In that scenario, they rely on database administrators or Information Stewards to manually access, understand, and document metadata to try to keep a form of understanding in place. This enormous task wastes valuable resources across the enterprise with no guarantee of completeness. An automated approach that enables analytics to be derived to review change and progress offers the chance for an enterprise to begin to integrate common information across the enterprise. This helps to remove redundancy and better exploits information across differing silos to gain deeper insight into their business.

The following walkthrough uses Figure 8.1 to describe a Discovery scenario in a proactive style. For this and subsequent figures, the numbers in the figures relate to the numbers in the walkthrough lists:

1. An analyst (1) using a frontend GUI-based tool accesses the Discover Component (2) to identify the various databases within the data domains. This can be one or many of the various types of data structures, such as operational, master data, or Unstructured Data.

2. The Discover Component (2) reads the DDL or similar metadata and uses any Metadata Services (3) available from the respective data source to gather an assessment of that data source. The results are stored in the analytical data store as metrics (in component [5]) or models of the underlying data structures as metadata (in component [4]).

3. Subsequently, this information captured can now be accessed either by the analyst (1) or through a business process service (7). This allows a repeatable process to be enabled and checks placed against "as was" (previous) and "as is" (present) states of the databases.

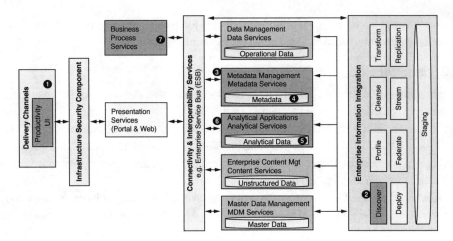

Figure 8.1   Discovery scenario

4. Inconsistencies and changes can be rapidly analyzed using the Analytical Services (6) against the data stored in the analytical data (5) and appropriate action taken to manage any changes, such as remapping data structures against ETL processes.

The Discover process has become more than a one-time investigation. It is now embedded as a business as usual process and from it, several benefits occur:

- The business can easily monitor changes and react to them.

- New developments or acquisitions can be swiftly incorporated and understood in context with the existing business.

- The laborious manual processes (often within silos) to understand systems has been removed, and an enterprise view of the business can now be maintained, which considerably assists the design efforts going forward.

8.3 Profile

This stage focuses on the *content* of the data within the repositories to gain insight into implicit relationships across columns, tables, and databases. Increasingly, these techniques are applied to incoming data feeds (structured or semi-structured) to assess the quality of the data *before* it enters any system. Couple this with Cleansing Services (see the next section) to proactively fix any issues by alerting relevant operations or Information Stewards of the issue and these become powerful tools in driving data quality throughout the business.

8.3.1 Profile Capabilities

Profile capabilities provide insight into the quality and usage characteristics of the information. They can also help uncover data relationships across systems through, for example, foreign key affinity mapping. This enables us to understand how data quality changes over time and ensures that assumptions and business rules defined on the data still hold true. Some core capabilities associated with this step are:

- **Deep profiling capabilities**—Provide a comprehensive understanding of data at the column, table, and source levels.

- **Multi-level rules analysis (by rule, by record, by pattern) unique to the data profiling space**—Provides the ability to evaluate and compare data structures across the enterprise. Creates and executes targeted data rules to validate key business requirements in an easy-to-use user interface.

- **Shared metadata foundation**—Integrates metadata discovered by profiling with other aspects of metadata (for example, Cleansing, Transform, and Federation Metadata) to support the enterprise.

- **Data quality management**—Identifies proactively data quality issues and patterns, and sets up baselines for tracking deteriorating data quality.

This analysis aids you in understanding the inputs to your integration process, ranging from individual fields to high-level data entities. Information analysis also enables you to correct problems with structure or validity before they affect your systems. In many situations, analysis must address data, values, and rules that are best understood by business users. Questions to ask in this analysis include:

- Is a unique column really unique when all data points are analyzed?

- Are integer values always created as such in the database (changing data types after initial creation of data in a table may have spurious results)?

- Does a business rule embedded in the database always hold true?

For comprehensive Enterprise Resource Planning (ERP), Customer Relationship Management (CRM), or Supply Chain Management (SCM) packages, validating data against business knowledge is a critical step before attempting to cleanse and move that data to any other repository or clean that data so it is used more effectively within the application itself. This exercise forms the basis for ongoing monitoring and auditing of data to ensure validity, accuracy, and compliance with internal standards and industry regulations. Although profiling of source data is a critical first step in any integration project, it is important to continually monitor the quality of the data beyond the initial integration. This is calling for more than a single step solution. An effective solution has the capability to continually audit the data sources to track results against business metrics for completeness and quality of data as an ongoing process that can be run and tracked over time.

Understanding the quality and contents of data sources is important. However, as a result of this profiling, a metadata map of source systems is created. This significantly builds on the Discovery stage by reflecting the actual data structures and implicitly identifying relationships between data. As mentioned in the previous Discovery stage, metadata is crucial, and a metadata map can be automatically created by data profile tooling and kept in some form of Metadata Repository.

This stage greatly assists an information governance program by swiftly identifying areas of misunderstanding, concern, or mismatch across systems. After it is in place, it can be run systematically to continually reassess the data and map to previous exercises to understand whether downstream (for example, cleansing) activities have a significant positive impact on the overall data quality and understanding of data.

Newer Profiling Services also include techniques such as using metrics and indices that are visible to end users and give them an indication of how trustworthy the data is based on the analysis performed in this stage. Indicators, such as tags to enable users to indicate their rating of the data in terms of quality, value, and so on, can be added to the overall profile, which makes a complete set of ratings around each data element. By making these indices visible to the end users, these Analysis Services are increasing the overall worth of that data to anyone who wishes to use it to make an informed decision.

What if such a service isn't available? The IT department would struggle to identify quality of information within its business. For example, the department might review only systems believed to be critical, because the exercise might become too time-consuming. The sheer effort of revisiting this to ensure there hasn't been change or degradation in what was understood might be too difficult to even complete.

Without this component and its reusability, knowledge gained about the content and context of your data would always be poor. It's worth remembering that most companies believe 20–30 percent of data degrades each year, so this simply cannot be a one-off exercise. The discovery and profiling phases must be repeatable and consistent in their approach to drive quality through all areas of the business. The results from these components are routinely added to reporting dashboards and scorecards in today's IT operations to ensure that the visibility of progress can be seen by the business. Where quality begins to slip, appropriate action can be taken internally, and if necessary with external suppliers of data to ensure the business continues to operate on optimal, consistent, and high-quality information.

8.3.2 Profile Scenario

Assume you are to build a new MDM System. To do this, you have a number of source systems that are to be used with the new MDM System. Each source system needs to be profiled across all its attributes to identify data content issues and define a set of business rules that can be applied to cleansing routines to populate a core MDM solution later in the process. The MDM System you plan cannot be deployed in one step, but in a phased approach to mitigate risk and ensure each step is managed correctly with a subset of the data sources added to the MDM System in each phase. The Profiling Component should be run periodically against the new MDM core system and the results obtained should be assessed against previous results. The Profiling Component will identify if any new relationships in data can be observed as the data is constantly cleansed (using the Cleanse Component). This information can be used to report back to other operational systems and their users on the quality of data they supply and as a way to challenge third-party sources regarding improvement of their data feeds into the enterprise. It also allows the monitoring of the master data within the MDM System to ensure it complies with the initially defined data profiling metrics.

This scenario uses the Profile Component and the Deploy Component to enable a reusable service that can be invoked by any user or process as part of a Service-Oriented Architecture (SOA) style deployment. The Deploy Component (this is explored in more detail in section 8.9) takes this idea and looks in more detail at how Service-Enabling Components fundamentally changes the way in which such routines are used across the enterprise.

The following walkthrough uses Figure 8.2 to describe a typical Profile scenario:

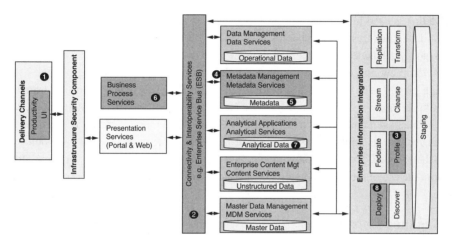

Figure 8.2   Profile scenario

1. Assume that initially a user (1) has run the Profile Component (3) that reviews a number of sources of data from the various data stores; these can be operational, analytical, unstructured, or even other master data domains.

2. From this, the user elects to deploy this as a service using the Deploy Service (8) to store a profiling routine and hold the appropriate metadata within the Metadata (5) layer, driven from the Metadata Service (4). (This is basically some form of registry or repository from which access to metadata is granted.)

3. Subsequently, a Business Service (6) or user running an ad-hoc request (1) requests the Profile Service via the Enterprise Service Bus (ESB) (2).

4. The Deploy Service (8) works with the Metadata Service (4) and Metadata Repository (5) to identify the Profile Service. This finds the appropriate service, invokes it, and runs the service, building the latest view of the data structure, relationships, and quality assessments associated with that data.

5. These latest definitions are stored in a suitable analytical repository (7) for comparison with other results, and the associated metadata for when the service is run and a status are returned to the Metadata Repository (5) for subsequent use.

   This history of information becomes valuable when assessing the progress a business is making around its information governance policies; it can be used to drive a frontend tool that builds a dashboard of the status of certain key data items relationships, structures, quality, or general health of the data within the business.

8.4 Cleanse

The data that is used in business systems often comes from a lot of source systems with many different data structures. As companies grow, they often find it difficult to phase out old legacy systems and yet businesses by necessity need to deliver new functions and augment existing systems with new and improved systems. As these solutions expand and grow, the overall IT landscape grows, data becomes more confused and difficult to manage, and the same data is used multiple times in different areas of the business, subject to differing definitions, business rules, and management. Often data is also used for the incorrect purpose it was originally designed for. For example, users simply add useful comments or identifiers to fields to help them in their day-to-day roles that were not envisioned when first designed. This leads to confusion about the use of the data and valuable insight being hidden from only those who understand where to look.

8.4.1 Cleanse Capabilities

Generally, when applying cleansing procedures to review, there are three areas of concern:

1. Profile a number of source systems existing data. The goal is to understand the nature of any problems that may exist within the data. This step requires the definition of metrics regarding data quality to all data from data stores to ascertain data quality levels. It is important to use as large a sample size as possible to ensure no hidden relationships or issues are missed. Review the results of this analysis to ensure that any issues are clearly reported into the business so that the impact of data quality issues can be quantified in business terms. These should link to real business impact and to financial, operational, or strategic benefits that good data quality helps to improve.

2. Profile the target system data and understand the discrepancies between source and target systems. Use the Discovery and Profile stages to identify the gaps between analyzed source systems versus the target systems. This step clarifies and helps the business understand the scale of work to enable change that is required.

3. Complete detailed alignment and harmonization requirements for each relevant data element. This stage uses the Cleanse Component and applies data quality measures to the identified data elements, ensures standardization and matching support these need,

and translates these results to business terminology. The Cleanse Component then creates the detailed reports, charts, and summaries that portray the standardization and matching levels against preset targets.

Without high-quality data, strategic systems cannot match and integrate all related data to provide a complete view of the organization and the interrelationships within it. If the data is not consistent, business managers and leaders cannot rely on a return on the investments made in critical business applications. As briefly described in Chapter 5, there are a number of substages to this stage, as discussed in the following sections.

8.4.1.1 Investigation Step

This step is strongly linked to the previous Profile Service; although the investigation step is more related to understanding the quality aspects of the source data records and gives complete visibility into the actual condition of the data. Values might be held as free text format and embedded as aggregated information; for example, a street name might capture house numbers, street names, and house names. By analyzing this and determining suitable logic to separate these pieces of information, a standard approach to defining these data items can be enabled. This is the first step toward breaking down this information into suitable atomic elements. Clearly, this requires domain-specific knowledge. (For example, in some countries, addresses have no postal code or zip code numbers and must be managed accordingly, and the United States uses direction indicators, such as "98 East Main Street," which is uncommon in many other countries.)

8.4.1.2 Standardization Step

This step conditions the data records further and structures these records according to standards of the source data and given quality improvement rules. It reformats data from multiple systems to ensure that each data type has the correct content and format, as specified in rules defined by the users. Typical standardization steps can include:

- Converting numbers held as text to integers.
- Checking whether values in fields that hold information such as postal codes, area codes, or phone numbers comply with the correct format.
- Ensuring differing name formats are identified and standardized (name standardization). For example, Max could be a nickname or abbreviation for Maxwell, Maximilian, or Maximo. (Note this can be a complex task with certain names; for example, the same person in Africa could have very different name spelling across countries.)
- Cleansing addresses to have them consistently available in a standardized form (address standardization). For example, *Sunset Blvd.* would be replaced by the standardized version, *Sunset Boulevard.*

8.4.1.3 Matching Step

During this step, matches are determined through deterministic or more sophisticated probabilistic matching capability and dynamic weighting strategies. Deterministic matching is based on business rules and algorithms to define a match. The advantage of this method is that it provides a clear answer (obviously, this is based on the rules and algorithms used to define that match, that is, the rules can still define false positives), such as two records do or do not match. The rule set is often the limiting factor with the rules and algorithms categorized with a degree of simple or medium complexity. The probabilistic method leverages statistical algorithms and fuzzy logic to indicate a match. This approach uses more powerful mechanisms to identify a match and provides the probability that records match, such as 93%. The degree of confidence in the match should be balanced against the value of the information being addressed and the cost to determine the match. These techniques help to ensure data integrity by linking records from one or more data sources that correspond to the same customer, supplier, or other entity. Matching can be used to identify duplicate entities that are caused by data entry variations or account-oriented business practices.

8.4.1.4 Determination Step

The final step includes the decision about which data records will survive and which ones get discarded. This step allows a single record (or even field within a record) to survive from the best information across specified data sources for each unique entity. The business rules for this are held in the Metadata layer. Records that fail the survivorship test are always maintained in some form of suspense or dump file for interrogation by Information Stewards. Based on the matching rules, the designer specifies survivorship rules that determine which record and attributes of a record reflect the correct information and are carried forward, and records that need to be removed are discarded. Cleansing Services can be deployed in a traditional sense as a set of algorithms that manage the influx of data in batch processes. However, increasingly, they are seen as an approach to deal with data immediately as it arrives in real time (either as a trickle feed or as it is physically keyed into an application). The data might enter the business by using an SOA-style service that allows for standardization and matching of individual input rows and fields. For example, a single name or address can be cleansed and returned in a standardized format, or if probabilistic matching is used, returned along with a set of possible candidates that are identified in that process. When Cleansing Services are used as data is entered into systems in real time, (note that Chapter 6, section 6.5.2 describes real-time operational patterns to support such a scenario) this immediately improves data representation (for example, consistent coding for regions, states, and other codification style) and increases the odds of finding a duplicate before it is persisted. Avoiding the problems caused by duplicates in advance is far less costly than trying to correct them afterward.

Without a Cleansing Component, the good work of the Discovery and Analysis Components simply cannot be part of the day-to-day operations. By enabling a set of reusable cleansing routines, you can introduce a standard enterprise-wide approach to managing the same data feeds in the same way; whether that data arrives through a message, a batch feed, or a web service, it can all be dealt with in an identical manner.

8.4.2 Cleanse Scenario

In this scenario, consider how the Cleansing Component can be reused across multiple differing data feeds. Assume you have a scenario in which you want to cleanse addresses and postal codes, and there is an enterprise-wide data model that is physically maintained by an MDM solution. The requirement is for addresses to be verified against postal codes at a number of touch points with the master data solution, which might include:

- **A batch data feed**—This takes some of the operational data and processes it overnight to synchronize that data with the MDM System.

- **A message queue-based feed**—This trickles data from web-based frontends that allow a customer to enter his name and address when requesting new services from the business. This is an example of an asynchronous check.

- **An SOA service call**—Part of the requirement is to call an address—postal code matching service.

Figure 8.3 is used to describe how the same Cleanse Component can be used by these requests to ensure a consistent algorithm is supplied to manage this across all entry points into the business. The following walkthrough list describes a typical Cleanse scenario:

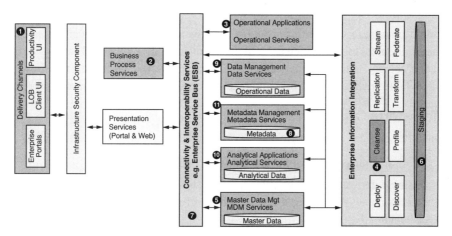

Figure 8.3 Cleanse scenario

1. Data is presented to the Cleansing Service through multiple channels, a user interface on the web (1), or a business process that triggers a batch load (2). The same Cleansing Component (4) is used across all these channels. This requires that the component is capable of running against individual transactions or large batch loads. The logic remains the same, but the operational model to call the component might differ for different requests.

2. As each differing request calls the Cleanse Component (4), it invokes the necessary logic to check the postal code against the address and return a response that can be managed differently for the differing requests. For example, batch records that fail the check are written to a suspense file—using the staging area (6) so an Information Steward can fix the data and rerun the failed transactions. A message queue returns the response to a queue via the ESB (7), and the applications, in layer (1), use this response to either fail or allow the transaction to continue.

3. After verification of the data is complete, it can then be written to one (or more) of the backend services—(5), (8), (9), (10), (11), (12)—to complete the transaction. The data can be written to the MDM System first and then propagated on to the downstream systems, for example, (9) and (10). At this point, this becomes a master data scenario rather than a cleansing issue.

4. The Metadata Service (11) is used to gather any statistics associated with whether the transaction passes or fails the cleanse step, and metadata (8) regarding the transactions is captured and stored for subsequent analysis to assist the Profile Service in determining whether quality of overall service is improving.

8.5 Transform

In its simplest form, this stage performs some form of transformation (driven by rule sets) on the data while it manages movement from source systems to target systems in either batch or real time. The data sources might include indexed files, sequential files, relational databases, archives, external data sources, enterprise applications, and message queues. During the transform stage, a target file or table might find itself becoming the source file for subsequent processing.

8.5.1 Transform Capabilities

The Transform stage can be used to manage any of the following styles of transform:

- String and numeric formatting and data type conversions
- Business derivations and calculations that apply business rules and algorithms to the data (examples range from straightforward currency conversions to more complex profit calculations)
- Reference data enforcement to validate customer or product identifiers
- Conversion of reference data from disparate sources to a common reference set, creating consistency across these systems
- Aggregations for reporting and analytics
- Creation of analytical or reporting databases, such as data marts or cubes

This stage requires that the component be capable of connecting to a wide range of mainframe, legacy, enterprise applications, databases, and external information sources. It needs to be capable of managing transformations in batch mode, where it might potentially deal with tens of millions of records per hour[3] and single records delivered in real time via, for example, a message queue. This requires a highly scalable and flexible architecture that can manage parallel processing and integration with ESBs as and when necessary. In an SOA context, there are increasingly new ways to invoke the transform process in an on-demand manner rather than in a batch-driven process. Traditional, non-SOA transform solutions are typically used to manage scenarios like the following:

- **Data Warehousing**—Data needs to be transformed from multiple source systems to generate a single version of the truth suitable for use by Business Intelligence (BI) toolsets. This is often seen as the classic use for transform capabilities and has been exploited for many years. Data transformation is critical to helping companies provide this single version of the truth from a wide range of sources.

- **Consolidation of multiple applications into a reduced set**—One of the tasks in consolidating applications (today, many companies consolidate multiple SAP R/3 systems into a single SAP Netweaver instance) is to transform the data associated with the multiple legacy databases into a form suitable for merging with the new, consolidated database(s).

- **MDM**—In some master data scenarios, the master data resides in many isolated systems and is stored and maintained in different formats, which creates a high degree of inconsistency and incompleteness. To produce an accurate and consistent set of information that can be managed in a central MDM System, data needs to be gathered, transformed into the master data model, and consolidated into the master data repository.

8.5.2 Transform Scenario

Consider a global company that tries to manage its inventory. The inventory details lie in multiple heterogeneous databases. To identify the inventory of all stock, the data needs to be gathered from all the differing sources and brought together. Issues such as differing locations using different part numbers for the same part can seriously impact any consolidated effort to get a global view of stock. This must be resolved before such a view of stock can be made available. This scenario uses the Transform Component to take the various feeds, map the source to target definitions, and apply any checks and aggregations of data to deliver a concise view of product data into an MDM System.

We require that this data be near real time to ensure inventory levels are as accurate as possible when purchasing decisions are made. This is achieved using one of the replication scenarios from Section 8.6. This increases the probability that the master data system is in sync with operational systems and reduces batch windows as data is continuously updated, ensuring the business maintains a single consolidated view of product master data. The Cleanse Component from Section 8.4 can also be used to enhance the quality of the data by applying Standardize, Match, and Filter Components to augment the delivery of an accurate result set.

---

[3] See reference [1] describing grid computing techniques that allow massive throughput of such transformations.

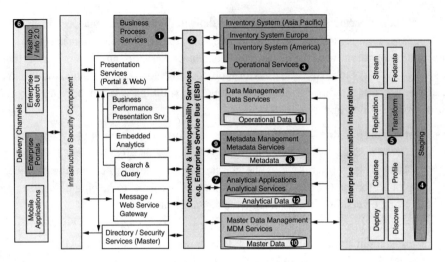

Figure 8.4   Transform scenario

The following assumptions are made about the typical Transform scenario depicted in Figure 8.4:

- Mapping of source to target data model and any merge process into the target model has been previously defined for data flows. The target model has been defined to enable this scenario. If this is not the case, then techniques found in Section 8.2 must be completed to gain an understanding of what exists to apply the Transform stage to!

- Data is replicated (1) using Q replication (detailed in section 8.6).

- Data can be cleansed (2) as a precursor to the step, but we do not delve into details on the Cleansing Component.

The following describes a typical Transform scenario in sequential order:

1. Some business processes (1) drive replication in the EII layer to present information over the ESB to the staging layer (2). This step simply moves and maps the data from source (operational systems [3]) to target (staging area [4]) in preparation for processing.

2. The Transform Component (5) can be accessed by either a business process (1) that triggers events every time new data arrives or a time-based business process that enables data to be transformed in sets of data (for example, every 5 minutes) or based on counts of new data arriving (for example, every 500 transactions). It can even be triggered manually through an event raised from one of the delivery channels (6), such as a user requesting a refresh of a local dataset.

3. The Transform Component (5) uses the Metadata Repository (8) and Metadata Services (9) to map and drive the transform of the newly arrived data into a suitable format to

meet the downstream systems needs. These might use, for example, any of the repositories—(10), (11), and (12)—for use with their appropriate services.

4. After the transform job is complete, metadata is written back into the Metadata Repository (8) with suitable statistics of rows processed, rows failed, and other status information. This can then be reviewed at any suitable time by an Information Steward or operations support analyst to check the job and initiate any remedial actions necessary.

8.6 Replicate

Replication solutions are varied and use both hardware and software techniques to manage the movement of data from one system (or more) to another. Hardware solutions include such technologies as disk-to-disk mirroring and machine clustering to enable copies of data to be supported on a number of systems. For the purposes of this book, we concentrate on some specific information-intensive options and examine only those of particular interest here.

8.6.1 Replicate Capabilities

Techniques such as load/unload, exports, and FTP can be used to manage this function; however, these techniques often struggle with managing latency, audit, or performance issues. In addition, they often require additional custom code or scripts to implement them, which make them difficult to tie into any overall data movement and Metadata strategy.

Log shipping is sometimes addressed as a specific type of replication—one that is used to get an exact duplicate of the database to another server. This method is typically used to create a high availability solution where the business can accept only a few minutes of data loss.

In contrast, a pure Replication Service is used to create copies of a specific table, set of tables, or subset of data within a table or tables from a source database onto one or many target databases. The data can be pushed in near real time or on a schedule depending on the requirements of the application and the connectivity which the network can support. Replication can be setup to send the same data to several servers at the same time.

One final point to note is that tools that can accommodate the Transform stage can also work to move data from one location to another, with good performance. The solutions described here can be used instead of a transform style solution if, for example, such tooling is not available. For this reason, we have elected to focus on approaches that have gained in popularity especially around the area of delivering data in near real time, which is a need that is becoming more prominent with increasing data volumes to deal with faster decision making needed to gain competitive advantage. There are several differing techniques that can be used to accomplish these functions.

8.6.1.1 Trigger-Based Replication

Trigger-based replication captures Insert, Update, and Delete operations by using the corresponding trigger on all tables to be replicated to capture changed data into separate queues or control tables. The advantage of this approach is that triggers are part of most database systems so the option can be developed at little cost. It does not require changes to any application that the underlying database might support. The disadvantage of this approach is that it degrades the Insert, Update, and Delete performance of the underlying database because Structured Query Language (SQL) Trigger statements are compiled into the executable of the Insert/Delete/Update (I/D/U) statements, which can make response times unacceptable in some cases. An important thing to keep in mind when contemplating a trigger-based replication solution is the action taken via a trigger is synchronous with respect to the triggering data-change operation. For example, an insert statement aimed at a table on which an insert trigger has been defined does not complete successfully until the action taken by the trigger has also completed successfully.

This being the case, it's often essential that the target system is not updated using the trigger on a captured data change because that takes too long and slows down the source data change operations too much. A better design is to place the captured data change information onto another table from which an apply process running on the target system can retrieve it. An alternative for temporary storage of the captured, to-be-applied data changes is a message queue, and this technique can make use of the same messaging technology as that described in the following Queue replication scenario.

8.6.1.2 SQL Replication

Figure 8.5 shows a configuration for SQL replication. Note that the key requirement for this form of replication is that the underlying database creates suitable transactional logs and these are well formed and understood by the capture routines. The advantage of such an approach is that it has little or no impact on the performance of the underlying transactions being run. This section briefly assesses the capabilities of this technique.[4]

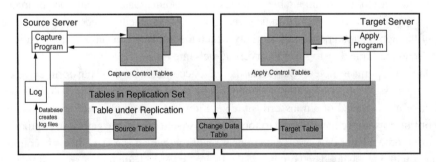

Figure 8.5   SQL replication

SQL replication allows you to replicate data from source databases and transmit those changes to targets by first running a *Capture* routine that writes changes to staging tables on the

---

[4] More details can be found in [2] and [3].

source system and then an *Apply* routine on the target system retrieves that data and writes to the target tables. The Capture program normally reads transactional logs of a database for changed source data and saves the committed changed data to said staging tables. Normally some form of audit capability (often simply more tables within source and target systems) can track the information that they require to do their tasks and to store information that they generate themselves (more Metadata). This includes information that you can use to find out how well they are performing. Note that it is feasible to use SQL replication to work across heterogeneous databases if suitable federation capabilities exist that allow changes from one type of database system to be mapped to another. This technique has some shortcomings when trying to manage high-volume and low-latency solutions and is best used for relatively simple scenarios that include only a few source-to-target databases.

Queue replication has been developed to help with the scenarios with much more complex requirements around real-time integration requirements.

8.6.1.3 Queue Replication

Queue replication is a high-volume, low-latency replication solution with the idea that changes in a source system are captured and published to a message queue (a middleware application) to manage and transmit transactions between source and target databases or subsystems. Queue replication solutions are asynchronous, which means that they describe a process where, at a given instant in time, the copy and the source data are out of sync with each other. The delay (or latency) can range from a few seconds or a few minutes to many hours. Asynchronous replication has the following potential advantages:

- Being able to cope with the unavailability of the target system or communication system
- Minimizing the overhead on the updating transaction in the source system
- Enabling sub-setting and merging of source data, and data transformations
- Using optimization algorithms such as grouping multiple updates to the same row on the source system to a single update on the copy
- Working in situations where network performance is harder to guarantee, for example, over long distances

The potential disadvantage is that the copies are out of sync with the sources from which they are generated. Figure 8.6 shows a simple configuration of Queue replication. Queue replication allows you to replicate committed transactional data from many different database sources by using two programs that are often named Q Capture and Q Apply. Of course, the database must have the capabilities to create a log of database changes for this to be possible. The Q Capture program runs on the source system and reads the source database transactional logs for changed source data and writes the changes to one (or many) message queues. The Q Apply program generally runs on the target system and retrieves captured changes from queues and writes the changes to targets.

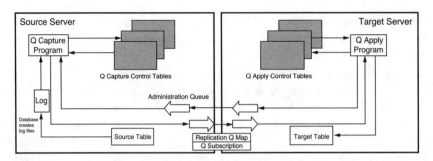

Figure 8.6   Queue replication

Most commercial tooling to support Queue replication creates database tables to track the information that they require to do their tasks and to store information that they generate themselves (Metadata). This includes information that you can use to find out how well they are performing. These tables contain information about your replication sources, the targets that correspond to them, and which queue manager and queues are being used by the Q Capture program. It is possible to replicate between remote servers or within a single server, and replication changes can be in a single direction or in multiple directions. Replicating in multiple directions can be bidirectional (useful for managing standby or backup systems) or peer-to-peer (useful for synchronizing data on production systems). Chapter 6 describes the operational patterns (see sections 6.5.2, 6.5.3, and 6.5.4 for three applicable patterns) that support such Q-based replication scenarios.

8.6.2 Replication Scenario

An increasingly accepted technique for the population of an enterprise DW is the scenario that uses Queue replication to trickle feed data from a variety of sources. Using the Component Overview Diagram from Chapter 4, we can describe how the Replicate Component works in conjunction with the various data stores and other elements to provide such a service. A real-life example of the practical application of this could be the real-time collection of POS (Point of Sales) data from retail outlets to drive the core DW to deliver critical sales and stock information more quickly or used to drive supply chain systems to manage the replenishment of stock on a shorter cycle.

In Figure 8.7, the Component Model from Chapter 5 has been abbreviated to show the key components working together for this scenario. In this scenario, the assumption is that the Replication Services to capture information (the Q capture routines) are running against the target applications (for example CRM, ERP, or legacy apps) and building a queue ready for use by whatever service reads that queue. The following walkthrough list describes a typical Replication scenario:

1. A Business Service (1) (traditionally a batch process, event, or time based, more recently an SOA enabled call to implement a service) invokes the Replication Service. The data could be from many of the data domains, typically:

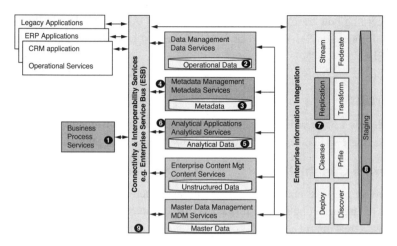

Figure 8.7 Replication scenario

- **Operational data (2)**—These are data elements from legacy, CRM, ERP packages, and so on.

- **Master data (3)**—The core data entities that make up a business, such as customer, location, account, or product, that can be from an MDM solution or maintained within one of the existing applications.

- **Analytical data (4)**—This data can come from other third-party sources, which are possibly statistical or marketing related, or from internal data that has previously been created, such as customer segmentation metrics.

  Data from content repositories can be involved but it has probably gone through some other process first (for example, text mining) to produce data that can be consumed by another more structured, data store. The data is moved over the ESB (9) to the Replication Component (7) as a message queue that handles authentication, authorization, and assured delivery.

2. Data is captured using the Replication Component (7). This might be because the Business Service has simply requested an update or the Replication Service might be monitoring the queue for any changes to the data and applying those changes when they arrive.

3. The data is then moved into the staging layer (8) (the target tables) from which processing of this data can be done as appropriate. This can mean building up sets of data to process, such as where some form of summarization is needed, or taking each row as it arrives and processing it (possibly with the Cleansing Component, but not necessary). The data is moved into the analytics data repository—for example, a DW (4)—for use with the Analytic Services (for example, BI) using replication services (7).

4. Throughout this process, Metadata regarding the source and target systems structure and message queues structure is held in the Metadata Repository (3) alongside any Metadata

concerning how to invoke these services as an SOA-style service. In this way, the specific Replication Services can be found and reused with other solutions within the overall EIA.

8.7 Federate

The Data Federation stage is different from replication or data movement in general. Its purpose is to provide a single virtualized view of one or more source data systems.

8.7.1 Federate Capabilities

Federation has strong links into SOA-style solutions. When designing such solutions, the core services require aggregated, quality information often from multiple sources. Additionally, with the increasing interest in grid and cloud computing, federation might become a much more prevalent technology than is currently the case. An increasing number of grid applications manage data at large scales of both size and distribution. The complexity of data management on a grid arises from the scale, dynamism, autonomy, and distribution of data sources. These complexities can be made transparent to grid applications through a federation layer that contributes to enabling ease of data access and processing, dynamic migration of data for workload balancing, parallel data processing, and collaboration.

Federation can help by efficiently joining data from multiple heterogeneous sources. A federated server can access data directly (for example, by accessing a relational database) or access an application that creates and returns data dynamically (such as a Web service). For example, when an application issues a query, a data federation engine retrieves data from the appropriate source data systems, integrates it to match the virtual view, and then sends the results back to the calling system. Data federation always pulls data from source systems on an on-demand basis. Any data transformation is done as the data is retrieved from the source systems and can make use of the Transform stage described earlier in this chapter.

A federated system uses Metadata held within a Metadata store or specifically within the federation tool itself to help access the source data. This Metadata can be the view definition of the query that links several source databases or might be more sophisticated where federation is mapping spreadsheets, flat files, or XML sources. This more extensive Metadata information can help the federated solution optimize access to the source systems.

Federated solutions should provide business Metadata that describes key linkages between critical data elements in the source systems. An example is customer data within an MDM system that is deployed using the Registry Implementation style. The Metadata might contain a common customer identifier that is mapped to the various customer keys in the source systems ensuring the federated query can access the source systems where the MDM solution is deployed in this Registry Style manner.[5]

---

[5] Chapter 11 has more information about this style of integration and [4] describes this in complete detail.

The advantages of a federated approach are that it provides access to current data and removes the need to consolidate source data into another data store. This approach is not necessarily well suited for retrieving and dealing with large amounts of data or for applications with ·significant data quality problems in the source data. Another consideration is the potential performance impact and overhead of accessing multiple data sources at run time. Data federation should be used when the cost of replicating or consolidating data is greater than the business benefits it accrues. Federation scenarios are usually those where ad hoc, well-defined, and known performance characteristic style queries are run across multiple well-defined sources. Federation scenarios also benefit from supporting technology such as using caching techniques to try and reduce the overhead on rerunning similar queries against source systems each and every time data is requested. Federation can play a role where data security and license issues don't allow the data to be copied out of the source system(s) in place. Federation can be used as a short-term technique (for example in testing scenarios or quick pieces of work to manage systems that have been acquired through mergers) to swiftly derive benefit before a longer-term strategy is thought out.

A federated solution can have the following capabilities:

- Correlate data from local tables and remote data sources, as if all the data is stored locally in the federated database.

- Update data in relational data sources, as if the data is stored in the federated database.

- Move data to and from relational data sources, through the use of SQL statements.

- Use data source processing strengths by sending requests to the data sources for processing.

- Compensate for SQL limitations at the data source by processing parts of a distributed request at the federated server.

- Access data anywhere in your enterprise, regardless of what format it is in or what vendor you use, without creating new databases and without disruptive changes to existing ones, using standard SQL and any tool that supports Java DataBase Connectivity (JDBC) or Open DataBase Connectivity (ODBC).

In the traditional context, applications typically use standard relational interfaces and protocols to interact with a federation server. The federation server in turn connects through various adaptors, or wrappers, to a variety of data sources such as relational databases, XML documents, packaged applications, and content management and collaboration systems. The federation server is a virtual database with all the capabilities of a relational database. The requesting application or user can perform any query requests within the scope of their access permissions. Upon completion of the query, a result set is returned containing all the records that meet the selection criteria.

In an SOA context, a service might need to retrieve comprehensive information from within some business process; for example, accessing a customer's known policies/purchases and credit checks in the case of an online purchase from a website or opening a new insurance policy as part of the process of validating and processing the request. This information almost certainly resides in multiple systems that might be external to the business processing the request. Data federation joins the information from multiple sources so that it can be surfaced as a service to the requestor. In this case, the federation server can act as service provider, a service consumer, or both, which leverages SOA conforming interfaces. When the data federation server exposes integrated information as a service provider, a service consumer can access the integrated information through a service interface. The data federation server can also consume and then integrate services provided by multiple information sources. Most successful SOA projects focus first on the most important, most widely used business functions that are exposed as services. These often span multiple backend systems. Gathering information from multiple heterogeneous sources is an important requirement and capability that SOA relies on. The service is not a query in the traditional data access context; it is a request for a business entity (or entities) the Federation Service might fulfill through a series of queries and other services.

8.7.2 Federation Scenario

Consider Figure 8.8. It merges data from existing legacy mainframe data repositories and a new XML database. The mainframe data source is used to hold critical operational transactions that are captured each day (for example, ATM transactions for a bank). The XML engine is used to hold details regarding products that a customer is involved in, for example, a third-party insurance program that runs under the Banks brand or mortgage applications derived from other subsidiaries of the bank. These are gathered on a daily batch basis from external sources and loaded into the XML engine overnight.

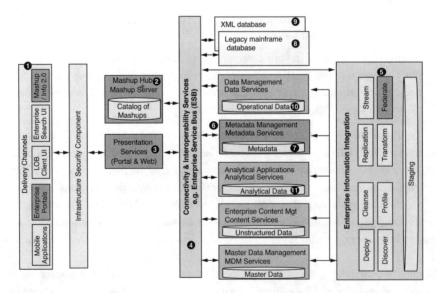

Figure 8.8   Federation scenario

The aim is to marry this data to gain insight into the likely risk associated with any new requests for loans from the customer. This step might be one of many in a larger enquiry regarding mortgages loans. The requirement is to map data held in the mainframe (for example, total withdrawals per day) against the customers other related data requested from the XML engine with the goal of gaining a wider view of the customers' current points of contact with the bank and potential risks associated with offering new services.

An assumption is made that the Federation server has already been set up to manage access to multiple back ends, in this case the legacy mainframe database, using an appropriate wrapper, for example, VSAM, and an analytical store using an XML database, for example, DB2 pure query engine. The applications (8) and (9) maintain the data normally, but we have decided to access the databases simultaneously using one of the front-end channels in (1).

The following list describes a typical Federation scenario:

1. User submits request through one of the channels shown in (1).

2. One of the components (2) or (3) manages that request and converts the request into a SQL query, passing this over the ESB (4).

3. The Federation Service (5) takes this SQL request and reviews whether data is already available in a pre-prepared cache.

4. If data is not available, the Federation Service takes the query and breaks it down into its constituent parts using the Metadata Service (6) and Metadata Repository (7) which holds definitions for access paths to the relevant data, which have been configured previously.

5. After query paths have been identified, the queries are sent out to each relevant data source—mainframe (10) and XML engine (11)—in an optimized format for that engine and the results are returned to the federation server.

6. The Federation server caches the results and sends the result set back to the ESB which forwards it to the appropriate frontend server for further processing and rendering—(2), (3), and (4)—before returning the completed results to the front-end channel (1).

8.8 Data Streaming

Data streaming is a new range of services that changes the way in which architects can view the processing of information coming into the business.

8.8.1 Data Streaming Capabilities

We are constantly bombarded with information in ever greater volumes (primarily through Unstructured Data sources, such as video, audio, e-mail, and so on) and with greater velocity. (Transactions processing seems to be constantly increasing through the use of things such as embedded sensors to gather structured information, for example, Radio Frequency Identification

[RFID] to track supply chain data.) We must manage this influx in some manner to make sense of what is happening and look for potential improvements. Consider Figure 8.9 which describes the myriad number of ways in which data can now move around a business.

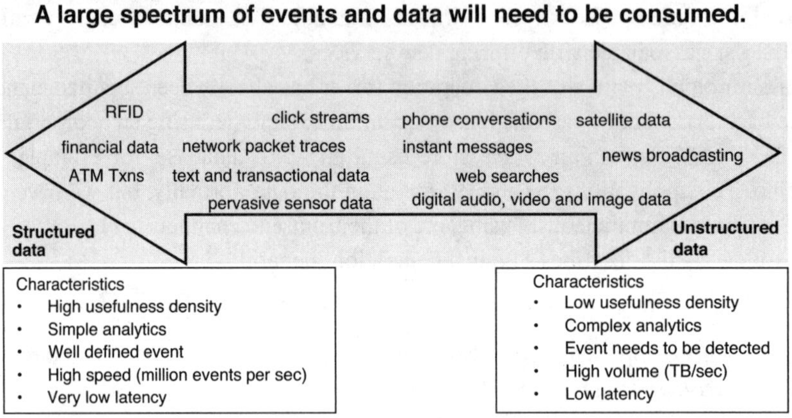

A large spectrum of events and data will need to be consumed.
RFID
click streams
phone conversations
satellite data
financial data
network packet traces
instant messages
news broadcasting
ATM Txns
text and transactional data
web searches
pervasive sensor data
digital audio, video and image data
Structured data
Unstructured data
Characteristics
High usefulness density
Simple analytics
Well defined event
High speed (million events per sec)
Very low latency
Characteristics
Low usefulness density
Complex analytics
Event needs to be detected
High volume (TB/sec)
Low latency

Figure 8.9 The increasing spectrum of data that needs to be managed in an EIA

To leverage this information, we need to ensure that we can analyze it in a way that offers greater insight to allow competitive advantage through access to more timely information. We need to be able to understand the data as it's constantly being generated and minimize our time to react based on that understanding. Without this approach, our actions are too late, wrong, or both. Consider Figure 8.10.

Data at rest analysis
Data
Data Warehouse
Queries & Analysis
Results
Streaming and Memory based Data analysis
Data
Queries & Analysis
Results
Information Integration
Data Warehouse

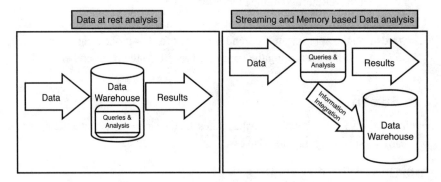

Figure 8.10 Traditional query management versus streaming data

This diagram demonstrates a new way of considering how data can be processed. Rather than building up sets of data over time into some form of information repository and then running differing queries against them to obtain results (note the left side of Figure 8.10), we can now stream the data directly into a set of queries and obtain results dynamically because that data is consumed by the queries (note the right side of Figure 8.10). Data of high value can be stored in traditional analytic stores. Of particular concern in business analytics and optimization solutions (see Chapter 14 for more details on streaming scenarios) are the challenges for optimization of transport and placement of the data when the volumes of information being consumed is so huge that the transport itself is a challenge and the storage requirements would become difficult and expensive to manage—for example, data in message streams for a stock trading. The following list describes several examples where streaming can be applied:

- **Traffic congestion into a city**—With a traditional approach, we can gather data about cars entering the city and analyze what time of day congestion arises. With a streaming approach, we can constantly monitor data entering our systems regarding the traffic entering the city and identify much earlier when traffic might start to look as though it could become congested (based on previous history, previous weather patterns and other feeds) to start to tackle the problem in near real time. This approach relies on a new set of interconnected devices. For example, the car needs devices embedded within it to be able to announce where it is. You need to be able to access online city street maps, online weather conditions, and known areas where roads are under repair, CCTV images around the city, radio warnings, and so on. By analyzing all this information in near real time, it's possible to redirect traffic before running into a problem. It may also be possible to offer additional information on other transportation options to give citizens alternatives to the car if this mode is blocked.

- **Health care monitoring**—Stream computing has been used to perform better medical analysis with significant reduction on a doctor's workload. What regularly takes doctors, nurses, and other medical personnel a significant amount of time to study by streaming biomedical data from a network of sensors monitoring a patient, the analytical application can use known medical patterns to detect early signs of disease and health anomalies faster. Stream analysis can also use this data to detect correlations among multiple patients and derive insights about the efficacy of treatments. These novel applications of the business analytics and optimization technologies in the health-care industry have already been demonstrated with tangible advantages at several institutions.

- **Banking and Financial Services (Trading)**—Success in many segments of the financial services industry relies heavily on rapidly analyzing large volumes of data to make near-real-time business and trading decisions. For example, any large stock exchange in North America, Europe, or Asia requires the ability to analyze real-time streaming data from external sources such as information supplied by financial market data providers, such as Reuters and Bloomberg L.P. Additionally, information provided by other exchanges from around the world—information in audio and video feeds from news agencies and weather forecast, energy demand maps, and models—can also be used to help deliver insight into decision making. To be truly useful, this information requires real-time analysis and correlation to provide traders with a solid information advantage before trading decisions are made.

The previous scenarios are around Business Analytics and Optimization (BAO) and are described in greater detail in Chapter 14. This chapter focuses on one example.

Being able to perform analysis on streaming data is required to deliver the extremely low latency requirements for business insights that many operational BI environments need to effectively derive value and enable timely business decisions. In addition to its ability to ingest large volumes of Structured, Semi-Structured, and Unstructured Data, the streaming environment delivers a repository of data source adapters and analytical operators such as filter, join, aggregate, transform, and others to efficiently design an analytic application. Extreme flexibility is achieved by its ability to add new operators and adapters including advanced analytical functions using open standards-based tooling and an application development environment. When this powerful feature is exploited, the Streaming Services technology is capable of consuming and processing any data source. This means we look at multiple styles of data (Structured/Unstructured) that includes huge volumes of data and historically aggregated data all coming together on a second-by-second basis.

Streaming aligns itself tightly with the concept of virtualization (grid and cloud computing) that ensures the appropriate resources can be assigned to specific streams of work in a dynamic manner. The goal of virtualization is to ensure the optimal use of resources across a wide and demanding set of processing tasks. In this way, managing streaming data can benefit from grid- and cloud-style computing. Operationally, to manage such dynamic workloads, we might need to virtualize many of the physical assets and use intelligent systems management. Chapter 6 describes a number of virtualization patterns. (For example, read section 6.5.15 for a description of a cloud-based provisioning pattern that is useful in this scenario.)

Such ideas are important, and we need to see that streaming is the application of existing technologies in a new paradigm that does the following:

- Continually adapts to new inputs and new categories of input.
- Integrates existing EII Components exposed as services and new providers to cater for more complex data forms such as video and audio or newer types of feeds such as RSS and Ajax style feeds.
- Seamlessly manages all forms of data (structured/unstructured) in near real time.

Figure 8.11, extended from Chapter 5 (the overall component model for an EIA), details the high-level Architecture and Core Components of the streaming analytics environment. It shows how a streaming analytics application is created from the various data-source adapters and analytic operators through the application development environment. The designed streaming application can be visualized as a flow graph through the tooling. It has the flexibility to adapt to many target architectures and, after it is deployed, it is optimized for the specific platform where the application runs.

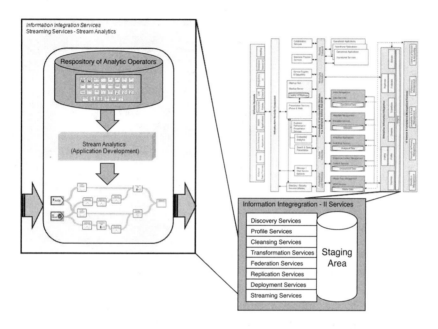

Figure 8.11   Architecture of the Stream Analytics platform

In the example that follows (a stock trading scenario), consider the volumes and variety of information being processed. Although a traditional environment can be adopted that assigns resources to specific tasks, it's possible to see how cloud models can optimize such a solution by constantly associating work classes with incoming work and dynamically adjusting the infrastructure to accommodate the requirements.

8.8.2 Data Streaming Scenario

Consider a financial trading scenario. Figure 8.12 describes typical feeds that are consumed in such a process, where there is an increasing demand for sub-millisecond identification and response to opportunities identified when using near-real-time market data. Many forms of data might need to be correlated and managed to enable a sensible assessment to be derived that can be the basis for automatically making a decision on purchasing or selling stock on the financial stock exchange.

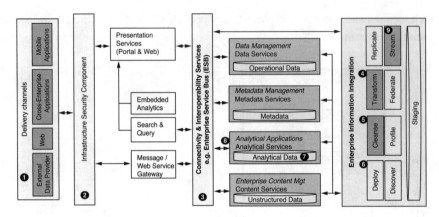

Figure 8.12   Typical streaming data flow and operators enabled against them

Existing information from the New York Stock Exchange (NYSE) along with data from SEC Edgar (Securities and Exchange Commission, Electronic Data Gathering, Analysis, and Retrieval), weather, news, and radio channels are used to gather intelligence in near real time to align with existing historical information from a DW to make those informed decisions. Looking at Figure 8.12, we can describe the steps to manage a streaming-based solution:

1. Data arrives from multiple channels (1) in multiple formats, web feeds (weather), Structured Data (SEC Edgar and NYSE), and unstructured content (Video news) is passed through the security layer (2) to verify its authenticity and then driven though the ESB (3) to be consumed by one of the components on the EII layer.

2. The EII layer must consume these feeds in near real time. The streaming capabilities of the EII layer coordinate the various resources required, including services to enable transforms (4) and cleansing (5) routines that could already be in place and available to invoke as services enabled using the Deploy Component (6).

3. The Streaming Component (9) manages the coordination and run time of these other components to assemble the output as required and posts the results to the analytic data store (7) via the Analytic Service component (8). Figure 8.12 helps to describe the new forms of analytics that might take place upon the differing feed types. For example, the NYSE Feed might be managed by existing components—cleanse (4) and transform (5)—whereas the video and weather feeds might be subject to specific algorithms to scrape useful information from those feeds that might exist within the video or weather feed that is normally difficult to extract. Such techniques could be deployed using Mashup Components that could rapidly be re-engineered if necessary to accommodate external feeds that are often liable to outside change and influences.

4. The results are combined and returned to the user (1) or, more likely in a near-real-time scenario, a business process calls the results based on time- or event-based needs and uses the results to drive a decision to buy or sell stock.

5. Useful aggregated information can be stored within the analytic data store (7) for subsequent reuse, for example when calculating the VWAP[6] in Figure 8.12.

Figure 8.12 simply outlines the typical practical steps taken to process such information into real, actionable insight on the trading floor.

8.9 Deploy

This section focuses on how to take the services described in the previous sections and physically deploy them to the information infrastructure, in such a way that they are easily located and consumed when needed.

8.9.1 Deploy Capabilities

The Deploy Component provides a unified mechanism for publishing and managing shared SOA services across data quality, data transformation, and federation functions, allowing any calling service-enabled application to find and easily deploy these services for any information integration task and then to consistently manage them. Key is that the components built can be published and always available for use and that these services include the Metadata Services, which provide standard SOA and analysis of Metadata across the platform. We now find ourselves in a position to be able to swiftly reuse the logic and processing associated with these services through this Deploy Component using standard protocols and interfaces to enable this in an easy to identify and consume manner.[7] Some key characteristics of this component are:

- **Scalable**—To enable high performance with large, unpredictable volumes of requests.

- **Standards-Based**—The services are based on open standards and can be invoked by standards-based technologies including EAI and ESB platforms, applications, and portals.

- **Flexible**—Services can be invoked by using multiple mechanisms (bindings). At a minimum the service should be capable of binding these components as Java Message Service (JMS), JavaScript Object Notation (JSON), Really Simple Syndication (RSS), Representational State Transfer (REST), Enterprise Java Beans (EJB), and Web Services (SOAP/HTTP).

---

[6] Volume Weighted Average Price (VWAP): A trading benchmark used especially in pension plans. VWAP is calculated by adding up the dollars traded for every transaction (price multiplied by number of shares traded) and then dividing by the total shares traded for the day.

[7] See [5] for more details.

- **Reusable**—The services publish their own Metadata, which can be found and called across any network.

- **Manageable**—Monitoring services within the component enables the timely reporting of system-wide performance data. This facet is important when these deployed services are working within critical business processes.

- **Reliable and highly available**—Along with operational characteristics, this component must be capable of identifying where failures occur and be capable of rerouting a service request to a different server in the pool.

- **High performance**—Load balancing and the parallel processing capabilities (possibly exploiting grid capabilities) must be engineered into the overall solution when these services are used enterprise wide. Virtualization for these services might also be necessary to ensure the quality of service measures can be met.

8.9.2 Deploy Scenario

Consider the case of an international credit checking agency company that currently manages name and address matching through a batch service (from suppliers such as banks and building societies) that validates names and property addresses. The company has previously used automated tooling to improve the quality of its data, but is increasingly finding that the batch process is running beyond the overnight window and data can be out of date often.

The company has seen a huge increase in the number of customers using its web site to monitor their credit details and have decided to include some additional information in the web front end to allow users to validate their names and addresses online. The business plans to use this data to augment their back-end systems. This is done in real time to ensure that all channels can make use of this enhanced data as soon as possible. Existing logic to manage the standardization and quality rules has been identified (see previous sections), and this has been selected as a candidate to be wrapped as an information service. This is invoked when the message from the user front end is delivered to that service. Initially, the data arrives in secure, asynchronous, and assured delivery as a message queue (see Chapter 6, section 6.5.4 for an appropriate pattern), and then it is shredded. The relevant data passed across the Cleansing and Transform Services and from there added in to the relevant back end systems through the appropriate service (for example, MDM Service or an Analytical Service). Figure 8.13 depicts this scenario.

1. The company's master data system (1) is used to present a web form with name and address details to a user through a variety of delivery channels such as PDAs, PCs or smart phones (2) (note that the service could be enabled through a mashup Deployable Service) (3).

2. The user validates and/or changes these details and sends this back to the business as an XML data stream.

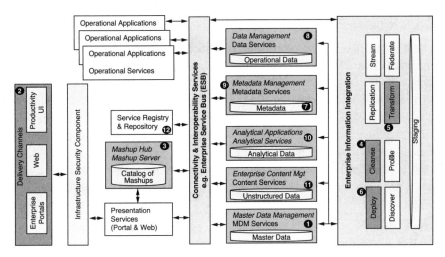

Figure 8.13   Deploy scenario

3. This stream travels over the Internet, is authenticated, and is passed over the ESB where it is shredded and processed by the Cleanse (4) and Transform (5) Components. Both these components have been enabled as web services (it could be other standards used) and their details held in the Metadata Repository (7). The Cleansing Service could for example include:

   - **Matching Services**—These enable data integration logic to be packaged as a shared service that can be called by enterprise application integration platforms. This type of service allows reference data such as customer, inventory, and product data to be matched to and kept current with a master store with each transaction.

   - **Transform Services**—These can enable in-flight transformation, which enables enrichment logic to be packaged as shared services so that capabilities such as product name standardization, address validation, or data format transformations can be shared and reused across projects.

4. The Deploy Component (6) takes the request, which holds details of the service required. The service registry and repository (12) is queried to identify the services and bind them to the calling routine. The Deploy Component makes use of the service registry and repository to identify the details of the context of the service (what it does) and the appropriate interfaces required of the service.

5. The services are bound to the calling routines, invoked, and run. Any Metadata derived from these services is captured by passing the Metadata to the Metadata Services (9) for storage in the Metadata Repository (7).

6. After processing is complete, another service (1, 8, 9, 10, 11) might take this data and propagate it into any or all of the repositories (12) for use in other areas of the business.

8.10 Conclusion

In this chapter, we discussed more of the work described in Chapters 3, 4, and 5 by describing the role and function of the EII layer. We described how the specific components in this layer of the EIA Reference Architecture can be used in a variety of design, build, and run-time scenarios. One key point to observe in all the scenarios is that they are somewhat academic in that most real-life scenarios use several of the EII Components to build meaningful, long-term solutions. However, the scenarios describe how the EII components interact with the other components and offer guidance as to how they can be deployed along with each other in real life.

Next, Chapter 9 examines how the various components we have explored so far can be deployed in a real-life scenario and takes the user through this process in more detail.

8.11 References

[1] Appleby, R. et. al. 2006. *Patterns: Emerging Patterns for Enterprise Grids.* http://www.redbooks.ibm.com/abstracts/ sg246682.html (accessed December 15, 2009).

[2] IBM: 2008. *Introduction to Replication and Event Publishing,* Version 8.2. ftp://ftp.software.ibm.com/ps/products/ db2/info/vr82/pdf/en_US/db2gpe80.pdf (accessed December 15, 2009).

[3] Alur, N., Jaime Anaya, J., Herold, S., Kim, H. Tsuchida, M., Wiman, M. 2006. *WebSphere Replication Server for z/OS Using Q Replication: High Availability Scenarios for the z/OS platform.* http://www.redbooks.ibm.com/ abstracts/sg247215.html?Open (accessed December 15, 2009).

[4] Dreibelbis, A., Hechler, E., Milman, I., Oberhofer, M., van Run, P., and D. Wolfson. *Enterprise Master Data Management—An SOA Approach to Managing Core Information.* Indianapolis, Indiana: IBM Press, 2008.

[5] Alur, N., Balakrishnan, S., Cong, Z., Mlynski, M., Suhre, O. 2007. *SOA Solutions Using IBM Information Server.* http://www.redbooks.ibm.com/abstracts/sg247402.html (accessed December 15, 2009).

## CHAPTER 9

Intelligent Utility Networks

In this chapter, we discuss how the EIA Reference Architecture and the related Component and Operational Model can be applied to the utility industry. We introduce typical business scenarios for the utility industry and apply the logical architecture and operational patterns for a new solution concept that is called the Intelligent Utility Network (IUN). First, we explain the requirements and needs that shape the Information Services in the IUN.

In the utility industry, the convergence of environmental pressures, energy costs, regulatory transparency, aging infrastructure, and the demand for improved customer services, insight, and risk management require a new level of enterprise information and integration to enable informed decision making. The IUN—a concept for this new level of enterprise information management and integration services—provides automated metering based on smart devices, process optimization through interconnected systems, a new level of interaction with partners and employees, and informed decision making that is based on business and infrastructure analytics. For instance, the ZigBee Alliance[1] (an open association of companies that works together to enable reliable, cost-effective, low-power, wirelessly networked monitor and control products) and ESMIG[2] (the European Smart Metering Industry Group that covers all aspects of smart metering, including electricity, gas, water, and heat measurement) have announced a collaborative effort to identify where smart metering and Advanced Analytics for the European utility provider can be rolled out across the 27 member states of the European Union (EU). The two organizations plan to evaluate

---

[1] The ZigBee Alliance was created to address the market need for a cost-effective, standards-based wireless networking solution that supports low data rates, low power consumption, security, and reliability. For more information, see [1].

[2] The ESMIG member companies cover the entire value chain from meter manufacturing, software, installation, and consulting to communications and system integration. For more information, see [2].

ways to maximize the benefits of a standardized smart metering program for consumers, utility service providers, and the environment.

At the core IUN is the continuous sensing, IP-enabled information network that overlays and connects together a utility's equipment, devices, systems, customers, partners, and employees. It enables automatic data collection and storage from across the utility based on a Common Information Model (CIM)[3] and SOA. Advanced predictive analytics, simulation, and modeling are performed to support the optimization of energy provision, energy consumption, and the management of assets and operations to deliver efficient system reliability and performance.

The IUN also enables diagnostics of problems on the power grid with advanced predictive analytics and faster allocation of problem areas by exploiting self-healing techniques. This is achieved by installing diagnostics into the power grid equipment, such as transformers or power isolator switches, which extend the life of the utility assets and more accurately predict failures of aged devices or affected transmission lines. The IUN is also designed to meet regulatory, financial, compliance, and customer expectations.

9.1 Business Scenarios and Use Cases of the IUN

This section introduces the increasing issues with energy consumption, the demand for new business models, and the resulting building blocks of IUN information services. We explore why new solution patterns that meet specific use cases common in IUN solutions are needed. The concept of IUN applies to the operation of utility networks and energy resources such as oil, water, and gas. In the following sections, however, we focus on electricity and power networks.

9.1.1 Increasing Issues Concerning Electrical Energy

The demand for electricity continues to outpace the ability to build a new generation power grid and apply the necessary infrastructure needed to meet the growing population across the globe. Although the electrical grid and devices in the consumer environment have become more efficient, the electrical consumption in areas of flat growth has increased. This is probably attributed to an increasing reliance on electronics and automation in society. In addition, because most electrical energy is generated worldwide by burning fossil fuels, environmental pollution continues to grow at significant levels.

An increasing demand for electricity, aging power assets, reliability issues, and revenue constraints are acute issues in today's power infrastructures around the globe. There is also growing recognition that current difficulties in power delivery are compounded by inefficiencies in energy infrastructure. Examples are issues related to refining capacity, controlling transmission lines, and balancing the load of electric-generating facilities. Governments and companies around the world are beginning to address pain points related to reliability, resource consumption,

---

[3] See Utility Communications Architecture (UCA) and related working groups in [3]. More information concerning enterprise information exchange standards using Common Information Model (CIM) can be found in [4].

efficiency, national security, and environment. Governments recognize the need for the implementation of an IUN that is smarter in its approach to operate power networks.

9.1.2 The Demand for New Business Models

A traditional utility business model is based on the purchasing power for higher prices during
peak periods in an electrical system. Due to the fact that the supply of energy is dwindling and the
costs and environmental pressures to produce energy are increasing, business models of the electrical utility industry are changing around the globe. Utilities now have to focus on the abilities of
consumers to make intelligent choices to reduce and time their energy demand, to examine their
complete environmental effects, and to understand the impacts on the costs they pay every month.
In short, the utility cannot charge increased costs to the rate payer. However, in many countries,
there is no incentive for utilities to focus on reduction of energy demand and environmental
impacts. In fact, currently, most costs are passed to the consumer whether they are costs of repairs,
environmental impacts, or even bad management. Thus, regulatory changes need to take place in
most regions to entice the utility companies to help consumers reduce energy consumption.

As a result, there is a demand for a new business model and an optimized energy value chain
consisting of the availability of electrical energy (supply side) and the delivery and consumption of
energy (demand side). In the electrical utility industry, the initial step in the energy value chain is
the generation of electrical energy. Additional generation capabilities and peaking generation have
been developed to pick up the load between base generation layers and to supplement the variable
load within the demand cycle. Storage solutions are implemented to fill the gap between generation
and demand, especially when a generation source is not available or sufficient to offset the demand.
To move the energy from the generation site to the consumptive site, a delivery system is provided.
Typically, various electrical devices are included to help buffer, switch, and handle power quality
issues in the delivery network. Finally, in the energy value chain, there is the consumer.

The optimization of this energy value chain occurs at many levels in the electrical utility
and in the consumers' households. Technically, in the scope of the EIA Reference Architecture,
specific information domains have to be coordinated to provide the optimized energy value chain.
These domains include the following:

- The sensing and acquisition of metering devices, related data, and system information in
  real time or near real time across the power grid

- The real-time or near-real-time analytics of relevant data and its correlation and integration with business rules and infrastructure services

- The integration of predictive business analytics that determine future demand levels,
  necessary optimization tools, and applications needed during the course of an operational period

- The dashboard capabilities for both customer and utility through presentation services
  that combine technical analytics and portal services. (Chapter 5 discusses these capabilities in analytical and presentation services.)

The basic building blocks of the IUN solution are shown in Figure 9.1.

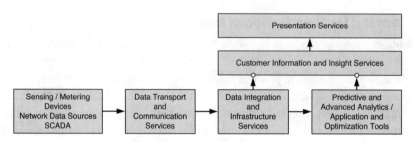

Figure 9.1   Basic building blocks of the IUN

The new generation IUN solution demands the exploitation and integration of various information sources. Basic building blocks are the sensing and metering devices, which are integrated with automated meter management and network data sources. Additional infrastructure services such as IP-enabled Supervisory Control and Data Acquisition (SCADA)[4] enable the standard-based data acquisition process. With these services, power providers are enabled to extend equipment life, prioritize the replacement of assets, defer costly network upgrades, and prevent network failure. Properly managed metered data enables utilities to predict system load and usage to avoid imbalances and reduce off-network purchases.

Other building blocks are the Data Transport and Communication Services that ensure the collection, consumption, diagnostics, and tracking of data from energy and metering devices, and then transferring that data to a central database for billing, troubleshooting, and analysis. The next-generation architecture takes into account that meter data analysis can be treated as streaming in real time prior to feeding the data into a Data Warehouse (DW), billing system, or settlement system.

With the Data Integration and Infrastructure Services, power grid events can be correlated with meter data and energy consumption data. With these services, timely information can be coupled with near-real-time business analytics and distributed information systems to better control the use, production, and consumption of electric energy.

The building block of Predictive and Advanced Analytics helps pinpoint over- or under-utilized infrastructure, improves system throughput, speeds service restoration after outages, and more. With modern network analytics tools, sensor and meter data can be mined[5] to support key

---

[4] See more information on Supervisory Control and Data Acquisition (SCADA) applied to the utility industry in [5].

[5] Typically, in IUN solutions, static meter device data is correlated with streamed energy consumption data. This refers to the real-time Analytics Services and Master Data Management (MDM) components in the EIA Component Model.

strategic imperatives. One strategic option might be to target the investment in components that are about to fail or are running near full capacity; in this case, the major objective is about avoiding network downtime. Another strategic imperative might enable real-time reconfiguration in the event of a blackout. In this case, the major objective is to reduce downtime and revenue loss while maintaining a positive public reputation. Furthermore, utility providers can gain an advantage in the billing and accounting process by implementing downstream application and optimization tools such as outage management systems.

The Presentation Services build on Customer Information and Insight Services, which implement EII capabilities. The Presentation Services can be implemented as a utility dashboard to gain more customer insight or as a consumer portal that links customer demand to utility services. The latter implementation enables customers to make better informed decisions about their energy usage. The ability for a consumer to control energy consumption coupled with data to manage and improve bill accuracy is a huge benefit. Likewise, the customer benefits from better tariffs that fit the appropriate consumption pattern. Modeling products[6] that enable operators and generators the capability to predict consumption behavior will evolve along with products that can model prices and forecast demand. This will become increasingly important as the move to real-time pricing continues. Companies that manage utility peak demands and loads must also be hooked into these systems to fully manage availability of energy and reduce peak buying or generating needs.

9.1.3 Typical Use Cases

This section explores why we need an information-centric architecture and an infrastructure that supports the integration of customer information, Advanced Analytics and optimization tools, a customer portal, and intelligent reader systems throughout the utility network.

This use case for the IUN starts with a controlled steady state, which means that all parts of the system run optimally and at capacity. Various organizational units of the utility monitor their respective systems, performing various analytics and preparing contingencies in the event an incident occurs. The distribution and energy management systems are determined to monitor power waveform, power flows, and the stability of the distribution network. These systems are also aware of the load demands, the proposed generation levels over the next few hours internally, and the current state of the generation facilities.

Advanced outage analytics makes recommended actions about how power can be rerouted due to various outage scenarios. There are no planned outages for maintenance; however, all crews are put on alert status because of predicted bad weather conditions in certain areas. The utility is prepared to take action to position service crews, equipment, and resources into those areas in an attempt to reduce response times and outage duration in the event of an outage. This is done by the

---

[6] Some types of generation sources might not be directly controlled by the utility. Therefore, modeling products determine how much energy should be available during a given period of time. This is applied by the collaborative method of use of Product Master Data, which is integrated with consumption forecasts.

Mobile Workforce Management System, which tracks all the workers, their skills, their locations, and the roles that might be needed over the next few hours. There are considerations underway to pre-stage equipment and resources in geographic areas that are deemed to be impacted by exceptional weather conditions. Advanced weather modeling tools such as IBM's Deep Thunder might also be used.[7] A major triggering event in this use case is bad weather conditions that destabilize the steady state of the systems. Assume that a series of lightning strikes hit a transmission line from one of the generating stations, which causes a surge in two of the phases. This power surge can severely damage the generation facility if it is not detected immediately and if corrective action is not taken. Power line sensors and remote terminal units embedded in the transmission infrastructure constantly monitor the state of the transmission and generation systems. In this case, a transmission line fails and the online transient stability control system indicates that the next generator needs to be tripped offline. The system takes the appropriate action to protect the generator. If there were actions to tip off customers, the Outage Management System would need to be alerted about why these units were taken offline so crews would not be dispatched to fix a problem that did not exist. In addition, the Distribution Management System is used to rapidly figure out how many circuits can be reenergized after the transmission and generation systems are taken offline to minimize the impact.

Another use case is the fact that an ice storm or heavy winds cause trees to fall on circuits, impacting the distribution network. During this period, the Fault Management System and the Outage Management System detect these events and send alerts of the outages via the data transport network. By correlating and integrating alerts and message data with the enterprise asset management system, downstream analytics can identify affected assets and take appropriate actions to prevent instability that could cause a major outage to the utility and perhaps spread to surrounding systems. The customer information system, which makes use of MDM capabilities related to utility consumer data, is alerted of the outages and has preconfigured measures to execute the contingencies for these events. This includes, for instance, proactively calling the effected customers, automatically posting information about the events to the utilities main page on the Internet, and providing an easy-to-use access on the enterprise portal to gain information about the event through all external phone numbers.

Meanwhile, during recovery time, the Mobile Workforce Management System dispatches crews and equipment to restore those customers who are without power. In addition, the Outage Management System identifies the problem that occurred and prioritizes appropriate actions to bring the generator back online as rapidly as possible. It incrementally assigns a load to its full capacity[8] and restores the customers who were taken out of service. Through Advanced Analytics,

[7] IBM Deep Thunder is a service that provides local, high-resolution weather predictions customized to business applications for weather-sensitive operations up to a day ahead of time. See further information in [6].

[8] Generators require a ramp-up time to incrementally add load when they are not acting as a spinning reserve. This time is dependent on the generation type with hydro taking just a few minutes, petroleum fuel-driven generators 10 minutes, coal fire taking one or more hours, and nuclear taking days.

a set of switching plans is produced to circumvent the problem areas that enable parties adjacent to the problem to have their power restored faster. As soon as the energy management system has determined there is sufficient power to enable these customers, their power is restored. At that point, the system is back in full service and all systems are in a steady state again. The customers who are still out of service are scheduled for repairs as the utility work crews perform the restorations and energize the downed lines.

9.2 Architecture Overview Diagram

We introduced the basic building blocks of the IUN solution and described use cases to demonstrate how different components of the system work together. Now, we introduce the Architecture Overview Diagram (AOD) of an IUN solution. The AOD helps transform the way power is delivered, managed, analyzed, and used.

The information-centric components of the IUN solution can be modeled using multiple layers, as shown in the AOD in Figure 9.2.

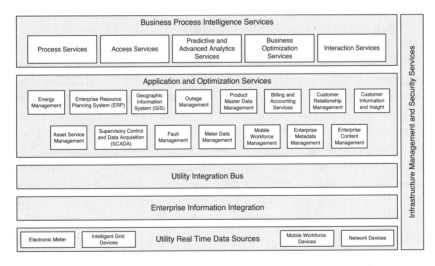

Figure 9.2   AOD of an IUN

The layers shown in the AOD range from Utility Real Time Data Sources, which are the simplest layer at the bottom of the stack, to Business Process Intelligence Services, the most complex layer. We briefly introduce the layers and their relevant capabilities of the AOD:

- **Utility Real Time Data Sources**—These are typically electronic meters with some amount of computing power and a large amount of memory to store data. They are far ahead of the traditional meters they replace, which provided only a mechanical counter where the energy consumed by the clients was recorded. The capability of these meters is to provide an articulated measurement engine of the consumed energy, making a diversified pricing scheme possible. Other data sources are intelligent grid devices that can provide self-healing procedures such as the automated interrupt of a short-circuit current. There are also network devices and mobile workforce devices such as PDAs.

- **Enterprise Information Integration**—This layer provides the EII capabilities already introduced in Chapter 5 and discussed in Chapter 8. For the IUN, the EII services provide data collection and integration for subsequent processing by the utility company's analytical service.

- **Utility Integration Bus**—This layer provides services that we already introduced as Connectivity and Interoperability Services in Chapter 5. In IUN solutions, these services are implemented as utility real-time Enterprise Service Bus (ESB), acting as a communication backbone between applications and data transport requests.

- **Application and Optimization Services**—These encompass various application domains such as CRM services to facilitate the management of a customer's relationship over the lifetime of the relationship. Another domain is ERP services processing customer, product, order, shipment, fulfillment, and billing data. The latter data is provided by Billing and Accounting Services. The Asset Service Management capabilities are typically implemented as a repository for product, meter, and location data. SCADA is used to monitor and control networks from a master location. It gathers real-time information such as the status of switching devices and information about faults and leakages in distribution systems. Meter Data Management Services are used to remotely manage electronic meters such as the assignment of each meter to a single concentrator building a meter topology. The Energy Management Services provide more detail of grid load and energy usage profiles across the utility network. The Fault Management and Outage Management Services provide error detection and recommended actions to prevent major outages. In case of outages that impact consumers, the Mobile Workforce Management Services are implemented to send work orders to be executed by crews in the field to fix a problem. The Geographic Information System (GIS) Services are used to store and mine asset locations on the distribution network. The Customer Information and Insight Services provide data on customer segments and demographics, which is typically computed in a DW. Advanced data management capabilities are provided by Product Master Data Management, Enterprise Metadata Management, and Enterprise Content Management that all were introduced in Chapter 5.

- **Business Process Intelligence Services**—This layer provides Process Services, Access Services, Business Optimization Services, and Interaction Services, which is not further elaborated. Exceptions are the Predictive and Advanced Analytics Services, information-centric elements that leverage outage intelligence by making power and waveform analytics available, providing quality metrics and correlating fault events.

- **Infrastructure Management and Security Services**—This layer represents overarching services for the previously discussed layers. These services include administration and configuration services, end-to-end system monitoring, capabilities to secure the company from information leaks, and secure access for information.

9.3 The Logical Component Model of the IUN

Next, we introduce the Logical Component Model of the IUN. Describing the major components and their relationships illustrates how smart metering and the right applications can provide faster turnaround for customers, utility employees, and the mobile workforce. These foster good relationships by allowing customers to pick when they want service. They also make service order dispatch necessary in far fewer cases. Outage updates can be available in multiple access points, giving customers flexibility that works for them. As a consequence, energy supply and availability through better service and outage management translates to local economic gains.

Figure 9.3 shows the relevant components in the Logical Component Model.

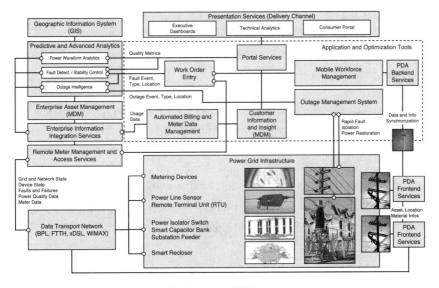

Figure 9.3   The Logical Component Model of the IUN

Next, we describe the relevant components of the Logical Component Model, which will further detail the building blocks and capabilities discussed in the AOD.

9.3.1 Power Grid Infrastructure

The remotely managed electronic metering devices are one element of the power grid infrastructure that is installed at each end point—at the customer premises. They are devices of the next generation that can measure energy based on the moment in time when the energy is consumed. Another consumption recording feature that is typically available on these meters is the possibility to manage supply with prepayment. It's like the rate option that is available on cellular phones. You pay a given amount of energy (kilowatt-hours); this amount is stored on the meter and takes care of delivering to you what you have paid for and takes care of interrupting the supply when the paid amount is exhausted. An additional option of energy recording is provided when customers agree to sign a contract with limited maximum power but want to retain the capability to go beyond that threshold, paying a different rate for peak consumption. To satisfy this requirement, the meter is capable of recording energy consumption based on the amount of power being absorbed. With that, different pricing rates that depend on real-time data about consumption trends or high consumption during peak time can be applied.

There are also additional devices that complement the smart power grid infrastructure, including:

- **Power isolator switch**—These are switch devices that can carry and interrupt normal load current and disconnect portions of the power network.
- **Circuit breaker**—These devices can automatically interrupt short-circuit currents. Circuit breakers are always paired with a relay that senses short-circuit conditions using potential transformers and current transformers.
- **Smart recloser**—These devices are similar in function to circuit breakers, except they also have the capability to reclose after opening, open again, and reclose again, repeating this cycle a predetermined number of times until they lock out.
- **Power line sensor**—This gives control and consequently the possibility for secure optimization of power grid operation. These devices identify unoccupied capacity in existing power lines and open the possibility to enhance the transfer of electricity.
- **Intelligent substation feeder control unit**—Devices that function as a programmable logic controller or Remote Terminal Unit (RTU) monitoring power quality and acting as fault and event (waveform) recorder.

9.3.2 Data Transport Network and Communication

The Data Transport Network and Communication layer provides for the transmission of data, such as metering device data, and for broadband services to connect utilities and their consumers. In recent years, increasing requirements for bandwidth-intensive applications have resulted in increasing demands for higher broadband bandwidth provisioning. In addition, the broadband services market is forcing broadband service suppliers to deliver combined services such as voice, data, and next-generation video (Video on Demand, High Definition TV) by a single connection. As a result, a myriad of competing fixed-line and wireless technologies provide the bandwidth required to deliver services for IUN solutions. However, each technology has its limits in terms of bandwidth, reliability, cost, or coverage. For the purposes of this book, we describe the technologies by which most activities are based.

In general, the technologies can be classified in two groups: fixed-line technologies and wireless technologies. The fixed-line technologies include solutions such as Hybrid Fibre Coax (Cable TV solutions), Digital Subscriber Lines (xDSL), Fibre to the Home (FTTH) solutions, or Broadband over Power Line (BPL) technologies. It is an unchallenged fact that fibre as a communication medium has highly advantageous benefits, such as almost-infinite bandwidth and high levels of security and reliability. As a consequence, direct fibre connections to each and every home are a desirable concept. Up until recently, the cost of customer premise equipment has been prohibitively high. However, economies of scale have driven the cost of equipment down to new, more affordable levels.

As already mentioned, Broadband over Power Line (BPL) is a fixed-line technology that allows Internet data to be transmitted over utility power lines. BPL is also sometimes called Power-Line Communications (PLC), which can fill in the broadband gap in rural areas. BPL systems enable high-speed data transmission over existing power lines and do not need a network overlay because they have direct access to the ubiquitous power utility service coverage areas. However, given the cost and the lack of an upgrade path to higher data rates, it seems unlikely that BPL will emerge as a leading broadband technology, but will remain as a niche fixed-line broadband option for IUN solutions.

Those fixed-line technologies operating over existing copper, coax, or power lines are bandwidth-limited by the nature of the transmission medium. Wireless technologies that use the radio spectrum are also bandwidth-limited, but in their case, by the amount of available licensed radio spectrum. Of these, WiMAX is the most promising technology for metro-based broadband provision. WiMAX stands for Worldwide Interoperability for Microwave Access. It is a standard-based technology[9] whose purpose is to deliver wireless broadband data over long distances. This can be achieved in a number of ways that are point to point or through the use of cellular technology.

9.3.3 Enterprise Information Integration (EII) Services

At the end of the communication channel, an implementation of EII services in which specific coordination and correlation of all meter management and utility network data takes place and data collection for subsequent processing by the utility company's analytical software is performed. For instance, asset data and network topology data from the Enterprise Asset Management are integrated with meter data and device state information to locate and access specific meter

---

[9] WiMAX is based on the IEEE 802.16 standard and the latest amendment to facilitate mobile services. In a typical cell radius deployment of 3–9 km, WiMAX systems aim to ultimately deliver capacity of up to 75 Mbps per channel for fixed and portable access applications.

devices. Another example is the information integration of energy consumption recorded data with consumer-related contract data, which subsequently can be computed by the Automated Billing Service. See Chapter 8 for more details about EII capabilities.

9.3.4 Remote Meter Management and Access Services

Instead of sending personnel on site for contractual changes, for read-out operations, or any kind of nondefect actions, the IUN solution provides Remote Meter Management and Access Services to control the meters from a central computer site. One of the major remote management processes has to address the location and configuration data of meters and concentrators. This data is the fundamental cornerstone of these services. The association between the meters and their concentrators is also referred to as *commissioning*. The commissioning process assigns each meter to a single concentrator. The source data comes either from the topology database or from the installation reports hosted by the Enterprise Asset Management System.

Another feature provided by these services is a remote management capability for meters with customizable energy consumption behavior. For instance, the preferable consumption of power during lower cost periods (off peak) can be remotely configured for the consumers' electronic meters.

9.3.5 Automated Billing and Meter Data Management

The data collection for Automated Billing purposes is performed directly on a cyclical process by the concentrators. At the scheduled time, the Meter Data Management Services simply issue a request to the concentrators to transfer the collected data upstream. The data is moved to the billing application using the message queuing protocol and then integrated with the consumers' contract data.

Another capability of Meter Data Management is the automated installation of a new electronic meter using the Personal Digital Assistant (PDA) of mobile workforces. In this case, the worker feeds back the data collected at installation to the automated metering system. The collected data is stored and passed over to the concentrator. The concentrator uses the obtained data to verify the connection with the assigned meters.

9.3.6 Enterprise Asset Management

The Enterprise Asset Management System acts as a repository for product, meter, and location data. Instances of asset data are typically implemented as Master Data, providing trusted information resources that are centralized for improved management in the MDM System. It also implements a real-time asset health and conditioning monitoring service, and it supports the analysis and comparison of asset performance across the grid.

9.3.7 Work Order Entry Component and Mobile Workforce Management

The Work Order Entry Component manages work orders as they come in from the Analytics Services. The Work Order Entry Component also maintains work orders, the history of work orders, and the company structure in terms of responsibilities and ownership. The Mobile Workforce Management Component takes on the work order, registers it in a database, and performs a first assignment by choosing between a remote execution (Remote Meter Management) or forwarding it to the PDA Backend Services.

PDA Backend Services are the modules that manage the operation with hand-held devices. They consist of server-side (backend) and client-side services (frontend PDA application). The server-side data model maintains the PDA device data, the requests currently being executed, and data collected in the field. This data model is the base for synchronization with the client side. The PDA Frontend Services provide the list of work orders and capabilities to support the mobile workforce for problem resolution tasks.

9.3.8 Customer Information and Insight with Portal Services

The Customer Information and Insight Services typically provide data on customer segments, demographics, and customer-related operations. Typically, this data is computed in a DW and aggregated results are persisted in attributes in an MDM System for further use in downstream systems. This information, coupled with the Meter Data Management Services, can help build a picture of what customer segments are interested in, certain rates, and which rates should be offered.

Portal Services are used to integrate business processes and information within the utility. They also provide Presentation Services across delivery channels and a secure unified access point in the form of a web-based user interface. They allow information subscription, aggregation, and personalization for utility internal portals (for example, executive dashboards) and consumer portals.

9.3.9 Outage Management System

The Outage Management System consists of disciplines and functions of system maintenance via programs and outage recovery planning meant to ensure that utility personnel are prepared in the event of an emergency outage. In case of an outage, it immediately isolates which circuits are down, pinpoints the cause of the outage, fixes the problem, restores service, and communicates with affected rate payers.

Furthermore, the Outage Management System can be linked with customer access and outbound notification preferences. Historical data can help develop accurate and timely load forecasting for future generation planning or short-term needs and profiling or modeling to determine how to best handle outage situations.

9.3.10 Predictive and Advanced Analytical Services

At all times, various management agents monitor their respective systems, performing various analytics and preparing contingencies in the event an incident within or external to their system occurs. For example, management systems within the power grid infrastructure are able to monitor voltage and reactive power[10] levels, power flows, and the stability of the distribution network. During this time, the available load can be calculated and shed with the current voltage levels and assumed load type. Outage intelligence services also make decisions about how power can be rerouted due to various outage scenarios.

In addition, there are energy management systems that monitor power quality and power flows on the transmission networks both within and adjacent to the utility's network. These systems are also aware of the load demands, the proposed generation levels over the next few hours, and the current state of the generation facilities. Operators use power waveform analytics to monitor the state reported by theses systems and the phase angles for all the transmission networks to make sure they are not getting out of tune.

There are also fault-detection and stability-control services implemented that not only monitor the transmission network for anomalies that can cause an instability, but also build contingencies that are preloaded into various distributed computers to be used in the event of a problem. Every few minutes, these contingencies evaluate new set loads that are ready to perform the processes outlined to prevent a cascading or significant event.

9.3.11 Geographic Information System (GIS)

GIS services are designed to digitally map a variety of sources including satellite images, aerial photographs, GPS field data, and existing maps leading to the GIS database creation. Today, most utilities now integrate GIS services with the Predictive and Advanced Analytics because of the threat of competition and because of their capability to respond to public, regulatory, and legislative inquiries that are geographic in nature.

The underlying data of the GIS is organized to yield useful knowledge, often as colored maps and images, but also as statistical graphics, tables, and various on-screen responses to interactive queries. GIS services have functional capabilities for data capture, input, manipulation, transformation, visualization, combination, query, analysis, modeling, and output. For IUN solutions, the GIS services are used to display and analyze spatial data that is tied to the operational systems of the utility. This connection is what gives GIS its power: Maps can be integrated with Advanced Analytics and data can be referenced from the maps.

9.4 Component Interaction Diagram

We introduced the components of the IUN when we discussed the Logical Component Model. Now, we describe the relationship and interactions of a few of these components. We cover how smart metering and data integration can help to monitor and control activities in the IUN

---

[10] Electrical systems usually have inductors and capacitors, which are referred to as reactive components. Ideal reactive components do not dissipate any power, but they draw currents and create voltage drops, which makes the impression that they actually do. This "imaginary power" is called reactive power. Its average value over a complete AC cycle is zero; it does not contribute to net transfer of energy, but circulates back and forth between the power source and the load and places a heavier load on the source.

remotely. We also provide a Component Interaction Diagram that illustrates how asset-related information can be integrated with the location information of GIS services with the use of mashup technology (see more details on mashups in Chapter 12). Finally, we describe the interactions of PDA Backend and Frontend Services with data replication technologies to illustrate how relevant information is offloaded to control and dispatch work force personnel.

9.4.1 Component Interaction Diagram: Smart Metering and Data Integration

We start with a remote meter management and control scenario for electronic devices installed at the consumer's premises. Each step in this scenario is indicated with a number in Figure 9.4 to illustrate the concept of smart metering and subsequent data integration.

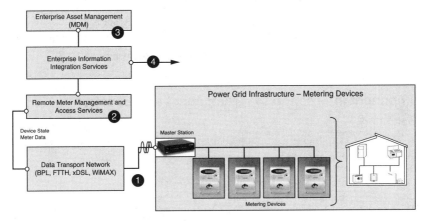

Figure 9.4   Component Interaction Diagram—Smart Metering and Data Integration

1. The first step in the interaction diagram is the communication with smart metering devices. Many devices are able to connect to Home Area Network (HAN) technology that enables consumers to remotely connect to and control many automated digital devices throughout their houses. For effective management of the metering devices, a master station acts as an intermediary between all connected meters and the network. Certain commands[11] for meter management are broadcasted out from the master station to the meters, enabling the reconfiguration of the network, or to obtain readings and process specific messages. In return, the meter device responds with a message that carries the desired value.

---

[11] Part 9 of the IEC 61968 standard specifies the information content of a set of commands and message types. More information on this standard can be found in [7].

2. The Remote Meter Management and Access Services are deployed as Web-based applications that are used by the utility's control room operators to monitor and control activities in the utility network remotely. These services communicate to the master stations interfacing the Data Transport Network. Some of the monitoring events, meter data, and device state messages are forwarded and subsequently correlated by the Enterprise Information Integration Services.

3. To analyze and compare asset performance across the grid, the forwarded real-time events and status messages are correlated with data from the Enterprise Asset Management repository. This provides an asset health and condition monitoring leveraging root cause analysis and policy enforcement through event enrichment. The asset data from the repository is comprised of configuration and location data and various parameters for meter commissioning, meter configuration, version level, and so on.

4. After cleansing and transforming data from Enterprise Asset Management and Remote Meter Management with EII Services, the data can be forwarded to downstream systems such as billing and settlement systems through the use of an ESB.

9.4.2 Component Interaction Diagram: Asset and Location Mashup Services

Figure 9.5 shows the Component Interaction Diagram; it illustrates how asset-related information and location data can be integrated by Mashup services.

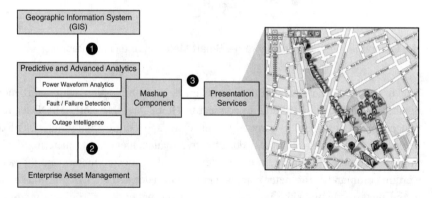

Figure 9.5   Component Interaction Diagram—Asset and Location Mashup Services

1. The first step in the interaction diagram is the integration of GIS services with the Predictive and Advanced Analytics Component that provides status and analytical data from the grid network. Operational grid device data is mapped with GIS-related data including satellite images, aerial photographs, and existing maps.

2. With the help of the Common Information Model (CIM),[12] which is considered the basic domain ontology for the electric utility domain, data from the Enterprise Asset Management is loaded. This data provides additional information sources for building network topology and part assembly views, and for connecting configuration data to the analytical process. The data is exposed as feed data source to be integrated into Mashup applications.

3. The Mashup Component interfaces with the GIS and asset data sources. The Mashup Component transforms and sorts data from GIS and Enterprise Asset Management to create a mashup widget. Then the Mashup Component is invoked by the Presentation Services. The Presentation Services are typically implemented as a portal that provides the runtime infrastructure for information services delivery to consumers or to the utility provider. These users have the ability to assemble custom situational information solutions, and they do so from asset data, operational analytics, and geographical information sources using graphical maps.

9.4.3 Component Interaction Diagram: PDA Data Replication Services

This section describes the data replication scenario with PDAs when relevant information has to be offloaded to handheld devices to control and dispatch work force personnel. Figure 9.6 shows the relevant component interactions. The steps to replicate work orders and related data to the PDA frontend devices are the following:

1. The Mobile Workforce Management Component is typically invoked by the Work Order Entry Component that transfers work orders as they come in from external systems. The Mobile Workforce Management database maintains these work orders and their history. Changes to this database trigger data replication events that provoke the PDA Backend Services' database to be updated with work order tables, workforce dispatching, or device-related data such as updated software versions for each PDA.

2. Both application data and nonapplication data synchronization is performed between PDA Backend and Frontend Services; work order downloads and collected data uploads are managed by the client-side PDA application and the server-side PDA Backend Services. Conflicts and priorities are managed by data synchronization logic. Additional check and resume policies govern processes to resume the data transfer after an interruption.

---

[12] The IEC standard 61970—Part 301 is a semantic model that describes the components of a power system at an electrical level and is known as the Common Information Model (CIM) for power systems. See more details in [8].

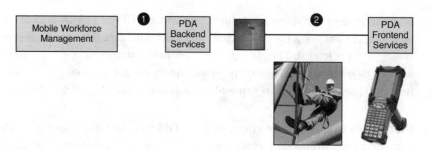

Figure 9.6   Component Interaction Diagram—PDA Data Replication Services

9.5 Service Qualities for IUN Solutions

According to the service qualities[13] (which were discussed in Chapter 6), we applied the most relevant service qualities for IUN solutions. For the purpose of managing the different perspectives of service qualities related to Information Services of the IUN, the service qualities are categorized as functional, operational, security management, and maintainability.

9.5.1 Functional Service Qualities

The listed functional service qualities for IUN solutions are attributes applied to request-driven provisions of new information objects or required data flows due to compliance and regulatory reasons. They are:

- **Data synchronization**—The data synchronization module of Mobile Workforce Management is responsible for data transfers between PDA devices and the central database. This synchronization should be implemented in both push mode and pull mode depending on the data type.

- **Data consistency for PDA services**—Session data is kept persistent on the PDA device so that an accidental reset or device breakdowns do not cause data loss. If the device starts after a reset and the same user logs on, the session is resumed. If a different user logs on, data collected by the previous user is synchronized back to the server side. The persistence support acts as a backup support for the device.

---

[13] In accordance with the taxonomy of The Open Group Architecture Framework (TOGAF), we introduced the notion of service qualities that represent a set of attributes, also known as non-functional requirements. See [9] for more information.

9.5.2 Operational Service Qualities

Operational service qualities for IUN solutions typically include the following requirements for service availability, scalability, and performance characteristics:

- **Scalability**—The scalability in the IUN solution is obtained due to the usage of clustered and load-balanced web and application servers, and the capability of network services that can work in cluster configurations. Scalable communication management functions allow real-time data interchange with the concentrators and through them, the consumers' meters.

- **Performance and real-time characteristics**—In sophisticated systems such as IUN solutions, faults must rapidly be identified and isolated by detecting anomalies in the utility network. This can be in the form of current or voltage sensors, spot meter reads, or detection of the load just prior to the tripping event. Thus, the communication backbone between applications and transport requests has to provide high performance and throughput. This also impacts related analytics systems, which need to be configured for near-real-time computation.

- **File system configuration**—To obtain high-performance levels of response time and elaboration time of data on disk subsystems, a physical separation of file systems should be implemented. This means that different file systems refer to different physical volumes. With the dedication of different disks, an optimal load distribution can be achieved.

9.5.3 Security Management Qualities

Security management qualities for IUN solutions typically include requirements concerning the protection of information from unauthorized access, identity control, authentication services, and key management.

- **Security on application level**—Authentication in the dialogue set up between central applications or the messaging backbone on one side and the meter devices on the other side is based on the usage of the standard MD5 algorithm.[14] Moreover, the data exchanged between the central server and the concentrators should be encrypted using the same algorithm.

- **Security on PDA device level**—Basic identification data such as serial number and hardware identification code, and management data such as installed software version and last logged user, should be maintained in the server-side PDA Backend Services.

---

[14] See more details on the MD5 algorithm in [10].

- **Security on meter device level**—The meters are protected against unauthorized operation with the use of access keys. For each meter, typically two keys are defined. One is used for local access via the PDA device and one is used for remote access from the central server via the communication channels. In addition, the users need to be authorized to access the system through passwords.

9.5.4 Maintainability Qualities

Maintainability qualities for IUN solutions typically include centralized capabilities such as user profiling, the use of open standards, and capabilities for repairing and upgrading components in a running system. Consider the following list of these types of qualities:

- **Centralized user profiling**—User profiling is addressed with a single point of user authentication and authorization to an arbitrary number of application modules. A single menu is presented to the user, where domain module function entry points can be arranged together in an arbitrary and dynamic tree structure. User profiling is implemented as an independent module that dynamically manages user access to application modules.

- **Use of system software and middleware standards**—To provide effective maintenance, the application modules of the IUN solution are implemented following the Java 2 Platform Enterprise Edition (J2EE™)[15] standard architecture. For queuing and messaging, the ESB is implemented as a Java Message Service (JMS) provider. JMS is the J2EE standard for queuing and messaging systems. The PDA application is developed according to the Open Service Gateway Initiative (OSGi)[16] standard. OSGi provides a standard way to connect devices such as home appliances and security systems to the Internet. The related framework provides a flexible and powerful component-oriented environment. This ensures standard portability across different PDA operating systems such as PalmOS, Symbian, or Linux®.

---

[15] J2EE is specified by SUN for building distributed enterprise applications. J2EE comprises a specification, reference implementation, and set of testing suites. See SUN resources and explanations of technologies in [11].

[16] More information on the OSGi consortium and related technologies that assure interoperability of applications and services can be found in [12].

9.6 Applicable Operational Patterns

We discussed operational patterns in Chapter 6. Operational patterns enable the architect to improve the Information Services design. According to the introduced component interaction diagrams and related service qualities of IUN solutions, Table 9.1 shows how appropriate operational patterns to the IUN business scenarios can be applied.

Table 9.1   Operational Patterns Applied to IUN Business Scenarios

IUN Business Scenarios	Required Service Qualities	Applied Operational Patterns
Smart Metering and Data Integration—This involves communication with smart metering devices and a mechanism to forward real-time events and status messages. Messages and data are subsequently integrated with downstream systems such as the Enterprise Asset Management repository.	**Scalability requirements**—These have to be obtained through the use of clustered and load-balanced HTTP and application servers. Communication management functions have to be tailored to work in cluster configurations. **Security requirements**—These have to be obtained through the implementation of encrypted data communication that uses appropriate algorithms. **Performance and real-time characteristics**—These have to be implemented to meet appropriate service levels for real-time events in the distribution network.	**Multi-Tier High Availability for Critical Data pattern**—This allows the overall system to service a higher application load than provided by a single node configuration. In addition, one can add more nodes to the system when service levels demand higher transaction throughput. **Near-Real-Time Business Intelligence pattern**—This provides access to information about business actions and it provides it as soon as possible. **Encryption and Data Protection pattern**—This provides protected data communication that is managed by key lifecycle management services.
Asset and Location Mashup Services—The major objective is to integrate business analytics with GIS services and asset data. Operational grid device data and geographical data are integrated by situational mashup services.	**Centralized user-profiling requirements**—These should be obtained by dynamically managing user access to application modules.	**Mashup Runtime and Security pattern**—This provides for easy-to-configure mashups that have implemented secure access to data feeds.

Table 9.1   Operational Patterns Applied to IUN Business Scenarios

IUN Business Scenarios	Required Service Qualities	Applied Operational Patterns
PDA Data Replication Services—These provide continuous updates of PDA backend services and handheld devices to control and dispatch work force personnel.	**Data consistency for PDA services requirements**—These have to be obtained by data management capabilities that ensure accidental reset or device breakdown to not cause data loss.	**Data Integration and Aggregation Runtime pattern**—This ensures that users and PDA applications do not make changes to critical operational systems that are not allowed. Data replication is implemented as two-way synchronization with additional capabilities such as managing conflicting updates. **Compliance and Dependency Management for Operational Risk pattern**—This provides dependency and topology services for PDA devices, ensuring that work orders are properly assigned.

9.7 Conclusion

In this chapter, we discussed the EIA Reference Architecture and the related methodologies and artifacts that can be applied to the IUN. We introduced typical business scenarios for the utility industry and then we discussed the logical Component Model, Component Interaction Diagrams, and operational patterns.

You saw how service qualities specific for IUN solutions can be derived from component interactions and typical deployment scenarios. You also understand how the IUN scenarios determine the requirements for scalability, performance, security, and maintainability. Finally, we applied operational patterns to the appropriate IUN business scenarios and requirements.

The IUN business scenarios illustrate how architects can make use of the methodologies and reusable architecture patterns to improve the implementation of Information Services. This chapter's discussion of the major EIA Reference Architecture building blocks can now be extended by delving into deployment scenarios of Enterprise Metadata, Master Data, Mashups, Dynamic Warehousing, and Business Analytics and Optimization Services.

9.8 References

[1] The ZigBee Alliance homepage: *Control your World™*. http://www.zigbee.org/ (accessed December 15, 2009).

[2] The European Smart Metering Industry Group (ESMIG) homepage: *We Make Metering Smart*. http://www.esmig.eu (accessed December 15, 2009).

[3] The Utility Communications Architecture (UCA) International Users Group homepage: *UCA International Users Group*. http://www.ucaiug.org (accessed December 15, 2009).

[4] The Common Information Model Users Group homepage: *CIM Users Group*. http://www.cimug.org (accessed December 15, 2009).

[5] Wallice D. 2003. *How to Put SCADA on the Internet. Control Engineering*. http://www.controleng.com/article/270907-How_to_put_SCADA_on_the_Internet.php (accessed December 15, 2009).

[6] IBM Research, Project Announcement. *Deep Thunder—Precision Forecasting for Weather-Sensitive Business Operations*. 2006. http://www.research.ibm.com/weather/DT.html (accessed December 15, 2009).

[7] International Electrotechnical Commission (IEC). *"Application Integration at Electric Utilities—System Interfaces for Distribution Management, Part 9: Interfaces for Meter Reading and Control."* IEC 61968-9 Ed. 1.0 en: 2009. http://webstore.ansi.org/RecordDetail.aspx?sku=IEC+61968-9+Ed.+1.0+en%3a2009 (accessed December 15, 2009).

[8] International Electrotechnical Commission (IEC). *"Energy Management System Application Program Interface (EMS-API)—Part 301: Common Information Model (CIM) Base."* IEC 61970-301 Ed. 2.0 en: 2009. http://webstore.ansi.org/RecordDetail.aspx?sku=IEC+61970-301+Ed.+2.0+en%3a2009 (accessed December 15, 2009).

[9] The Open Group homepage: *The Open Group Architecture Framework TOGAF—Version 9 Enterprise Edition*. http://www.opengroup.org/togaf/ (accessed December 15, 2009).

[10] The RSA Laboratories homepage: *What are MD2, MD4, and MD5?*. http://www.rsa.com/rsalabs/node.asp?id=2253 (accessed December 15, 2009).

[11] The SUN Microsystems Developer Network: *"Designing Enterprise Applications with the J2EE Platform, Second Edition."* http://java.sun.com/blueprints/guidelines/designing_enterprise_applications_2e/ (accessed December 15, 2009).

[12] The OSGi Alliance homepage: *"OSGi™ - The Dynamic Module System for Java™."* http://www.osgi.org/Main/HomePage (accessed December 15, 2009).

## CHAPTER 10

Enterprise Metadata Management

Why include a chapter on enterprise metadata management? Metadata is increasingly important in achieving the synergistic alignment of business and IT domains. This chapter describes new aspects of metadata, how it relates to the mapping of business terms to IT objects, and the increasing role enterprise-wide metadata management has in information-centric use case scenarios.

We also describe the emerging role of metadata and its management capabilities in architecturally mature environments. The goal is not to deliver an exhaustive description about all facets of metadata; there are already a number of great books available.[1] Instead, we concentrate on the aspects of metadata depicted in Figure 10.1.

10.1 Metadata Usage Maturity Levels

The maturity levels of metadata usage are:

- **Level 1**—An example of this lowest level of metadata is the DB2 catalog,[2] which is a set of tables that contain information about the data that DB2 controls. The DB2 catalog tables contain information about DB2 objects such as tables, views, indexes, stored procedures, user-defined functions, and so on.

- **Level 2**—Defining and consuming business metadata is essential for today's enterprises. A good example of business metadata is the description of business terms and business rules.

---

[1] See [1] for more information specifically about business metadata, and see [2] for more information specifically about Metadata Models.

[2] See [8] for more information.

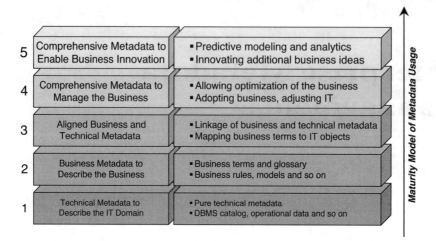

Figure 10.1   Maturity Model of metadata usage

- **Level 3**—The next level of maturity in terms of generating and consuming metadata is alignment. That is, there needs to be a link between the business and technical metadata.[3]
- **Level 4**—The next level of metadata usage is characterized by metadata use case scenarios that enable management and optimization of the business. This enables a sales leader to articulate requirements to adopt dashboards or generate new ones by using business language, where—through exploitation of metadata—those requirements are translated to the IT domain.
- **Level 5**—Gaining improved business insight, innovating additional business ideas and opportunities, allowing predictive business modeling and analytics,[4] further analyzing and optimizing the business—all of these need to be orchestrated through appropriate exploitation of business and technical metadata.

Before we dive into this subject, we spend some time defining important terms.

10.2 Terminology and Definitions

Simply defined, metadata[5] is "data about data." In the IT domain, metadata provides information about or documentation of other data and information managed within systems, middleware

---

[3] Other scenarios and benefits of aligning business and technical metadata can be found in [3], specifically as it relates to the financial services industry.

[4] Predictive business modeling and analytics comprise a set of methods and tools to analyze current and historical data to make predictions about future business models and behavior.

[5] This is also referred to as metainformation.

software, and applications. This usually includes descriptive information about the structure or schema of the primary data domain.

In this section, we elaborate on metadata according to the following four dimensions, which are depicted in Figure 10.2:

- **Categorization of metadata**—This includes the descriptive, structural, and administrative metadata.

- **Levels of detail of metadata**—This includes the contextual, conceptual, logical, physical, and implementation level.

- **Types of metadata**—This is business and technical metadata.

- **Sources of metadata**—This includes various IT systems, applications, documents, and people.

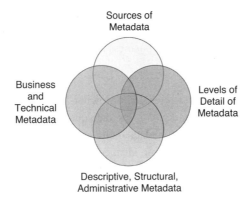

Figure 10.2   Metadata dimensions

10.2.1 EIA Metadata Definition

There are different levels of details for metadata that correspond to the EIA Reference Architecture. We propose the following levels of detail. In addition to the conceptual, logical, and physical level, we add a contextual level at the highest level and an implementation level at the lowest level:

- **Contextual level**—Describes the context of all metadata objects and serves as a general foundation to further describe the circumstances and conditions for specifying the metadata objects at subsequent levels.

- **Conceptual level**—Provides a high-level description of the metadata objects. This might include a high-level description of the data structures and relationships including taxonomies.[6] This level corresponds to the conceptual level of the EIA Reference Architecture.

- **Logical level**—Contains the logical level details of metadata objects, such as components and their relationships. This corresponds to the logical level of the EIA Reference Architecture and includes detailed diagrams of the metadata model, such as detailed descriptions and interactions of metadata objects.

- **Physical level**—Describes all metadata objects at the physical level. This corresponds to the physical level of the EIA Reference Architecture and contains operational aspects, such as who owns a particular metadata object, where it is located, who is permitted to consume the metadata, and so on.

- **Implementation level**—Contains the lowest level description of the metadata objects that are related to implementation and execution aspects. This is also related to the product implementation and product mapping.

As you have already seen in the introduction where we described the dimensions of metadata, we distinguish between two types of metadata: business and technical metadata. The following sections describe these two types of business and technical metadata in more detail.

10.2.1.1 Business Metadata

This type of metadata defines business rules such as ownership of the rules, business definitions, business data, business terminology and glossaries, data quality, business algorithms, and lineage using a business language. Business metadata includes the contextual information about the information retrieved, taxonomies that define business organizations, product hierarchies, other business taxonomies, and the vocabulary used to define business terms.

Following are a few examples of business metadata:

- **Business model**—The business model is a general working description that addresses internal and external factors of the ongoing operation of the enterprise. In more mature business architectural environments, the business model is a framework that enables transformation of innovative ideas into commercial value for the enterprise.

- **Business rules**—These rules govern business processes and include validation rules, usage rules, and other imperatives and guidelines to control proper execution of all business processes.

- **Business performance management and planning**—These are the Key Performance Indicators (KPIs) and other performance metrics. Furthermore, this includes metadata that enables and channels financial planning and forecasting, reporting, and

---

[6] A taxonomy is the practice and science of characterization and classification.

management of the business performance. This should be supported through products and tools.[7]

- **Business data quality rules**—There are rules to manage the business data quality. For instance, these rules enable business data governance to be implemented properly.

- **Business glossary**[8]—This captures the business data dictionary and business vocabulary, which are those entities and elements used in business schemas and other business definitions.

- **Report and dashboard**—This metadata contains the specifications and definitions of business reports, dashboards, and scorecards. It describes the content, structure, coherence, ownership, and reasoning of all reports.

- **Operational procedures and policies**—These are the rules or policies that describe the operational aspects of the enterprise. Examples are:

  - Procedures to manage the relationship with business partners and suppliers
  - External communication and reporting policies
  - Business conduct guidelines

10.2.1.2 Technical Metadata

Technical metadata defines the structure of IT systems, applications, database systems, Enterprise Information Integration systems, Master Data Management (MDM) Systems, Data Warehouse (DW) systems, including data marts and other technical environments. Ideally, technical metadata should be derived from the business and functional specifications, where a significant portion of the metadata is automatically generated by the previous systems. Automated tools exist to enable end users to quickly extract metadata from databases, for instance. Technical metadata refers to the location of the data sources, access protocol, and physical and logical schemas of the data sources, such as the entity-relationship models, object models, and ontological models.[9]

---

[7] See [9] for more details about IBM's Cognos Business Intelligence and Performance Management software.

[8] The business glossary can also be viewed as part of the business model. Most enterprises today actually start their business metadata journey with a business glossary, followed by a more comprehensive business-modeling exercise.

[9] An ontological model of an IT system contains definitions of fundamental concepts such as components and subsystems, and the relationships between those components. This model can then be used to describe operational properties of the IT system.

Let's have a closer look at the different areas of technical metadata:

- **Technical model**—These are logical and physical data models, multi-dimensional models, such as Online Analytical Processing (OLAP), Multidimensional Online Analytical Processing (MOLAP), Relational Online Analytical Processing (ROLAP), and other cubes, data-mining models (including predictive models), industry-specific models, and master data models for specific master data domains.

- **Navigational metadata**—This describes data linkage and data movement within the environments listed previously and includes business hierarchies, source and target locations, mapping specifications, source columns and fields, source data extraction design, transformation design and specifications, data quality rules and design points, derived fields, and target columns and fields.

- **Operational metadata**—This describes how the data in a system is managed from creation to an end point. Such metadata is used to describe the lifecycle aspects of data within the system(s) it resides in. These are related to batch jobs, applications, and data integration applications and jobs.

- **Deployment metadata**—This includes SOA-related artifacts in the enterprise, deployment models, and service models and their WSDL descriptions managed in a service registry or relationships of services to existing models like databases.

- **Report and dashboard metadata**—This includes Business Intelligence (BI) report specifications, report generation and scheduling, ownership, and usage models.

- **Security metadata**—This includes authorization and authentication to access and modify metadata, a security matrix for metadata generation (user controlled and system based), and a usage security matrix for exploitation of metadata.

- **Systems and applications metadata**—This includes name and description, owner and usage matrix, data scope and usage, and versioning.

10.2.1.3 Sources of Metadata

What are the sources of metadata? In other words, where do we typically find metadata in the enterprise and even beyond? It might be difficult to specify a comprehensive list of all potential metadata sources. Nevertheless, you might identify metadata in the following organizations, IT systems, and other parts of the enterprise:

- **Operational systems**—These are, for instance, industry-specific systems, such as core banking systems, Operational Support Systems (OSS) in the Telco industry, or claims-processing systems in the insurance industry.

- **Middleware software**—Metadata is contained in all middleware software, such as Enterprise Information Integration (EII) and Enterprise Application Integration (EAI) software, but also Enterprise Content Management (ECM) systems.

- **Database systems**—All database management systems contain metadata, such as descriptions of tables, indexes, and other database objects. This metadata is used for maintenance and performance optimization purposes.

- **Applications**—This includes packaged applications (for instance, Enterprise Resource Planning [ERP], Customer Relationship Management [CRM], Supply Chain Management [SCM], and Product Lifecycle Management [PLM] systems), other industry-specific applications such as Anti-Money Laundry (AML)[10] or fraud-prevention applications, mobile applications, web applications, and so on.

- **DW**—This includes metadata contained in the DW and the data marts. An example of metadata in this context is the specification of OLAP cubes.

- **BI reporting tools**—This metadata is associated with the generation of BI dashboards, KPI measurements, and other analytical reports including those for performance management purposes.

- **Tools**—Best practices, rules, guidelines, and patterns are in development tools, business process modeling tools, and data modeling tools[11]; and they are an essential part of the modeling tasks.

- **Documentation**—This can be spreadsheets, requirement and specification documents, EIA deliverables, and other documents.

- **Policies and procedures**—Policies, or at least certain parts or attributes of policies, might be considered metadata. Procedures—for instance, to back up a database or to perform other maintenance tasks to any IT system or application—can be viewed as a description or set of imperatives to be followed.

- **Processes**—This applies to business and technical processes alike. They are characterized through attributes and detailed specifications. Business processes might also be linked to regulations to which they need to comply.

- **People**—This might sound odd, but people (project managers, solution architects, business partners, and also customers) are one of the best sources of metadata, and their knowledge about data still influences the execution of business processes.

10.2.2 What Is Metadata Management?

Up to this point, we have elaborated on the definitions of metadata. This section describes the management aspects of metadata. Following is our own definition of metadata management:

> Metadata management is comprised of all capabilities and activities associated with ensuring that metadata is properly managed throughout its entire lifecycle. This

---

[10] See [6] for more information on AML.

[11] See [7] for more information on IBM's InfoSphere™ Data Architect data modeling tool.

includes tasks to create and capture, store and archive, and control metadata to properly manage inconsistencies and redundancies. This also includes capabilities to enable the consumption of metadata in the context of operational use case scenarios and to address governance of metadata throughout its entire lifecycle.

Figure 10.3 illustrates the metadata management tasks in the context of the information lifecycle management process. There are five major tasks. Metadata is generated in each phase and consumed in subsequent phases. This section provides examples of metadata that are generated in each phase and how metadata is exploited in subsequent phases.

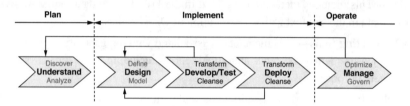

Figure 10.3   Information lifecycle management process

Let's further explain the tasks in Figure 10.3:

- **Understand**—This is the planning phase, which includes the discovery and analysis of any source data, whether the data is structured (for instance, relational data), semi-structured (for instance, XML data), or non-structured (for instance, content, e-mails, videos, or documents). Examples are statistics of value distribution of certain columns in a table, similar or even identical to XML data components in different XML schemas in different systems.

- **Design**—One of the key tasks in this phase is the definition of target models or schemas. The business metadata generated in this phase can be a target business glossary for a new set of KPIs to be analyzed and reported via a dedicated data mart.

- **Develop and Test**—This includes linking business terms to IT objects, data transformation and quality improvement jobs, reports and dashboards for business performance management, and so on. Examples of the metadata are the technical specification of data transformation jobs and rules for business and technical data quality improvements.

- **Deploy**—After the artifacts have been developed and tested, they obviously need to be deployed, which is the final implementation step. This includes the deployment of the previous artifacts. Examples of metadata that are generated through these tasks are run-time metadata of data transformation jobs, databases, tables, and columns of deployed database schemas as part of a new DW or data mart, and links between BI reports and dashboards to IT objects.

- **Manage**—This phase aims for further business and IT optimization, governance of business and technical data quality, and innovation of business ideas and opportunities.

Exploitation of both business and technical metadata needs to support these goals. For example, the link between business and technical metadata can increase trust in business reports and dashboards.

Metadata management, including the generation and consumption of business and technical metadata, needs to be delivered through a comprehensive set of products and tools. Later in this chapter, we present IBM's metadata technology mapping in the context of certain metadata-related use case scenarios.

10.2.3 End-to-End Metadata Management

End-to-end metadata capabilities imply the existence of people, processes, and technologies to deliver metadata standardization and consolidation that play a role in business process optimization across the enterprise. This requires establishing a data and information governance board within an enterprise to foster the end-to-end view on metadata management. Thus, end-to-end metadata implies that there is an *enterprise* data model and a business vocabulary to help minimize conflicts and duplication across business units. Enforced governance policies stop local groups from changing the metadata without informing other stakeholders and changes initiated in one place will be managed and propagated to other places. Tools and methods are available to exchange metadata between different groups throughout the entire enterprise.

The enterprise metadata strategy should include a repository that delivers a centralized or federated view of the *enterprise metadata assets* including technical metadata and business metadata. The end-to-end metadata management capability also implies the exploitation of metadata in use case scenarios that involve a variety of different business users, IT personnel, and specific subject matter experts collaboratively gaining improved business insight, analyzing business and technical anomalies, or innovating new business ideas. We introduce the term end-to-end metadata management because this collaboration of business users and technical personnel across the company, and the enterprise-wide scope in generating and exploiting business and technical metadata, justifies it.

10.3 Business Scenarios

This section provides some metadata-oriented business use cases and business patterns. We start with the business patterns, as these patterns can serve as an underlying foundation from which to develop and describe higher-level business use case scenarios.

10.3.1 Business Patterns

In approaching metadata-oriented business patterns, we use the maturity levels of metadata usage, which were introduced earlier in this chapter. These derived patterns support more complex and sophisticated business use case scenarios that are associated with end-to-end metadata management.

Figure 10.4 is a high-level depiction of the categorization of metadata business patterns. This categorization is far from complete; it should be viewed as a sample approach that leaves room for completion to be done in the context of a chosen business scope.

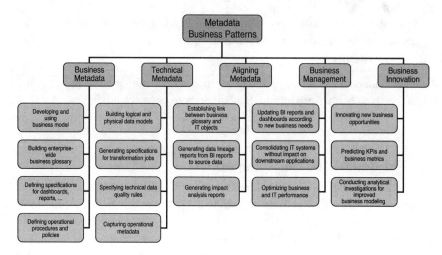

Figure 10.4   Metadata business patterns

Depending on the underlying business use case scenarios, the metadata business patterns might be individually deployed. For instance, the **Building Logical and Physical Data Models** pattern can serve as a base for a new risk and compliancy regulation. In architecturally more sophisticated environments, an appropriate combination of the patterns can yield metadata solutions that are more pervasive and have an end-to-end metadata foundation. Some of the patterns in Figure 10.4, in the categories Business Management and Business Innovation, assume conciliation with some patterns in the Technical Metadata and Business Metadata categories.

The following section briefly discusses some possible use case scenarios.

10.3.2 Use Case Scenarios

Following is a description of some exemplary use case scenarios with the generation and usage of business and technical metadata in the context of the previously described metadata patterns:

- **Building a new dynamic warehouse or data mart**—This requires a thorough understanding of the data source landscape, defining the business glossary, linking this to IT objects, modeling at various levels (such as conceptual and business requirement models), reporting specifications, and specifying dynamic replication and ETL jobs, business data, and technical data quality rules.

- **Adjusting BI reports and dashboard**—This is based on the business requirement to comply with new government regulations by adjusting existing BI dashboards to address new KPIs. The translation of this business requirement to the IT domain, implementing required changes to the DW environment, and updating BI reports and dashboards are among the required tasks.

- **Implementing master data schemas**—An enterprise-wide business model is required that defines and models the master data domains, specifications of synchronization, and replication needs between the master hub and legacy systems, specifications to consolidate and materialize master data, and master data governance rules and policies.

- **Consolidating SAP ERP and CRM systems**—This requires metadata generation related to SAP source systems, target models, transformation specifications from multiple SAP source systems to single-SAP systems, data quality improvement rules, and so on.

- **Increasing trust in existing BI reports and dashboards**—This requires metadata-based data lineage capabilities to gain insight into BI reports and dashboards that link to corresponding data sources and the transformation of data from data sources to underlying data marts.

- **Implementing a Telco predictive churn analytics dashboard**—This requires business modeling to define predictive churn analytics use cases, logical and physical data modeling based on Call Detail Records (CDR),[12] a churn-related Business Glossary containing the business terms, mapping of business metadata to IT objects, report and dashboard specifications, and so on.

10.4 Component Deep Dive

This section outlines in more detail the Metadata Management Component in the context of the EIA Reference Architecture. We present the Metadata Management Component Model for the Metadata Management Component introduced in Chapter 5, describing its components in detail and depicting the relationships among the components.

The EIA Reference Architecture is the underlying premise of the Metadata Management Component Model. This model is an abstraction and serves as a foundation to develop end-to-end metadata management systems that provide the required capabilities in the context of the business use case scenarios that we described previously.

10.4.1 Component Model Introduction

As you remember from Chapters 2 and 5, the term component model is associated with the description of the components, the component relationship diagram to describe the static relationship, and the component interaction diagrams to capture the dynamic relationship in the context of a specific deployment scenario. Figure 10.5 is a depiction of the Metadata Management Component Model. It illustrates the key components and their relationships. We describe the components shown in the diagram in the next section.

---

[12] CDRs are the pervasive data records that are produced by a telecommunication exchange that contains details of a particular call, such as the origination and destination addresses of the call, the time the call started, and the time the call ended.

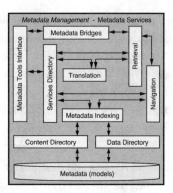

Figure 10.5   Metadata Management Component Model

The service registry, the metadata, and the models are not included in this list of components. The reason is that business models or logical and physical data models are considered metadata. The service registry is considered a metadata repository, which itself contains a set of capabilities and services. These components are related to each other. We don't include a lengthy, in-depth explanation for all possible component interactions and relationships. Instead, we highlight just a few interactions. Following are the key relationships that we discuss:

- Metadata Tools Interface relationship to Services Directory
- Metadata Tools Interface relationship to Metadata Bridges
- Metadata Bridges relationship to Retrieval
- Services Directory relationship to Retrieval
- Services Directory relationship to Navigation
- Navigation relationship to Metadata Indexing
- Metadata Indexing relationship to Data and Content Directory
- Services Directory relationship to Translation
- Retrieval relationship to Translation

10.4.2 Component Descriptions

The Metadata Management Component is comprised of the following services or subcomponents. Notice that this list is already described in Chapter 5. Here, we provide a complementary view of these metadata services:

- **Services Directory Services**—These are the metadata services, such as a data lineage service, a service to assign a term to a selected metadata asset or object, an impact analysis service, and so on. The Services Directory also provides information where the metadata services can be found.

- **Data Directory Services**—Example services provide a Business Glossary capability with the semantics of individual terms, and related IT objects, such as database tables, transformation stages, and so on.

- **Content Directory Services**—These services manage unstructured (content) metadata such as business model images or requirement model images.

- **Metadata Indexing Services**—These enable simple or advanced searches of metadata within the entire metadata repository.

- **Translation Services**—These enable translation of metadata from proprietary formats to a unified standardized metadata format.

- **Retrieval Services**—These retrieve the contents and services of the Metadata Management Component and obtain information that can be useful when transforming information, improving quality of source data, and so on.

- **Navigation Services**—These enable navigation through the diverse types of metadata to fulfill a defined user need.

- **Metadata Bridges Services**—These import and export metadata from heterogeneous sources such as physical databases from a heterogeneous set of databases or export metadata into Excel spreadsheets or PDF documents.

- **Metadata Tools Interface Services**—These enable metadata modeling tools to read, modify and write data to the metadata repository.

- **Metadata Models Services**—These establish metadata models for a defined set of problems, tasks, use case scenarios, or business processes.

10.4.3 Component Relationship Diagrams

In this section, we comment on some of the key component relationships. All of these interfaces can be different, depending on the implementation of the metadata management strategy and products chosen. Examples are APIs, interface protocols, messaging interfaces, Structured Query Language (SQL) language and data formats such XML, and other standards-based interfaces, such as the Open System Interconnection (OSI) reference model:[13]

- **Metadata Tools Interface relationship to Services Directory**—The metadata tools interface allows a link to the services directory; for instance, a request to a metadata service can be triggered.

- **Metadata Tools Interface relationship to Metadata Bridges**—In addition to establishing an interface to the services directory, there is a direct interface to the metadata bridges to facilitate the incorporation of metadata from heterogeneous sources.

[13] See [10] for more information.

- **Metadata Bridges relationship to Retrieval**—This interlock allows for retrieval of the required metadata through the corresponding metadata bridges. It facilitates the retrieval of the required metadata for further processing (for example, translation into the format of the corresponding metadata repository).

- **Services Directory relationship to Retrieval**—An interface to the retrieval component to retrieve the requested metadata is needed. This might be an XML-based or a parameterized interface that generalizes the interface so that it can be used with a wide variety of objects.

- **Services Directory relationship to Navigation**—This interface provides additional capabilities to allow navigation through a potentially large number of metadata services and business and technical metadata. The interface should assist the requestor in navigating through the metadata services by linking the business context or problem that suggests the exploitation of metadata to the appropriate metadata services (for instance, in a data lineage scenario).

- **Navigation relationship to Metadata Indexing**—This interface might be implemented in a way that metadata indexing services are implicitly requested by the navigation component. Depending on the tasks that involve the navigation component, this interface leverages indexing services for accelerated identification and visualization of the metadata.

- **Metadata Indexing relationship to Data and Content Directory**—After identification through the metadata indexing services, the data and content directory finally allows access to the required metadata. This can be a business, functional, or more technological or data-oriented interface depending on the structure of the metadata.

- **Services Directory relationship to Translation**—The translation component might be called from the services directory to convert proprietary metadata formats to common metadata standards.[14] This interface might be especially important in a federated metadata environment, where metadata across business units or beyond the enterprise need to be synchronized.

- **Retrieval relationship to Translation**—The translation component might also be called from the retrieval component. This is the case when accessing or storing metadata in the repository requires transformation from proprietary metadata formats to common metadata standards.

10.5 Component Interaction Diagram—Deployment Scenario

Metadata management is not an end unto itself; it serves a business purpose and has a pivotal role in enabling efficient execution of business use case scenarios. In this section, we use the Metadata Management Component Model as a foundation for a deployment scenario. This is possible for

---

[14] See [11] for more information on existing metadata integration solutions.

all use case scenarios. However, because of space constraints, we just present one example: "Adjusting BI Reports and Dashboards."

10.5.1 Business Context

As described previously, this scenario is based on the business requirement to comply with new government regulations in terms of adjusting existing BI reports and dashboards to address new KPIs or other business metrics. Adjusting existing BI reports and dashboards can be motivated by a variety of different scenarios, such as widening the business scope, adding additional business metrics, improving business insight, and so on. However, we limit our scope to regulatory compliancy issues.

This deployment scenario applies to many enterprises in different industries. Updates to existing regulations, such as the Basel II, Acord, SEPA, MiFID, USA Patriot Act, or emerging regulations, such as Solvency II (details and references for regulations can be found online in Appendix C), drive the need to adjust reporting on the compliancy to those regulations.

These requirements are typically articulated using pure business language. Business leaders and business subject matter experts derive new KPIs or other metrics from these regulatory requirements. To enable a translation from the business to the technical domain and to update the IT system to address these business requirements, exploitation and interpretation of both business and technical metadata is required.

10.5.2 Component Interaction Diagram

We discuss in the Component Interaction Diagram the following tasks that orchestrate the exploitation of business and technical metadata:

- Translating the business requirements, business language, KPIs, and other business metrics into the IT domain
- Identifying and understanding relevant data sources: The data sources can reside in legacy systems, packaged applications such as SAP ERP or CRM systems, or in an MDM System.
- Reflecting changes to the business model, conceptual model, logical, and physical data model
- Adjusting relevant enterprise information integration jobs, such as data transformation and quality improvement jobs
- Implementing required changes to the DW environment or a specific data mart
- Updating BI reports and dashboards

In Figure 10.6, look at the Metadata Management Component Model, which illustrates how this deployment scenario works in the context of the EIA Component Model. Figure 10.6 depicts the various steps that need to be executed.

The following list is a description of the steps; we concentrate on the key steps only. Needless to say, this flow needs to be adjusted depending on the specific project and customer requirements.

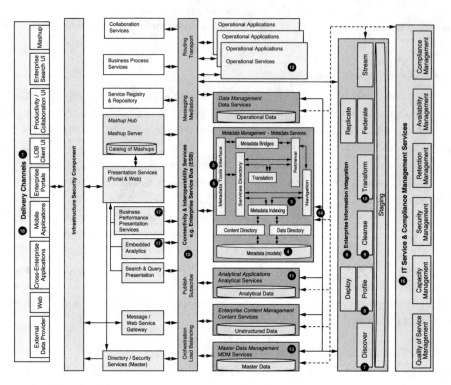

Figure 10.6   Adjusting BI reports and dashboards—deployment scenario

1. Business requirements need to be captured and articulated. This step documents business requirements, business specifications such as the new or modified KPIs, and the adjustments of existing BI reports and dashboards.

2. Based on the deliverables from Step 1, relevant business metadata needs to be identified. These are business models with the corresponding Business Glossary, conceptual models with business solution templates, and so on.

3. Relevant sections of the business metadata need to modified and enhanced according to requirements. For instance, the business model needs to be adjusted and new business terms and the KPIs have to be added to the Business Glossary.

4. This step ensures the update of the business metadata in the metadata repository. In this scenario, we assume a single enterprise-wide metadata repository. In real life IT environments, however, federation services provide federated access to multiple metadata repositories.

5. Linking business to technical IT objects is the key objective of this step. Achieving this synergistic vision between the business and IT domains is core to transforming business requirements into technical tasks. The services directory lists the functional capabilities that achieve this linkage. An example is to identify source systems, tables,

or transformation jobs that are associated to a set of KPIs or a specific BI report or dashboard.

6. Modeling tools can be used to modify the logical and physical data model according to business needs. New or updated metadata from previous steps will be taken as input for these technical modeling tasks. Depending on the business requirement and the existing IT environment, there are a variety of EII tasks that might have to be executed.

7. Searching through the data legacy infrastructure to discover new data sources that are required or relevant for adjusting BI reports is the objective of this step. This can also include new data sources that have not been relevant for the existing BI reports and dashboards.

8. Identified systems, applications, and data sources have to be analyzed for required data components. An example is to identify the overlap of data from different data sources maintained in different systems.

9. The quality of the identified source data might be insufficient and might need to be improved. Cleansing the relevant data is the objective of this step. The deliverables from this step are harmonized and consolidated data records.

10. According to the updated physical data models that will serve as the base for the DW or data mart, and consequently, the BI reports and dashboards that need to be adjusted, existing transformation jobs are adjusted or new ones are built. In executing this step, metadata from previous steps will be used. The outcome of this step is either specifications for transformation jobs (which is metadata) or executable transformation jobs.

11. Executing the transformation jobs from the previous step transforms and loads the data into the analytical systems. In case of local data marts or local BI systems, these transformation jobs might extract data to load them into an enterprise BI system.

12. Operational systems serve as a source for different EII tasks. For instance, operational data is the base for any DW project, where cleanse and transformation services access data in those source systems, thus preparing and loading it to the DW. This process needs to be facilitated by corresponding metadata.

13. The same is true regarding the MDM System. This system contains metadata related to their master data domains such as customer or product. Certain EII tasks access the MDM System to extract and transform the master data for loading it into the dimension tables of a BI system. These EII tasks exploit the metadata of the master data.

14. The previously listed EII-related steps all generate and exploit metadata. Updated and new metadata will, of course, be captured and stored in the metadata repository. For instance, the data modeling that is generated in Step 6 will be used as a target model for the transformation jobs from Step 10.

15. Connectivity & Interoperability services will be used for communication among systems. Step 15, therefore, contains services that will be requested at various points in this flow.

16. IT Service & Compliance Management Services are an underlying foundational set of services at the operational level. For instance, availability and quality of service capabilities are particularly important for the pervious steps, where metadata is accessed, modified, and stored.

17. Finally, after building the data marts, executing the transformation jobs, and populating the data mart with corresponding data records, the required BI reports and dashboards can be built. Reporting tools are used for this, where business metadata (business models) and technical metadata (report specifications and physical data models that serve as the base for the data mart) will be exploited.

18. The business requirements have been answered. BI reports and dashboards can now be used by the requesting business unit through various delivery channels.

This deployment scenario illustrates how business and technical metadata can support the implementation of important business tasks. In the next section, we explain how IBM products and tools efficiently support this deployment scenario.

10.6 Service Qualities for Metadata Management

In this section, we introduce the service qualities representing the non-functional requirements that are related to the end-to-end metadata management scope. Because metadata management is not a key component in the mission-critical operational schema of any enterprise, the service qualities are somewhat less strict compared to core business systems and mainstream applications. Typically, metadata is less challenging from a data volume or capacity perspective. Furthermore, systems management, operations management, or other non-functional requirements are less critical. Having said that, metadata still has a pivotal role in generating trusted information, improving business insight, and enabling business innovation. However, the core requirements for an end-to-end metadata management are geared toward capabilities such as function, integration, and ease of interpretation and consumption.

Table 10.1 describes the non-functional requirements and indicates their relevance in the metadata context. As you can see, we categorized just a few service qualities as "High."

Table 10.1   Non-Functional Requirements

#	Non-Functional Requirement	Description	Relevance
1	Performance	Performance needs to be acceptable. There are critical needs in exploiting metadata to quickly implement new BI reports; but data volume, a high number of users, and transaction throughput are not key metrics for metadata management.	Medium

Table 10.1 Non-Functional Requirements

#	Non-Functional Requirement	Description	Relevance
2	Capacity Management	Because the metadata volume is relatively small, capacity management has a somewhat low relevance.	Low
3	Growth and Scalability	Because metadata volume is small compared to transactional and DW data, these requirements have relatively low relevance.	Low
4	Continuous Availability[15]	The importance of metadata can become mission-critical, especially if the enterprise relies on its innovative capabilities and needs to frequently gain an improved insight into the business. However, continuous availability with the defined scope is still less relevant for metadata management.	Medium
5	Maintainability	Metadata has to be maintained. This is not necessarily a negligible task. But considering maintenance for other data domains, these requirements are less relevant.	Medium
6	Systems Management	In the context of other systems, the requirements for a metadata management system are moderate.	Medium
7	Operations Management	Operation management requirements against the metadata management system are moderate.	Low
8	Change Management	Change management is important for metadata, because the structure describing metadata might vary broadly depending on other IT systems used. Thus, the metadata system must ease the adaptation to new types of business and technical metadata as well as changes in existing metadata.	High
9	Configuration and Inventory Management	Although metadata itself is derived from configuration and inventory management, these requirements might be less relevant for the metadata management system.	Low

---

[15] Continuous availability is comprised of high availability, which addresses unplanned outages and continuous operations to address planned outages. High availability also contains disaster recovery and can be achieved by applying fault-tolerance techniques.

Table 10.1   Non-Functional Requirements

#	Non-Functional Requirement	Description	Relevance
10	Security Management	Metadata itself is critical, sensitive, and even personal. It can describe some of the key business metrics or the structure of the entire enterprise business model. That's why security is a critical requirement. Another aspect is that a malicious change in metadata might be disruptive in an environment when other systems depend on it (e.g., metadata representing service descriptions).	High
11	Problem Resolution	Problems will occur, especially in the accuracy, relevance, and link of business and technical metadata. Problem resolution capabilities to maintain and even improve metadata, the meaning, and relevance are important.	Medium
12	Help Desk	In the context of metadata, this is limited to access of associated metadata for timely service provisioning.	Low

10.7 Applicable Operational Patterns

To be consistent with the context of operational patterns we introduced in Chapter 6, we elaborate on the metadata-related operational patterns according to the following three "Scope of Integration" categories. All three categories apply to the business and technical metadata domain:

- **Discrete Solution Scope**—This addresses predominately the generation and consumption of metadata in a single line of business or even smaller organizations. This category reduces the scope and volume of metadata considerably. However, the business use case scenarios that we introduced earlier in this chapter still apply. For instance, building a new dynamic data mart or implementing a Telco predictive churn analytics dashboard still requires almost identical metadata. However the number of business users and IT personnel involved in the generation and exploitation of metadata is significantly smaller compared to the next two categories.

- **Integrated Solution Scope**—This is typically related to our end-to-end metadata management scope with the generation and consumption of metadata across the enterprise and across different user roles. As we described earlier in this chapter, the "end-to-end" aspect of metadata management includes the tasks and needs of different business users, IT personnel, and specific subject matter experts for them to collaboratively gain improved business insight, analyzing business and technical anomalies, or innovating new business ideas. Although the structure, scope, and instantiation of the metadata itself is similar to the discrete solution scope, the security requirements, change management needs, entire metadata lifecycle management aspects, and the end-to-end (meaning enterprise-wide) implementation almost certainly means more complex operational patterns for metadata.

*   **Cross-Domain Solution Scope**—This is the generation and consumption of metadata in a cross-enterprise context, typically through the interconnection with suppliers and partners, customers or regulatory organizations. In this category, we might actually derive additional metadata structures and instantiations, depending on the nature of the collaboration with supplier, partners or third-party vendors. Similar to the integrated solution scope, the security requirements, cross-enterprise change management needs, and the broader metadata lifecycle management aspects requires a more secure and sophisticated metadata operational pattern. In addition, in this scope, the operational pattern is characterized by the existence of multiple metadata repositories with—at least to some degree—overlapping and possibly even inconsistent metadata structures.

It is worthwhile to conduct a similar exercise with some of the other operational patterns. However, for space reasons, we have chosen the federated metadata pattern. What are the key characteristics of this operational pattern? Table 10.2 outlines just a few characteristics. The solution scope column indicates for which previously discussed scope the characteristic is particularly applicable.

Table 10.2 Characteristics of Federated Metadata Pattern

Characteristics	Description	Solution Scope
Multiple Metadata Repositories	These repositories might be distributed throughout the enterprise (integrated) or beyond the enterprise (cross-domain), requiring additional operational capabilities to include various branch offices, system zones, and so on.	Integrated or Cross-Domain
Business and Technical Metadata Integration	The integration of metadata management in terms of allowing the collaborative execution across all relevant user roles in the planning, implementation, and operation is already sophisticated in the integrated solution scope. However, the synergistic operational capabilities that are required in the cross-domain scope are considerably aggravated simply through challenges in the inter-enterprise collaboration.	Integrated or Cross-Domain

Table 10.2 Characteristics of Federated Metadata Pattern

Characteristics	Description	Solution Scope
Metadata Quality Issues	Metadata quality issues including duplicates, inconsistencies, and so on, are less likely to occur in the integrated scope, but almost surely exist in the cross-domain scope. Metadata inconsistencies in the cross-domain scope require more sophisticated operational capabilities.	Integrated or Cross-Domain
Sophisticated Security Schemas	Although security is equally essential for the integrated solution scope, the cross-domain scope requires sophisticated operational security schemas to account for individual privacy needs of the involved business units or enterprises.	Integrated or Cross-Domain
Change Management	Of course, change occurs in all of the three scopes. For the discrete scope, this is a fairly straightforward task. For the integrated and definitely the cross-domain scope, change management can develop into a major undertaking.	Discrete, Integrated or Cross-Domain
Performance	We do not consider performance a critical operational issue. However, in the cross-domain scope, operational performance needs to be addressed, mainly because of the existence of the federation pattern, stronger security needs, inconsistency of the metadata, transformation, and synchronization needs.	Cross-Domain

10.8 IBM Technology Mapping

Next, we look at how IBM products and tools can accommodate the demand for end-to-end metadata management solutions. We are confident that you will be motivated to dive into IBM's metadata management product portfolio and study some of the exciting capabilities that these products offer. In conducting the IBM technology mapping, we use the deployment scenario "Increasing Trust in Existing BI Reports and Dashboards" as an example.

10.8.1 IBM Technology Overview

The following is the IBM metadata management-related set of products: IBM InfoSphere Information Server, IBM InfoSphere Metadata Workbench, IBM InfoSphere Business Glossary, and IBM InfoSphere Data Architect.

In addition to the previous metadata management-related products, the following IBM products are used in this deployment scenario: IBM Cognos 8 Business Intelligence, IBM Telecommunications Data Warehouse, and DB2 9.7. All these products exploit and also generate metadata. Appendix A (online) provides references to more details on these offerings.

10.8.2 Scenario Description Using IBM Technology

We have chosen the telecommunication industry as an example. Figure 10.7 presents a Cognos BI-based Telco Churn dashboard. The underlying DW and data mart are derived from IBM's Telecommunication Data Warehouse (TDW) models. The dashboard depicts the churns that occurred over a certain time period, separated between private and corporate customer types. In addition, the top ten churns are listed by tariff group to gain insight. Finally, the churned subscribers are presented in an accumulated fashion by tariff group to illustrate their significance in the context of all churns.

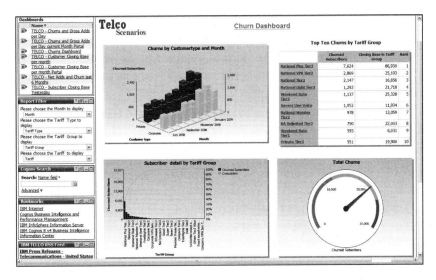

Figure 10.7 Telco churn dashboard

Prior to continuing with our scenario "Increasing Trust in Existing BI Reports and Dashboards," we need to point out that some of the IBM products, such as IBM InfoSphere Information Analyzer, DataStage, and QualityStage, have been used to build the DB2-based Telco DW. Business and technical metadata has been generated during this DW build process and is stored in the single shared metadata repository, which is part of IBM InfoSphere Information Server. IBM's TDW comes with a set of Telco-specific industry models, such as conceptual and requirements models and logical and physical data models. These models are modified and adjusted to specific project needs using the InfoSphere Data Architect (IDA) and Enterprise Model Extender (EME) plug-ins. In addition, these tools are used to map the conceptual model to the physical model. The InfoSphere Data Architect can synchronize a data dictionary with the InfoSphere Business Glossary, where the Business Glossary can be used to manage and visualize the link of business terms to underlying IT objects, such as database tables. Finally, the Cognos BI Framework Manager is used to design report- and dashboard-related metadata models that are also linked to the underlying database tables.

Thus, the following four categories of metadata are stored in the single shared metadata repository of the InfoSphere Information Server:

- **Business Metadata**—Primarily generated via the InfoSphere Business Glossary including the link to IT objects.

- **Business Metadata and Data Models**—Incorporated from the TDW models using the IDA and EME tools. This includes the conceptual models, the physical data models, and the mapping between them, including the mapping of source-to-target data models for the data mart generation.

- **Technical Metadata Related to EII Tasks**—This metadata is generated by InfoSphere Information Server components, such as Information Analyzer, DataStage, and QualityStage. It contains for example operational metadata, data transformation, data quality specifications and rules.

- **Technical Metadata Related to Report and Dashboard Design**—This is the metadata that is generated by the Cognos BI Framework Manager and is incorporated into the InfoSphere Information Server and stored in its metadata repository.

Figure 10.8 illustrates the first step in gaining insight into the terms used in the Cognos BI reports and dashboards. Directly from anywhere in the Cognos report, the Business Glossary can be called to explain the meaning of a specific term and to better understand IT assets that are related to this term. In our example, the term *churned subscribers* is explained. Using IBM's Business Glossary, details concerning the related IT assets can be displayed, such as the row counts, number of columns of a particular table, foreign key violation counts, and so on. Thus, the Business Glossary provides the first level of insight by explaining terms used in a report including related IT assets and technical details of those assets.

The next step is to increase trust in the report content (for instance, certain churned subscriber figures) to better understand where the data comes from and what happened to the source data records along the way. Among many other capabilities, the IBM InfoSphere Metadata Workbench enables data lineage and job lineage reports to understand the complete traceability of information across the EII tools, which allows data elements in Cognos reports to be traced back to their sources, leveraging a unique seamless view across the different categories of metadata that were mentioned previously.

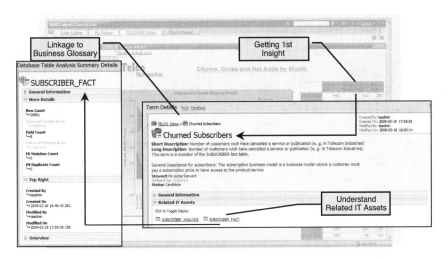

Figure 10.8   Link to Business Glossary

Figure 10.9 (on the following page) is a depiction of a data lineage report that displays the Telco Churn dashboard on the lower right side and enables tracing modifications and transformations back to the SRC_Product DataStage DB2 UDB stage. Depending on which objects are chosen (for instance, BI reports or parts of a report, tables or columns of a table, DataStage stages, and so on), the data lineage report yields different results and provides improved insight into the flow of source data to specified BI reports.

10.9 Conclusion

This chapter looked at the role of metadata and metadata management in business use case scenarios. In addition, it described how metadata management can help to support you in addressing business challenges, gaining insight into the current business, improving trust in BI reports and dashboards, and accelerating implementations to address new requirements or new business opportunities.

Metadata is not an end to itself; it should be seen as an enabling factor for other topics, such as data and information governance, efficient EII implementations, predictive modeling tasks, and—last but not least—the facilitation of a structured dialogue between the business and IT organization.

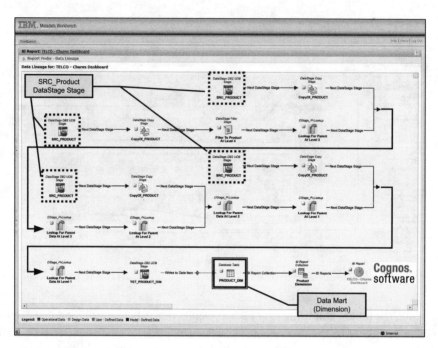

Figure 10.9   Data lineage

10.10 References

[1] Inmon, W. H., O'Neil, B., and L. Fryman. *Business Metadata: Capturing Enterprise Knowledge.* Burlington, MA: Morgan Kaufmann, 2007.

[2] Marco, D. and M. Jennings, M. *Universal Meta Data Models.* Indianapolis, IN: John Wiley & Sons, 2004.

[3] Wegener, H. *Aligning Business and IT with Metadata: The Financial Services Way.* Chichester, West Sussex, UK: John Wiley & Sons, 2007.

[4] Agrawal, P., Benjelloun, O., Das Sarma, A., de Keijzer, A., Murthy, R., Mutsuzaki, M., Mutsuzaki, M., Sugihara, T., J. Widom, 2007. *Trio-One: Layering Uncertainty and Lineage on a Conventional DBMS.* Stanford University InfoLab. http://infolab.stanford.edu/trio (accessed December 15, 2009).

[5] Widom, J. 2007. *Trio: A System for Data, Uncertainty, and Lineage.* Dept. of Computer Science. Stanford University.

[6] Gough, T. *Anti-Money Laundering: A Guide for Financial Services Firms.* London, UK: Risk Books, 2005.

[7] IBM. 2009. IBM InfoSphere Data Architect. http://www-01.ibm.com/software/data/studio/data-architect/ (accessed December 15, 2009).

[8] Baklarz, G. and P. C. Zikopoulos. *DB2 9 for Linux, UNIX, and Windows—DBA Guide, Reference, and Exam Prep,* 6th Edition. Indianapolis, Indiana: IBM Press, 2007.

[9] IBM. 2009. *Cognos Business Intelligence and Financial Performance Management.* http://www-01.ibm.com/software/data/cognos/ (accessed December 15, 2009).

[10] Wetteroth, D. *OSI Reference Model for Telecommunications.* NY, NY: McGraw-Hill Professional Publishing, 2001.

[11] Metadata Integration Technology, Inc. 2009. *Metadata Integration Solutions Through Pictures.* http://www.metaintegration.net/Products/Overview/Solutions.html (accessed December 15, 2009).

## CHAPTER 11

Master Data
Management

Defining data models for key business entities such as customers, products, invoices, or orders is part of the metadata creation and metadata lifecycle management explained in Chapter 10. This chapter builds on what we have discussed about metadata and introduces how to handle master data that represents the second layer in the Enterprise Information Model. Master data appears in many relevant operational business processes, such as order entry and billing.

This chapter shows typical business scenarios that implement Master Data Management (MDM).[1] We discuss the inner structure and subcomponents of the MDM component of the EIA Reference Architecture. A Component Interaction Diagram shows the viability of the MDM component in the EIA.

Relevant operational aspects of the deployment of MDM solutions such as non-functional requirements and appropriate operational patterns from Chapter 6 complement the discussion of MDM's architectural aspects.

11.1 Introduction and Terminology

We introduced several of the relevant dimensions of MDM such as *master data domains*, *methods of use,* and *implementation styles* in Chapter 5 when we initially positioned the component delivering MDM Services. An MDM System can be characterized by these three dimensions. The term *Multiform MDM* is typically used to describe MDM Systems with full support for these three dimensions. The initial scope in each dimension for the first implementation and the subsequent rollouts must be determined based on business priorities and use cases.

---

[1] See the MDM book [1] for more details on MDM architecture. You will find, for example, unique security and operational aspects and new solution areas covered here that are not available in that book.

In an ideal world, a single copy of master data would be managed by an MDM System, where all application consumers of master data would interact with this MDM System whenever any read or write access to the master data was necessary. In such a scenario, the MDM System is the *system of record* and the single, authoritative source of truth of master data for an enterprise. Technically, a system of record can be composed of multiple physical subsystems in such a way that this is transparent to the other systems (using the federation technique introduced in Chapter 8).

Unfortunately, this ideal world for an MDM System cannot always be achieved or is difficult to achieve due to various confounding factors. The first of those confounding factors is legal constraints that might limit MDM across geopolitical boundaries. Legal aspects regarding employee and customer information in European countries are examples. Another factor is master data that can be locked in packaged applications or in a Line of Business (LOB). Packaged applications from SAP require a local copy of master data in the database used by the SAP application to properly function. Other factors are cost, complexity in current IT infrastructure, requirements for performance, and availability in a complex distributed world that might prevent the ideal world. These factors share the fact that copies of master data are created that can be partial or full copies. In some cases, the replicas are integrated and synchronized extensions of the MDM System managed with proper data quality and integrity. Replicas of this type are also known as *systems of reference*. Because the synchronization with the system of record might not be real time, a system of reference might not always have the latest version of all master data records. Because the system of reference is synchronized with the system of record, it is also an authoritative source of master data.

Next, we look at the different implementation styles in more detail and understand how they are related to the two concepts of system of record and system of reference.

11.1.1 Registry Implementation Style

The Registry Implementation Style is useful for providing a read-only[2] source of master data to consuming applications with a minimum of data redundancy. An MDM System deployed with this implementation style materializes a thin slice of cleansed and validated master data attributes within the MDM System. This set of attributes is often needed to uniquely identify a master data entity so it is relevant for uniquely registering the new entity (hence, the name of this style). However, sometimes there are more attributes persisted than just the ones needed for assuring uniqueness; the scope depends on the concrete implementation. Master data attributes not moved in the MDM System remain unchanged in the source application systems and are linked from the MDM System using cross-reference keys. Thus, whenever a master data record is retrieved from such a system, it is a two-step process:

---

[2] There are many variations possible. For instance, there are Registry Implementation Style deployments where part of the master data attributes managed within the MDM System are also created and updated in MDM and synchronized to the LOB systems where the records are expanded.

1. The identifying information and the related cross-reference keys are looked up in the MDM System.

2. With the cross-reference information, all relevant attributes are retrieved from their respective source systems.

Deploying an MDM System with this implementation style can be done quickly because most master data is still managed in the source system. Thus, authoring processes do not need to change, providing quick business results. On the downside, attributes in the master data from the source system might lack proper data quality and can be changed creating conflicts that are not resolved across the sources. Another disadvantage is that the collaborative method of use is difficult (or impossible) to implement because of the high integration needs for workflows that span across all involved source systems.

11.1.2 Coexistence Implementation Style

This style is used if master data changes happen in multiple locations and involve an MDM System that fully materializes all common master data attributes and synchronizes with all other systems that change master data. In an environment where the MDM System is deployed using this style, the synchronization between other systems changing master data and the MDM System can be unidirectional (from another system to MDM System) or bidirectional.[3] Also, any change executed in the MDM System can be published to read-only, consuming applications of master data. Because it is not the single place of master data changes, it is not a system of record for all attributes. One of the advantages of this implementation style is that it is not intrusive to the current application systems. Another benefit is that this style is able to provide full capabilities of an MDM System. A clear disadvantage of this style is that the master data in the MDM System is not always up to date, due to the delay in the propagation of master data changes from other systems to the MDM System.

11.1.3 Transactional Hub Implementation Style

The Transactional Hub implementation style[4] is the most advanced implementation style for MDM, providing centralized, complete master data in a system of record, which *is* the *single version of the truth*. An MDM System deployed with this style executes MDM service requests in a transactional fashion and is thus part of the operational fabric of an IT environment. Any read or change request is executed against this system if this implementation style is used for an MDM solution. While MDM Services execute, incoming master data is cleansed, validated, matched, and enriched to maintain high master data quality. Any change of the MDM System can be distributed

---

[3] In this case, special care must be taken to avoid cyclic propagation of changes. In addition, proper conflict resolution must be implemented.

[4] For more details on this implementation style or for a comparison of them, see [2].

via batch processes or using a Publish/Subscribe mechanism on message queues where consuming applications can register.

Security, high availability, performance, and Information Governance requirements are the highest for this implementation style because a system of this type represents a single point of failure for *all* applications that need access to master data (and the fact that an attacker gaining access to this system can compromise a complete and up-to-date set of master data). There are significant benefits of an MDM System deployed as a Transactional Hub: As a system of record, it provides centralized access, centralized governance, and centralized security to master data that is consistent, correct, and complete with full support for all methods of use. There are only two disadvantages of this implementation style: cost and complexity. Both are incurred because this implementation style requires that all applications with master data needs must be integrated with this system so that whenever a master data operation occurs, this is performed against the MDM System. This is typically a more intrusive and complex step compared to the other two implementation styles, particularly as it relates to packaged applications. Thus, this implementation style is typically reached incrementally over time through other entry points such as either the Registry or Coexistence Implementation Style.

11.1.4 Comparison of the Implementation Styles

Implementing MDM is never a *big bang* approach. It requires at least the third level of information maturity, as introduced in Chapter 2, to implement it successfully. Furthermore, parallel to implementing and running an MDM solution successfully over time, any enterprise must establish a strong Information Governance group working horizontally across all lines of business within an enterprise to reach a common agreement on master data models and how master data is used in business processes. Adequate information maturity and Information Governance are the foundation for a phased end-to-end rollout of MDM across an organization. The scope of the first phase has to assure that the business stakeholder remains committed to the MDM journey and must be selected in such a way that a good return on investment can be shown and that it can be done successfully in a relatively short amount of time (usually six to nine months). Subsequent phases then broaden the initial deployment by adding functionality or master data domains. Another possibility is that a subsequent phase moves from a more basic style such as the Registry Implementation Style to a Coexistence or even a Transactional Hub Implementation Style to deliver more business value either for one, a subset, or all instantiated master data domains in the MDM System. A business must decide which implementation style delivers the appropriate business value while still considering implementation cost.

Implementations today are often a true hybrid. Many Transactional Hub implementations are the system of record for the vast majority of attributes and a system of reference for a few exception attributes. For example, tax identifiers or other external identifiers are created outside the MDM System and the MDM System just stores and distributes them next to the attributes for which the MDM System is the system of record. This enables consumers to get the full master data record from a single system. Another typical approach is that companies start with a single domain and add other domains over time where a different implementation style by domain is chosen.

11.1.5 Importance of Information Governance for MDM

Each LOB has a different view of the same master data object such as customer, asset, account, location, or product. An Information Governance group is key for governing master data model changes effectively over the rollout after there is agreement about an initial master data model.

Establishing trusted master data requires minimal levels of data quality. For example, duplicates should be removed while the MDM System is initially deployed and they should be prevented after deployment. Reconciliation processes—automated or Information Steward driven processes—are a governance decision that is driven by business requirements. Using the duplicate prevention problem as an example for one aspect of data quality, Information Governance drives technology decisions, such as selecting and deploying matching technology. More importantly, process and governance aspects define why and how technology should be used to address data quality to create and maintain trusted master data.

Certain types of master data, such as customer or employee information, might need management according to legal requirements to comply with retention or data privacy constraints. Establishing governance to enforce and audit compliance consistently is something an Information Governance body in an enterprise can work across organizations to facilitate consistent, enterprise-wide treatment of compliance. Thus, for a successful MDM initiative, a complementary Information Governance program should be established.

11.2 Business Scenarios

Master data exists across all industries because a typical enterprise tries to sell something (a product) to someone (a customer). Not surprisingly, solving master data problems is a topic for many enterprises. We do not discuss all possible business scenarios in which an MDM would be a good fit; instead, we provide a brief summary for the most commonly known scenarios across various industries. Let's start with a couple of new scenarios and then consider existing, well-established scenarios that need support.

As part of the Smarter Planet business scenarios, we see the rise of the asset and an increase of importance related to the location domain for MDM. As seen in Chapter 9, an electricity grid is built from many pieces—the individual assets forming the grid. Similarly, all deployed sensors in these networks are assets. Furthermore, it is crucial to know where these assets are located. Without trusted information about these assets and their locations, it is hard to make these networks more efficient because you are unable to easily identify where leaks are if you have redundant, inconsistent, and inaccurate data for these assets. For smarter traffic system solutions, another Smarter Planet scenario, the assets managed are streets. Without consistent, reusable asset master data, the various constituencies in this solution such as government agencies and transportation companies are not able to efficiently provide the smarter traffic system solution.

In the telecommunication industry, there is a change in the product domain with increased importance given to the location domain for MDM. The products in this industry tend to become more short-lived, and at the same time, more tailored to smaller customer segments. The driving force is the need for differentiation in an ever-increasing and more competitive market, such as in Japan, Europe, and North America. One dimension of this differentiation is the rise of location-dependent, on-demand services for cell phones. The implications for the management of product and location master data in these context-sensitive environments are twofold: Not only must the collaborative authoring of a product be simplified to bring it to the market faster (using an efficient implementation of the New Product Introduction [NPI] process based on MDM), but also the consistent management of the location domain becomes more important. Without consistent location information, it is almost impossible to offer reliable, location-dependent services unless you have them consistent and accurately available and linked to attributes such as land-line availability, distance to nearest hub, available cell coverage, digital cable and DSL bandwidth availability, and attributes that provide information about local competition.

Track and Trace solutions improve the supply chain and typically require access to product, location, and customer master data. A new scenario here is the Returnable Container Management (RCM) business model in the automotive industry. Track and Trace solutions also support Smarter Planet scenarios such as farm-to-table tracking[5] for reducing waste of food while at the same time optimizing the supply chain and improving food security by assuring compliance with permissible temperature ranges for perishable food items. Regulations drive the need for Track and Trace solutions in the healthcare industry. In some countries (or states in the United States), it is required by law that a package of medicine is traced end-to-end from the point of manufacturing to the point of dispensing to a patient using an electronic pedigree (hence, the name e-Pedigree solutions).

An Enterprise Master Patient Index (EMPI) solution is a typical MDM solution for healthcare. In healthcare, patients use healthcare services, for instance, provided by hospitals, doctors, and pharmacies, which are paid by the healthcare insurers. The Master Patient Index solution addresses the need to efficiently manage information about patients and healthcare providers alike.

Improving cross- and up-sell capabilities is a major driver in banking and insurance. Various insurance companies one of the authors worked with had an IT department per LOB. The organizational structure of IT was in silos, each with redundant and inconsistent customer master data. Simple questions such as, "Does this customer who has car insurance also have risk life insurance?" are difficult (or even impossible) to answer. Finding an answer is, in such a scenario, a manual and costly exercise. Introducing a centralized MDM System that manages customers (including household information), product, and customer-product relationships enables efficient cross-selling and up-selling.

---

[5] See [4] for more information on this scenario.

In the public sector, demand for MDM solutions also exists to improve homeland security by keeping the bad guys out and letting the good guys in.[6] Homeland security services involving master data include processing passport applications and screening passports, visas, and registered traveler programs. In addition, governments provide services to their citizens through various channels; services include pension services, social services, veteran services, or educational services, and so on. For homeland security and other government services, consistent, high-quality citizen master data is important.

Cost savings and efficiency improvements are common in cross-industry business scenarios. IT systems, labor, and money are limited resources for an enterprise; smart use of them is equivalent to maximum returns on investment. Investing in customer care representatives across various channels, for example, requires the ability to identify the most profitable customers. This depends on high-quality customer master data delivered by an MDM System. If master data is unmanaged and a customer changes an address, this often requires keying in this information multiple times across various systems. Using an MDM service for this can simplify this situation significantly.

11.3 Component Deep Dive

Figure 11.1 shows the MDM Component[7] introduced in Chapter 5 as part of the Component Model for the EIA. We show the MDM Component with its subcomponents for all specialized services introduced in the Component Model description.

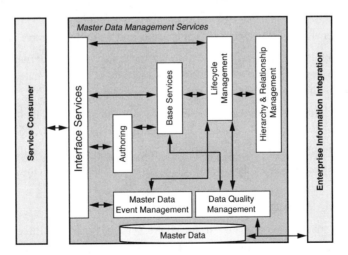

Figure 11.1   Subcomponents of the MDM Services Component

---

[6] An example of a government that received bad publicity in 2005 can be found in [5]. The government declined entry to legal citizens or held them in detention because of inconsistent citizen data.

[7] The presentation in this section is aligned where possible with the presentation in Chapter 3 in [1].

We discuss the subcomponents of the MDM Services in the following sections and show how a service is delivered by the subcomponents.

11.3.1 Interface Services

As mentioned in the Component Model description of the Master Data Management Component, the Interface Services provide an abstraction layer to an MDM service. This means the same service implementation is available through a variety of protocols that should be open and based on industry standards. The interface services should enable real-time and batch integration. The interface services provide the following specific group of services for the Master Data Management Component:

- **Batch Services**—For import and export of master data, the interface services provide a batch service capability that can be used on demand or periodically on a scheduled basis.

- **Web Services**—Seamless consumption of MDM Services particularly in an SOA environment is enabled through support of Web Services. Note that Web Services are listed as an example protocol to support in SOA. REST and similar protocols should be supported, too.

- **Messaging Services**—A comprehensive set of messaging service capabilities allows seamless consumption of the MDM Services through message-based protocols such as Java Message Service (JMS). Furthermore, these messaging services must support the implementation of notification and Publish/Subscribe patterns so that appropriate consumers can be made aware of it when certain events happen within the MDM System.

- **XML Services**—These process the incoming and outgoing data that is in XML format.

- **EII Adapter Services**—These seamlessly integrate with an external Enterprise Information Integration Component for consumption of specific data quality and data integrity functions such as name and address standardization.

- **Security Adapter Services**—These seamlessly integrate with the external Directory and Security Services Component for authentication and authorization.

- **Out-of-the-box Adapter Services**—External components such as the Business Process Services Component or the external data providers integrate with these.

11.3.2 Lifecycle Management

For all supported master data domains of the MDM System, the MDM Lifecycle Management Services provide business and information processing to manage master data end-to-end, performing holistic Create, Read, Update, and Delete (CRUD) operations on it. These services also apply relevant business logic and invoke Data Quality Management Services and Master Data Event Management Services. These services are coarse- and fine-grained, depending on the task they accomplish. If implemented with appropriate compliance to core SOA principles such as re-use, the coarse-grained services consume fine-grained services. For example, a coarse-grained *createCustomer()* service might invoke the fine-grained services *addAddress()*, *addRelationship()* and *addContactInformation()* under the hood, and they can also be invoked individually for an existing customer record. In addition to these base functions, these services must also support state management to reflect that a product is in a draft, review, active, inactive, or archived state.

The specific types of services provided by the MDM Lifecycle Management services include coarse-grained and fine-grained services for inquiry and update operations and service composites. Examples include demographic services to create and maintain customer information or location services to create and maintain address and contact information. Services supporting Information Governance are Data Stewardship Services capable of analyzing master data and allowing manual reconciliation of duplicates.

11.3.3 Hierarchy and Relationship Management Services

Hierarchy and Relationship Management Services can be categorized as three types:

- **Relationship Services**—Relationships exist either within a domain (such as household relationships) or they are cross-domain, such as customer-product or product-supplier relationships. Relationships can be bidirectional (is-spouse-of) or unidirectional (is-father-of). Thus, the relationship services must manage all the various types of relationships comprehensively. From a business perspective, the relationships are valuable because they enable the identification of cross- and up-sell opportunities by looking at the existing customer-product relationships.

- **Versioning Services**—Managing the state of a master data instance over its entire lifecycle requires the ability to capture and manage changes appropriately with versioning. This enables point-in-time inquiries (for example, show me the product as of November 12, 2009). As seen in section 11.2, in the telecommunication industry, the products become more differentiated and there might be different versions of telecommunication services or cell phones with slightly different feature sets at the same time. This requires strong versioning capabilities to be given by the versioning services. In the apparel industry, the capability to version product catalogs for spring (on sale) and autumn (in creation) collections would exploit the versioning feature to have different states available for each product. Regulatory compliance is another driver for this feature, such as tracking versions of tariffs for compliance reporting and adherence.

- **Hierarchy, Roll-up, and View Services**—Managing organization and product hierarchies require hierarchy services to create and maintain hierarchies. For example, associating or mapping Dun & Bradstreet information as a legal hierarchy to a set of individual organization customer records depends on the availability of the hierarchy services. Creating product hierarchies to view products by a product type hierarchy or through a vendor hierarchy is another typical use case for these services. Roll-up services operate on hierarchies to accumulate information across nodes in a hierarchy. View services enable the inquiry of master data from the MDM System based on taxonomies that indicate that the result of the same MDM service might vary based on views associated with roles of the person requesting the MDM Service.

11.3.4 MDM Event Management Services

Actionable master data enables more intelligent use of master data. For example, a product might have a date attribute indicating when the product is permissible to be sold through an e-commerce channel. When this date is reached, based on a date-driven event, the MDM System might publish this product to a subscribed e-commerce application. Thus, the MDM Event Management Services are a critical subcomponent service group for the MDM Services. Using them, intelligence can be derived by defining events within the MDM System as either service requests or date- and time-driven. It is possible to configure events so that they are executed before the MDM Services execute or when the MDM Services are done but before the result is returned to the caller. The events can be defined as business and data integrity rules or scheduled events. Notification capabilities are part of the MDM Event Management Services and they can notify users (for instance, with e-mail) or other systems (via a certain message placed onto the ESB) that a specific event requiring action has occurred.

11.3.5 Authoring Services

Authoring Services provide capabilities to author, augment, and approve the definition of master data, including the capability to author master data in collaborative workflows. Depending on the software selection for an MDM System, the workflow capabilities are either part of the base services or they seamlessly integrate with the Business Process Services Component. For the authoring of master data, this subcomponent provides the following services:

- **Master Data Schema Services**—They define the logical and physical data models for the various master data objects. The output of these services is metadata about the master data and should be integrated with the metadata infrastructure in the enterprise.

- **Hierarchy and Relationship Services**—For the creation and maintenance of hierarchies, views, and relationships, this subcomponent leverages the Hierarchy and Relationship Services previously discussed in section 11.3.3.

- **Grouping Services**—Creating and maintaining collections of related master data instances can be done using Grouping Services. For example, for a product, a product bundle can be defined consisting of a digital camera, a memory card, and a case for transporting the digital camera.

- **Attribute Services**—As the name implies, they operate on an attribute level performing a default value population or setting and changing attribute values.

- **Check-in and Check-out Services**—If multiple users can access the same master data instances, concurrency issues arise. Check-in and Check-out services enable concurrency but at the same time ensure consistency by preventing concurrent updates on the same attribute at the same time from different users.

11.3.6 Data Quality Management Services

Master data without proper master data quality has limited usefulness. Thus, the MDM Services must manage master data with proper data quality. The subcomponent Data Quality Management

Services is responsible for the master data quality. On a high-level, there are three types of services provided:

- **Data Validation and Cleansing Services**—These enable the specification and enforcement of data integrity rules, standardization, external data validation, and exception processing. For example, you can specify that if the age attribute has a value smaller than 18, then the profession column might contain only the value "child" or "student." Standardization such as name and address can also be delivered by integrating appropriate services from the Enterprise Information Integration Component with appropriate cleansing services. External data validation might leverage services to validate if an address exists based on address dictionaries that are usually available on a country by country basis. If a data integrity issue is detected, the exception processing might invoke an event to notify a Data Steward to manually fix an entry.

- **Reconciliation Services**—These services include deterministic and probabilistic matching services, conflict resolution services, collapse and split services, and self-correcting services. Conflict resolution, collapse, and split services enable a Data Steward using a Data Stewardship UI to manually reconcile or split master data entities with appropriate survivorship rules. Self-correcting services would be scheduled periodically to perform a fully autonomic validation of the master data, assuring appropriate levels of master data.

- **Cross-Reference Services**—These provide the capabilities to uniquely create IDs, cross-reference keys, and perform equivalency management. Whenever a unique ID for a customer, product, account, contract, or location is needed, the capability to create such a unique ID is provided through the Cross-Reference Services. For the Registry Implementation Style, in particular, maintaining data lineage is a key capability that provides a 360-degree view of a master data entity that has unique cross-reference identifiers to find attributes not maintained in the MDM System. Equivalency management capabilities enable the consistent retrieval of master data across master domains and systems.

11.3.7 Base Services

The Base Service subcomponent has a wide range of capabilities. We limit the discussion to an introduction of the four major subdomains that are:

- **Security and Privacy Services**—These services provide a comprehensive set of capabilities such as service authorization (who can invoke which service) and data authorizations. Data authorizations are granular, granting no access, read access, or read-write access on the attribute level. Authentication is taken care of by the Interface Services, which interface with external authentication providers for this task.

- **Audit Logging Services**—These provide the capabilities to audit the services (who called which service and when), the data (who changed which attribute, when, and to what value), and the events (when did an event occur and why). The audit trail for the data is a complete history with all changes tracked on the attribute level. Audit capabilities are often required to satisfy regulatory requirements.

- **Workflow Services**—Workflow Services are necessary features for the definition and execution of workflows (supporting use cases such as the NPI process) with business rules and appropriate monitoring. Note that business processes in an SOA environment might span across multiple systems where the MDM System might be only one service provider in the scope of the process. In such a case, the process might be driven by the external Business Process Services Component and this subcomponent would use capabilities of the Interfaces Services to appropriately interface with this external component. Delegation is also possible in other cases.

- **Search Services**—Exact, partial, and wild card search capabilities, and support for predefined and ad-hoc queries, are functions provided by Search Services.

11.4 Component Interaction Diagram

After understanding how the MDM Component works internally, this section uses a Component Interaction Diagram to demonstrate MDM capabilities in a broader solution—the Track and Trace solution for RCM. The name Track and Trace solution is closely linked to the capability to track and trace how supplies move through the supply chain. The main point we focus on is the inefficient treatment or loss of containers, which means their locations are unknown and they are more often empty instead of used for a delivery. The particular Track and Trace solution addressing this issue is known as RCM. The automotive industry suffers from the following business pain points:

- High cost due to loss of returnable containers
- Missing materials or missing containers, causing production downtime in the worst case
- Lack of supply chain visibility
- Non-used containers

The goals of the RCM solution are:

- Reduced container loss
- Increased container availability, avoiding one-way packaging
- Increased container track and trace capability internally and externally
- Increased container turnover
- Increased container flow visibility
- Improved reporting and analytic capabilities, enabling smarter decision making for a more efficient supply chain

The objective of a Track and Trace deployment is to break down the walls around each of the IT islands in the supply chain and to bring all parties of the supply chain together in an end-to-end manner using the concept of *product serialization* that is the basis of the product movement. This means the manufacturer of a product assigns a unique ID to each instance of the product. However, to make this idea work for commercial exploitation, three things would have to come together:

- **Standardization of the data carrier layer**—The introduction of standards[8] and certifications of devices against them to make sure the way the data is physically encoded in a tag is consistent. This facilitates seamless collaboration between supply chain participants.

- **Standardization of the data encoding layer**—The data carrier layer standardizes the mechanism that places data into a tag. The standardization of the data encoding layer defines the content of the data encoding into a tag. Here, the key concept is an Electronic Product Code (EPC) that uniquely identifies a product. Leveraging existing global standards such as the Global Trade Identification Number (GTIN) for unique product identifiers from GS1[9] maximizes the value of the product data used by adding serialization generating the Serialized Global Trade Identification Numbers (SGTINs).

- **Price and performance**—RFID is a technology from the 1970s. Recent advantages in mass production have reduced manufacturing cost, and technology improvements have overcome these obstacles.

The Component Interaction Diagram in Figure 11.2 is based on the Component Relationship Diagram in Chapter 5. For space and complexity reasons, components that are not center stage for this solution have been omitted in Figure 11.2. Here, we introduce the new components; all others were introduced previously. We also assume that RFID technology is used for serialization. Thus, RFID Readers (3) read the serialization information. The raw RFID read events are processed first by the RFID Middleware (23) to remove duplicate read events of the same tag and perform an initial aggregation. The EPCIS Partner (1) Component represents other participants in the supply chain that either execute the previous or the subsequent step in the supply chain. The EPCIS system (20) has two standardized interfaces:

- The EPCIS Capture Interface receives standard RFID events from the RFID Middleware (23) based on the Application Level Event (ALE).

- The EPCIS Query Interface offers query capabilities for EPC events.

The EPCIS system uses data services (18) to persist the operational data in an EPCIS repository. Trading partners in the supply chain synchronize with the EPCIS System Component (20) through the EPCglobal network, which is used to synchronize static product instance data (such

---

[8] EPCglobal is an industry body (see [9]) that defines the relevant standards in this space. Just a few of the important ones are EPC, Electronic Product Code Information Service (EPCIS), ALE, EPCIS Capture Interface, and the EPCIS Query Interface. RFID is a technology used for product serialization that fixes barcode-based serialization issues.

[9] GS1 defines the relevant standards such as GTIN for the Global Data Synchronization Network (GDSN). See Appendix B online for details.

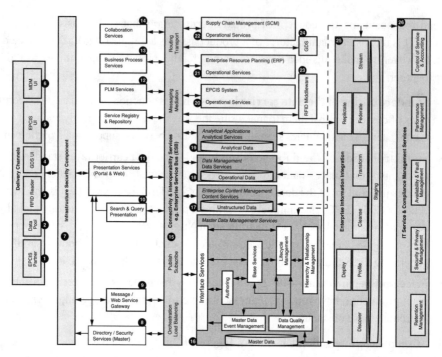

Figure 11.2 Component Interaction Diagram for the Returnable Container Management solution based on Track and Trace

as the SGTIN) and dynamic product instance data (such as temperature measurements). For the administration of the EPCIS System (20) Component, administrators use the EPCIS UI (5). With the EPCIS UI (5), an administrator can define what EPCIS Partner (1) can see and what EPC events are based on subscriptions to ensure appropriate security. EPC events must be actionable; the EPCIS system might use the Collaboration Services Component (14), for example, to send e-mail notifications to an appropriate user (such as, "The container didn't arrive at the distribution center on time") or trigger the start of an appropriate workflow driven by the Business Services Component (13) with a message notification. Finally, for the analytical insight, the EPCIS system must be integrated with a BI solution such as a Data Warehouse (DW) application that leverages Analytical Services from the Analytical Application Component (19). For the presentation of the analytical insight into the supply chain, dashboards and scorecards using Search and Query presentation services (10) are used. Typical reports include the status of the container assets and their current location against their supposed status and supposed location (such as, "Is a supply delivery on time?"). Optimizing the container turnaround, time reports can be done on how long a container sits "idle" in a distribution center and based on this, appropriate action can be taken.

The RFID and EPCIS components are mandatory components for this solution. The ERP system (21) and the SCM system (22) use Data Services (18) to persist their operational data.

Both systems consume master data, such as product from the MDM System (16) and relevant information from the EPCIS system (20) for optimizing the supply chain and improving the resource planning.

The Master Data Management Component (16) provides the following capabilities for the RCM solution, demonstrating enterprise-wide information integration capabilities based on the EIA Reference Architecture according to the architecture principle 14 introduced in Chapter 4:

It enables the creation of a centralized MDM System to create and manage master data over its lifetime using the Enterprise Information Integration Services (25) during the Master Data Integration (MDI) phase of an MDM deployment. After the MDM System is operational, it also allows streamlined creation and maintenance of master data.

The Data Pool Component (2), the GDS UI Component (4), and the GDS Backend Component (24) are used to synchronize with the Global Data Synchronization Network. These components are optional and largely depend on whether or not at least some of the participants in the supply chain network use the GDSN for the exchange of static master data, such as attribute values applicable to all instances of the same product and the unique identifier such as a GTIN that is also applicable to all instances of the same product. Similarly, trading partner and location master data is available through the GSDN. If they are used, the static master data can be received by the MDM System (16) through the GDS Component. Static product information can also be synchronized from the MDM System to resellers through the GDS Component.

If base product information is received through the GDS, using the MDM UI (6) workflow-from in-house, master data enrichment can be done. If the GDS components are not present, collaborative authoring of product master data can be done through the MDM UI.

The MDM System provides a single place to onboard information from the Product Lifecycle Management (PLM) System Component (12), which is complementary to the Product Information Management (PIM) capabilities of the MDM System (16). In engineering departments in the automotive industry, often PLM systems are used. An MDM System is designed to operationalize master data into all processes, particularly also sales and marketing processes that are complementary capabilities to the PLM capabilities. Thus, the MDM System can be used to bring together a 360-degree view of product information with input from internal departments such as engineering using PLM systems and external participants using GDS to provide a foundation for further enrichment of product, trading partner, and location master information.

Product information often contains Unstructured Data as well, such as images or documentation in PDF. Scanned contracts with trading partners are Unstructured Data. An ECM Component (17) manages the Unstructured Data. The centralized MDM System uses Unique Resource Identifiers (URIs) to link the Unstructured and Structured master data together for seamless and consistent consumption.

The MDM System can also be used to manage all customer and car dealership information. The MDM Component (16) simplifies the distribution of master data to other applications such as the EPCIS System (20) and a Data Warehouse delivered by the Analytical Applications Component.

For a Track and Trace solution, bringing together EPC events with master data enables a deeper understanding on what is going on in the supply chain. For example, within the EPC event, you might find the GTIN number as part of the SGTIN representing the serialized, unique identifier for a product instance or information such as a Global Location Number (GLN) and indicating where the tag read event took place. The master data capability is used to find out the name of the product and its attributes (such as temperature boundaries for a perishable good) using the GTIN number. Using the GLN, the MDM System can be inquired to retrieve the addresses of the distribution centers the container in the RCM solution passed through. The EPCIS system requires a slice of master data that it receives during setup through a batch approach. Afterwards, the integration of the MDM System and EPCIS system can be done in two ways: Either a periodic batch (such as every night) with deltas is created by the MDM System and applied to the EPCIS system, or an ongoing, more real-time focused integration is built where the EPCIS system would subscribe on a message queue and where the MDM System posts master data updates using a Publish/Subscribe pattern.

When the DW is initially built, it receives clean master data from the MDM System (16) for the dimension tables using EII services (25). Later on, these dimension tables are kept up to date with trickle feeds from the MDM System. The report quality significantly improves not only for the Track and Trace reporting, but also for other reports.

We conclude the discussion of this use case with two flows specifically targeting the Track and Trace aspects of the Returnable Container Management solution. The first flow shows how an EPC event for a container is received through a read from a RFID reader through the RFID middleware into the EPCIS system:

1. The first step happens when an RFID reader (3) reads the tag of a container.

2. Through the Message and Web Service Gateway Component (9) and the Connectivity and Interoperability Services Component (15), the raw RFID information from the device is sent with a message to the RFID Middleware (23).

3. The raw RFID information is processed by the RFID Middleware (23) and duplicate reads are removed. Compliant with the ALE specification, higher-level events are published and sent to the EPCIS Capture Interface of the EPCIS Component (20).

4. The EPCIS Capture Interface of the EPCIS system (20) stores the EPC event unchanged into the repository of the EPCIS system that calls a data service (18) through the Connectivity and Interoperability Services Component (15).

The second flow illustrates how trading partners collaborate regarding the exchange of information of the tracked containers. This demonstrates efficient enterprise information integration capabilities across enterprises, according to architecture principle 14:

1. Based on a subscription on the EPCIS system of the EPCIS Partner (1) owning the previous step in the supply chain the EPCIS system (20) receives appropriate EPC events as message. The message reaches the enterprise network through the Infrastructure Security Services Component (7), the Message and Web Service Gateway Component (9), and the Connectivity and Interoperability Services Component (15) to apply appropriate security measures. An example of such a received EPC event is when the container leaves the distribution center of the EPCIS partner owning the previous step in the supply chain.

2. Upon arrival of the container, its content is processed and the container is filled with new or additional materials and shipped again. All these steps are tracked through RFID readers (3) and the RFID Middleware (23), aggregating and cleansing the raw RFID information before appropriate higher-level events are published as compliant with the ALE specification to the EPCIS Capture Interface of the EPCIS system (20).

3. The EPCIS system (20) publishes appropriate EPC events to notify the owner of the previous step that the container has arrived and the owner of the next step in the supply chain that the container has been shipped again as well as the products within the container.

Through this, at any given point in time, the location of where the container has been "seen" the last time can be automatically inquired as can the next location where it is supposedly arriving. This provides the visibility of the containers in the supply chain.

11.5 Service Qualities

For all data domains, non-functional requirements define operational, security management, and maintainability service qualities. In this section, we do not cover all service qualities related to non-functional requirements for any MDM solution. We describe only the ones that are important to MDM. High Availability is important for MDM as well; however, we cover that aspect with a dedicated operational pattern in the next section.

11.5.1 MDM Security

Introducing MDM in an enterprise shifts the use of master data from the situation on the left side to the situation shown on the right side, as shown in Figure 11.3.

The situation on the left side means that from the perspective of an attacker who has the intent to gain access to customer records, the attacker must compromise multiple systems, potentially protected in subnetworks through firewalls. Even if the attacker is able to compromise all these systems, the attacker only gets access to inconsistent, incomplete, and nonstandardized customer records. Thus, the value of the data due to poor data quality might not be as good as the attacker would need it to be. As a result, without proper master data integration, the customer data might be of little use to the attacker. A part of the security in an IT environment as shown on the left side in Figure 11.3 is security by obscurity, meaning that it's not clear where a customer record can be found or which version is the right one.

The situation on the right side means an attacker compromising a single system gives access to the most valuable information a company has: the entirety of its master data. Because the master data is now managed by an MDM System, the customer data is of high quality due to cleansing and enrichment and it doesn't require data quality improvements to be useful for the attacker.

This creates the following paradox situation: MDM increases the value of your core business entities by centrally managing it with high quality. For the same reason, it decreases it at the same time, making it a prime time target for attackers, unless of course, appropriate security for the MDM System is in place. On the positive side, the introduction of the centralized MDM System provides a

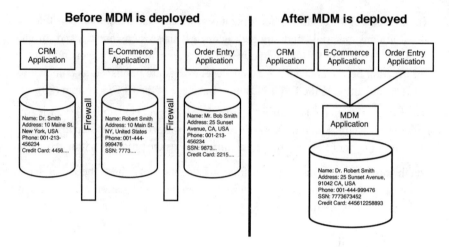

Figure 11.3   Introducing MDM—before and after

holistic view about master data, enabling a holistic risk assessment and a single, centralized place to enforce security. For information assets such as master data, there are three types of risks:

- **Operational risk**—An example is Denial of Service (DoS).

- **Regulatory and compliance risk**—An example is a fine due to noncompliance with a legal requirement for information assets.

- **Reputational risk**[10]—An example is the loss of customers if they don't trust the enterprise anymore because their data is compromised.

For each risk, three principal actions can be taken:

- **Mitigation/Reduction**—An example is an internal attacker using a tool that examines network traffic (*threat*) to obtain master data because the master data flows unencrypted over an internal network (*vulnerability*) and the malicious insider sells that information to identity thieves (*risk*). A solution might be to use either encryption of the communication channel (such as SSL), message encryption, or both.

- **Accept**—An organization decides to live with the risk.

- **Transfer**—An enterprise buys insurance or some other coverage against loss from another party.

We explore only the option of risk mitigation or risk reduction.

---

[10] Two examples where banks lost sensitive customer data are described in [12].

It is out of scope of this book to discuss a complete Enterprise Security Architecture that would provide the architecture context for an MDM solution from a security perspective.[11] However, we show in the context of the Component and Operational Model of the EIA Reference Architecture where security aspects for an MDM solution must be addressed.

In the Component Model shown in Figure 11.2, the Infrastructure Security Component (7), the Directory / Security Services Component (8), the Message and Web Services Gateway Component (9), and the Security and Privacy Services (part of the IT Service & Compliance Management Services Component [26]) provide the functions for risk mitigation.

The Security and Privacy Services that are part of the IT Service & Compliance Management Services Component (26) provide a number of relevant functions; we highlight just two of them. The first one is to deliver protection of data at rest using encryption services from this group delivering the necessary protection of backups of the database used to store master data. The second one is data masking services to comply with privacy requirements in software development and test environments for sensitive, personal information.

The MDM System is responsible to deliver data authorization (who can see what and enforcement of read versus read-write access). It is also responsible for a complete history of all master data changes on the attribute level. Finally, either this component—by itself or by integration with the IT Service & Compliance Management Services Component—needs to deliver full audit capabilities regarding who called which master data service and when and what has been changed.

The MDM System offers services that support XML either on a protocol level (such as Web services) or the data format as outlined in section 11.3.1. Protection against a variety of XML attacks such as recursive elements, metatags, or XML flooding techniques must be taken[12] to appropriately secure the MDM system.

11.5.2 Privacy

Privacy is an issue whenever Personally Identifiable Information (PII) is electronically created and processed. Risks related to privacy span across two risk categories of regulatory and reputational risks. From the regulatory side, there are legislations such as EU Directive 95/46/EC, HIPAA, and the California Senate Bill 1386, which cover privacy of information of customers or patients.

Many privacy-related requirements can be addressed by security services such as authentication and authorization. However, privacy preferences cannot be addressed by these means. Customers or employees can inform the company under which circumstances they might be called or if they want to receive mail advertisements. Customers might choose to opt out of notifications if they intend to limit the contact initiated by an enterprise. These privacy preferences need to be managed by the MDM System and communicated to and honored by the master data-consuming applications.

---

[11] See Chapter 3 for an introduction to key security capabilities. For more comprehensive discussion of MDM and security, see Chapter 4 in [1] and [15].

[12] An overview of XML threats can be found in [12], and the ways to protect against them can be found in [13].

There is a challenging problem related to PII information, though. This problem arises when software developers and testers for an MDM solution need to work with PII with the intent to verify that the solution works on real customer data used in production instead of using random data that might not have the same characteristics as the production data. In the development and test environments for software development, security requirements are typically less restrictive than in the production environment. Thus, PII moved from production environment into a development or test environment might be exposed to PII breaches from a privacy point of view. Simply removing PII from the data set used for development and test purposes makes it essentially useless from a test result perspective. Data de-identification (also known as data masking) is a suitable solution for this problem. It is a technique that uses statistical algorithms to maintain the same characteristic as the original data, but mapping it in such a way that it cannot be translated back to the original sensitive PII.

11.6 Applicable Operational Patterns

Chapter 6 introduced several operational patterns and some of them are particularly relevant for the MDM space. We start with the operational patterns for data integration. The Registry Implementation Style is implemented with the operational Data Integration & Aggregation Runtime Pattern (see section 6.6.3) to deliver the federation layer for the MDM Services.

The next areas of operational patterns are availability and disaster recovery. An MDM System deployed using the Registry Implementation Style depends on the availability of the source systems. If the number of sources grows in such a deployment, the availability can decrease quickly. In this case, making the MDM System more available than the source systems is not feasible. The Multi-Tier High Availability for Critical Data Pattern discussed in section 6.6.6 provides insight on using the Registry Implementation Style from an operational perspective to address availability demands. It is critical to note that the source systems can still be operational even if the MDM System is not.

MDM solutions that are deployed in the Transactional Hub Implementation Style create a single point of enterprise-wide failure because all applications depend on the availability of the MDM System regarding master data. Using this implementation style has the advantage of an availability perspective that shows there is no dependency on the source systems like there is with the Registry Implementation Style. However, because a system of record created with the Transactional Hub Implementation Style is a single point of failure with enterprise-wide impact, the MDM System should be made highly available using redundant components. A variation of the operational Multi-Tier High Availability for the Critical Data Pattern introduced in section 6.6.6 is needed for the Transactional Hub Implementation Style. Using the IBM InfoSphere MDM Server (see Appendix A online), this variation is shown in Figure 11.4. It exploits horizontal and vertical clustering techniques of the WebSphere® Application Server (a J2EE Application Server) on which the MDM Server (a J2EE application) is deployed and load distribution is done with a load balancer. For the persistency given by a relational database, appropriate features must be selected to make the database highly available and continuously operational. Addressing the disaster recovery requirements enables the operational Continuous Availability & Resiliency Pattern introduced in section 6.6.5 to be applied.

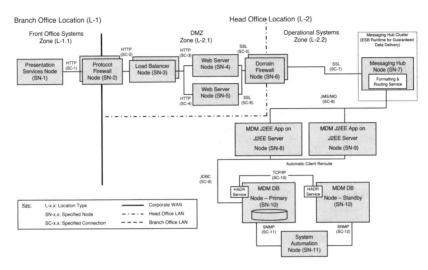

Figure 11.4   Multi-tier high availability for Critical Data Pattern for Transactional Hub deployment

The next area of operational patterns is related to security and data privacy. Backups of databases containing master data should be protected through encryption techniques. If the master data is affected by data privacy, then using encryption for backups might already be required for data privacy reasons. The operational Encryption & Data Protection Pattern described in section 6.6.12 outlines how this can be done from an operational perspective. For other security aspects, the discussion of operational patterns is beyond the scope of this book.[13]

The last area of relevant operational patterns is compliance. Generally speaking, depending on a country's legal requirements for master data, there can be regulations related to retention of master data where compliance is mandatory to avoid penalties. The Retention Management Pattern introduced in section 6.6.1 describes how to deal with retention. For other regulatory requirements, the Compliance & Dependency Management for the Operational Risk Pattern introduced in section 6.6.10 provides useful insight into the operational aspects of compliance.

11.7 Conclusion

This chapter detailed the MDM Services Component of the EIA Reference Architecture by showing the need for it in various businesses. On the technical side, the description of the component

---

[13] For more details on security from an architecture and implementation perspective see [15] and [16].

conceptually showed how the architectural foundation for an MDM solution can be derived based on the EIA. Operational aspects and operational patterns flesh out the critical parts of an MDM solution.

11.8 References

[1] Dreibelbis, A., Hechler, E., Milman, I., Oberhofer, M., van Run, P., and D. Wolfson. *Enterprise Master Data Management—An SOA Approach to Managing Core Information*. Indianapolis, Indiana: IBM Press, 2008.

[2] Berson, A. and L. Dubov. *Master Data Management and Customer Data Integration for a Global Enterprise*. New York, NY: McGraw-Hill, 2007.

[3] Hechler, E., Oberhofer, M., and P. van Run. 2008. *Implementing a Transaction Hub MDM Pattern Using IBM InfoSphere Master Data Management Server*. http://www.ibm.com/developerworks/data/library/techarticle/dm-0803oberhofer/index.html (accessed December 15, 2009).

[4] IBM homepage for Smarter Planet: *Smarter Food*. http://www.ibm.com/smarterplanet/us/en/food_technology/examples/index.html (accessed December 15, 2009).

[5] Report by the Commonwealth Ombudsman, Prof. John McMillan, under the Ombudsman Act 1976, REPORT NO.11|2007, published August 2007, ISBN: 9780980387827, publisher: Commonwealth Ombudsman, Canberra Australia. http://www.ombudsman.gov.au/commonwealth/publish.nsf/AttachmentsByTitle/reports_2007_11/$FILE/report_2007_11.pdf (accessed December 15, 2009), © Commonwealth of Australia 2007.

[6] White, A. and G. Abrams. *Service-Oriented Business Applications Require EIM Strategy*. Gartner Group, ID Number: G00124926, 2005.

[7] Alvarez, G., Beyer, M., Bitterer, A., Blechar, M., Chandler, N., Newman, D., Radcliffe, J., Sholler, D., Steenstrup, K., White, A., and D. Wilson. *Hype Cycle for Master Data Management*. Gartner Research, ID Number: G00169421, 2009.

[8] Kalogirou, J. and S. Nayak. 2009. *Simplifying IT with Master Data Management and SOA*. Information Management Special Reports. http://www.information-management.com/specialreports/2009_147/integration_master_data_management_service_oriented_architecture-10015593-1.html?portal=master_data_management (accessed December 15, 2009).

[9] The GS1 homepage: http://www.gs1.org (accessed December 15, 2009).

[10] The EPCglobal homepage: http://www.epcglobalinc.org/home (accessed December 15, 2009).

[11] News Articles on Banks Who Lost Customer Information. http://www.guardian.co.uk/money/2008/apr/07/scamsandfraud.consumeraffairs and http://news.cnet.com/8301-10784_3-9959976-7.html (accessed December 15, 2009).

[12] Hines, C. 2006. The (XML) *Threat Is Out There....* http://www.ibm.com/developerworks/websphere/techjournal/0603_col_hines/0603_col_hines.html (accessed December 15, 2009).

[13] Fot, D. and M. Oberhofer, M. 2009. *Leverage DataPower SOA Appliances to Extend InfoSphere Master Data Management Server Security Capabilities*. IBM developerWorks. http://www.ibm.com/developerworks/data/library/techarticle/dm-0908mdmserversecurity/ (accessed December 15, 2009).

[14] Blakley, B. *Defusing the Personal Information Time Bomb*. Burton Group, White Paper, 2007.

[15] Ashley, P., Borret, M., Buecker, A., Lu, M., Muppidi, S., Readshaw, N. *Understanding SOA Security Design and Implementation*. http://www.redbooks.ibm.com/abstracts/SG247310.html (accessed December 15, 2009). IBM Redbook, 2007.

[16] Schneier, B. *Applied Cryptography. Protocols, Algorithms and Source Code in C*. New York, NY: John Wiley & Sons, 1996.

## CHAPTER 12

Information Delivery
in a Web 2.0 World

In this chapter, we consider the use of mashups as part of the next phase of informational applications. In the context of Enterprise Information Architectures, a mashup is something that exhibits many of the properties of a Web 2.0 application (as defined by Tim O'Reilly[1]). We describe how mashups fit into Web 2.0, and then outline mashup architecture, its place within the component model described in Chapter 5, and some scenarios that use mashups to enable the user to understand typical mashup applications in practice.

12.1 Web 2.0 Introduction to Mashups

A *mashup* is a lightweight web application that is often created by end users and combines information or capabilities from more than one existing source to deliver new functions and insights. Widgets[2] and feeds that are mashed together often come from independent sources and do not change when mashed. Mashups are built on a web-oriented architecture (Representational State Transfer [REST] and Hyper Text Transfer Protocol [HTTP][3]) and leverage lightweight, simple integration techniques (asynchronous JavaScript and XML [AJAX], Really Simple Syndication [RSS], and JavaScript Object Notation [JSON]). The result is the fast creation of rich, desktop-like web applications.

In addition to being able to rapidly build new applications from mashups, there are other equally important requirements that form part of an enterprise-wide solution. These include

---

[1] See [1] for more details.

[2] A widget can be defined as a piece of code that can be installed and executed in any separate HTML-based web page by an end user without requiring additional compilation.

[3] See Appendix B online for definitions and references of these standards and technical specifications.

governance, performance, security, and several other requirements that are needed to deploy a full blown Web 2.0-based application into production. Connecting to a business's SAP, Oracle, Siebel, and other Enterprise Resource Planning (ERP) solutions alongside any Operational Data Stores (ODS), Data Warehouses (DW), and information-based integration platforms is not the same problem as developing a relatively simple application that can show a point on a map based on a simple query from a tactical data source. This means the mashup environment must be capable of working with relatively simple data sources (for example, news feeds and maps) and also be capable of developing wrapper style services that encapsulate enterprise-wide data (structured or unstructured) that is developed and controlled through appropriate governance to expose the data to users developing the mashup solution.

12.2 Business Drivers

The term mashup is borrowed from the pop music scene, where a mashup is a new song that is mixed from the vocal and instrumental tracks from two different source songs (usually belonging to different genres). Like these songs, a mashup is an unusual or innovative composition of content (often from unrelated data sources) made for human (rather than computerized) consumption.

So, what might a mashup look like? The EveryBlock Chicago crime website[4] is a great intuitive example of what's called a mapping mashup. This mashup combines crime data from the Chicago Police Department's online database with maps from Google Maps. Users can, for example, query the mashup to show graphically (with highlighted areas using marker pins) the details of all recent burglary crimes in a specified area of Chicago. This has proven to be an excellent combination of two different forms of data (crime statistics and geographical data) that reveal new insights into crime prevention in Chicago.

However, although becoming widespread and familiar, mapping mashups are the simpler style of mashup that supports individuals and businesses. The following is a list of some of the mashup styles that can be used:

- **Mapping mashups**—Mapping mashups use the huge amounts of data collected about things and activities, and links them to data that holds location information. When Google created its Mapping API, it opened the floodgates for this style of mashup. Web developers can now mash many kinds of data to maps from Google. Others followed shortly after; Microsoft®, Yahoo, and AOL all have APIs that deliver similar capabilities.

- **Video and photo mashups**—The ability to use images or videos and attach tags or other data to them has allowed such data to be combined with other information available. Photo hosting such as Flickr[5] and other social networking tools with APIs that expose photo sharing has led to a variety of mashups. These types of mashups use metadata that is embedded within the images or video (for example, who took the picture,

---

[4] For more details, see [2].

[5] For more details, see [3].

when it was taken, etc.) and can be linked with other data that has similar metadata to produce aggregated information that offers more than merely a picture. For example, a picture of a singer could be linked to the albums he or she has written and other interesting information; it could identify similar photos and build a library of such images. If those photos were tagged by users of the website, it could offer links to news feeds or blogs about the singer.

- **Search and shopping mashups**—These forms of mashups have been available for some time. Comparative shopping tools such as BizRate, PriceGrabber, MySimon, and Google's Froogle[6] used combinations of business-to-business (B2B) technologies or screen scraping to aggregate comparative price data. Recently, with Web 2.0 technologies, emerging companies such as eBay and Amazon[7] have released APIs for programmatically accessing their content to allow tagged content to be exploited.

- **News mashups**—Companies such as the BBC or Reuters[8] have been using Web 2.0 technologies (such as RSS and Atom feeds) since 2002. These have been used to distribute news feeds related to various topics. Users can subscribe to specific mashups that can aggregate information and present it in a bespoke fashion to that user over the Web. For example, a user can create a personalized newspaper based on feeds from many external sources about favorite topics of interest. An example is Doggdot.us,[9] which combines feeds from the technically oriented news sources Digg.com, Slashdot.org, and Del.icio.us.[10]

- **Structured data (aggregation) mashups**—The creation of feeds using simple protocols (REST, RSS, and so on) to access enterprise applications (SAP, Siebel Enterprise Data Warehouse and so on) enables small data sets to be made available to users to aggregate across those data sources and to drive other more visually rich mashups (such as the mapping mashup mentioned previously).

Basically, mashup adoption in the enterprise has been driven by two common business needs: driving up revenue and controlling costs. Businesses have always needed to grow their revenue through increased sales and services. In today's economy, though, it's more likely that businesses need to retain existing customer loyalty to secure existing revenue streams. Similarly, the other need, to reduce operational costs, also justifies investment in enterprise mashups.

---

[6] For more details, see [5].

[7] For more details, see [6].

[8] For more details, see [7].

[9] For more details, see [8].

[10] For more details, see [9].

Reducing the need for skilled IT staff to develop applications and enabling them to focus on core tasks offers a chance to directly affect the bottom line of a business by moving simpler development needs directly into the business's hands.

Businesses are beginning to work out how to use mashups in new, innovative ways to address these business needs. This has been forced somewhat by the sheer workload of application development within a typical IT department in today's large enterprises. Lines of Businesses (LOB) also want to have more control when dealing with specific issues their departments may have (as opposed to enterprise wide solutions) which enables them to quickly develop specific solutions to their requirements. On the other hand, IT departments are continually under pressure to deliver applications more quickly with less funding. They are also turning to mashups for non-mission-critical applications, because they can be built by less skilled staff and developed in shorter timeframes. IT organizations use mashups to supplement less Web knowledgeable business users who are not able to fully author their own Web-based applications, often at lower costs then traditional techniques would yield.

These generic style mashups can be used to provide specific solutions across many sectors in many business scenarios, such as the following:

- Access to supply chain information (stock, location of vehicles, performance of suppliers, location of stores close to stocking out of critical products, and so on) for a retailer.

- Aggregate customer account details so a bank can quickly select all accounts, documents, and recent transactions with a specific client to assist in targeting new promotions, offer specific customers access to accounts, find branch offices and ATMs, and supply information to enable customers to quickly contact call centers through a variety of channels such as phone, e-mail, or mail.

- Aggregate different data sources to allow management at a service company to view historical performance, the pipeline of activity for the business, and skills associated with the organization to match roles to work and search options to identify potential customers.

The basis for a set of business requirements to drive use case scenarios can be developed from an assumption that mashups will help businesses achieve the following:

- **Increase revenue**—Enable sales and service teams with solutions that combine a variety of data in an easy-to-use interface.

- **Reduce costs**—Rapidly focus on areas of the business that might not have been targeted as quickly in the past.

- **Better collaboration**—Bring together solutions that give small, focused teams the ability to understand issues, discuss them, and then take action where necessary.

- **Secure customer loyalty**—Use a multiplicity of channel-driven information to better understand your customers' wants and needs; share information with different groups in your business to better understand the lifetime needs of customers; deploy mashups rapidly to customers to offer a competitive advantage over others; enable data-driven solutions so customers can extend mashups to suit their needs; and tag solutions to give added value to the customer and others who use the mashup.

To achieve these aims, the solutions developed have a number of specific goals predicated specifically for a mashup environment:

- **Improve decision making**—Enable the end user of the mashup to make decisions in a timelier manner and over a wider range of areas than the corporate level, enterprise-wide, monolithic applications currently do. These mashups might also incorporate broader, non-traditional data sources (web-based data, unstructured sources, and so on), and they might require the management of large volumes of data and new visualization techniques to offer greater insight into the data being consumed.[11] The mashups might become incorporated into the enterprise-wide view or they might be discarded if the decisions are for a specific, little, repeated event.

- **Optimize the productivity of individuals**—Enable users to wire their own mashups to develop new widgets and become empowered to use data in ways that the IT department cannot or does not have the time to deliver. This enables the long tail of applications as seen in Figure 12.1. Tim O'Reilly[12] outlines this idea as being the applications that IT departments don't have time to develop normally. These applications are generally high value for a small user community but not applicable to the needs of the majority of the business community.

- **Improve informal business processes**—Develop situational applications that enable small numbers of groups or teams to collaborate more effectively.

- **Minimize dependencies on expensive IT skills**—Open mashups to a wider audience and let them develop solutions that meet local, tactical needs. Of course, you should harvest and develop the best of these for exploitation to a wider audience. Users become able to use and enhance existing widgets (internally and externally created) based on a catalog of items that can be commented on and tagged by other users to allow new users to quickly identify the most used or most relevant function.

- **Quickly demonstrate new business opportunities**—Allow new solutions to be rapidly prototyped using enterprise-wide assets along with external data and local content to show new ways of managing, analyzing, and exploiting available data. Emerging standards help widgets become much more useful. Information can be passed between them to enable data to be aggregated and consumed in new and interesting ways. These mashups can be stored as the aggregated view of widgets as well as other mashups to

---

[11] See [10] and [11].

[12] See [1].

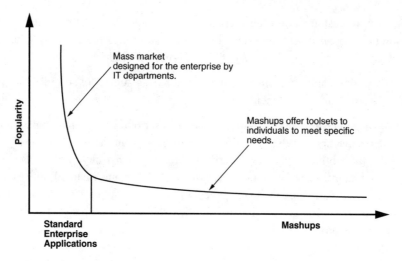

Figure 12.1   The long tail of situational applications can now be developed.

build more mashups that can be cataloged and reused by the whole community, quickly
building richer applications that demonstrate new solutions.

The benefits of mashups vary according to their usage; following are some of the benefits:

- **Faster answers**—Mashups give the user access to internal and external information
  without needing IT resource. Mashups exploit internal and external data sources to
  develop solutions that provide specific insight into a business problem. This combines
  data in ways that probably have never been done before, offering faster routes to new
  business insight. Because of this, mashups provide answers faster than almost any other
  information-management technique. For business scenarios, where performance is crucial, mashups provide the fastest way to access critical business information. Note that
  this implies that access to those critical systems can be rapidly achieved.

- **Improved resource use**—Mashups give business users the ability to develop their own
  solutions. IT is freed to address other tasks while previously underutilized data sources
  become more relevant. This is a difficult balancing act for IT departments that wish to
  manage data centrally. They must maintain all their existing systems alongside mashups
  that add extra load while still ensuring acceptable performance and not stifling innovation and access to that information.

- **New opportunities**—The PC is no longer the only tool to develop web-based solutions
  for. Mashups can be deployed over a variety of channels, from thin client portal-based
  front ends, to remote terminals or handheld devices such as mobile phones or PDAs.
  More than one billion people are now online (many now using phones to access the
  internet, for example). Mashups enable the development of solutions that suit a wide

range of devices. Not developing solutions for such users misses on vast, new opportunities in this changing marketplace.

By their nature, these styles of applications bring differences around architectural principles within the enterprise and can cause challenges around managing the solutions deployed. For all the benefits these solutions can offer, IT departments should be wary of such situational applications because of the following:

- Some developments become organic and are developed without any IT involvement, which might result in solutions that at best augment existing solutions, and at worst, supplant them with solutions that were never designed to be used by large numbers of users. This has some resonance with the explosion of spreadsheets in the '80s and '90s with little formal control of data that resided within them. The benefits (and issues like governance of several similar spreadsheets delivering no single version of the truth) need to be carefully considered. However, many critical mashup applications should reside in the IT-managed service landscape to provide some important distinctions around opportunities for management and governance that are much harder to implement in a pure desktop environment.

- The development and growth of solutions perceived to be in a state of perpetual beta—never completed and never designed—are where some aspects of governance might be useful. IT departments need to identify solutions developed with mashups that have become steady state and are showing greater usage and value across the community. They need to review the data feeds and transformations used by mashup solutions to ensure they can be reused in the context of a Service-Oriented Architecture (SOA).

- There are no real best practices when creating mashups; some loose rules can be defined, but being too prescriptive can slow down development or prevent some of the innovation these solutions promise. However, the lack of best practices and standards can be challenging to IT departments.

- Business users have to understand, embrace, and exploit this new paradigm, and therefore, some training is required.

12.2.1 Information Governance and Architectural Considerations for Mashups

Section 3.3 in Chapter 3 considered Information Governance. This chapter extends that thinking into specifics for a mashup environment. When considering how mashups access the data used, the governance of that data can become a crucial element as greater volumes of end users adopt mashups. Consider the following issues that can arise:

- Many of the data feeds created are relatively fine-grained (simple queries or feeds) and become accessible to those who have appropriate security access. This contrasts with large-scale applications where it is the application that controls access to the data. By developing new fine-grained services, additional, unexpected loads on back-end solutions can occur unless they are carefully managed.

- Mashup style applications are built quickly, and performance isn't considered in the same rigorous way as traditional developments. Gathering data from several heterogeneous sources might be the only way to get to that data and might require inefficient or complex federated queries, which might include screen scraping for mainframe data and web services for other sources of data. There is a trade-off between making data available in situations where it simply wasn't available in the past and making it perform to levels that are deemed acceptable to the end users. A governance set of procedures that ensures mashups are monitored and the more complex solutions are considered for enterprise-wide style solutions (if their value dictates) can be enabled, or the mashups can simply be revoked if appropriate.

- Access to some data sources might be difficult to obtain in practice, (for example, a lot of web pages provide data in HTML, and web-scraping software is not always reliable and is error-prone). In addition, IT departments have built solutions that operate to rigorous service levels over time, and deploying mashup style solutions over them might impact performance, causing operational problems. In addition, where silos of data still exist, without good governance in place, it might be difficult to gain clearance to access specific data in certain lines of business.

- Mashups can be shared by those who have access, and new mashups can be built upon these, so scalability might become a concern if usage is rapidly consumed.

- Systems and operations management can become more complex when dealing with fine-grained feeds and multiple mashups (potentially hundreds or more). How the IT department monitors which mashups impact which data stores and how problems are resolved easily when solutions are business-driven become a key concern.

12.3 Architecture Overview Diagram

The high level components that make up the architecture are described in this section. At its simplest level, the core components required to deliver a mashup-enabled system are depicted in Figure 12.2. These are a tiered layer of components ranging from the various data available to be mashed through the interfaces to access them, the actual software that employs that data (widget), and the tooling to assemble these for wide-scale deployment.

The various components shown in Figure 12.2 are:

- **Mashups**—A *mashup* is a situational application that is built from a number of different components wired together to create a new application that offers greater value than the individual applications on their own.

Figure 12.2   A simple view of components that are needed to make up a mashup

- **Mashup makers (or builders)**—A *mashup maker* is the assembly area that allows for the running and creation of mashups. It offers users a GUI-based environment to build mashups by integrating private and public information services. The user can visually manage content no matter what its source (for example, static content, such as a Web page with dynamic content, a SOAP, a REST service, or an RSS feed). The mashup maker provides a collection of widgets, which are software components that provide access (normally coarse-grained) to one or more services.

- **Widgets**—Widgets tend to be designed with a focus on consumption and customization to ensure they are flexible. With Web 2.0 design and the wide array of data to be consumed, it is difficult to understand in advance how content developed is to be used. Widgets can be visual (display a chart), or nonvisual (build a transform of data to be used elsewhere). Using the mashup maker, a widget can be dragged from a GUI-based palette onto a canvas, its properties opened, reviewed, and then used to connect the appropriate inputs and outputs between those widgets, with the creation of a mashup as the end result.

- **Data Service Interfaces**—For there to be sufficient widgets to build up a large enough set to build useful mashups, interfaces to the many sources of information are needed. A data service interface uses feeds, such as REST, WSDL, AJAX, or XML Remote Procedure Calls (XML-RPC) to make available information needed in a mashup.

- **Content**—Content simply refers to the various information that can be accessed via the data services, whether it's ERP solution, spreadsheets, flat files, databases, unstructured information, or semi-structured information. It is simply the various repositories available to be used across all the data domains we have defined.

12.4 Component Model Diagram

In this section, we decompose the Mashup Component introduced in Chapter 5 into its relevant subcomponents.[13]

Figure 12.3 depicts a suitable architecture to meet the needs of a mashup environment.

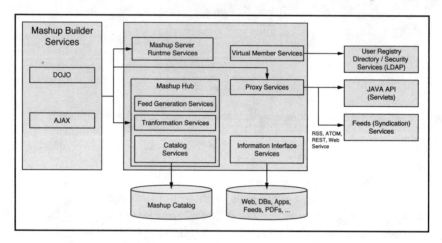

Figure 12.3   Architecture overview

The various subcomponents within the architecture are described in the following list. The logical runtime subcomponents that are utilized in the architecture patterns are:

- **Mashup Builder Services**—The mashup runtime in the browser provides a JavaScript framework for rendering the mashup UI that consists of widgets, data sources for managing the interactions, and a link between the widgets and services acquired from another vendor. After widgets are loaded and rendered in the browser, they are considered part of the Browser Mashup Runtime Component. This aligns with the Presentation Services available in the Component Model.

- **Mashup Hub**—The Mashup Hub Component delivers an environment for IT and business professionals to work with all forms of data, including Web, local, departments, and enterprise wide-based data available in any organization. The Mashup Hub Component interfaces with these data sources and creates Atom feeds. In addition, the Mashup Hub Component can aggregate, transform, or sort data from any data source to create a consolidated feed, referred to as a *feed mashup*.

- **Mashup Server Runtime Services**—The Mashup Server Runtime Services Component provides the runtime infrastructure for deploying and hosting mashup applications.

---

[13] The decomposition is aligned with the excellent articles by Holt Adams in the IBM developerWorks website found in [12] and [13].

After calling a mashup application from a user's browser to the Mashup server, the Mashup Server Component loads any required server-side components and sends any Mashup Builder services components and associated widget components to the browser.

- **Virtual Member Services**—This subcomponent uses a layer of abstraction that delegates the authentication of users to a suitable security system (for example, WebSphere Application Server security). Within the security system there is a virtual member management database, local operating system, LDAP, or custom user registry, which will be used for the authentication of user, credentials.

- **Proxy Services**—This subcomponent enables widgets running in the Mashup Builder Services Component to access domains other than the one from which the mashup application was loaded. Browsers enforce a same origin policy that prevents client-side scripts, such as JavaScript (which widgets are based on), from loading content from an origin that has a different protocol, domain name, or port. The Proxy services allow the data to be accessed and shared with appropriate security rules considered.

- **Feed (Syndication) Services**—Feed Services provide XML data that supports RSS or Atom formats. The formats and associated protocols are used to syndicate content that is updated frequently.

- **User Registry Component**—The User Registry component is a repository that holds user account information such as user ID and password, permissions, and roles. This is used to provide authentication and authorization of Web resources. This data source clearly must also support the virtual member services.

- **Catalog**—A Repository for catalog services, the Catalog consists of page structures, feeds, widgets, and other objects used by the Mashup Hub.

- **Java API (Servlet) Component**—The servlet component is a Java server-side component that enables widgets running in the browser to access the Java APIs of components and applications deployed on a Web server to extend the capabilities of mashup applications. Use it with the Proxy Services Component.

- **Information Interface Services**—These services are used whenever the information service to be consumed by the mashup does not have an easy-to-consume interface. For example, an information service with a COBOL[14] interface might need to be wrapped in a REST-based interface to be consumable within a mashup. Obviously, interface mappings are usually done by the Connectivity and Interoperability Component previously introduced, but if the software selected for this component lacks a certain mapping capability, the Information Interface Services of the Mashup Hub Component must fill the gap.

---

[14] COBOL is short for Common Business Oriented Language and is one of the oldest programming languages.

It's worth considering how mashups and an SOA strategy can be employed to reuse services developed at the enterprise level. Many of the services a mashup can consume can be developed through a set of enterprise-wide services and can be used to build momentum to become self-sustaining. Many businesses consider SOA a strategy, but opening up services to mashup developers is necessary for mashups to take their place as valuable assets next to the existing IT infrastructure.

12.5 Component Interaction Diagrams

After the mashup ecosystem is in place, you can use the model of assemble, wire, and share to build situational applications via a mashup maker. Let's break this down into each action. The responsibilities of the roles in the various phases of the model are displayed in Figure 12.4.

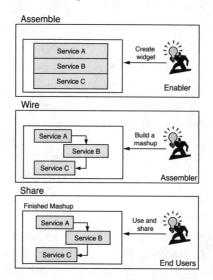

Figure 12.4   The assemble, wire, and share model

The following lists describes each role and interaction shown in Figure 12.4:

- **Assemble**—The enabler can create a catalog that contains all the widgets (built internally or from external sources) that might be used in a given area of the business. The mashup maker is used to access the catalog to identify and use components they may need in building a mashup. The catalog can also be used as a central point of governance, with appropriate security defined around widget access from which mashups can or cannot be accessed.

- **Wire**—The assembler uses the mashup maker to connect widgets found in the catalog to create a mashup. For example, a form-based widget can be placed on a page, allowing a user to enter data. This data can be connected to the input of a widget that provides some form of Web service invocation (for example, querying a database based on the input data from the form). The output of the Web service response can be connected to a further widget that renders a visual display (for example, a chart or map based on the returned data).

- **Share**—The assembler shares the mashup to make it publicly accessible. It is then available to end users.

There are three distinct roles in this process:

- **Mashup enabler**—The mashup enabler writes the widgets and adds them to the catalog. They often work with the assemblers to design widgets that will meet the needs of specific projects and are deployed within the catalog for reuse elsewhere over time. This is usually an individual from the IT department or someone with sufficient technical skills to write software.

- **Mashup assembler**—This is typically an end user or subject matter expert. The mashup assembler builds mashups by wiring together the widgets and any preassembled mashups already available within the catalog.

- **End users**—These personnel normally only use the mashup as it was intended and do not build any new components. They do, however, contribute to the overall use of the application by using social tools such as rating tags and comments, which are used to provide feedback so the application can be improved by the mashup assemblers and enablers on future iterations.

What makes the mashup ecosystem so effective? We see at least the following reasons:

- The standardization of key technologies, such as SOAP, REST, and AJAX, has seen a growth in the use of SOAs on the Web and inside the enterprise. This has led to these technologies reaching a tipping point. There are now many sources of reusable Web-based APIs and mashups that are easily obtained within the Web.

- This is an easy to understand programming model. It is simple to adopt due to the many business and power users who are familiar with Internet-based applications (and simple scripting languages such as PHP) and can do tasks such as writing Excel macros.

Chapter 5 describes how information can be viewed as a set of services and how those Information Services can be exposed directly into a business service or utilized with other services to build composite services that make up part of a business service.

Mashups play directly into these themes. Whether the mashup is a pure feed that is used to transform, modify, or somehow manipulate data from a content source and deliver this directly to an end user (say a federated or transformed query), or it is a composition and choreography of data retrieval and visualization (a composite service) to deliver new insight to an analyst. The range of business services discussed in Chapter 5 can be delivered using these mashup style solutions.

But how do all these components interact? Figure 12.5 shows generically what is *functionally* needed to deploy a set of components (therefore, the virtual member services are not shown here) to enable a mashup-based solution.

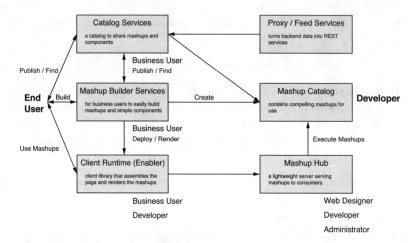

Figure 12.5   Component Interaction Diagram

Based on the description of the Mashup Components from Chapter 5, Figure 12.5 depicts how these components interact with development and end-user communities to successfully deploy a mashup-based solution. The specific items shown in Figure 12.5 are:

- **Mashup Builder Services**—These are mandatory components. The Mashup Builder is the tool to wire widgets and feeds together into new mashup. The Mashup Builder Services can also be used to use mashups as sources themselves: wire them together and create new mashups. The Mashup Builder is deployed on a browser mashup runtime architectural component and uses the Mashup Hub Runtime Services (transform, feed generation, see Figure 12.3) to create new mashups and widgets.

- **Client Runtime (Enabler) Component**—An additional optional component, this is an end-user tool that enables the use of mashups only. This component is required in scenarios where the users of mashups are different from (and probably more numerous than) the creators of mashups. The Mashup Enabler is deployed on the browser mashup runtime architectural component.

- **Mashup Catalog Services and Mashup Catalog**—This is mandatory; it provides cataloging and characterization of feeds, mashups, and widgets so that available resources can be discovered by mashup makers and mashup users. Collaborative features enable end-user tagging and sharing of resources. The Mashup Catalog is deployed on the Mashup Hub Component.

- **Mashup Hub**—This is mandatory; it provides server-side support to mashup makers and user environments, including the execution of transformations on input feeds and management of security (such as how browser technology places limits on the way in which information from multiple Web domains can or can't be combined to prevent hacking). A mashup hub can overcome this by acting as a proxy domain. The mashup server is deployed on the Mashup Server Architectural Component.

- **Proxy/Feed Services**—These services are used to develop feeds and widget adaptors to develop new widgets or convert non-Web information sources (databases, applications, and spreadsheets, for example) into feeds, services, and widgets.

We now explore how these components can be used in various scenarios (use cases) to highlight likely functional solutions to a variety of problem scenarios.

12.5.1 Component Interaction Diagrams—Deployment Scenarios

We have developed a number of deployment scenarios that use the components previously described to show the flexibility and uses of mashups in CRM style solutions and integration in an enterprise-wide SOA.

12.5.1.1 Scenario 1: Improved Customer Relationship Management

In Figure 12.6, mashups provide an improved Customer Relationship Management (CRM) experience for end users to better understand how their customers react to changes in policies, promotions, and offers by rapidly gathering data from multiple channels (data sources) and combining it to create new views about customer segmentation and to identify how changes affect buying behaviors.

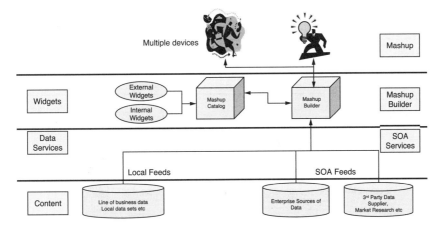

Figure 12.6 CRM mashup

Driving this approach is the difficulty in swiftly gathering knowledge of customer interaction and transaction history across multiple systems. Mashups can partially help gather this data (possibly from predefined SOA services already in place for a Master Data solution, for example) and new sources of data (external statistics, mapping widgets, and so on) to deliver new ways of visualizing customer buying behaviors by time, demographic, competitor performance, and so on.

By sharing this mashup across Customer Relationship Managers, it can be used to increase effectiveness in responding to customer interactions. For example, mashups can be embedded in an existing business process to help client advisors at point of sales offer better service to clients by augmenting the existing analytic tools with new information not previously available to those staff.

12.5.1.2 Scenario 2: User Interfaces to SOA

The example described in Figure 12.7 (access to SOA services) can be applied to any industry. It is useful to understand how mashups can be used to exploit existing SOA-enabled services. By adopting an SOA approach to development, mashups can easily exploit the services built due to the open nature in which they are built and a rigorous approach to standards, which means it is easy to connect to these services. In addition, the adherence to non-functional aspects of the solution that are controlled at the enterprise SOA level means mashups should be able to exploit the services with well defined service levels. In addition, mashups that access, manipulate, and transform data[15]—although invisible to the end user—can supplement the enterprise-wide services to add value in small communities by solving their specific problems without necessarily involving the IT department.

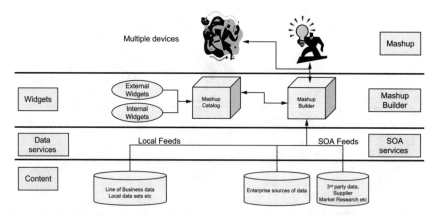

Figure 12.7   Access to SOA services

---

[15] See [14] for a demo on this topic.

Mashups enable the easy exposure of SOA services, rapidly exposing them to end users in an environment that supports the rapid creation of dynamic user interfaces. The purposes behind this solution are to quickly prototype or develop new composite services based on enterprise-wide work done in an SOA environment to date. It also has a mechanism that enables end users to exploit the enterprise-wide services and have them managed by the IT department to ensure security; performance, availability, and so on are in a controlled environment where access to data is critical to the business.

In the example in Figure 12.7, mashups are created based on services already existing or simple widgets created from one (or a few) SOA services that can be exposed on a variety of different end-user devices. Consider channels such as the phone, a PDA, television, or the Web. Exposing these services for use (and reuse) in existing social networks can offer new routes to market. For example, offering a simple location and search feature that can be run from a phone to identify the nearest bank branch or retail outlet might bring new customers to that business.

12.6 Service Qualities for Mashup Solutions

To understand how the Service qualities of a solution are derived, you need to consider the non-functional requirements (NFR) of the solution. NFRs of a mashup might differ from that of traditional web applications, and it is worth considering how the two styles of applications (traditional and mashup), development, usage, and maintenance are considered. There are a number of similarities, but some distinct differences. It isn't always obvious which style of solution has an advantage over the other. It's worth stepping back and reviewing these points before deciding on an approach; mashups may not always be the most appropriate solution.

If the application has the following characteristics, the application is core to the business and cannot afford to be anything other than industrial strength:

- The solution will be deployed across large parts of the business and will have a structured support service and rigorous Service Level Agreements (SLA) associated with it.

- The application has a formal design methodology associated with it to address a comprehensive set of business requirements and well-defined User Interface (UI).

- Things like complex data integration, business process workflow, or document workflow need to be rigorously managed.

- The solution needs to be highly available, and outages must be minimized at all costs.

These characteristics should point toward a traditional web application to ensure resilience, availability, and support, and a well-defined interface that does not change and is embedded within the solution.

If, however, the application has the following characteristics, then a mashup solution might be viable:

- The business needs something fast and the solution is seen as throwaway.
- Users have some experience of the data behind the solution and are comfortable with web-based concepts.
- The solution needs to use internal, enterprise, or LOB data with external data sources to provide new insights.
- Prototyping and using agile methods (rapid iterations to get to an end point) are required to shape solutions rather than have them formally defined.
- Business users can build large parts of the solution and extend the solution if the right infrastructure is enabled.
- Solutions need to be merely sufficient to address a specific need.
- Data sources required can be accessed by the simple Web 2.0 methods mentioned earlier such as RSS, Atom, or REST style interfaces.

As you can see from this set of requirements, a more fluid style of development—with access to data through simple interfaces and solutions that are good enough to meet a need now—is a different proposition than a traditional web application. It is worth making the point at this stage that there might be governance models that can be put in place for user-driven mashups that can effectively promote those that are rapidly used and seen as adding value to a widening community. IT departments might have to learn how to harvest these assets and enable them through more robust frameworks for enterprise-wide style deployments.

Table 12.1 outlines some of the key NFRs of both styles and how they differ.

Table 12.1 Differing NFR Requirements Between Traditional and Mashup Developments

#	NFR	Traditional Web Application	Mashup Application
1	Performance	These solutions need to be high performance and manage hundreds or even thousands of transactions per second. SLAs are strictly defined and enforced	Performance is not critical, but should always be considered; delivering new insight is critical.
2	Capacity	Data stores can be many terabytes in size.	Large data sets can be reused; however little is stored, it is merely accessed from internal or external data sources. There is little data held in the mashup environment itself.
3	Growth and Scalability	Often required for thousands of users.	Much smaller numbers normally; however, solutions should be capable of being deployed to larger numbers of users if necessary.

Table 12.1   Differing NFR Requirements Between Traditional and Mashup Developments

#	NFR	Traditional Web Application	Mashup Application
4	Reliability/ Availability	Such systems often require very high up time (up to 99.999 percent)	Managed on best endeavors (see system management features).
5	Required Service Time	There are minimal windows for outages.	Most targets are generally online only for the working day (for example, 8 am to 6 pm). This is driven by the availability of multiple data sources and whether industrial strength mashup production environments are required.
6	Disaster Recovery (DR)	Normally there is some form of failover solution that is based on "heartbeat" monitoring of the production system. This can redirect users to a DR capability if failure occurs.	If the solution goes down, it is simply restored from backups.
7	Maintainability	Any solution probably uses some form of autonomic features to assist with maintenance and alerting of issues.	Mashups are designed to be reused by building and breaking down their components over time. IT departments can struggle to support such solutions because a steady-state solution is often not the preferred end point.
8	Systems Management	All the areas are physically managed by IT to ensure the solution is maintained and managed in an acceptable way to the business.	Many of these areas are managed locally or in an ad-hoc fashion.
9	Availability, Operations, Performance, and Capacity Management	IT feedback on system metrics ensures SLAs are met and any issues are identified and resolved.	There are no formal targets for mashups; "good enough" is the target. Any solutions that take on more traditional attributes should be formally managed and redeveloped into that space, and governance of mashups is required to enable this.

Table 12.1   Differing NFR Requirements Between Traditional and Mashup Developments

#	NFR	Traditional Web Application	Mashup Application
10	Change Management	A formal change process is in the place of a developed solution.	Ad-hoc development; mashups are adapted and saved in a catalog, there is self-policing of the solution through tagging, and comments are available on each mashup developed.
11	Configuration Inventory Management	License management and system configuration are managed from a central point.	Little or no requirement.
12	Security Management	User administration is managed centrally and access control to system resources is managed from the IT department.	Mashup security is still difficult to solve and will be a concern as Web 2.0 applications become more ubiquitous. For example, it will be necessary to keep code and data from each of the sources of information separate to prevent unscrupulous developers from hacking others' source data.[16]
13	DR Continuity	Normally a full test plan around DR is in place and continuity testing is formally planned annually.	Mashups generally have little design consideration such as a failover capability in infrastructure or in a DR solution.
14	Problem Resolution	Formal logging and tracking is engaged to resolve issues.	Problem resolution is managed at a local level with minimal IT support.
15	Help Desk	Help desk is available to manage user issues.	There is not a help desk; there is a self-serve spirit within the user community.

Clearly, these are significant differences. Mashups can be constructed and potentially discarded quickly. As such, they form excellent candidates for deployment in a virtual or cloud-style type operational pattern. This not only enables new environments to be quickly deployed, but also enables non-planned growth in a dynamic fashion with an easy-to-redeploy model for the assets and for when the mashup is no longer required.

---

[16] IBM recently announced WebSphere sMash, which addresses a key part of the browser mashup security issue by keeping code and data from each of the sources separated, while allowing controlled sharing of the data through a secure communication channel. More details can be found in [15] and [16].

12.7 Mashup Deployment—Applicable Operational Patterns

Operational Models are used to describe an IT Infrastructure and have been described in Chapter 6. This section describes some simple scenarios for deploying mashup services on differing operational models to meet the needs of NFRs or service qualities.

This section reviews only the Conceptual Model for mashups. Physical characteristics are defined during the design phase of a typical specific project. The Operational Model determines the shape and outlines the distribution style of the solution. More precisely, it provides a first, technology-neutral view of the operational architecture, and it focuses on the requirements of the business and the underlying characteristics of the business (locations and roles).

Drawing on Chapter 6 and the example in Table 6.4, we can define a few simple scenarios that show how a mashup environment can be built to become increasingly more resilient. The goal here is to support greater refinement and critical service qualities.

12.7.1 Scenario 1: Simple Deployment Model

When building such a simple model, you might prototype and then develop small subsystems used by individuals or small groups of users; availability is not an issue and the system can be down for anything up to a few days without any real impact on those using it. A summary of the key requirements is shown in Table 12.2.

Table 12.2 Simple Mashup Deployment Scenario

#	Exemplary Component Interaction Diagram	Major Data Domain Involved	Typical Requirements on Service Qualities	Exemplary Operational Pattern Selection by Scope of Integration		
				Discrete	Integrated	Cross-Domain
1	Swiftly build ad-hoc analytics making use of existing internal systems, small groups of users in single LOB	Analytical Data	Limited requirements, simple service level around restoring service within a few days		—	—
			Provisioning of data of best endeavors			
			Security limited to that required for internal group of users	Mashup Runtime & Security Pattern		

In Figure 12.8, the model uses a single server to run the operational components required for a basic mashup service that consists of builder services (optional enabler service on this operational node), catalog services, and additional widget services that are served up from the server service. A single application server such as WebSphere Application Server can be used to enable this model. It is assumed that the internal and external feeds already exist and can be exposed as services (RSS, Atom feeds, and so on) that any mashup could then exploit. The core services and data in this scenario can be held in a variety of applications and legacy systems, running, for example, within WebSphere Application Server, CICS®, IMS™, or DB2. The WebSphere Application Server Feature Pack contains features to enable applications and data to be exposed as RESTful services; so does the IBM WebSphere MQ HTTP Bridge.[17] Alternatively, an appliance such as IBM WebSphere DataPower® SOA Appliances[18] can be used to transform between Web services, native XML feeds, and RESTful protocols.

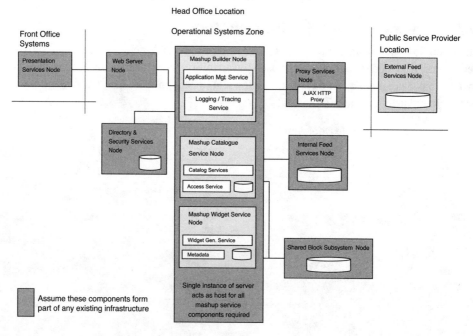

Figure 12.8   Simple Deployment Model

12.7.2 Scenario 2: High Availability Model

This scenario adds to the previous model and starts to split the various operational components to physically run on separate, clustered application servers that can act as failover to each other. Table 12.3 describes the key requirements for such a solution.

---

[17] See [17] for more details.

[18] See [18] for more details.

Table 12.3 Clustered Servers for Resilience—Server for Catalog and Widget Building Remains on the Same Platform

#	Component Interaction Diagram	Major Data Domain Involved	Typical Requirements on Service Qualities	Operational Pattern Selection by Scope of Integration		
				Discrete	Integrated	Cross-Domain
1	Build resilient solutions that can be deployed to large groups of users and ensure infrastructure can support reliability and availability characteristics required.	Analytical Data	Service levels are well defined and require uptime that is at least during working hours (always). Service should be restored within hours if an issue occurs. Security is limited to that required for internal groups of users. Data is still dependant on underlying applications and databases. This option requires an additional pattern to enable resilience within the solution and it offers improved availability, where anything up to 24 hours, 7 days a week, and 365 days a year access could be enabled.		Mashup Runtime & Security Pattern Multi-Tier High Availability for Critical Data Pattern	—

Figure 12.9 describes the Mashup Components required to deliver a high-level availability scenario. The Mashup Builder Server Nodes can appear as a group of independent nodes interconnected and working together as a single system. A load-balancing mechanism such as IP spraying, as previously discussed, can be used to intercept the HTTP requests and redirect them to the appropriate node on the cluster through an HTTP plug-in, providing scalability, load balancing, and failover as part of the Web Application Server of choice. In addition, the catalog and widget services can be run separately as an additional server node. The split has been dictated at this stage to ensure those services associated with the creation of new mashups and those associated with actually using and running the mashups are separated. In this way, developers can continue to build or users can continue to run mashups even if failure of one subsystem is catastrophic.

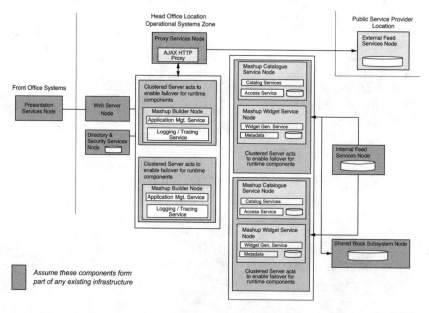

Figure 12.9   Mashup Components deployed for high-availability scenario

It's worth noting that this approach can be extended to any of the other nodes in Figure 12.9. Indeed, it is assumed that in any enterprise environment, things like web server nodes are already clustered and these services will simply use (possibly extend) the server nodes already in place. Finally, this solution does not cater for loss of data that the mashups consume; if external or internal feeds lose their data source access through failure of the underlying applications or databases, then the service would fail.

12.7.3 Scenario 3: Near-Real-Time Model

The previous scenarios were designed only to cater for external and internal data feeds that might be somewhat out of date (for example, daily updates from suppliers on stock availability or updates on statistics from external government agencies). However, there are now large amounts of data that many businesses are retrieving in near real or even real time. This has been fueled by an explosion in instrumentation that enables companies to access data faster and in finer grained slices. One example is RFID tagging on stock movements, on line instrumentation in the oil industry to track oil flow and automation of energy monitoring and tracking in the business and home. All these initiatives mean greater volumes of data and richer sets of data can be made available for mashups to integrate with other internal and external data for use. Table 12.4 describes the requirements for just such a solution.

Table 12.4 Mashups Scenario that Exploits Near Real-Time Analytics

| # | Component Interaction Diagram | Major Data Domain Involved | Typical Requirements on Service Qualities | Operational Pattern Selection by Scope of Integration | | |
				Discrete	Integrated	Cross-Domain
1	Build resilient solutions that can be deployed to large groups of users and ensure infrastructure can support reliability and availability characteristics required. Data is driven in near real time or real time, and a mashups consume data that is as recent as possible.	Analytical Data	Highly available, reliable, and integrated into existing enterprise-wide information assets; makes use of any enterprise-wide SOA solutions that expose information already in place.	Mashup Runtime & Security Pattern Data Integration & Aggregation Runtime Pattern ESB Runtime for Guaranteed Data Delivery Pattern	Multi-Tier High Availability for Critical Data Pattern	—

Figure 12.10 is a simplification of what is in Chapter 6. The Mashup Pattern is used to depict how any such environment can act as the source for data for a mashup solution, whether it be data fed directly from any ESB via message queues (potentially as an event-driven feed) or via a feed from a Data Warehouse, an Operational Data store, or even a data mart to supply Analytical Data that can then be mashed up with other sources from other external feeds. This solution also recognizes that an existing ESB and data integration program of work are probably already in existence and integrates the mashup infrastructure into this environment.

The three patterns are relatively simple in their nature; however, they account for differing levels of NFRs. However, they are useful to describe so that the reader can easily identify how operational patterns can be linked together with the Mashup Pattern to describe how innovative solutions can be swiftly built around a mashup style infrastructure.

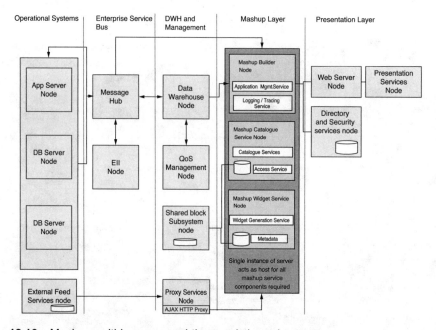

Figure 12.10   Mashups within a near-real-time analytic environment

12.8 IBM Technologies

The diagram in Figure 12.11 depicts the current set of IBM technologies that make up the mashup offering.

IBM Mashup Center combines all the user mashup capabilities from IBM Lotus® Mashups and the information access and transformation capabilities of IBM InfoSphere Mashup Hub into one tightly integrated, comprehensive mashup offering.

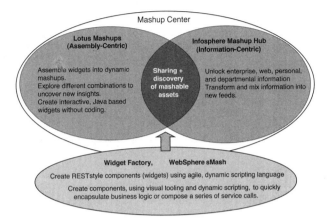

Figure 12.11   IBM Software Stack

12.8.1 Lotus Mashups

IBM Lotus Mashups provide a lightweight mashup environment for assembling personal, enterprise, and web content into simple, flexible, and dynamic applications. With Lotus Mashups, users with limited web-based knowledge can easily create and share new applications that address their immediate business needs. Please note that at the time of this writing, this product was supposed to be renamed Mashup Builder.

12.8.2 InfoSphere Mashup Hub

IBM InfoSphere Mashup Hub is a lightweight information management environment for IT and business professionals who want to unlock and share Web, departmental, personal, and enterprise information for use in Web 2.0 applications and mashups. IBM InfoSphere MashupHub includes visual tools for creating, storing, transforming, and remixing feeds to be used in mashup and situational applications; it also includes a central catalog where users can tag, rate, discover, search, and share mashable assets.

Please note that at the time of this writing, this product was supposed to be renamed Data Mashup Builder.

12.8.3 WebSphere sMash

IBM WebSphere sMash[19] is an agile dynamic scripting environment that enables developers to build and run REST-based components using visual tooling and dynamic scripting languages such as PHP and groovy. Scripting developers can use WebSphere sMash to quickly create widgets that can be assembled into new web applications using IBM Mashup Center.[20] Figure 12.12 describes IBM's Mashup Center in more detail.

---

[19] See [15] and [16].

[20] For more details, see [19].

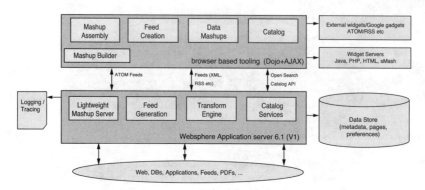

Figure 12.12   IBM Mashup Center architecture

The Feed Creation, Data Mashups, and Catalog components are provided by InfoSphere MashupHub. Users can register widgets, mashup pages, and existing feeds accessible within the Intranet or the Internet. The InfoSphere MashupHub creates and registers feeds and feed mashups built using a simple browser-based UI. The browser-based tooling also enables a mashup author to discover and share any registered feeds and widgets to further reuse in mashup applications with Lotus Mashups. After they are created, the mashup applications can be stored in the catalog for discovery and use by others.

For deployment of mashup applications, Lotus Mashups includes a lightweight mashup server, whereas InfoSphere MashupHub is more comprehensive and includes a feed generation component and a transformation engine. The mashup server is the target of mashup URLs for accessing mashup applications and loads the page and its associated widgets to the browser. When widgets access feeds registered in the InfoSphere MashupHub catalog, any metadata is retrieved which is required to interface with the data source. That metadata is then used by the feed generator to connect to the data sources and to invoke the transformation engine when data is aggregated or transformed from one or more of the data sources.

12.9 Conclusion

This chapter attempted to describe a new style of development that removes itself from tightly coupled applications that are closely linked to the data they perform their actions upon. Mashups offer end users and developers the opportunity to develop a new breed of solutions that can satisfy the long tail of user requirements that are so often difficult to keep up with. The construct associated with mashups is such that previous developments can be easily exploited and a large set of internal and potentially external widgets can be used to create, assemble, and deploy solutions rapidly. These solutions can be augmented, reused, or even discarded with a speed that is not possible in most of today's IT shops. Couple this with the ability to deploy these assets in a cloud style environment and their uses become efficient and economical while still being highly effective in targeting solutions that are important for critical business requirements for short periods of time or to develop things that might never have been possible, delivering new ways of working.

12.10 References

[1] O'Reilly, Tim. 2005. *What Is Web 2.0? Design Patterns and Business Models for the Next Generation of Software:* http://www.oreillynet.com/pub/a/oreilly/tim/news/2005/09/30/what-is-web-20.html?page=1 (accessed December 15, 2009).

[2] Chicago Crimeblock web site: http://chicago.everyblock.com/crime/locations/neighborhoods/englewood/ (accessed December 15, 2009).

[3] Flickr web site: http://www.flickr.com/ (accessed December 15, 2009).

[4] CNN web site: http://www.cnn.com/ (accessed December 15, 2009).

[5] Various web sites: http://www.bizrate.co.uk/, http://www.pricegrabber.co.uk/. http://www.mysimon.com/, and http://www.google.co.uk/prdhp?hl=en&tab=wf (accessed December 15, 2009).

[6] Various online trading web sites: http://www.ebay.co.uk/ and http://www.amazon.co.uk/ (accessed December 15, 2009).

[7] Various news web sites: http://www.bbc.co.uk/ and http://uk.reuters.com/ (accessed December 15, 2009).

[8] Doggdot: http://doggdot.us/ (accessed December 15, 2009).

[9] Slashdot: http://slashdot.org/ (accessed December 15, 2009).

[10] Robinson, Rick. 2008. *Enterprise Web 2.0, Part 1: Web 2.0—Catching a Wave of Business Innovation:* http://www.ibm.com/developerworks/webservices/library/ws-enterprise1/index.html (accessed December 15, 2009)

[11] Robinson, Rick. 2008. *Enterprise Web 2.0—Part 2: Enterprise Web 2.0 Solution Patterns:* http://www.ibm.com/developerworks/webservices/library/ws-enterprise2/index.html (accessed December 15, 2009).

[12] Adams, Holt. 2009. *Mashup Business Scenarios and Patterns, Part 1 and 2:* http://www.ibm.com/developerworks/lotus/library/mashups-patterns-pt1/ (accessed December 15, 2009).

[13] Adams, Holt. 2009. *Mashup Business Scenarios and Patterns, Part 2:* http://www.ibm.com/developerworks/lotus/library/mashups-patterns-pt2/ (accessed December 15, 2009).

[14] Feed server demo on YouTube: http://www.youtube.com/watch?v=dHXSiGpWxno (accessed December 15, 2009).

[15] IBM WebSphere sMash web site: http://www-1.ibm.com/software/webservers/smash/ (accessed December 15, 2009).

[16] Cloud: IBM WebSphere sMash: http://www.ibm.com/developerworks/downloads/ws/ws-smash/learn.html?S_TACT=105AGX28&S_CMP=DLMAIN (accessed December 15, 2009).

[17] WebSphere Message Queue web site: http://www-01.ibm.com/software/integration/wmq/httpbridge/ (accessed December 15, 2009).

[18] DataPower web site: http://www-01.ibm.com/software/integration/datapower/ (accessed December 15, 2009).

[19] IBM Mashup Center web sites: http://www-01.ibm.com/software/info/mashup-center/ and http://www-10.lotus.com/ldd/mashupswiki.nsf (accessed December 15, 2009).

## CHAPTER 13

Dynamic Warehousing

This chapter describes some of the new approaches in Data Warehouse (DW) solutions with particular focus on the capabilities required to implement an agile, flexible, responsive, and timely Business Intelligence (BI) and analysis infrastructure that enables organizations to quickly respond to the changing needs in business expectations. This chapter explores the role of the Enterprise Information Architecture (EIA) Components in the Dynamic Warehousing (DYW) approach, which is considered an evolutionary step as far as traditional DW development and is aimed at addressing the demands for real-time data access, the requirements to deliver more dynamic business insights, and the need to process large amounts of information. All of these approaches enable organizations to respond on demand to unscheduled analysis requests as events trigger the need for information throughout the day.

DW and BI have significantly evolved in the past few years. The "traditional BI" approach was to manage historical information to assist with strategic decision making often using daily, weekly, or even monthly snapshots of data for insights into real time and near real time business transactions. Because flexibility and agility requirements of businesses change, data volumes exponentially increase, which requires timely decisions and applications and systems to better leverage business insights in the daily business operations.

Today's global economy demands that organizations adapt to both the constantly changing needs of the business and their customers. The speed and dynamic nature of these requirements often impose significantly shorter intervals for decision making than the long-term planning and time-consuming implementations associated with the development of traditional decision support systems. The BI solutions that are designed and developed today need to actively support operational decision making. This puts significant pressure on the DW and the infrastructure where it is deployed to deliver "dynamic" characteristics, such as higher levels of flexibility, scalability, and performance while ensuring the quality and reliability of the information they store.

DYW represents this next step in the DW evolution; it defines a framework for delivering right-time, contextual information intelligence used for operational processes, tactical decisions, and strategic planning. This new approach to warehousing involves defining the strategy for harvesting, integrating, transforming, and analyzing large volumes of Structured and Unstructured Data stored in operational systems and other repositories inside and outside the enterprise. Creating a DYW solution involves the provisioning of capabilities that extend beyond the traditional approach, including the use of BI, analytics, and reporting tools to support the large number of business processes and applications that require dynamic business insights.

13.1 Infrastructure for Dynamic Warehousing

The infrastructure used to deploy a DYW solution leverages most of the components of the EIA including Enterprise Information Integration (EII), metadata, master data, Enterprise Content Management (ECM), and the analysis and reporting capabilities of the Analytical Services. Figure 13.1 depicts a layered high-level view of the extended information infrastructure associated with the DYW approach.

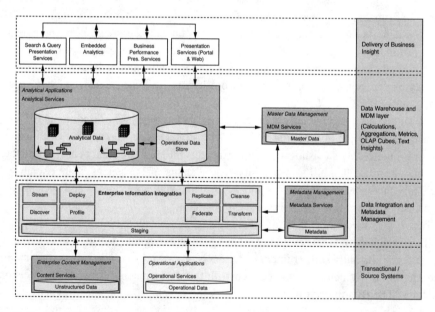

Figure 13.1   The DYW extended infrastructure

Some readers might be familiar with the term Active Data Warehouse (ADW),[1] which has been used often in the technical literature to refer to the core characteristics of the DYW approach discussed in this chapter. Several detailed comparisons of the two approaches can be found in industry publications and books. Lou Agosta, PhD,[2] in several of his publications, offers the most illustrative arguments for differentiation. He successfully makes the case for the distinctiveness of DYW by correctly highlighting how the ADW approach lacks the exploitation of the autonomic capabilities of the database. In the ADW, the implementation of a closed-loop, real time processing framework is primarily developed by hand coding and does not offer much in terms of capabilities to provide useful insights to both operational and BI processes.

The Operational Data Store (ODS),[3] a commonly implemented repository in DW solutions, is used to address the operational needs of business users and it stores volatile data. Some operational data moves directly into the DW through the EII layer, whereas other operational data passes from the operational sources through the EII layer into the ODS and into the DW. The ODS is an integration platform of data from various source systems that leverages the same standard extraction and transformation practices of the EII used to feed the DW. As illustrated in Figure 13.1, the ODS is a core component of the DYW infrastructure.

13.1.1 Dynamic Warehousing: Extending the Traditional Data Warehouse Approach

The extended infrastructure of the DYW illustrated in Figure 13.1 leverages the EIA Components to provide a set of capabilities well beyond what is offered by the traditional DW solution. This section introduces these additional capabilities and how they enable the delivery of right-time, contextual information used for operational, tactical, and strategic analysis and business operations. We begin by exploring in more detail the high-level principles that identify the DYW approach:

- Provide trusted, timely analytics and business insights in context
- Extract and integrate knowledge from Structured and Unstructured Data
- Introduce industry-specific blueprints to accelerate the return on the investment
- Leverage the EIA to handle varying service level agreements (SLA)

The following sections explore in more detail these specific principles.

---

[1] The ADW represents an extension of the traditional enterprise data warehouse to provide operational intelligence. ADWs are generally capable of supporting near real-time updates, fast response times, and mixed workloads by leveraging well-architected data models, optimized ETL processes, and the use of workload management.

[2] See [1] and [2] for details.

[3] The Operational Data Store represents an integrated, real-time, subject-oriented repository structure designed to serve the real-time integrated processing of operational users. The subject of operational data stores is discussed in detail in [3].

13.1.1.1 Provide Timely Analytics and Business Insight in Context

Enabling the delivery of timely analytics implies that the intelligence derived from the data stored in the DW platform must be available at the "right-time"; that is, the data must have the correct level of currency to meet the needs of the application or business process that requires it. Data currency, measured by how well the data in the intelligence reflects the current state of the business, should match each application and each user's specific requirements for information timeliness.

Right-time BI optimizes the time latency between when a business event occurs and when appropriate action is taken. This is a fundamental requirement to bring the benefits of BI to a broader population within the enterprise, ensuring that people and processes at all levels of the enterprise can take advantage of the power of this insight for better decision making.

This better use of information intelligence turns the DYW approach into the ideal framework for the adoption and deployment of Operational Business Intelligence.[4] All the required components are present to enable the collection and assembly of data from the business as it happens, so it can be analyzed and made available to employees, business processes, and applications to help drive decisions across the enterprise. To deliver timely, in-context BI, the DYW approach relies on the assembled components of the EIA to deliver the following key capabilities:

- **Speed and low latency**—The DYW system must provide answers to ad-hoc queries within the particular requirements for right-time. Usually, the SLA for analysis latency is measured in seconds and minutes, and answers must be provided quickly no matter where the request for rapid access to analytical information has been initiated.

- **Scalability**—The deployed infrastructure must be able to serve everyone in the organization who is involved in the key operations of daily business and scale easily as the number of applications grows. This often implies that the DYW platform must be able to incrementally scale to potentially thousands of concurrent users and to terabytes of data, while maintaining query speeds of seconds or minutes.

- **Flexibility**—The deployed DYW infrastructure must support a variety of schemas and queries to meet the business needs; that is, the EIA Components must be capable of processing transactions and analytical requests at the same time while delivering the agreed SLAs. Additionally, the DYW solution is an approach flexible enough to guarantee that changes in the organization's business models can be implemented without affecting the usage of the BI solution. The use of open standards for the DYW facilitates ease of integration within the EIA and adds flexibility by facilitating the integration of the solution within the existing enterprise infrastructure.

- **Embedded insights**—These provide real time analytics that can be embedded in business processes. DYW should facilitate access to the intelligence using any available delivery channel in the organization. A particular focus area is on enabling easy,

---

[4] When discussing Operational BI, it is assumed that all the data must reflect its most current state (real-time); however, capturing and providing every piece of information used by the organization in real time is both expensive and usually unnecessary.

omnipresent access within the users' familiar environment and it is the access layer component of the EIA, with its multiple information delivery channels, that provides the mechanisms for end users, applications, business processes, or external systems to access this information. Embedded insights demand that the intelligence is simple to use, deploy, and customize. Consuming applications, processes, and business users should have access to operational environments that connect transactions and analytics into a single composite analytic application where they see and understand things and can immediately take adequate actions. Embedded analytics transforms BI from sets of stand-alone products to enterprise services that make BI easier to use and pervasive.

Figure 13.2 shows how the available mechanisms in the DYW approach deliver business insights to applications, users, and processes. The lower half of the figure represents the extended infrastructure of the DYW; the upper half shows the variety of EIA Components that can be leveraged to deliver the insights to any application, user, and process. Timely and in-context information delivery is achieved using a variety of integration technologies such as:

- EII technologies
- Integrating BI and transactional systems using the Connectivity and Interoperability services such as an Enterprise Service Bus (ESB)
- Delivery of information based on an event or a request via Web Services

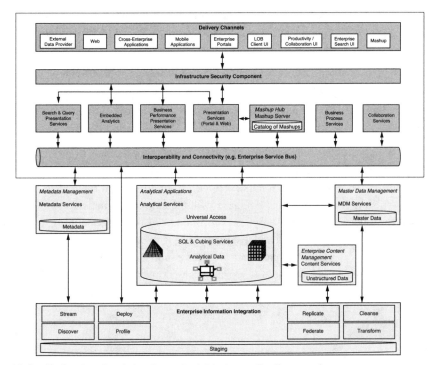

Figure 13.2   Delivering timely business insights to applications and users

Any decision on the specific technology solution to guarantee right-time delivery should be driven by the data currency and latency requirements of the business.

13.1.1.2 Extract and Integrate Knowledge from Unstructured Data

Intuitively, insights derived from various information sources are vital to the decision-making processes; nevertheless, in the traditional warehousing environment most analysis is performed only with structured data. The capability to mine intelligence from the information stored in unstructured and semi-structured sources (documents, voice calls, e-mails, text fields, video, XML documents, and so on) can significantly increase the accuracy of the BI analysis, making it more insightful. The difficulty has traditionally been that unstructured analysis is an expensive and time-consuming process. The key to unlocking the business value of Unstructured Data is tied to automating the process of extracting information from unstructured sources and providing analysis tools that can make effective use of this information.

Most of the unstructured information stored as free-form text in call-center notes, problem and repair reports, insurance claims, customer e-mails, and product reviews that exist in applications disseminated across the enterprise cannot be used with most existing BI tools to help in answering pressing business questions such as:

- Can we identify and address the top types of problems encountered by the most profitable customers to reduce loyal customer churn?

- Can we analyze the customer ratings on our own and competitor's products, by crawling through possibly our own site blogs or third-party blogs and social services?

- Can we uncover ways to increase our share of the customer wallet by analyzing call-center notes, e-mails, and blogs to find interest in other related products (cross-sell and up-sell) or new products (growth)?

- Can we analyze claims data and patient records to identify insurance fraud using text analytics and pattern detection techniques?

The DYW approach establishes the framework to solve these kinds of problems using the Unstructured Information Management Applications (UIMA) standard for text analytics. UIMA delivers the capabilities needed to extract structured information from the text in Unstructured Data sources and store it in a relational database with the associated metadata. This enables the BI tools used for reporting, Online Analytical Processing (OLAP),[5] data mining, and advanced analytics to benefit from the text analysis results and use it to enrich the BI results and improve the predictive power of data mining and other predictive models. Figure 13.3 illustrates how the components of the EIA interact to discover, extract, transform, and deliver text analysis results to the DW platform in the DYW approach.

---

[5] See [4] for more details.

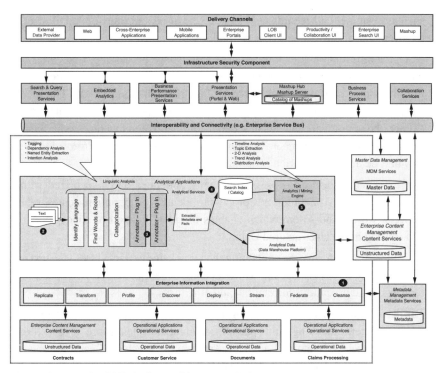

Figure 13.3 Extend the DW platform with text analytics

Text analytics enables organizations to understand the content and what users are looking for and their application context without manual tagging beyond today's typical solutions limited to keyword/full-text search. Contextual understanding interprets the intent and application context to help in finding information based on what it means as opposed to what it directly says. This is accomplished by uncovering the knowledge buried within free-form text fields that contain most of the supporting details (for example, comments, notes, description, and so on) using linguistic capabilities such as:

- Distinguish between different meanings of the same term: rock (stone) versus rock (music) versus rock (to sway) versus ROCK (as an acronym)

- Provide an understanding of domain-specific terms (for example, auto parts, chemicals, and so on)

- Understand concepts and identify facts (for example, entity relationships): people, places and organizations or parts, problems, conditions and actions (for example, is the person "located at" a place or are they "talking about" it?)

Next, we briefly walk through the steps of information flow in this example:

1. The EII Component extracts content from the unstructured sources identified by the variety of operational applications. The extracted information contains the original data,

such as customer call records, and must be cleansed and transformed to meet the input requirements of the text analytics technology.

2. Next, the information goes through natural language processing. Categories, rules, and dictionaries are used to recognize information more specific to the particular topic. The information is parsed and tokenized to identify individual words. The extraction of structured data uses functions, such as regular expression patterns (commonly used to extract phone numbers and social security numbers), and leverages other IT infrastructure assets such as the company's Lightweight Directory Access Protocol (LDAP) directory to look up authentication information.

3. The extracted information can be optionally annotated and categorized with features found in the text. Annotation is a process to identify proper nouns, dates, relationships between words, and so on, which enables the identification of concepts, entities, and facts buried in the Unstructured Data.

4. The snippets of information containing the knowledge extracted from the text are tagged appropriately and then indexed using techniques that enable a high-speed retrieval of requests for aggregation, correlation, and other uses.

5. Further insight is derived from using additional text analysis capabilities such as text mining, pattern matching, and specialized linguistic rules. More advanced techniques and tools such as Natural Language Processing, Machine Learning, and statistical approaches are also widely used in this phase.

6. The intelligence accumulated in the warehouse platform is then used to enhance the BI reports, provide extra data elements to data mining and other predictive models, and other uses that directly impact the higher quality of the BI generated.

Examples of industries where the DYW solution has been deployed to take advantage of the unstructured information analysis capabilities include:

- **Health care**—Text analytics used for the ad-hoc discovery of frequent phrases used by clients, to execute spot analysis for instant feedback and enable drill down on positive and negative sentiments to source comments using terms such as nurses, rooms, hot water, and so on, and to develop trend analysis of negative or positive sentiment over time.

- **Manufacturing**—Text analytics used to implement root cause analysis of issues with the capability to drill in from reporting to the actual document using semantic search on keywords for quick ad-hoc narrowing of results (for example, fire, break, crack, and so on) and alerting when specified phrases or correlations exceed specified conditions.

- **Telecommunications**—Text analytics used to help address customer churn by ad-hoc discovery of frequent phrases and exclamations used by customers and implementing alerts when phrases corresponding to "likely to depart" are defined correlation/frequency.

13.1.1.3 Introduce Industry-Specific Blueprints to Accelerate ROI

Traditional DW deployment efforts suffer from issues associated with cost and slow development due to frequent scope changes, lack of the right industry knowledge, and difficulty in finding the right skills in-house. The resulting DW infrastructure is often inflexible to new business requirements and introduces problems with the consistency of the intelligence generated in addition to higher levels of data redundancy and fragmentation of key data entities.

To address these pains and ensure the delivery of trusted data and business metrics, organizations often turn to proven industry-specific solution templates as a starting point for their BI efforts. These templates or blueprints provide common, industry-specific data and business process definitions across the enterprise, including the business vocabulary, data repository design guidelines, data mappings, integration patterns, and multi-dimensional analysis and reporting templates. These blueprints are based on successful implementation experiences with organizations in that industry, and they ensure that the DW structures are based on industry best practices, avoiding costly re-architecture efforts and fragmented, legacy solutions.

The IBM Industry Models are among the leading examples of these blueprints; they span several industries and contain business terminology, process, service, and data models alongside a set of corresponding Key Performance Indicators (KPI). One key advantage of these models and specifically IBM's is the availability of open standards-based tooling extensions to enable developers and architects to quickly map out a complete top-to-bottom framework from which business processes, information services, and data models can be meshed together from an early stage in the solution development process. This is a real differentiator and adds value as it significantly shortens the overall design effort.

13.1.1.4 Leverage the EIA to Handle Varying SLAs

In addition to providing the foundation for housing and managing the organization information over time, the DYW approach is a principled approach that can be used as a guide to achieve the level of integration that is required between the EIA Components to ensure quick, constantly optimized access to that information, while minimizing storage requirements. Additionally, the approach also sets the framework to guarantee information quality, reliability, and security as it uses the industry proven best practices to deliver a flexible warehousing infrastructure that at the same time is transparent, incurs minimal data redundancy while maximizing its capability to efficiently serve all types of analytical needs.

We briefly look at a simplified high-level view of the EIA Component Model in Figure 13.4, which illustrates the role played by the EIA Components previously introduced in the DYW approach; these are the most relevant components:

- **Operational Applications Component**—This component represents the transactional systems and applications the enterprise uses for the day-to-day operations. These applications act as the traditional DW sources, and they generate and manage the structured and often unstructured information needed to conduct the business operations.

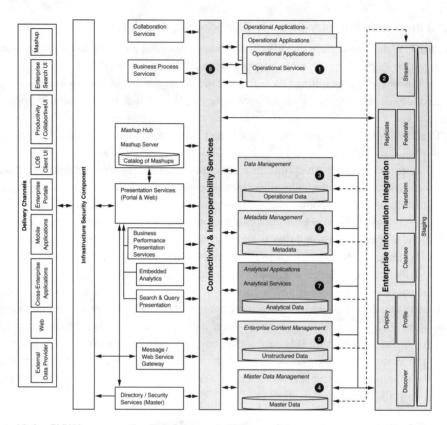

Figure 13.4   DYW leverages the EIA Components

- **Enterprise Information Integration**—The capabilities are used to discover, profile, and catalog the information from all the disparate data sources across the enterprise. The information cataloged from these sources is then aggregated, cleansed, transformed, and delivered to the DYW platform in the Analytical data domain. Timely delivery of data and extreme scalability is ensured by leveraging the batch, near real time and real time capabilities of the EII Component and through the use of subcomponents such as Change Data Capture (CDC) and Streaming Services, which are capable of trickle-feed changed data into the warehouse as changes occur or ingest high volumes of streaming data for analytic processing before the data lands in the DW.

- **Data Management**—These represent the data repositories where information is stored and provide the foundation for the storage of operational information. This component also includes core management, administrative, and query services, some of which are leveraged in the DYW approach.

- **Master Data Management**—This is used to ensure a common view of customers, partners, and products across different applications. MDM holds quality "governed" dimensions for master data domains including customer, supplier, product, location, distributor, asset, account, employee, citizen, parts, and so on. By utilizing the data standardization, duplicate identification, and merge capabilities of the MDM Component, a single version of the truth about each dimension is created before it is loaded in the DYW platform that makes MDM's architecture and functionality play a key role in enforcing data quality and data governance in the DYW context.

MDM maintains the enterprise cross-reference for key DYW dimensions such as customer and product. MDM maintains the ID of every connected system and the ID of the object in each connected system. MDM cross-reference capabilities include understanding multiple duplicates in each system and across systems. When the DYW platform uses this master cross-reference data, it can correctly combine the trickle-fed entries for accurate fact table reconciliation. This is key consideration for accurate BI reporting and analysis because when fragmented data is not recognized as the same entity, the BI applications can lead to misleading intelligence and poor decision making.

MDM holds the official hierarchy information used by the operational applications. This hierarchy information is needed for the proper functioning of key business processes and critical for proper rollup of aggregate information by the BI tools. MDM management of clean governed operational hierarchies also extends to managing multiple alternate hierarchies across multiple dimensions, which is critical for accurate reporting of the downstream analytical applications. DYW encourages the use of the hierarchy information provided by the MDM Component because the direct impact this has on the quality of the intelligence needed to effectively manage enterprise core business processes such as profitability analysis, risk assessments, and enterprise performance management budgeting and forecasting.

- **Enterprise Content Management**—This encompasses the repository and management of the organization's Unstructured Data. Unstructured text data held here can be analyzed and the results made available to the DYW to provide a more complete view and understanding of the DYW dimensional data and more accurate results from data mining and other predictive models.

- **Metadata Management**—This is one of the cornerstones of any successful warehousing approach. End-to-end Metadata guarantees the integration of all other components and enables traceability and data lineage from the intelligence reports all the way back to the data sources. These are often business requirements that facilitate trust and transparency of the information, and consequently they determine how fast business users and decision makers embrace the BI infrastructure.

- **Analytical Application**—These represent the heart of the DYW platform, which includes the repository where data is housed and provides seamless integration to business processes, portal applications, BI reporting, analytics, and data-mining tools through universal access capabilities using MDX, XMLA, or ODBO (see Appendix B, online for more details on these standards); in addition, low latency and right-time analysis is enabled through the use of "no-copy analytics" (see Chapter 5, section 5.3.14 for details) and cubing service capabilities that enable data movement and transformation and OLAP cubes to be created without extracting data from the DW platform.

- **Connectivity and Interoperability Component**—This represents the backbone used by all IT systems in the extended DYW infrastructure to communicate with each other, and it also enables connection to other components beyond the enterprise.

13.2 Business Scenarios and Patterns

In this section, we examine a few business scenarios to illustrate how the extended infrastructure of the DYW leverages the components of the EIA to deliver flexibility and agility to the business beyond the capabilities of the traditional DW approach. We recognize that the traditional approach to warehousing plays a critical role in enabling companies to look back at historical data to evaluate business performance for strategic and tactical planning purpose; however, this focus on analysis of historical structured data does not satisfy the dynamic nature of the business decision-making processes today. DYW delivers the framework to expand the traditional approach by enabling access to Structured and Unstructured Data and by enabling real time views into the business operations and helping to deliver these views to a much larger audience. Both of these characteristics are increasingly standard requirements because they are critical to facilitate effective business decisions.

To materialize effective decision making, the EIA must be the enabler of two critical conditions that should exist simultaneously:

- The information available must be trusted and correct.
- The information must be current and available at the time and in the context of the decision.

When these conditions exist, companies in all industries are able to leverage their business insight as a competitive differentiator; the information infrastructure and the information assets are facilitating the implementation of new or improved business services, such as:

- Employees are able to provide better answers to customers at the point of contact.
- Better information is provided to suppliers to optimize the supply chain.
- Customers can use better insights to extend their purchases and their relationship with the organization.

In almost every industry, business users and IT professionals acknowledge that the capability to rapidly put actionable insights in the hands of the right decision makers translates into positive business outcomes—whether that means selling more products, reducing operational costs, meeting compliance requirements, or better understanding market conditions.

13.2.1 Practical Business Applications

Now we look at some business scenarios taken from recent implementation experiences with a variety of organizations where that DYW approach has been successfully used to deliver business flexibility resulting in improved business results:

- **Telecommunications Industry Use Case**—In the telecommunications industry, the capability to quickly and accurately extract customer data from the company's call detail records (CDR)[6] containing the customer activities and behavior has a direct impact on the bottom line of every service provider. Using the DYW for reporting and analytics solutions with visibility into the customer's behavior is one of the most valuable tools service providers have to spot potential fraud, predict service satisfaction and loyalty, and run a wide variety of advanced analytics to better align services with market demand and to determine how the subscribers are using the network infrastructure. By reviewing the customer CDRs and compiling lists of all incoming and outgoing calls made by the subscriber base, the BI solution can then build groupings and hierarchies and identify patterns that when combined with the historical data can yield critical KPIs, such as the levels of customer attrition (churn).[7] These KPIs and other metrics calculated in near real time can be used to make immediate strategic business decisions and adjustments using marketing campaigns or introduce new or modified services, products, and so on.

- **Customer Service Use Case**—In the customer service area, DYW can trigger business transformation and improvements by using the information that exists across the organization to identify related issues or concerns a customer might have. A banking institution can use these insights to understand the likelihood of a customer leaving for the competition or closing the account. This customer intelligence can also be used to derive guidance on the most promising cross-sell and up-sell opportunities and make this accessible while the Customer Service Representative (CSR) is engaged with the customer at a touch point. For example, when a customer contacts a call center, the CSR gets the typical information made available in the Customer Relationship Management (CRM) system. With a DYW, additional customer insights can be embedded in the application used by the CSR. This additional customer insight is analytical information such as customer profitability, customer buying patterns, and customer credit scoring. Using this additional data, the CSR is now able to address the customer's problems more quickly and suggest personalized discounts or product alternatives. These improvements in services are

---

[6] CDRs are the pervasive data records that are produced by a telecommunication exchange containing details of a particular call, such as the origination and destination addresses of the call, the time the call started, the time the call ended, and so on.

[7] Customer churn, also known as customer attrition, customer turnover, or customer defection, is a term used by businesses to describe the loss of clients or customers. See [5] for details.

generally contributors to higher levels achieved in customer satisfaction and retention, and can often turn the customer support efforts into revenue-generating opportunities.

- **Retail Industry Use Case**—Sales efforts in the retail industry can be dramatically improved if the sales representative can better understand relevant information about the specific customer served at the point of sale, instead of just using this information for historical analysis and reporting. This can directly impact profit margins by identifying more relevant cross-sell opportunities and improving the employee's negotiating position.

- **Government Use Case**—Governments and policing organizations use DYW capabilities to more effectively fight crime. Before these capabilities, they used to focus primarily on reporting and analysis of crime statistics. Now, they aggregate and analyze relevant information as soon as they receive an emergency call reporting a crime. An insightful and relevant report can be generated and sent to the detectives dispatched to the crime scene, enabling them to identify related incidents and potential suspects before they even arrive at the scene.

A common thread in these industry examples is that the warehousing capabilities are used to enable real-time analysis of all types of information in support of process optimization, outcome prediction, and risk reduction. The ultimate goal of these DYW projects is to free information from the silos in which it resides, so it can be processed to extract intelligence and knowledge that is delivered as a service, in the right context and format to any business process or user on demand. By unlocking the value of information and servicing the insights to applications and users across lines of business, DYW acts as a tool that empowers business users and can service multiple applications and business lines for both strategic planning and operational purposes.

13.3 Component Interaction Diagrams—Deployment Scenarios

This section provides two examples that illustrate in further detail how the EIA Components interact with each other in the context of specific business scenarios. The section also explains how the provided services are used to deliver the required business functionality to illustrate the usage of the component model for application- and industry-specific needs, and furthermore to validate the relevance and interrelationship of some of the components in the context of these use-case scenarios. These two use-case scenarios are:

- Dynamic Pricing in Financial Industry
- Addressing Customer Attrition/Churn

13.3.1 Dynamic Pricing in the Financial Industry

Dynamic Pricing and Profitability Management is one area of business that has increasingly been used in banking and other financial institutions as a tool to help improve their bottom-line and differentiate themselves from the competition by leveraging a customer-focused product and pricing management approach to deliver personalized services that improve service, satisfaction, and retention while capturing a larger size of the customer business.

Instead of the traditional BI prediction of customer behavior based on the customer segmentation analysis, the strategy is to personalize the services and offers with the specific focus on the benefits to the individual consumer.

13.3.1.1 Business Context

Although traditional pricing schemes are used pervasively today in some industries, many organizations are finding unique advantages in implementing pricing schemes where customized prices to individual consumers or business customers are based on the customer purchase history, relationship with the business, and potential for future revenue. Financial institutions have been among the adopters of this strategy and have implemented price segmentation techniques that rely on access to trusted customer data and products. The strategy enables companies to offer better deals to their best customers, or to strategically price items and product bundles.

The intense commoditization of banking products is making it harder for banks to differentiate themselves in the market, and this accentuates the already decreasing loyalty. Despite heavy investments to understand customer value and potential, many banks continue to target customers who are profitable today while not paying enough attention to those who will be profitable later. The strategy to address this challenge is to develop a better understanding of what financial incentives they can offer to customers that will create more value and incentives for loyalty and still enable them to remain profitable.

A key requirement for this strategy to succeed is to have a comprehensive view of the customer managed over time and across contact channels and products; additionally, advanced analytical techniques are used in the development of profitable bundles of products across lines of businesses that provide incentives for customers to use additional banking offerings. By pricing these bundles dynamically and transparently, the bank enables consumers to make choices about using offerings in ways that reward them resulting in increased loyalty, wallet share, and bank profitability.

13.3.1.2 Component Interaction Diagram

Let's now work on the translation of the business requirements into the technical domain, and illustrate their interactions using Component Interaction Diagram.

The Dynamic Pricing solution generally uses a common banking interface to provide analysis of the best product bundles and prices based on BI insights around product usage, customer behavior, product and customer profitability analysis, customer segmentation, and forecasting. The process then maps customer, product, price, and transactional data to propose the most appropriate product bundles and offers dynamic pricing to the customer consistently on any channel where the customer interacts with the bank.

Figure 13.5 highlights the basic architecture components and interactions for offering Dynamic Pricing to customers in the banking industry.

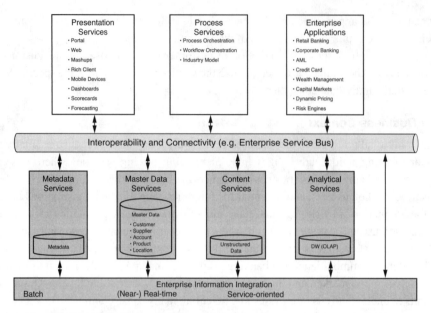

Figure 13.5   Architecture Overview Diagram (AOD) for a Dynamic Pricing solution

The core components in this type of solution (noted in dark gray in Figure 13.5) follow:

- **Enterprise Applications**—Generate and manage the transactional information from customers from where the intelligence is to be derived. These systems include banking applications such as credit cards, retail and corporate banking, wealth management, lending, and so on.

- **Enterprise Information Integration Services**—Collect, profile, aggregate, transform, and deliver transactional data from the Enterprise and deliver this information to the Analytical Services and MDM Components.

- **Metadata Services**—Are repeatedly invoked to help with the understanding of the data and the mappings needed among data elements. Data feed to the DYW platform and the MDM Services layers in real time or near real time that enables the infrastructure to deliver right-time analysis, that is, up-to-date customer insights is available to every channel, business user, or process whenever there is customer contact.

- **Analytical Services**—Represent the DW platform where transactional data is stored and the relevant intelligence information about customer and products is derived for use in the other applications and processes. These services often invoke MDM Components to pass the required customer intelligence so it can be served, in the context of the customer information, to the required processes and applications.

- **MDM Services**—Deliver the trusted single view of customers, products including hierarchies and other groupings, and other master data elements, which can be leveraged as DYW dimensions. MDM also enables the cross-master data domain view (for example, customer-product-location, which when combined with the intelligence derived from the transaction analysis out of the warehousing layer creates a richer customer insight that can be made available to any of the channels to enable a consistent and personalized customer treatment).

- **Content Services**—Represent the storage and management of unstructured information that can be harvested using advanced text analysis and other techniques, to enrich the knowledge and the intelligence derived in the analytical component and dimensional data flows from the MDM Component.

Traditional and advanced Analytical Services and specialized calculation engines, such as the ones used for Dynamic Pricing, can leverage business rules to provide additional operational insights and suggestions about the customer to the various delivery channels. One example is when the customer visits a branch to apply for a loan: In addition to the traditional customer intelligence, the CSR has access to personalized prices and interest rates that can be suggested to better satisfy the customer needs while minimizing the risks to the bank. In many traditional banking scenarios that do not have these capabilities, this personalization will take additional time (sometimes days) because the information is not readily available. The Connectivity and Interoperability layer guarantees the integration of all components.

What does all of that mean for our EIA Component Model and specifically for the Component Interaction Diagram? Figure 13.6 is a depiction of the Component Interaction Diagram for this deployment scenario, where each step in a scenario is indicated with a number in the figure.

Let's go through this step-by-step:

1. All the relevant operational systems across the bank need to capture transactional information. These are the organization's systems used for the day-to-day operations and include core banking systems across the various lines of business and systems such as the CRM, legacy and in-house developed solutions, and any client information file. These systems are the source of all transactional information and data about customers, products, prices, and so on.

2. EII capabilities are used to discover profile and catalog information from the disparate operational systems across the enterprise. The cataloged information is then aggregated, cleansed, transformed, and delivered to the DW platform. Timely delivery of data and extreme scalability is ensured by leveraging the batch, near-real-time and real-time capabilities of the EII Components.

3. Metadata Services provide the common set of functionality and core services to enable communication, exchange, and consumption of data between all the involved systems. Metadata Services will be executed to optimize, validate, and execute the steps in the process. The relevant metadata needs to be identified, retrieved, and exploited. Metadata Services will help to identify relevant information and to establish the linkage between the business context and the underlying IT objects.

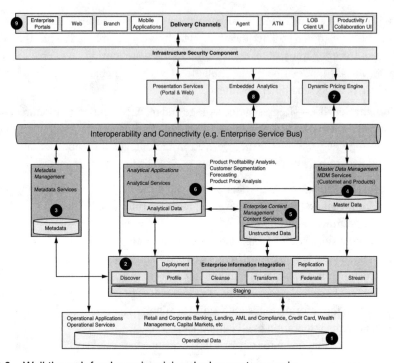

Figure 13.6   Walkthrough for dynamic pricing deployment scenario

4. MDM manages the trusted, single view of the customers and products that is required
   for a reliable use of the analytical techniques. Master data elements for customer and
   products are used as clean, trusted dimensions that feed the DYW platform. Trusted customer information needs to be retrieved and verified using the single source of truth from
   the MDM Component. This might even have to be done on demand, meaning in real
   time to enable current business processes to benefit from trusted customer information.

5. Content services in this context store and manage unstructured information about customers and products that can be analyzed to enrich the content of the DW.

6. A variety of analytical processes and techniques are invoked in batch and real time by
   the Analytical Services to help in assessing profitability performance and other customer metrics using historic and current data. The generated intelligence in the DYW
   about customers is made available to the MDM Component for its distribution on
   demand to applications and processes where trusted customer information is served; it
   includes product profitability analysis, customer segmentation, forecasting, and product
   price analysis.

7. Specialized engines are often invoked to perform advanced analytics and calculation
   such as streamlined profitability modeling that use customer behavior and associated
   revenue fees to design profitability calculations and customer valuation scoring or

analysis and optimization of product management and pricing decisions. This intelligence is added to the existing customer insights in the DYW platform and help in guiding the decisions about pricing for the specific customer.

8. Embedded analytics enables the combination of insight derived from the DW platform and analytical engines within the context of the specific application or business process so that the intelligence information is available in time and in context to help the decision-making process.

9. The delivery channel is responsible for communicating the intelligence to an end user or to an application. The delivery channel also serves as a user interface to help re-direct the customer to the suggested products and services derived from the analysis.

13.3.2 Addressing Customer Attrition/Churn

Marketing and customer intelligence is a general business area applicable to many industries where the delivery of embedded right-time business insight information to the specific market management, sales management, or customer service process can significantly improve the customer experience and loyalty, while minimizing risks and uncovering potential opportunities for additional sales. Minimizing customer attrition is the scenario from the customer service area, which is applicable to many industries including banking and financial services, insurance, and telecommunications, which we discuss in this section.

13.3.2.1 Business Context

Although the customer churn phenomenon is a more prevalent concern for businesses in highly competitive industries such as the telecommunications and mobile phone services, market trends such as deregulation and globalization have extended this pain to virtually all industries. More and more companies are focusing on improving the customer experience at every one of the organization's touch points and particularly the customer service center. The main focus around customer attrition involves the voluntary churn, which is due to a decision by the customer to switch to another company or service provider. It is in this area that most customer churn analysis tends to concentrate on, because it occurs due to factors that the organization can control.

Marketing research and surveys of various types are used to help better understand customers throughout their lifecycle. The information collected during this research and the information generated in the CRM, call logs, and e-mail systems during customer contacts are rich sources for intelligence that can help indicate whether a customer is satisfied and why. This information is often stored in free-form text fields and is difficult to analyze using the conventional analytical tools. Unstructured Data in external sources such as blogs, web pages dedicated to customer reviews, and the information discussed in social networking sites are also among the most valuable sources for customer and product insight. In general, it is safe to affirm that the intelligence seen from a DW is incomplete unless it represents the facts discovered in unstructured and semi-structured data.

Customer retention is an essential part of the business models in banking, financial services, insurance, and the telecommunications sectors where they have extensively used analytical models for predictive analytics and churn modeling that extract information from data and use it to predict future trends and customer behavior patterns (see Figure 13.7).

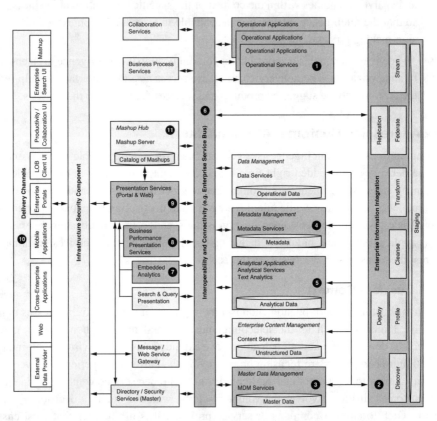

Figure 13.7   Walkthrough of addressing customer churn deployment scenario

The steps to address customer churn deployment follow:

1. Operational systems generate and maintain transactional information related to customer purchases and services contracted. These applications also store some of the Unstructured Data recorded as text containing customer inquiries and opinions generated during calls and e-mails to customer service representatives.

2. The EII services harnesses all the relevant transactional information that is used as a base for further transformation and preparation before it is loaded into the DYW platform. These are current transactional records, but also historical transactional records in order to allow for comparison, time analysis, and pattern-matching techniques. These

services are also invoked to provide connectivity to various structured and unstructured systems, and they deliver the scalability needed for fast processing of large volume of data, which translates in near-real-time delivery of insights. EII Components are also used to extract, transform, and load the master data into the MDM Component, often leveraging the same infrastructure used to load the DYW platform.

3. Master data including information about customer, products, suppliers, and so on, that is managed by the MDM solution is used to feed clean, trusted dimensions to the DYW. Specific information loaded into the warehouse from the MDM Component includes:

- **Dimensions**—MDM holds "trusted and governed" dimensions for customer, supplier, product, location, distributor, asset, account, employee, citizen, parts, and so on. Utilizing data standardization, duplicate identification, and merge capabilities, a single version of the truth about each dimension is created in the MDM system and leveraged by the DW platform.

- **Cross-references**—MDM holds the corporate cross-reference for key dimensions such as customer and product. MDM maintains the ID of every connected system with its source system management capabilities, and it maintains the ID of the object in each connected system. This master cross-reference data is used in the DW for accurate fact table reconciliation, and it is fundamental for accurate reporting and analysis.

- **Hierarchies**—MDM manages the hierarchy information used by the operational applications. This hierarchy information is used in key business processes such as catalog management and accounts payable. MDM also manages alternate hierarchies across multiple dimensions with appropriate cross-domain mappings (for example, product to cost centers, customer to product bundle, and so on). Making this hierarchy information available to the DYW is critical for accurate rollup and reporting of the analytical applications.

4. Metadata Services will be executed to optimize, validate, and possibly even re-execute steps. The relevant metadata needs to be identified, retrieved, and exploited. Metadata Services help to identify relevant information and to establish the linkage between the business context and the underlying IT objects.

5. Text data created in CRM logs and other systems generated during customer calls and other interactions such as e-mails and customer surveys are analyzed to extract knowledge and meaning for greater relevance and insight. The results are used to enrich the information in the DW. Insights from text analysis can also be extracted from e-mail archives, voice messages, and other unstructured content repositories.

For example, in the banking industry, a rules-based text analysis engine can detect the customer churn candidates by finding all occurrences of customer contacts regarding cash advances on credit cards; identifying the contacts where the customer has expressed complaints about the service (for example, identifying the terms "high rate," "overcharge," and so on); and correlating information about account status against these complaints and further identify higher correlation between customer complaints about cash advance, interest rates, and inactive accounts. These insights can be used to enrich the analytics in the DYW and increase the accuracy of predictive models that exploit patterns found in historical and transactional data to identify customers most at risk of attrition. In addition to text analytics, the Analytical Services deliver the capabilities for various customer segmentation, demographics, and behavior analysis for a more robust understanding of the likelihood of a given customer to leave.

Other advanced approaches for real-time predictive churn analytics are used in the telecommunications industry, where solutions that use the latest research algorithms—for instance, Timely Analytics for Business Intelligence (TABI), SNAzzy for Social Network Analysis (SNA), and Parallel Machine Learning (PML)[8]—are combined with IBM InfoSphere Streams to identify in near-real-time groups of related customers that are at risk of leaving their leaders and apply measures to prevent it including sign-on incentives and more focused and effective marketing campaigns.

6. The Connectivity and Interoperability services serve as the communication enabler between the various components, such as the operational applications, the EII services, the MDM hub, and so forth. These services are requested numerous times in this scenario.

7. Embedded Analytics enables the combination of insight derived from the customer churn analysis with the information on a given customer available at a point of contact in a timely manner, and this helps in personalizing the service level given to that customer particularly if it is a valuable one at risk of leaving.

8. Investigation and decision support is an essential step to understand, react, and find ways to even prevent customer churn. Business performance presentation services facilitate this investigation step. BI reports and dashboards with information and metrics on customer attrition rates and its causes are among the assets generated by this component.

9. In the context of our deployment scenario, there are services such as an alerting engine that can automatically send reports to a department that deals specifically with customer churn situations. Summarized information related to the customer spending and use of promotions and discounts can be, for example, part of the information in these reports. By proactively addressing customer churn situations, the organization improves its customer retention rates and improves customer satisfaction rates.

10. The Delivery Channels Component is responsible to finally communicate alerts to an end user or to an application. This can have different peculiarities, such as the delivery channel to be used in order to request an alert status update or to display alerts to an end user in real time to enable immediate reaction. The delivery channel also serves as a user

---

[8] These technologies are developed by researchers at IBM Haifa Research Lab in Israel, IBM T.J. Watson Research Lab in Yorktown Heights, NY, and IBM India Research. See [6] for details.

interface to launch further investigation and to execute the case management services. It is important to underline here that the information is delivered as a service so that the application running on each channel can operate according to its specific requirements (for example, Web, PDA, phone, thick client, and so on).

11. The final step is the creation of reports and dashboards with information and metrics on customer attrition rates and its causes to further understand, control, or prevent it. The reader can consult Chapter 12 for a more discussion on the delivery of business analytics and optimization techniques.

13.4 Conclusion

This chapter introduced the DYW approach and illustrated several business scenarios, how the solution can be described using the Component Model of the EIA Reference Architecture.

The discussion in the chapter illustrates how the DYW approach utilizes the components of an extended infrastructure to deliver a flexible, scalable, and agile BI solution that delivers trusted business insights to processes, applications, and business users in a timely manner and in context.

It is important to highlight how the dynamic characteristics of this approach to warehousing focus on satisfying the increasing need for organizations to process increasing volumes of data from multiple sources inside and outside of the enterprise and the shrinking levels of tolerance the business has for latency when delivering BI. These requirements for timeliness are addressed with the introduction and application of efficient approaches to information integration and the use of state-of-the-art algorithms and techniques for massive data collection and processing, advanced predictive modeling, and social network analysis.

Another area of focus in the DYW approach is the emphasis it places in leveraging newer capabilities provided by the DW platform that are elements of the technology race for delivering trusted results faster.

In the next chapter, we explore the new trends in the business analytics and business optimization disciplines. We explore how new analytics solutions that address specific business challenges are built, exploiting the infrastructure created by a DYW solution approach.

13.5 References

[1] Agosta, L. *The Essential Guide to Data Warehousing*. Upper Saddle River, NJ: Prentice Hall, September 1999.

[2] Agosta, L. 1999. *Data Warehousing Architecture Alternatives*. http://www.forrester.com/Research/Document/Excerpt/0,7211,35148,00.html (accessed December 15, 2009).

[3] Inmon, W. H. *Building the Operational Data Store,* Second Edition. Burlington, MA: John Wiley & Sons 1999.

[4] Becker, B., Kimball, R., Mundy, J., Ross, M., Thornthwaite, W. 2010. *The Data Warehouse Lifecycle Toolkit,* Indianapolis, IN: Wiley.

[5] van den Poel, D., Lariviere, B. 2003. *Customer Attrition Analysis for Financial Services Using Proportional Hazard Models,* http://ideas.repec.org/p/rug/rugwps/03-164.html (accessed December 15, 2009).

[6] Timely Analytics for Business Intelligence (TABI), Parallel Machine Learning Toolbox (PML), and Massive Collection System (MCS): http://telephonyonline.com/wireless/news/ibm-analytics-tapped-0415/ (accessed December 15, 2009).

## CHAPTER 14

New Trends in Business Analytics and Optimization

Today, it is generally accepted that effective business performance measurement and monitoring can be achieved only through optimized use of information. This imperative demands that the Enterprise Information Architecture (EIA) and all its capabilities enable the delivery of trusted, timely, and in-context Business Intelligence (BI) to the people and processes that require these insights to make the appropriate business decisions.

Optimizing information assets is becoming a priority in most organizations due to the pervasive nature of information silos across the enterprise. Most information environments are characterized by large and varied data volumes, high data creation rates, and the need for increasingly faster consumption and analysis of the information. The lower latency requirements that many business processes have when consuming intelligence to make effective decisions is also among the factors triggering the move toward overall optimization of the information supply chain.

Under these conditions of "information explosion," the key requirement in most organizations is to find an answer to how data is acquired, managed, and interpreted to drive business value. To answer this question, "smart" enterprises, which must have ready access to precise, relevant information from all sources for right-now decision making—and right-timed action—have been applying a set of common principles to the use of BI and business performance. These enterprises are among the core triggers for some of the new trends in analytics and business optimization that we discuss in this chapter.

These principles include:

- Serve BI to a wider audience, that is, to better empower employees to make effective decisions.
- Deliver actionable information to users and processes within the context of their everyday activities.

- Offer intelligence information as a service—BI capabilities in the form of services that can be displayed through portals, dashboards, and other types of business processes.

- Integrate search technologies and unstructured analysis into the BI environment.

- Deliver information through a variety of channels—from reports and dashboards to mobile devices containing the relevant metrics through automated alerts activated by business rules.

- Improve delivery time so that information is fresh enough to be useful for decision making.

- Reduce data latency by providing tools capable of real time analysis (for example, filtering, cleaning, correlating, transforming, integrating, and so on). The relevant data comes from a wide array of sources and formats, including Online Transaction Processing (OLTP), Online Analytical Processing (OLAP) applications, and from data streams.

Note that the dynamic and operational capabilities of the newer BI technologies and approaches prove that both the more traditional Data Warehouse (DW) and the Dynamic Warehousing (DYW) are not necessarily the only sources for deriving business insights. Thus, a new approach for Business Performance Management (BPM)[1] is needed that will be elaborated in the next section.

14.1 A New Approach to Business Performance Management

Although advanced analytical methods and complex algorithms have been available, primarily in the domain of academics for some time, today's tools and techniques have opened the door for their innovative use to solve formerly intractable business challenges and to provide superior insight and predictability to support management decision making.

Enterprise executives, performance managers, and business analysts have traditionally leveraged business metrics delivered in role-tailored tools such as scorecards, BI reports, and forecasts. A variety of business metrics are utilized to understand how well the organization—or a particular Line of Business (LOB)—aligns with the desired business goals. The traditional information flow framework from raw data to BPM shown in Figure 14.1 is significantly enhanced by the use of emerging analytics and business optimization techniques aimed to provide full support for collaboration within the decision-making cycle. This is leading to a more efficient use of the information intelligence. This higher maturity level in the use of business insights involves the full exploitation of the traditional BI technologies combined with the use of advanced analytical models, social network behavior techniques, predictive models, and other sophisticated analytical models. The new approach is also characterized by the use of real-time integration techniques, massive data collection architectures, and newly developed approaches

---

[1] The BPM acronym is sometimes used in IT to describe Business Process Management. This is not the same thing as Business Performance Management. As a result, instead of BPM, some people prefer the term Corporate Performance Management (CPM), and still others prefer Enterprise Performance Management (EPM).

that apply the analytics arsenal to streaming data to deliver the high degree of scalability and low latency demanded by many fast-paced business environments.

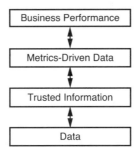

Figure 14.1   Traditional information flow in BPM

14.1.1 A Framework for Business Analytics and Business Optimization

Holistic approaches to Business Analytics and Business Optimization have emerged as trends to address the new BPM challenges. Incorporating all of the new and advanced BPM techniques and principles together with the business analysis and business performance optimization offers more thorough performance management. A holistic approach to Business Analytics and Business Optimization uses the EIA and the organization's Information Governance strategy and processes to align operational and strategic business objectives to fully manage the process of achieving the goals the enterprise has established.

The approach illustrated in Figure 14.2 defines a framework for how data is accessed, packaged into information, and measured. Business Analytics and Business Optimization require that the EIA deliver the capabilities to enable data to be collected and analyzed from anywhere (including internal and external sources, sensors, instruments, and other sources); access the wide variety of formats such as Structured, Unstructured and societal data; and grouped, categorized, and processed into information that business users can access and consume at the right time and in context. This approach also dictates that beyond the performance measurement, the business insights enable detection, direction, and prediction of business outcomes, which are core characteristics of optimized business processes across an integrated enterprise.

In addition to the new technology trends in Business Analytics and Business Optimization, which are the subject of the business scenarios in this chapter, organizations are required to consider several areas of competency and strategies. Such strategies include:

- **Creating a strategy for analysis and optimization**—An important consideration in this approach is the creation of an enterprise strategy to better align the organization's information assets with its business goals. This strategy describes how organizations achieve their business objectives faster, with less risk and at a lower cost by improving how information is recognized and acted upon across the enterprise, within a business

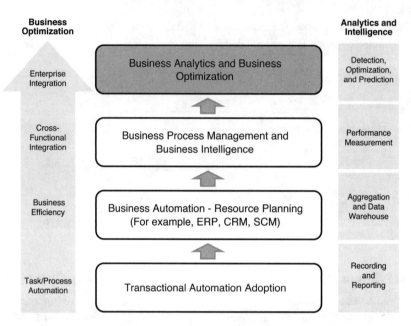

Figure 14.2   A framework for Business Analytics and Business Optimization

function or an LOB. An effective Business Analytics and Business Optimization strategy not only addresses what should be done with the information, but also how to act on it. That is, it defines the recommended actions at all levels: policy, analytics, business process, organization, applications, and data.

- **Designing an Enterprise Information Management (EIM) strategy**—The creation of an EIM strategy includes the methodology, practices, principles, and technologies needed to effectively manage disparate data. The EIM is a driver for impacting individual and organizational performance, and it is as well an enabler of BI standardization because the resulting EIM must ultimately ensure that relevant and timely information is delivered to business applications and users in a way they understand. The EIM strategy derived from the Business Analytics and Business Optimization framework focuses on solving specific information-related problems that have a direct impact in the creation of an organization-wide business performance strategy or the implementation of a specific advanced analytical solution. Common areas around which this EIM strategy is created include an EIA with components such as Enterprise Information Integration (EII), Master Data Management (MDM), and Enterprise Content Management (ECM). The EIA supporting the EIM is governed by Information Governance. Among the areas considered to create this EIM strategy, we include the EIA with focus on components such as the EII, MDM, and ECM, as well as Information Governance.

14.1.2 Performance Metrics

To provide context for the discussion of our use cases, we return to the BPM theme and briefly examine how metrics are used to quantify, monitor, and evaluate the performance of the business. Business metrics, or Key Performance Indicators (KPI), represent performance measurements for specific business activities. Each metric is associated to a specific business goal or threshold used to determine whether or not the business activity performs within the accepted limits.

BI and analytic techniques are used to monitor these KPIs periodically or in real-time and the values delivered to executives, managers, and other information consumers through personalized, role-based tooling to facilitate the assessment of the present state of the business and to assist in prescribing a corrective action to achieve the desired result. By implementing the definition, monitoring analysis, and tracking of KPIs, BPM provides business users and decision makers with the insights required for implementing actions aimed to optimize business performance. This mechanism turns BPM into a powerful enabler of the close link that must exist between the IT and business communities, which we consider one of the core EIA principles highlighted in this book. EIA principles are discussed in Chapter 4.

The following sections of this chapter present several business scenarios to discuss the new approaches to the traditional business analysis and BPM methods. This chapter also discusses new trends and techniques used by many organizations to provide packaged business insight in context and in a timely manner.

14.2 Business Scenario, Business Patterns, and Use Case

Let us look at a business scenario that involves many of the core elements of the holistic approach for Business Analytics and Business Optimization to establish a framework for a solution that addresses a common business challenge in the banking and financial sectors around Enterprise Risk Management (ERM).

ERM at a financial institution requires full transparency and visibility into the many areas of risk where the institution is exposed, and this requires the EIA to be the enabler of risk-related information management capabilities to:

- Facilitate the use of more robust risk modeling engines.
- Use a large number of risk metrics to capture and promote the understanding of the institution's full exposure.
- Provide an integrated view of risk information including correlation across the institution asset classes, portfolios, and the relationships of different types of risks.
- Enable real-time and intra-day information delivery capabilities to account for the rate of change of risk factors.

Under these conditions, the traditional risk reporting schedule aimed at compliance with government institutions and regulatory agencies is no longer sufficient to understand the overall risk the organization has and what are the different risk exposures by product, geography, business units, and other dimensions. To satisfy these wider and more up-to-date risk demands, organizations use advanced risk modeling engines and scenario analysis tools that use near real time or real-time analysis to predict external threats to the institution stability such as a change in the dynamics of the market. To satisfy the business requirements of today, risk officers and other business managers must be able to align risk management with the existing business silos to have visibility into an enterprise-wide view of risk exposures (for example, counter-party credit risk).

Among the main factors forcing banks and other financial institutions to define and implement effective ERM strategies are several industry regulations such as the Sarbanes-Oxley Act and the European Basel Capital Accord (Basel II).[2]

These regulations are also major drivers for implementing a wide array of enterprise Business Analytics and Optimization solutions beyond the ERM area. It is also interesting to note that for many financial institutions embarked in initiatives to support regulations such as the Sarbanes-Oxley Act, the legislation is seen as an opportunity to streamline systems and improve the efficiency of business processes. At the same time, supporting Basel II requires companies to implement a strategy to integrate data and processes that are often split between finance, operational, and risk-management functions, and this is another strong incentive to speed up the development of strategies to turn the EIA into a more streamlined, agile, and responsive asset that is capable of providing trusted and relevant insights for better risk management, better performance management, and better decisions around capital allocation.

14.2.1 Banking Use Case

We briefly examine the core requirements for an integrated ERM view at a banking institution and validate what capabilities the components of the EIA must deliver to meet the requirements of providing business insights into enterprise risk.

A comprehensive strategy for management of enterprise risks in the banking industry involves business capabilities such as:

- Understand the various financial risks across business silos, which involve obtaining accurate information about risk exposure across business lines.

- Detect and address the risks associated with internal and external financial crime and fraud. This involves analytical and business rules and the capacity to detect crime patterns in a timely manner while processing vast amounts of data from a large number of sources in real time.

- Anticipate and mitigate potential risk from failed internal processes, people, or systems including the capacity to understand correlation of risks across asset classes and risk types.

- Comply with risk-related regulations across jurisdictions where the organization operates, generates, and delivers useful risk insights to the right people.

---

[2] Details can be found online in Appendix C. For a reference, see [1] and [2].

In Figure 14.3, we present a high-level view of a framework for the information flow in a risk solution. The figure illustrates the major levels of this framework: an information integration layer to extract risk-related information from the enterprise operational systems, a trusted information delivery level that consolidates and makes information available in a timely manner, a level containing a rich set of traditional and advanced analytical and reporting capabilities to generate risk insight from the consolidated data, and a variety of delivery channels so risk intelligence can be made accessible to the users and decision makers in time and in context.

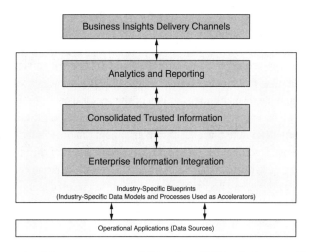

Figure 14.3 Information Management capabilities for a BPM solution to address enterprise risk

This framework highlights the core information architecture technical capabilities and major information flows, but it does not explicitly address key dimensions such as the latency allowed for the information intelligence to be available. We discuss these elements in more detail in later sections of this chapter.

14.3 Component Interaction Diagrams—Deployment Scenarios

In this section, we provide detailed business examples to describe how the EIA components interact with each other in the context of specific use-case scenarios that illustrate the application of Predictive Analytics and Business Optimization. The objective of this section is to demonstrate the use of the EIA Component Model to satisfy industry-specific application needs, and to validate the relevance and interrelationship of some of the components in the context of these use-case scenarios.

The business scenarios presented in this section expand and discuss the details of the examples introduced in Chapter 8 to demonstrate how newer approaches to BI Analytics are used to deliver Predictive Analytics and Business Optimization capabilities. These solutions use ultra-low latency intelligence generated while processing large amounts of data from structured and unstructured sources. These newer types of BI solutions are rapidly becoming a key requirement for most large organizations as they find new ways to enable quick and effective business decisions and successfully improve their capabilities to predict business events.

14.3.1 Predictive Analytics in Health Care

Before discussing this business case, look at the final report of a recent IBM study in the health care sector, Healthcare 2015 Study,[3] which includes a detailed description of the drivers that make today's health care environment fundamentally different from the past and looks at health care delivery systems across the globe identifying how many nations' health systems, including the ones in the developed nations, are approaching crisis and becoming unsustainable.

Organizations in the health care sector, both providers and payers, have experienced for some time now a strong pressure from government and society in general to significantly control the increasing costs associated with the delivery of services while improving patient care. Delivering on these requirements requires a deeper understanding of the sector using a clear business perspective so that timely and sound decisions that impact both customer care and the economic sustainability of the health care systems can take place. These requirements fuel the need for the extensive and innovative use of BI tools. Traditionally, these tools have been a part of the technological arsenal in sectors such as banking, retail, and manufacturing. Although these advanced analytics and BPM techniques are new, they are rapidly becoming part of the core group of technologies used to satisfy this increasing demand for real-time trusted insights into the business of patient care.

14.3.1.1 Business Context

Health care systems worldwide struggle to address increasing costs, inconsistent quality, and inaccessible care. Among the patient-centric common goals and strategic objectives of most health care providers, we can identify:

- Improved patient care by rapidly analyzing symptoms and communicating better with patients

- Increased patient satisfaction and drive loyalty by improving overall outcome and delivering a better patient experience

- Improved overall efficiency by shortening waiting times for required procedures and reducing the length of stay in the hospital

- Increased health care innovation with particular focus on patient care

IBM researchers and the University of Ontario Institute of Technology (UOIT) Health Informatics Research department[4] have successfully designed, deployed, and tested a "first of a

---

[3] This IBM Healthcare 2015 Study was conducted in 2008 by the IBM Institute for Business Value. See [3].

[4] This "first of a kind" Health Informatics Research initiative is aimed to help doctors detect subtle changes in the condition of critically ill premature babies. See [4].

kind" system based on the Stream Analytics technology to help doctors detect subtle changes in the condition of critically ill premature babies. This innovative application of new and advanced analysis techniques to specific areas of patient care demonstrates a significant impact in preventative patient care, in addition to the expected business results associated with effective BPM approaches. Eventually this win-win situation delivers significant costs to the health care system.

Currently, physicians monitoring premature babies rely on a paper-based process that involves manually looking at the readings from various monitors and sensors and getting feedback from the nurses providing the care.

The new software ingests constant streams of biomedical data, such as heart rate, blood pressure, oxygen levels, temperature, and breathing rates that are generated by medical monitoring devices attached to a premature baby. Monitoring premature babies is especially important because there are certain life-threatening conditions such as infections that might be detected up to 24 hours in advance by observing changes in physiological data streams.

14.3.1.2 Component Interaction Diagram

Figure 14.4 is a depiction of the Component Interaction Diagram for this deployment scenario, where each step in a scenario is indicated with a number.

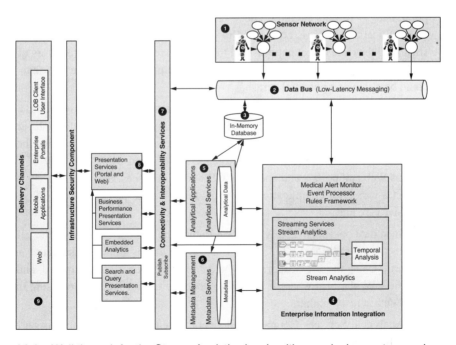

Figure 14.4 Walkthrough for the Stream Analytics in a health care deployment scenario

We go through this step-by-step in the following list:

1. Information from a network of sensors that constantly monitor the baby's vital signs constantly streams into the Streaming Analytics application. The data streams consist of a variety of monitored biomedical data that includes vital signs such as blood pressure, heart beat, other electro cardiogram (ECG) measures, saturation levels of oxygen in the blood, levels of specific proteins, and many others. These are normally used by medical personnel to evaluate the prenatal baby's condition and anticipate any complication. Traditionally, this information is reviewed from paper forms printed in the various devices by the intensive care unit nurses every 30 to 60 minutes.

2. The medical monitoring devices output data via a serial port using a variety of formats. All data communications are done using a queue-based, ultra-low-latency data bus for microsecond response.

3. An in-memory database adds relational capabilities to the technology, enabling high-speed data caching, persistent states for high availability, and the possibility to enrich the streamed data with metadata.

4. The Streaming Services Component of the EIA provides the analysis framework implemented in the stream analytical application engine. This framework includes a medical alert monitoring component, a rules management engine and repository, data validation and data interpretation functions, and a temporal abstraction layer used to support temporal analysis of data streams. The streaming application supports event management and notification, and it is configured to correlate the value of key indicators from the streaming data and detect patterns and trends that are known to be predictors of serious medical conditions. For example, if the oxygen saturation levels are less than 85%, it could be a sign of a potential "crash."

    If an alerting condition is detected, the event notification triggers signals and messages that are sent instantaneously to medical personnel through the connectivity layer so they can take the appropriate actions. Critical events are pushed primarily through the mobile applications channels, but other intelligence is delivered using a variety of channels such as Web and portals and specific LOB client interfaces. Stream Analysis is able to predict a variety of complications up to 24 hours before physicians and nurses in the intensive care unit.

    Streamed data once analyzed is then sent to the other subcomponents of the EII to provide the more traditional ETL services before the data is stored in the data warehouse platform. Using the DYW approach, the data is transformed, standardized, and loaded into the DW platform where it is used to generate further intelligence using the traditional data at rest paradigm.

5. The Analytical Services Component delivers the capabilities for analysis on the captured data stored in the DW repository. Data is stored in the DW platform by EII

services that are invoked by the Stream Analytics application. Advanced Analytics, BI reporting techniques, data mining, statistics, and predictive modeling are among the tools health informatics researchers use to derive insights into the patient health condition. It is in this layer that, for example, data from different patients can be correlated and intelligence derived on the effectiveness of a given treatment. Analytic Services are called to execute various facets of health analysis and can also generate new alerts and other events.

6. Metadata Services can be invoked by the streaming application to store new metadata from the data streams. These services are also used to enrich the information stored in the in-memory database engine that supports the data bus with relational capabilities.

7. The Connectivity & Interoperability Services enable the management and orchestration of events and alert messages in the infrastructure. This layer provides the subscription services to deliver alerts and intelligence information to the Presentation Services.

8. Presentation Services are responsible for providing the medical alerts and other intelligence information to the appropriate delivery channel. These services can package and generate embeddable insights that are delivered to the user interfaces in context.

9. Intelligence information, including alerts and exceptions, is delivered to the medical personnel using a variety of channels that include mobile devices, the Web, messages, and desktop applications.

Stream Analytics applied in this manner to the health care industry demonstrates the power and effective applicability of Predictive Analytics techniques. This approach becomes an important tool that helps create a proactive health ecosystem to support patient-centric health care. By using this approach for Business Analytics, health care professionals have immediate access to trusted information that has been consistently gathered and that can give them a faster and more complete perspective on the health of their patients while releasing them from time-consuming activities to concentrate on more effective care.

The use of real-time intelligence in the health industry sets the ground for implementing a system where timely intelligence is provided to stakeholders, patients, doctors, nurses, families, and others on the specific patient's health issues what course of action to take, and why. Patient care is improved by enabling a better communication with the patients and their families, which empowers them. Significant efficiencies are realized by freeing medical personnel from slow time-consuming activities to better concentrate on patient care.

Recently, a few initiatives have been launched at several hospitals and other health care organizations to extend the use of this technology to deliver real time health care insights using channels such as a patient portal with significant benefits to all.

14.3.2 Optimizing Decisions in Banking and Financial Services—Trading

The financial service industry faces the combined problems of unprecedented volatility, increased risk, and exponential growth in market data volume and velocity. These factors create complex challenges in risk management and force the current analytics and modeling used in the stock trade execution processes to deliver capabilities that are often beyond what these systems were originally designed to deliver. The newer generation of EIAs for the financial industry, particularly in the trading areas, need to combine optimized utilization of processing power with being able to process Structured and Unstructured Data including time series data. They also need to be able to perform complex analysis in real time. In this industry, to gain a competitive advantage, having robust capabilities for real time management of risk is a core imperative.

Enabling financial service firms to instantly understand and derive intelligence from vast quantities of streaming data from almost limitless sources can deliver that advantage to these organizations. Financial institutions with this knowledge are able not only to derive insights but also to build new models ahead of the news cycle faster than the competition to achieve higher margins and faster time to market. This innovative use of the company's information assets becomes a major factor in achieving a competitive differentiation and can deliver significant gains in the business performance optimization front.

14.3.2.1 Business Context

A brief reading through the most recently published studies and estimations on the measured effects of timely decisions in the stock market can quickly illustrate why having access to real-time intelligence is a strategic imperative in this industry. A recent publication by the TABB Group[5] has indicated that a one-millisecond advantage in market access can be worth millions of dollars a year in additional revenue. Today, sub-milliseconds or microseconds are the measurements that are used by traders wanting an advantage over their competition.

For many well-established professional trading groups from the United States, Asia, and Europe, having a flexible, low-latency, high-capacity EIA and underlying infrastructure enables the use of newer algorithmic trading tools, which require ultra low-latency trading services. Getting market data quickly and having a trading engine that can make fast decisions and swift execution are core requirements to accomplish this.

Streamlined network topology and an efficient combination of processes are key factors to significantly reducing latency, but the factor that brings the most improvement in speed is the capacity to process the increasing market data volumes combined with the speed of the trading algorithms and the ability to execute prompt risk identification and management. Stream Analytics offers the ideal platform to address these challenges with its capabilities to ingest limitless amounts of Structured and Unstructured Data in-motion and perform complex analysis, event detection, pattern identification, and routing, which are core to risk management, in microseconds.

---

[5] This study from TABB Group Research in 2008 looks at the need for speed and reduced latency to help improve the ability of brokers and trading desks for best execution. The study can be found at [5].

14.3.2.2 Component Interaction Diagram

The diagram in Figure 14.5 illustrates how the components of the EIA can be combined to implement an efficient trading platform.

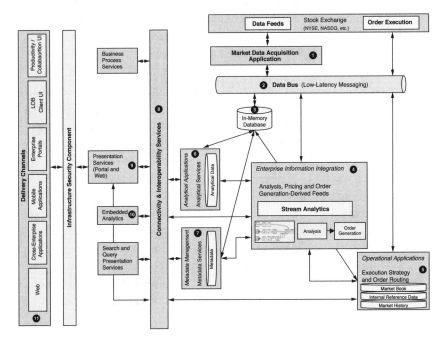

Figure 14.5 Walkthrough for the Stream Analytics in the financial service sector deployment scenario

In the following list, we walk through the steps highlighted to describe this interaction:

1. A Market Data Acquisition Application Component receives streams of data from a variety of market data provider institutions such as the stock exchanges (NYSE,[6] NASDAQ,[7] and AMEX[8]) and a large number of other mercantile exchange (both private and public) from around the world, weather information, financial and investment news feeds, and so on.

---

[6] The New York Stock Exchange is the largest stock exchange in the world by United States dollar value. NYSE is operated by NYSE Euronext, which was formed by the NYSE's merger with the fully electronic stock exchange Euronext.

[7] National Association of Securities Dealers Automated Quotations. It is the largest electronic screen-based equity securities trading market in the United States.

[8] Formerly the American Stock Exchange now known as NYSE Amex Equities.

2. Communication typically occurs using a low-latency Data Bus Component that enables microsecond response time. A product often used to implement this layer is the IBM MQ Low Latency Messaging.[9]

3. An In-Memory Database adds relational capabilities to the technology, enabling high-speed data caching, persistence of states for high availability, and the possibility to enrich the streamed data with Metadata. The In-Memory Database is enabled to interface with operational systems storing market reference. Historical or book data add additional possibilities for correlation and real-time trend detections.

4. The Streaming Services Component of the EII provides the analysis framework implemented in the stream analytical application engine. The streaming application is configured to ingest the data from many sources and apply a variety of analytical techniques and algorithms, using correlations, filters, and other supplied analytical functions. User-defined adaptors and filters can also be developed and deployed to enable rich analytical functionality. Examples are executing caption extraction and speech recognition from video and news feeds, using specialized hurricane forecast models to process the filtered weather information extracted from data streams, and identifying and scanning company earnings news and reports. Information is correlated, classified, aggregated, transformed, and often annotated to enable patterns and trend detection before the trade decision is made. The generated orders are then routed to the order execution engine. Data streams, once analyzed and filtered, and the information on the execution strategies are sent to the EII layer where it is standardized, transformed, and loaded into the DW platform for more traditional BI processing.

5. The Operational Applications Component in charge of the order execution strategy receives the trade decision results from the streaming analysis and is in charge of generating the order and routing it, using the low-latency data bus, to the appropriate gateway to be sent to the Stock Exchange for order execution.

6. Analytical Services execute a variety of traditional and advanced analysis for deriving intelligence from the data in the DW platform. BI reporting, multi-dimensional analysis, data mining, predictive models, and the use of time series analysis are among the capabilities that this EIA Component provides. In addition to the end-of-period reporting, this component also generates the intelligence information to provide intra-day visibility into various defined KPIs for measuring business performance, market risks, and other critical information required throughout the organization. The generated intelligence is packaged and delivered to the BI applications or Presentation Services through the Connectivity & Interoperability Services Component.

7. Metadata Services will be executed to optimize, validate, and execute other steps. The relevant Metadata needs to be identified, retrieved, and exploited. Metadata Services are also

---

[9] See details in [6].

invoked to store new Metadata from the data streams and to enrich the information managed by the In-Memory Database. Metadata Services will help to identify relevant information and to establish the linkage between the business context and the underlying IT objects.

8. Connectivity and Interoperability Services serve as the communication enabler between the various components, such as the Operational Applications Component, the EII Services, and so on. These services are requested numerous times in this scenario.

9. Presentation Services are responsible for providing the financial alerts and other intelligence information to the appropriate delivery channel. These services can be packaged to generate embeddable insights that are delivered to the user interfaces in context.

10. Embedded Analytics act as an enterprise BI Service that users and applications tap into to deliver information insights to users on demand so that users no longer need to shift software contexts when moving from operational processes to analytical ones.

11. Intelligence information, including alerts and exceptions, is delivered to the business users using a variety of channels that include mobile devices, the Web, messages, and desktop applications.

14.3.3 Improved ERM for Banking and Financial Services

This section focuses on the previously introduced ERM business scenario to illustrate and describe a particular business case requiring analytical capabilities with near-zero latency. We discuss how these newer and advanced real-time analytic methods are used to address the latency requirements of risk management in the stock trading area. Figure 14.6 highlights the basic architecture components and interactions to implement an integrated ERM solution in the financial services industry. The darker figures depict the EIA components that deliver the capabilities for ultra-low latency intelligence.

14.3.3.1 Business Context

ERM is an intrinsic part of doing business in banking and financial services, because most firms must be willing to take on a fair amount of risk to provide the most value to shareholders. The capabilities needed to successfully manage this risk must deliver a current, credible understanding of the risks unique to the organization across all types of risk (for example, credit risk, operational risk, market risk, liquidity risk, and trading risk). To accomplish this, the EIA must be flexible enough to support, measure, and monitor a wide range of business issues including:

- Use a large number of risk metrics to capture and promote the understanding of the institution's full exposure

- Provide an integrated view of risk information including correlation across the institution asset classes and portfolios and the relationships of different types of risks

- Enable real-time and intra-day information delivery capabilities to account for the rate of change of risk factors

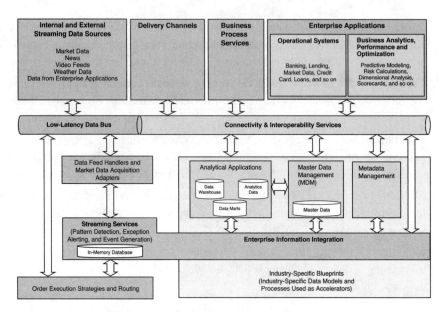

Figure 14.6   Architecture Overview Diagram for an ERM solution

We now explore how the capabilities represented in the Architecture Overview Diagram in Figure 14.6 are used to meet the requirements of an integrated ERM solution. The data required to define and monitor enterprise risk flows from the Operational Systems to the Analytical Applications Component. A variety of integration mechanisms available from the EII layer and data quality mechanisms by means of the MDM Component are used to deliver a consolidated view of trusted information in the risk area.

Metadata is generated, maintained, and managed by the Metadata Management Component, which also delivers the capabilities required to design, maintain, and trace the risk intelligence reports that are generated by the Analytical Services.

The Analytical Applications Component uses traditional and advanced analysis and reporting capabilities to generate consistent and reliable risk intelligence, which is delivered to business users using any available channel. Specialized risk analysis engines are often used for risk prediction, and the business rules engine can be used to implement automatic corrective actions based on defined criteria and thresholds set for the different KPIs that are specific to risk management, also known as Key Risk Indicators (KRI).

Industry-specific blueprints are used to accelerate the implementation of ERM because these blueprints and models encapsulate best practices for data and processes for that industry. They include prebuilt Metadata and data mappings, which save development time and increase data quality and accuracy.

For organizations that operate in the financial markets, having access to near-zero (milliseconds) latency intelligence has been demonstrated to provide a significant competitive advantage linked to the success of the trading operations and the financial success of the organization.

Using the Low-Latency Data Bus Component with access to real-time intelligence also contributes to minimize the institution's risk and exposures by significantly increasing the organization's capability for on-time detection of suspicious actions and patterns that might negatively impact the organization's risk position.

The Streaming Services consume and process streams of data from a number of sources such as market data from public and private marketplaces, mercantile exchange institutions, news and video feeds, weather forecasts, and so on. They have the capabilities for deriving instant intelligence including identifying trends and their correlations by scanning dozens of public and private marketplaces simultaneously. This insight is also used to trigger alerts, events, or automated actions that can significantly minimize the institution's operational risk by preventing potential losses or confirming advantageous conditions for a given trade decision. Streaming Services are often deployed together with a Low-Latency Data Bus, such as the IBM MQ Low Latency Messaging offering. This enables the analytics platform to detect, identify, and analyze patterns associated to risk factors before the orders are generated and passed to the Order Execution Strategy Components.

Risk intelligence information and KRIs are delivered to the user through a variety of channels. Using reports, scorecards, and dashboards, users are provided with intra-day visibility into risk information such as risk levels, regulatory capital requirements, trends in the organization's Value at Risk (VaR),[10] stress testing,[11] and other scenario analysis.

14.3.3.2 Component Interaction Diagram

This section details, the EIA components and how the services they provide are used to deliver the required view of risk using the ERM example introduced in the previous section. Figure 14.7 illustrates the EIA Components used in this example.

1. The EII capabilities are used to extract, transform, and load the required risk data from the operational systems into the DW platform. The broad capabilities of the MDM Component deliver high quality trusted master data to the Analytical Applications Component to enable business users to access a consistent set of information including the capability to explore and analyze risk data from multiple sources while enabling the BI solution with flexibility to respond to user demands as the business changes.

    Additionally, EII capabilities such as Change Data Capture (see more details in Chapter 8) are used to address many of the latency requirements associated with risk management

---

[10] In financial risk management, Value at Risk (VaR) is a widely used measure of the risk of loss on a specific portfolio of financial assets.

[11] Financial stress testing is a form of scenario analysis defining a scenario in the markets (for example, What happens if interest rates go up by at least y%?) and uses a specific algorithm to determine the expected impact on a portfolio's return should such a scenario occur. Stress testing reveals how well a portfolio is positioned in the event the forecasts prove true and it also provides insight into a portfolio's vulnerabilities. Several governmental agencies use this analysis as a regulatory requirement on certain financial institutions to ensure adequate capital allocation levels to cover potential losses incurred during extreme, but plausible, events.

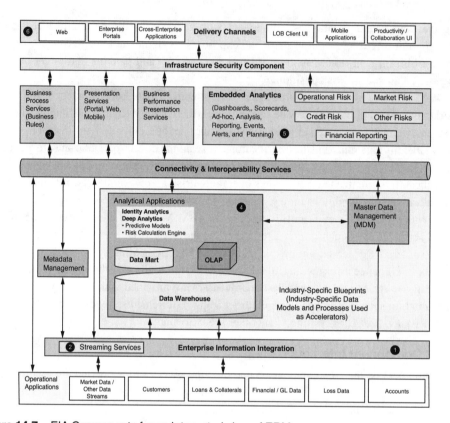

Figure 14.7   EIA Components for an integrated view of ERM

as they can be deployed to feed information in real time and near real time to the DW platform from the operational applications across the organization.

The analysis process to determine which data elements from which sources are relevant to risk analysis and how they should be transformed and used in the generation of risk insights can be accelerated using proven Industry-Specific Blueprints that act as implementation accelerators as they combine deep expertise and industry best practices in the risk management area. The IBM Industry Models[12] are among the leading blueprints for ERM in the banking industry. Industry templates and blueprints provide a fast track for successful ERM as they deliver configurable applications and solution templates with departmental and industry relevance, which are targeted to solving specific business problems.

2. The Streaming Services Component (see more details in Chapter 8) delivers the analytical capabilities that are used to address low-latency requirements inherent to financial

---

[12] Details about IBM Industry Models can be found in [7].

risk management for the detection of patterns that might indicate fraud or illegal activities around financial transactions or the identification of factors that can influence the levels of financial risks associated to the market transactions. This component provides the functionality to look at financial transactions as they occur and to monitor other types of risks such as the ones associated with the use of the enterprise infrastructure. The Streaming Services Component can be configured to detect patterns, perform analysis, and trigger actions on streaming data from the various sources before the data is persisted in the DW platform where it is consumed by more traditional BI and analytical tools for risk analysis.

3. Events, exception conditions, and alerts generated by the Streaming Services Component and other sources are sent to the Business Process Management Component from where business rules and policies are managed to implement actions that address the detected business condition. This closed-loop BI processing[13] is used to optimize business operations through specific actions from the derived risk intelligence. Many financial institutions implement this solution to automate many of the decisions, recommendations, and actions that mitigate enterprise risk.

4. The DW platform is used to store risk information that can be used to generate enterprise risk insights using a variety of traditional and advanced analytical capabilities. Identity Analytics Services are often implemented here to enable identity verification and resolution, non-obvious relationship discovery, and name recognition in heterogeneous cultural environments. Risk insights are generated by a variety of traditional and advanced analysis and predictive modeling tools as well as specialized risk engines.

5. The Embedded Analytics Component delivers the risk-reporting capabilities that include traditional enterprise governance and compliance dashboards, reports, financial risk analysis and reporting, real-time risk reporting, and monitoring that are primarily associated with operational risks. Business users in charge of making risk-related decisions can have instant access to risk insight using any channel. Information should be delivered as an easily consumable service to facilitate the quick decision-making process that is often associated with risk management.

6. The risk intelligence information is delivered to users through a variety of delivery channels, from the traditional BI reports on desktop applications to dashboards with dynamic capabilities and information provided to mobile devices.

This business scenario around ERM demonstrates how the newer BI and analytical technologies are used to implement a business optimization solution. To conclude this discussion, it is

---

[13] In the BI area, a closed-loop decision-making system monitors KPIs to provide business users with the information they need to make decisions as well as with information that enables them to see the effects of those decisions.

important to highlight some common trends that characterize these BI environments, which can be identified as key elements of a holistic approach to Business Analytics and Optimization:

- Traditional DWs and BI applications are not always successful in delivering trusted information in context at the right time to the right people. These critical requirements accelerate the evolution of BI environments and the EIA into high-performance, enterprise-wide analytic platforms with low-latency capability infrastructures that can generate and deliver actionable insights that go beyond the traditional DW and BI functionality.

- More and more, Analytic Applications are used to proactively deliver BI to users, rather than require them to discover it for themselves.

- In organizations that have achieved higher maturity levels in the use of Business Analytics, BPM and Business Optimization, these applications are used to deliver information insights about business operations. They are also able to predict business outcomes and events while delivering the intelligence information in context by comparing it against business plans, budgets, and forecasts.

- Tactical and strategic BI initiatives converge, requiring companies to become more responsive to business needs and customer requirements.

- Close to real-time or low-latency business information is becoming an important requirement in many organizations because they increasingly make use of BI for managing and driving the daily business operations.

14.4 Conclusion

The business scenarios discussed in this chapter provide examples of the newer trends in the use of advanced and traditional BI strategies and technologies to help enterprises and other organizations across all industries handle more information than ever before to derive business value and react to opportunities and threats. A key challenge faced by these organizations is the sheer volume of all this data. This makes it increasingly difficult to manage, analyze, and put information in the hands of people who need it in context and in a timely manner.

At the same time, the market demands better information and a new kind of intelligence to enable faster, more accurate decisions. Enterprises need the tools to tap into the intelligence of the entire value chain and leverage all the real-time information available to them from markets, supply chains, customers, smart devices, and Web 2.0 to make faster, more intelligent choices.

Factors such as the availability of powerful infrastructures now enable enterprises to capture, process, model, aggregate, prioritize, forecast, and analyze extreme volumes of data in new, faster, and deeper ways, paving the road to transform information into a strategic asset.

Stream Analysis has emerged as a key technology used to develop new trends in Business Analytics and Business Optimization, which enable organizations to shift the focus from sense-and-respond to situational awareness and prediction as a response to the new challenges and competitive threat. For example, in financial markets, competitive advantage is no longer just about being able to react to change, but being able to react in a matter of milliseconds. Stream Analytical Applications deliver EIA capabilities that enable enterprises to meet these new requirements by:

- Responding quickly to events and changing requirements
- Continuously analyzing data at rates that are orders of magnitude greater than existing systems
- Adapting to rapidly changing data forms and types
- Managing high availability, heterogeneity, and distribution for the new stream paradigm
- Providing security and information confidentiality for shared information

In today's new reality, it's not enough to simply respond to opportunities, threats, and risk. Successful businesses will have the intelligence and predictive capability to make the right decisions in anticipation of those events.

14.5 References

[1] The Sarbanes-Oxley Act of 2002. Online at http://www.gpo.gov/fdsys/pkg/PLAW-107publ204/content-detail.html (accessed December 15, 2009).

[2] The Basel Accords detail. Online at http://www.bis.org/about/factbcbs.htm (accessed December 15, 2009).

[3] IBM Institute for Business Value, IBM Global services. *Healthcare 2015: Win-win or lose-lose?* A study of Heath Care systems. Online at http://www-03.ibm.com/industries/healthcare/us/detail/landing/G883986O04888I88.html (accessed December 15, 2009).

[4] IBM and University of Ontario Institute of Technology collaboration with Canadian hospital to help predict changes in infants' condition. Online at http://hir.uoit.ca/cms/?q=node/24 (accessed December 15, 2009).

[5] TABB Group Research. 2008. *The Value of a Millisecond: Finding the Optimal Speed of a Trading Infrastructure.* Online at http://www.tabbgroup.com/PublicationDetail.aspx?PublicationID=346 (accessed December 15, 2009).

[6] IBM MQ Low Latency Messaging. Online at http://www-01.ibm.com/software/integration/wmq/llm/ (accessed December 15, 2009).

[7] IBM Industry Models. Online at http://www-01.ibm.com/software/data/industry-models/library.html (accessed December 15, 2009).

[8] Mosimann, R. and P. Mosimann, Dr. R. Connelly, M. Dussault, L. Trigwell, and F. McKeon. *The Performance Manager for Banking. Proven Strategies for Turning Information into Higher Business Performance.* Ottawa, Canada. Cognos, 2007.

Glossary

ABB (Architecture Building Block):   Specifies the services required in an organization's specific system.

ADW (Active Data Warehouse):   A data warehouse that is generally capable of supporting near- real-time updates, fast response times, and mixed workloads by leveraging well-architected data models, optimized ETL processes, and the use of workload management.

Agile methods: Methodologies that describe rapid iterations to get to a target in software development.

AMEX: Formerly the American Stock Exchange; now known as NYSE Amex Equities.

AML (Anti-Money Laundry):   Defines measures to prevent the transformation of the status of money earned from illegal methods into legal money.

AOD (Architecture Overview Diagram):   The AOD is a deliverable for defining the conceptual architecture of a solution.

Architecture: According to ANSI/IEEE, architecture is defined as "the fundamental organization of a system, embodied in its components, their relationships to each other and the environment, and the principles governing its design and evolution."

Architecture Patterns: Provide a proven solution in the architecture domain to a repeating problem in a given context.

405

Architecture Principles: Policies and guidelines that define the underlying rules that an organization uses to deploy business and IT resources across the enterprise.

ATM (Automatic Teller Machine): A machine used to for instance withdraw money from a bank account or inquire about the status of accounts within a bank account.

BI (Business Intelligence): This is a term that describes a broad variety of analytical applications used by an enterprise to get intelligent and meaningful insight into how the business performed in the past or is currently performing. This insight is typically used to make decisions, giving a business a competitive advantage. BI covers a broad field such as Data Warehousing, data marts, text analytics, data mining, or business reporting to name just a few.

Blog: Abbreviation for Web log, this is a Web page that serves as a publicly accessible personal journal for an individual.

BPL (Broadband Power Line): A fixed-line technology that enables Internet data to be transmitted over utility power lines. Note that this is sometimes also known as Power-Line Communications (PLC).

BPM (Business Performance Management): Provides a process to define business metrics (so-called Key Performance Indicators [KPIs]) and measure them with the goal to further optimize the business. BPM is also known as Corporate Performance Management (CPM) or Enterprise Performance Management (EPM).

CCD (Consistent-Change-Data): These tables are targets in subscription-set members that contain information about changes that occur at the source and have additional columns to identify the sequential ordering of those changes.

CCTV (Closed Circuit Television): This is a visual surveillance technology designed for monitoring a variety of environments and activities.

CDC (Change Data Capture): This is a process used to determine and track the data that has changed (known as deltas) in a database so that action can be taken.

CDI (Customer Data Integration): This is an MDM implementation focusing on the customer master data domain only. Two-three years ago this was a common approach to MDM.

CDR (Call Detail Records): These are the pervasive data records that are produced by a telecommunication exchange containing details of a particular call.

CPM (Corporate Performance Management): See BPM.

CRM (Customer Relationship Management): This is a packaged solution that delivers an end-to-end solution around contacting, understanding, and serving particular customer needs.

CRUD (Create, Read, Update, Delete): This acronym is commonly used to describe basic database functions.

Customer churn: Also known as customer attrition, this is a term used by businesses to describe the loss of clients or customers.

Data lineage: This provides the functionality to determine where data comes from, how it is transformed, and where it is going. Data lineage metadata traces the lifecycle of information between systems, including the operations that are performed on the data.

Data stewardship: This is known as a role assigned to a person that is responsible for defining and executing data governance policies.

DDU (Data Deployment Unit): This a unit of data that is assigned to one or multiple deployment nodes as part of defining the Operational Model.

DMZ (Demilitarized Zone): This is a firewall configuration for securing local area networks (LAN).

DoS (Denial of Service): This is a technique for overloading an IT system with a malicious workload, effectively preventing its regular service use.

DR (Disaster Recovery): This is a process that describes how to recover the IT environment after a disaster such as a fire destroying the IT building.

DSL (Digital Subscriber Line): Set of technologies that provides digital data transmission over the wires of a local telephone network.

DU (Deployment Unit): This is the smallest unit of data (see DDU) or a piece of deployable code or software (see EDU) assigned to one or multiple deployment nodes as part of defining the Operational Model.

DW (Data Warehouse/Data Warehousing): This describes the traditional approach to data warehousing covering structured information and supporting tactical or strategic reporting requirements.

DYW (Dynamic Warehouse Warehousing): The next evolutionary step of data warehousing aimed at addressing the demands for real-time analytics (also known as operational BI), the requirements to deliver more dynamic business insights, the need to integrate unstructured information into the analytical process, and the need to process large amounts of information.

EAI (Enterprise Application Integration):   A technique that allows business processes to span across different applications under a common integration paradigm increasing functionality, flexibility, and performance.

EC2 (Elastic Compute Cloud):   A commercial web service from Amazon that lets paying customers rent computing resources from their computing cloud.

ECM (Enterprise Content Management):   This is a discipline in information management dealing with Unstructured Data. For example, it must support content workflows, solutions for archiving e-mail and retention management for compliance solutions, among others.

EDU (Execution Deployment Unit):   This a unit of executable code or software that is assigned to one or multiple nodes as part of defining the Operational Model.

EIA (Enterprise Information Architecture):   The framework that defines the information-centric principles, architecture models, standards, and processes that form the basis for making information technology decisions across the enterprise.

EIA (Enterprise Information Architecture) Reference Architecture: Applied architecture levels that determine and customize the key reference architecture components for the specifics of the EIA.

EII (Enterprise Information Integration):   Provides the capability to access, cleanse, transform, and deliver data from disparate data sources.

EIM (Enterprise Information Model):   This consists of the Conceptual Data Model with the five data domains and their classification criteria and the Information Reference Model describing the relationships among the five data domains. The EIM is a key ingredient for the EIA.

EIS (Enterprise Information Services):   Services that support different data domains and types of decisions at different levels of the organizational hierarchy.

EMPI (Enterprise Master Patient Index):   This an MDM solution in the healthcare industry.

EMTL (Extract, Mask, Transform, Load):   Processes that are used during data masking.

Enterprise Architecture: A tool that links the business mission and strategy of an organization to its IT strategy. It is documented using multiple architectural models that meet the current and future needs of diverse stakeholders.

EPM (Enterprise Performance Management):   See BPM.

ER (Entity Relationship):   Also known as ERD (Entity Relationship Diagram).

ERD (Entity Relationship Diagram): This is a data modeling technique that creates a graphical representation of the entities and the relationships between entities in an information system.

ERM (Enterprise Risk Management): This is a process that provides full transparency into the risk exposures of an enterprise, enabling the management of these risks with a scorecard-based approach.

ERP (Enterprise Resource Planning): Integrated computer-based application software used to manage internal and external resources.

ESB (Enterprise Service Bus): An open standards-based distributed synchronous or asynchronous messaging middleware solution that provides secure interoperability between enterprise applications.

ETL (Extract, Transform, Load): Software and tools that enable businesses to consolidate their disparate data while moving it from place to place.

Federation: The integration of data from multiple systems into a unified, consistent, and accurate representation geared toward the viewing and manipulation of the data without replicating it.

GIS (Geographic Information System): In its simplest view, a GIS system is used to manage location information.

HA (High Availability): Availability is a characteristic describing the availability of an IT system for its intended use. High availability indicates that the IT system in question has strong requirements regarding this characteristic such as 24x7 operations.

HR (Human Resource): In the context of IT, the term HR typically refers to software solutions managing employee information—the human resources from an enterprise point of view.

HSM (Hierarchical Storage Management): This is a data storage approach that manages data cost optimized by distributing it appropriately on high speed (and thus high cost) and low speed (and thus low cost) storage media based on access patterns.

IaaS (Information as a Service): Describes a new paradigm to enable standardized access to the data by applying a standard set of transformations to the various data sources.

ILM (Information Lifecycle Management): This is a set of strategies, processes, policies, and tools that govern the lifecycle of information from its creation to its deletion based on business requirements associated with that information.

Information Agenda: Provides a strategy, information governance, a roadmap, and an enterprise information architecture and tools to solve information-intense problems.

Information Architecture: Provides the foundational information-relevant concepts, components, and frameworks of an organization's IT environment and defines its relationship to the organization's objectives.

Information Governance: The set of policies, roles, responsibilities, and processes applied to data domains that you establish in an enterprise to guide, direct, and control how the organization uses information and related technologies to accomplish business goals.

Information Maturity Model: An assessment technique that evaluates a baseline of the current enterprise information management infrastructure against best practices.

IOD (Information On Demand): This is a term coined by IBM in 2006. It defines a new approach to manage information more efficiently.

IT (Information Technology): Broad subject which deals with technology and other aspects of managing and processing information.

IUN (Intelligent Utility Network): The continuous sensing, IP-enabled information network that overlays and connects a utility's equipment, devices, systems, customers, partners, and employees.

KPI (Key Performance Indicator): KPIs are metrics defined to measure business performance of an enterprise. This term is related to BPM.

LAN (Local Area Network): A LAN is characterized by local scope and typically higher speed and greater bandwidth compared to Wide Area Networks (WAN) and connects local IT infrastructure such as servers, PCs, and so on.

LOM (Logical Operational Model): Describes the placement of specified components onto specified nodes, the specified connections between those nodes necessary to support the interactions between specified components, and the non-functional characteristics of those nodes and connections, acquired from the placed specified components and their interactions.

Mashup: A lightweight Web application that is often created by end users and combines information or capabilities from more than one existing source to deliver new functions and insights.

Mashup (Maker/Builder): An assembly environment for running and creating mashups.

MDB (Multidimensional Database): A type of database that is optimized for data warehouse and online analytical processing applications.

MDI (Master Data Integration): This is a process to integrate, cleanse, and harmonize master data from heterogeneous source systems while building an MDM system.

MDM (Master Data Management):   A system and services for the single, authoritative source of truth of master data for an enterprise.

MDX (MultiDimensional Expressions):   A multidimensional query language, it uses syntax similar to SQL and is used to query multidimensional cubes (OLAP databases).

MOLAP (Multidimensional Online Analytical Processing):   Related to analytical tools where data is stored in an optimized multidimensional array storage rather than in a relational DB (ie., in ROLAP).

MOM (Message Oriented-Middleware):   Infrastructure focused on sending and receiving messages that increased the interoperability between applications and systems.

Multi-tenancy: Enabling many users from different customers to use the services of a central utility.

NAS (Network Attached Storage):   This is a storage that is not built-in storage such as hard disks in a PC. Instead this type of storage is connected to servers through network infrastructure such as Ethernet.

NENR (Non-Erasable, Non-Rewritable):   This is a characteristic of a storage media indicating that it can be written only once and what has been written is not erasable with software applications. This type of storage media is often used for archiving of data.

NFR (Non-Functional Requirement):   Describes a requirement of a software solution that is not a function; typical examples include performance, scalability, maintainability, and security.

ODS (Operational Data Store):   A DB system designed to integrate data from multiple sources to allow operational access to the data for operational reporting.

OLAP (Online Analytical Processing):   An approach to quickly answer multidimensional analytical queries.

OLTP (Online Transaction Processing):   Class of systems that facilitate and manage transaction-oriented applications.

Online Social Networking Websites: Known as social sites that function like an online community of Internet users. Many of these online community members share common interests in hobbies, religion, politics, and so on.

Operational BI (Operational Business Intelligence):   A business intelligence solution where all the data reflects its most current state in real-time.

OS (Operating System): This is a specific type of software bridging between applications and hardware such as PCs or servers. It provides applications key services such as memory management, storage management, or process and threading management.

OTC (Order-To-Cash): This is a business process family consisting of processes covering the creation of an order, order fulfilment, creating a bill and receiving the payment (the cash) for bills.

OTO (Opportunity-To-Order): This is a business process family consisting of processes to create a prospect and related opportunities until the prospect becomes a customer by placing the first order.

PaaS (Platform as a Service): PaaS is defined as a computing platform delivered as a service.

Patterns: Patterns provide a proven solution to a repeating problem in a given context.

PDP (Policy Decision Point): PDPs contain security policies defined for an infrastructure. They are deployed by administrators through resource managers.

PEP (Policy Enforcement Point): Access to a resource is controlled by a resource manager applying PDPs at logical PEPs.

PII (Personally Identifiable Information): This is information related to an individual that is considered in many cases sensitive and therefore must be managed according to certain regulations.

PIM (Product Information Management): Two to three years ago, this MDM solution was often deployed as a single domain implementation for the product domain. This type of MDM implementation became known as product information management.

PLC (Power-Line Communication): See BPL entry.

PLM (Product Lifecycle Management): This is a management strategy of how products are moved through their lifecycle. Software solutions in this space focus on design aspects and manufacturing of products, whereas PIM software solutions are centered around maintenance of the product information to support selling and distribution of products. Thus, PLM and PIM are complementary in nature.

PM (Performance Management): This is a discipline of IT operations concerned about managing the performance of IT solutions over their lifecycle to meet user requirements from a performance point of view while at the same time trying to achieve this goal at minimal cost.

POM (Physical Operational Model): At this level, the hardware and software technologies needed to deliver the Operational Model's characteristics and capabilities are identified and configured. It documents the overall configuration of the technologies and products necessary to deliver the functional requirements and non-functional requirements of the IT system.

Pub/Sub (Publish/Subscribe):   An architecture pattern for implementing message queues.

Q-Replication (Queue replication):   A high-volume, low-latency replication solution with the idea that changes in a source system are captured and published to a message queue.

QoS (Quality of Service):   The QoS describes the non-functional aspects of a service such as performance.

RA (Reference Architecture):   Provides a proven template of an architecture for a particular domain that contains the supporting artifacts to enable their reuse.

RAID (Redundant Array Independent Disks):   A category of disk drives that employ two or more drives in combination for fault tolerance and performance.

RCM (Returnable Container Management):   This is a Track and Trace solution leveraging MDM and analytics on EPCIS event data.

RDBMS (Relational Database Management System):   Type of DBMS that uses SQL to store data in related tables.

ROI (Return On Investment):   This is a financial measure expressing how many benefits an investment yields. A negative number indicates that the investment is a loss not returning any benefits. A positive number expresses that the investment has measurable financial benefits and thus delivers a positive return.

ROLAP (Relational Online Analytical Processing):   Performs dynamic multidimensional analysis of data stored in a relational DB.

RPC (Remote Procedure Call):   Procedure that executes in another address space or on another computer.

RPO (Recovery Point Objective):   This is a measure to express how much data might be lost if a recovery is necessary to a certain point in time.

RTO Recovery Time Objective: This is a measure indicating how quickly after an outage IT infrastructure needs to be recovered to continue operations. The smaller the number, the quicker the solution must be able to be recovered.

SaaS (Software as a Service):   A kind of hosted application that enables organizations to access business functionality at a cost typically less than paying for licensed applications.

SAN (Storage Area Network):   This is an architectural approach to connect different types of storage through networks to servers and PCs.

SCM (Supply Chain Management):   To provision products or services to a network of inter-connected businesses.

SLA (Service Level Agreement):   A service level agreement defines the agreement characteristics expected by the service consumer that the service provider supposedly meets.

SOA (Service-Oriented Architecture):   An architectural style to enable loosely coupled systems and promote re-usable services based on open standards.

SoC (Separation of Concerns):   A concept that enables you to work on a specific aspect of an application without having significant impact on other parts of the application.

SRR (Service Registry and Repository):   This is the metadata repository for service descriptions.

SSO (Single Sign-On):   This is a security approach and technique for authentication, allowing a user to sign into multiple applications through authentication at a single point.

TCO (Total Cost of Ownership):   This is a cost measure expressing the total cost of purchasing, operating, and maintaining an IT solution consisting of hardware and software over its lifecycle.

TOGAF (The Open Group Architecture Framework):   An architecture framework that enables practitioners to design, evaluate, and build the right architecture for a particular business.

Trickle Feed: The process of feeding data from one system to another in either real-time or small time intervals.

UI (User Interface):   The User Interface is in essence what a user sees on a computer screen to interact with a software program by entering data, searching for files, and so on.

VaR (Value at Risk):   A widely used measure of the risk of loss on a specific portfolio of financial assets.

VOS (Virtualized Operating System):   This is an operating system not installed on hardware directly but inside a virtualization infrastructure such as XEN or VMware.

VSAM (Virtual Storage Access Method):   A record-oriented file system; in this kind of dataset, information is stored as a collection of records.

WAN (Wide Area Network):   Computer network whose communication links cross metropolitan, regional, or national boundaries.

Widget: A piece of code that can be installed and executed in any separate HTML-based web page by an end user without requiring additional compilation.

WiMAX (Worldwide Interoperability for Microwave Access):   This wireless technology is one of the most promising technologies for metro-based broadband provision.

Index

A

ABBs (architecture building blocks), 26, 77
absolute consistency, 58
access mechanisms, Operational Model Relationship Diagram, 158
accuracy, classification criteria of Conceptual Data Model (data domains), 58
active/active mode, 182
active/standby mode, 182
ADM (TOGAF Architecture Development Method), 44
adoption, mashups, 331
ADS (Architecture Description Standard), 147
AES (Advanced Encryption Standard), 193
AJAX (asynchronous JavaScript and XML), 329
aligning Information Agenda with business objectives, 19
alternatives, Component Interaction Diagrams (Component Model), 144

Analytical Applications
    Business Performance Presentation Services, 110
    Component Model
        high-level description, 131
        interfaces, 133
        service description, 132-133
Analytical Applications capability, Conceptual View (EIA Reference Architecture), 81
Analytical Applications Component, 398
analytical data domains, 56, 62-63
Analytical Services
    Cloud Computing, 220
    Component Model
        high-level description, 131
        interfaces, 133
        service description, 132-133

in Logical Component Model of IUN, 269-270
    Logical View, 101
"anticipate and shape," 7
AOD (Architecture Overview Diagram), 77
    for utility networks, 263-265
Apple iPod, 140
application abstraction by SOA paradigm, key drivers to Cloud Computing, 203
Application and Optimization Services layer (AOD), 264
Application Layer, Enterprise Architecture, 27
Application Platform Layer, Information Services, 159
Application Server Node, 184, 191
application services, EIA Reference Architecture, 48
application tier, multi-tenancy (Cloud Computing and EI), 210-211
architectural considerations for mashups, 335-336

415

O

OLAP (Online Analytical Processing), 286
OMG (Object Management Group), 120
Operation System Services, Technology Layer, 163
Operational Applications, Component Model, 114-116
  high-level description, 115
Operational Applications Component, 396
operational architecture, EIA Reference Architecture, 36
operational data domains, 56, 61
Operational Intelligence Services, Analytical Applications Component, 132
operational metadata, technical metadata, 286
Operational Model, 147-148
  Cloud Computing, 215
  connections, 149
  deployment units (DU), 149
  design concepts, 149-150
  design techniques, 150-151
  levels, 148
  locations, 149
  nodes, 149
  relationship diagram, 155
    access mechanisms, 158
    basic location types, 155, 158
    inter-location border types, 158
    logical, 167-168

standards of specified nodes, 158-159, 162-167
service qualities, 151-152
  examples, 152
  relevance of service qualities per data domain, 152, 156
operational patterns, 168-169
  Automated Capacity and Provisioning Management pattern, 196-198
  Compliance and Dependency Management for Operational Risk, 188-190
  Content Resource Manager Service Availability pattern, 184-186
  context of, 169-170
  Continuous Availability and Resiliency pattern, 180-181
  Data Integration and Aggregation Runtime pattern, 176-177
  Encryption and Data Protection pattern, 192-194
  ESB Runtime for Guaranteed Data Delivery pattern, 177-180
  Federated Metadata pattern, 186-187
  File System Virtualization pattern, 194-195
  for IUN, 277-278
  Mashup Runtime and Security pattern, 187-188
mashups, 349

deployment model, 349-350
high availability model, 350-352
near-real-time model, 353-354
for MDM, 326-327
Metadata Management, 300-301
Multi-Tier High Availability for Critical Data pattern, 181-184
Near-Real-Time Business Intelligence pattern, 170, 175
Retention Management pattern, 190-192
Storage Pool Virtualization pattern, 195-196
operational procedures and policies, business metadata, 285
operational service qualities for IUN, 275
operational systems, 115
opportunity anti-patterns, EIA Reference Architecture, 50
opportunity patterns, EIA Reference Architecture, 49
optimization of energy value chain, 259-261
organizational readiness, Information Governance, 15-16
Out-of-the-box Adapter Services in MDM Component Model, 314
Outage Management System layer (Logical Component Model of IUN), 269
outages use case (IUN), 261-263

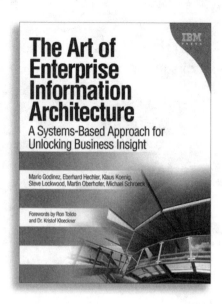

FREE Online Edition

Your purchase of **The Art of Enterprise Information Architecture** includes access to a free online edition for 120 days through the Safari Books Online subscription service. Nearly every IBM Press book is available online through Safari Books Online, along with more than 5,000 other technical books and videos from publishers such as Addison-Wesley Professional, Cisco Press, Exam Cram, O'Reilly, Prentice Hall, Que, and Sams.

SAFARI BOOKS ONLINE allows you to search for a specific answer, cut and paste code, download chapters, and stay current with emerging technologies.

Activate your FREE Online Edition at
www.informit.com/safarifree

> **STEP 1:** Enter the coupon code: OENJPXA.

> **STEP 2:** New Safari users, complete the brief registration form.
> Safari subscribers, just log in.

If you have difficulty registering on Safari or accessing the online edition, please e-mail customer-service@safaribooksonline.com